AGAINST
THE GODS

To my dearest Papa,
my guide + teacher.
To a Wonderful 2003!
All my love   —Myda

AGAINST THE GODS

THE REMARKABLE STORY OF RISK

PETER L. BERNSTEIN

JOHN WILEY & SONS, INC.

New York • Chichester • Weinheim • Brisbane • Singapore • Toronto

This text is printed on acid-free paper.

This publication is designed to provide accurate and authoritative
information in regard to the subject matter covered. It is sold
with the understanding that the publisher is not engaged in
rendering professional services. If professional advice or other
expert assistance is required, the services of a competent professional
person should be sought.

Library of Congress Cataloging-in-Publication Data:

Bernstein, Peter L.
    Against the gods: The remarkable story of risk/Peter L. Bernstein.
        p.   cm.
    Includes bibliographical references and index.
    ISBN 0-471-29563-9 (paper)
        1. Risk Management.   2. Decision-making.   I. Title.
    HD61.B4666   1996
    368—dc20   96-33861

Printed in the United States of America

20 19 18 17 16 15 14 13 12

For
Peter Brodsky

Contents

**1900–1960:
CLOUDS OF VAGUENESS AND THE
DEMAND FOR PRECISION**

**DEGREES OF BELIEF:
EXPLORING UNCERTAINTY**

Acknowledgments

The suggestion that I write a book about risk came from the late Erwin Glickes, then president of The Free Press. Erwin was a man who projected copious amounts of power, persuasiveness, and charm. Although he considered my long experience as a professional investor to be sufficient qualification for the task he had in mind, I soon discovered, as I had feared, that risk does not begin and end on the floor of the New York Stock Exchange.

The vastness of the subject matter is daunting. Risk touches on the most profound aspects of psychology, mathematics, statistics, and history. The literature is monumental, and each day's headlines bring many new items of interest. Consequently, I have had to be selective. I believe, however, that the omission of any important material was the result of a decision on my part rather than an act of oversight.

For this project, I have been far more dependent on other people than I had been in my earlier forays into writing books. Old friends as well as many complete strangers from a wide variety of disciplines have provided invaluable assistance combined with criticisms and creative suggestions. In this case, increasing the number of cooks was a clear benefit. My gratitude to them is boundless. There would have been no book at all without them.

Convention dictates that expressions of appreciation to spouses and editors should come at the end of the list of acknowledgments, but on this occasion I choose to mention my wife and my editor first. That is where they belong.

Barbara, my wife as well as my business partner, provided countless creative ideas, conceptual contributions, and positive criticisms, all of them essential to the task; there is barely a page that does not reflect her influence. In addition, her success in arranging our lives to accommodate this whole project made all the difference between progress and chaos.

Myles Thompson of John Wiley has been critically important to the project. I have been privileged to have his expert editorial suggestions, to enjoy his enthusiastic leadership, and to benefit from his professional management. Myles's colleagues at Wiley have cooperated with me in every way possible from start to finish. Everett Sims's copy-editing helped me to make sense where there was confusion, while his masterful use of the scalpel exorcised a great deal of fluff in the manuscript without harm to the content below.

A few people rendered assistance far beyond the call of duty. I owe a special debt to Peter Dougherty for his countless inestimable comments and suggestions. Mark Kritzman was a tireless pilot through the shoals of mathematical and statistical treatments. Richard Rogalski and his associates at the Baker Library at Dartmouth saved me untold hours by making their facilities available to me at long distance; Rich's good humor and eagerness to help added to the joy of having his generous assistance. Martin Leibowitz bestowed a gift of immensely valuable material that has enriched the content of the book. Richard and Edith Sylla were indefatigable investigators at points where the going was the roughest. Stanley Kogelman furnished me with a priceless tutorial in probability analysis. Leora Klapper served as an ideal research assistant: indefatigable, enthusiastic, thorough, and prompt.

Molly Baker, Peter Brodsky, Robert Ferguson, Richard Geist, and William Lee were good enough to read segments of early versions of the manuscript. They gave me the running start I needed in order to transform rough drafts into a finished material.

The following people also made significant contributions to my work and warrant my deepest appreciation: Kenneth Arrow, Gilbert Bassett, William Baumol, Zalmon Bernstein, Doris Bullard, Paul Davidson, Donald Dewey, David Durand, Barbara Fotinatos, James Fraser, Greg Hayt, Roger Hertog, Victor Howe, Bertrand Jacquillat, Daniel Kahneman, Mary Kentouris, Mario Laserna, Dean LeBaron, Michelle Lee, Harry Markowitz, Morton Meyers, James Norris, Todd Petzel, Paul Samuelson, Robert Shiller, Charles Smithson, Robert

Solow, Meir Statman, Marta Steele, Richard Thaler, James Tinsley, Frank Trainer, Amos Tversky,* and Marina von N. Whitman.

Eight people generously undertook to read the manuscript in its entirety and to give me the benefit of their expert criticisms and suggestions. Each of them, in his own way, deserves major credit for the quality of the content and style of the book, without bearing any responsibility for the shortcomings it contains. Here they are: Theodore Aronson, Peter Brodsky, Jay Eliasberg, Robert Heilbroner, Peter Kinder, Charles Kindleberger, Mark Kritzman, and Stephen Stigler.

I end with a note of thanks to my late parents, Allen M. Bernstein and Irma L. Davis, who inspired much of the enthusiasm that went into the creation of this book.

PETER L. BERNSTEIN

---

*Amos Tversky, who plays an important role in Chapters 16 and 17, died unexpectedly just as this book was about to go into print.

AGAINST
THE GODS

Introduction

Why hat is it that distinguishes the thousands of years of history from what we think of as modern times? The answer goes way beyond the progress of science, technology, capitalism, and democracy.

The distant past was studded with brilliant scientists, mathematicians, inventors, technologists, and political philosophers. Hundreds of years before the birth of Christ, the skies had been mapped, the great library of Alexandria built, and Euclid's geometry taught. Demand for technological innovation in warfare was as insatiable then as it is today. Coal, oil, iron, and copper have been at the service of human beings for millennia, and travel and communication mark the very beginnings of recorded civilization.

The revolutionary idea that defines the boundary between modern times and the past is the mastery of risk: the notion that the future is more than a whim of the gods and that men and women are not passive before nature. Until human beings discovered a way across that boundary, the future was a mirror of the past or the murky domain of oracles and soothsayers who held a monopoly over knowledge of anticipated events.

This book tells the story of a group of thinkers whose remarkable vision revealed how to put the future at the service of the present. By showing the world how to understand risk, measure it, and weigh its consequences, they converted risk-taking into one of the prime catalysts that drives modern Western society. Like Prometheus, they defied the gods and probed the darkness in search of the light that converted the future from an enemy into an opportunity. The transformation in attitudes toward risk management unleashed by their achievements has channeled the human passion for games and wagering into economic growth, improved quality of life, and technological progress.

By defining a rational process of risk-taking, these innovators provided the missing ingredient that has propelled science and enterprise into the world of speed, power, instant communication, and sophisticated finance that marks our own age. Their discoveries about the nature of risk, and the art and science of choice, lie at the core of our modern market economy that nations around the world are hastening to join. Given all its problems and pitfalls, the free economy, with choice at its center, has brought humanity unparalleled access to the good things of life.

The ability to define what may happen in the future and to choose among alternatives lies at the heart of contemporary societies. Risk management guides us over a vast range of decision-making, from allocating wealth to safeguarding public health, from waging war to planning a family, from paying insurance premiums to wearing a seatbelt, from planting corn to marketing cornflakes.

In the old days, the tools of farming, manufacture, business management, and communication were simple. Breakdowns were frequent, but repairs could be made without calling the plumber, the electrician, the computer scientist—or the accountants and the investment advisers. Failure in one area seldom had direct impact on another. Today, the tools we use are complex, and breakdowns can be catastrophic, with far-reaching consequences. We must be constantly aware of the likelihood of malfunctions and errors. Without a command of probability theory and other instruments of risk management, engineers could never have designed the great bridges that span our widest rivers, homes would still be heated by fireplaces or parlor stoves, electric power utilities would not exist, polio would still be maiming children, no airplanes would fly, and space travel would be just a dream.* Without insurance in its many varieties, the death of the breadwinner would reduce young families to starvation or charity, even more people would be denied health care, and only the wealthiest could afford to own a home. If farmers were unable to sell their crops at a price fixed before harvest, they would produce far less food than they do.

---

*The scientist who developed the Saturn 5 rocket that launched the first Apollo mission to the moon put it this way: "You want a valve that doesn't leak and you try everything possible to develop one. But the real world provides you with a leaky valve. You have to determine how much leaking you can tolerate." (Obituary of Arthur Rudolph, in *The New York Times*, January 3, 1996.)

If we had no liquid capital markets that enable savers to diversify their risks, if investors were limited to owning just one stock (as they were in the early days of capitalism), the great innovative enterprises that define our age—companies like Microsoft, Merck, DuPont, Alcoa, Boeing, and McDonald's—might never have come into being. The capacity to manage risk, and with it the appetite to take risk and make forward-looking choices, are key elements of the energy that drives the economic system forward.

The modern conception of risk is rooted in the Hindu–Arabic numbering system that reached the West seven to eight hundred years ago. But the serious study of risk began during the Renaissance, when people broke loose from the constraints of the past and subjected long-held beliefs to open challenge. This was a time when much of the world was to be discovered and its resources exploited. It was a time of religious turmoil, nascent capitalism, and a vigorous approach to science and the future.

In 1654, a time when the Renaissance was in full flower, the Chevalier de Méré, a French nobleman with a taste for both gambling and mathematics, challenged the famed French mathematician Blaise Pascal to solve a puzzle. The question was how to divide the stakes of an unfinished game of chance between two players when one of them is ahead. The puzzle had confounded mathematicians since it was posed some two hundred years earlier by the monk Luca Paccioli. This was the man who brought double-entry bookkeeping to the attention of the business managers of his day—and tutored Leonardo da Vinci in the multiplication tables. Pascal turned for help to Pierre de Fermat, a lawyer who was also a brilliant mathematician. The outcome of their collaboration was intellectual dynamite. What might appear to have been a seventeenth-century version of the game of Trivial Pursuit led to the discovery of the theory of probability, the mathematical heart of the concept of risk.

Their solution to Paccioli's puzzle meant that people could for the first time make decisions and forecast the future with the help of numbers. In the medieval and ancient worlds, even in preliterate and peasant societies, people managed to make decisions, advance their interests, and carry on trade, but with no real understanding of risk or *the nature of decision-making*. Today, we rely less on superstition and tradition than people did in the past, not because we are more rational, but because our understanding of risk enables us to make decisions in a rational mode.

At the time Pascal and Fermat made their breakthrough into the fascinating world of probability, society was experiencing an extraordinary wave of innovation and exploration. By 1654, the roundness of the earth was an established fact, vast new lands had been discovered, gunpowder was reducing medieval castles to dust, printing with movable type had ceased to be a novelty, artists were skilled in the use of perspective, wealth was pouring into Europe, and the Amsterdam stock exchange was flourishing. Some years earlier, in the 1630s, the famed Dutch tulip bubble had burst as a result of the issuing of options whose essential features were identical to the sophisticated financial instruments in use today.

These developments had profound consequences that put mysticism on the run. By this time Martin Luther had had his say and halos had disappeared from most paintings of the Holy Trinity and the saints. William Harvey had overthrown the medical teachings of the ancients with his discovery of the circulation of blood—and Rembrandt had painted "The Anatomy Lesson," with its cold, white, naked human body. In such an environment, someone would soon have worked out the theory of probability, even if the Chevalier de Méré had never confronted Pascal with his brainteaser.

As the years passed, mathematicians transformed probability theory from a gamblers' toy into a powerful instrument for organizing, interpreting, and applying information. As one ingenious idea was piled on top of another, quantitative techniques of risk management emerged that have helped trigger the tempo of modern times.

By 1725, mathematicians were competing with one another in devising tables of life expectancies, and the English government was financing itself through the sale of life annuities. By the middle of the century, marine insurance had emerged as a flourishing, sophisticated business in London.

In 1703, Gottfried von Leibniz commented to the Swiss scientist and mathematician Jacob Bernoulli that "[N]ature has established patterns originating in the return of events, but only for the most part,"[1] thereby prompting Bernoulli to invent the Law of Large Numbers and methods of statistical sampling that drive modern activities as varied as opinion polling, wine tasting, stock picking, and the testing of new drugs.* Leibniz's admonition—"but only for the most part"—was more profound than he may have realized, for he provided the key to why there is such a thing as risk in the first place: without that qualification, everything would be predictable, and in a world where every event is identical to a previous event no change would ever occur.

In 1730, Abraham de Moivre suggested the structure of the normal distribution—also known as the bell curve—and discovered the concept of standard deviation. Together, these two concepts make up what is popularly known as the Law of Averages and are essential ingredients of modern techniques for quantifying risk. Eight years later, Daniel Bernoulli, Jacob's nephew and an equally distinguished mathematician and scientist, first defined the systematic process by which most people make choices and reach decisions. Even more important, he propounded the idea that the satisfaction resulting from any small increase in wealth "will be inversely proportionate to the quantity of goods previously possessed." With that innocent-sounding assertion, Bernoulli explained why King Midas was an unhappy man, why people tend to be risk-averse, and why prices must fall if customers are to be persuaded to buy more. Bernoulli's statement stood as the dominant paradigm of rational behavior for the next 250 years and laid the groundwork for modern principles of investment management.

Almost exactly one hundred years after the collaboration between Pascal and Fermat, a dissident English minister named Thomas Bayes made a striking advance in statistics by demonstrating how to make better-informed decisions by mathematically blending new information into old information. Bayes's theorem focuses on the frequent occasions when we have sound intuitive judgments about the probability of some event and want to understand how to alter those judgments as actual events unfold.

All the tools we use today in risk management and in the analysis of decisions and choice, from the strict rationality of game theory to the

---

*Chapter 7 describes Jacob Bernoulli's achievements in detail. The Law of Large Numbers says in essence that the difference between the observed value of a sample and its true value will diminish as the number of observations in the sample increases.

challenges of chaos theory, stem from the developments that took place between 1654 and 1760, with only two exceptions:

In 1875, Francis Galton, an amateur mathematician who was Charles Darwin's first cousin, discovered regression to the mean, which explains why pride goeth before a fall and why clouds tend to have silver linings. Whenever we make any decision based on the expectation that matters will return to "normal," we are employing the notion of regression to the mean.

In 1952, Nobel Laureate Harry Markowitz, then a young graduate student studying operations research at the University of Chicago, demonstrated mathematically why putting all your eggs in one basket is an unacceptably risky strategy and why diversification is the nearest an investor or business manager can ever come to a free lunch. That revelation touched off the intellectual movement that revolutionized Wall Street, corporate finance, and business decisions around the world; its effects are still being felt today.

The story that I have to tell is marked all the way through by a persistent tension between those who assert that the best decisions are based on quantification and numbers, determined by the patterns of the past, and those who base their decisions on more subjective degrees of belief about the uncertain future. This is a controversy that has never been resolved.

The issue boils down to one's view about the extent to which the past determines the future. We cannot quantify the future, because it is an unknown, but we have learned how to use numbers to scrutinize what happened in the past. But to what degree should we rely on the patterns of the past to tell us what the future will be like? Which matters more when facing a risk, the facts as we see them or our subjective belief in what lies hidden in the void of time? Is risk management a science or an art? Can we even tell for certain precisely where the dividing line between the two approaches lies?

It is one thing to set up a mathematical model that appears to explain everything. But when we face the struggle of daily life, of constant trial and error, the ambiguity of the facts as well as the power of the human heartbeat can obliterate the model in short order. The late Fischer Black, a pioneering theoretician of modern finance who moved from M.I.T. to Wall Street, said, "Markets look a lot less efficient from the banks of the Hudson than from the banks of the Charles."[2]

Over time, the controversy between quantification based on observations of the past and subjective degrees of belief has taken on a deeper significance. The mathematically driven apparatus of modern risk management contains the seeds of a dehumanizing and self-destructive technology. Nobel laureate Kenneth Arrow has warned, "[O]ur knowledge of the way things work, in society or in nature, comes trailing clouds of vagueness. Vast ills have followed a belief in certainty."[3] In the process of breaking free from the past we may have become slaves of a new religion, a creed that is just as implacable, confining, and arbitrary as the old.

Our lives teem with numbers, but we sometimes forget that numbers are only tools. They have no soul; they may indeed become fetishes. Many of our most critical decisions are made by computers, contraptions that devour numbers like voracious monsters and insist on being nourished with ever-greater quantities of digits to crunch, digest, and spew back.

To judge the extent to which today's methods of dealing with risk are either a benefit or a threat, we must know the whole story, from its very beginnings. We must know why people of past times did—or did not—try to tame risk, how they approached the task, what modes of thinking and language emerged from their experience, and how their activities interacted with other events, large and small, to change the course of culture. Such a perspective will bring us to a deeper understanding of where we stand, and where we may be heading.

Along the way, we shall refer often to games of chance, which have applications that extend far beyond the spin of the roulette wheel. Many of the most sophisticated ideas about managing risk and making decisions have developed from the analysis of the most childish of games. One does not have to be a gambler or even an investor to recognize what gambling and investing reveal about risk.

The dice and the roulette wheel, along with the stock market and the bond market, are natural laboratories for the study of risk because they lend themselves so readily to quantification; their language is the language of numbers. They also reveal a great deal about ourselves. When we hold our breath watching the little white ball bounce about on the spinning roulette wheel, and when we call our broker to buy or sell some shares of stock, our heart is beating along with the numbers. So, too, with all important outcomes that depend on chance.

The word "risk" derives from the early Italian *risicare*, which means "to dare." In this sense, risk is a choice rather than a fate. The actions we dare to take, which depend on how free we are to make choices, are what the story of risk is all about. And that story helps define what it means to be a human being.

TO 1200: BEGINNINGS

1

The Winds of the Greeks and the Role of the Dice

Why is the mastery of risk such a uniquely modern concept? Why did humanity wait the many thousands of years leading up to the Renaissance before breaking down the barriers that stood in the way of measuring and controlling risk?

These questions defy easy answers. But we begin with a clue. Since the beginning of recorded history, gambling—the very essence of risk-taking—has been a popular pastime and often an addiction. It was a game of chance that inspired Pascal and Fermat's revolutionary breakthrough into the laws of probability, not some profound question about the nature of capitalism or visions of the future. Yet until that moment, throughout history, people had wagered and played games without using any system of odds that determines winnings and losings today. The act of risk-taking floated free, untrammeled by the theory of risk management.

Human beings have always been infatuated with gambling because it puts us head-to-head against the fates, with no holds barred. We enter this daunting battle because we are convinced that we have a powerful ally: Lady Luck will interpose herself between us and the fates (or the odds) to bring victory to our side. Adam Smith, a masterful student of human nature, defined the motivation: "The overweening conceit which the greater part of men have of their own abilities [and] their absurd presumption in their own good fortune."[1] Although Smith was keenly aware that the human propensity to take risk propelled economic progress, he feared that society would suffer when that propensity ran amuck. So he was careful to balance moral sentiments against the benefits of a free market. A hundred and sixty years later, another great English economist, John Maynard Keynes, agreed: "When the capital development of a country becomes the by-product of the activities of a casino, the job is likely to be ill-done."[2]

Yet the world would be a dull place if people lacked conceit and confidence in their own good fortune. Keynes had to admit that "If human nature felt no temptation to take a chance . . . there might not be much investment merely as a result of cold calculation."[3] Nobody takes a risk in the expectation that it will fail. When the Soviets tried to administer uncertainty out of existence through government fiat and planning, they choked off social and economic progress.

Gambling has held human beings in thrall for millennia. It has been engaged in everywhere, from the dregs of society to the most respectable circles.

Pontius Pilate's soldiers cast lots for Christ's robe as He suffered on the cross. The Roman Emperor Marcus Aurelius was regularly accompanied by his personal croupier. The Earl of Sandwich invented the snack that bears his name so that he could avoid leaving the gaming table in order to eat. George Washington hosted games in his tent during the American Revolution.[4] Gambling is synonymous with the Wild West. And "Luck Be a Lady Tonight" is one of the most memorable numbers in *Guys and Dolls*, a musical about a compulsive gambler and his floating crap game.

The earliest-known form of gambling was a kind of dice game played with what was known as an astragalus, or knuckle-bone.[5] This early ancestor of today's dice was a squarish bone taken from the ankles of sheep or deer, solid and without marrow, and so hard as to be virtually indestructible. Astragali have surfaced in archeological digs in many parts of the world. Egyptian tomb paintings picture games played with astragali dating from 3500 BC, and Greek vases show young men tossing the bones into a circle. Although Egypt punished compulsive gamblers by forcing them to hone stones for the pyramids, excavations show that the pharaohs were not above using loaded dice in their own games. Craps, an American invention, derives from various dice games brought into Europe via the Crusades. Those games were generally referred to as "hazard," from *al zahr*, the Arabic word for dice.[6]

Card games developed in Asia from ancient forms of fortune-telling, but they did not become popular in Europe until the invention of printing. Cards originally were large and square, with no identifying figures or pips in the corners. Court cards were printed with only one head instead of double-headed, which meant that players often had to identify them from the feet—turning the cards around would reveal a holding of court cards. Square corners made cheating easy for players who could turn down a tiny part of the corner to identify cards in the deck later on. Double-headed court cards and cards with rounded corners came into use only in the nineteenth century.

Like craps, poker is an American variation on an older form—the game is only about 150 years old. David Hayano has described poker as "Secret ploys, monumental deceptions, calculated strategies, and fervent beliefs [with] deep, invisible structures . . . . A game to experience rather than to observe."[7] According to Hayano, about forty million Americans play poker regularly, all confident of their ability to outwit their opponents.

The most addictive forms of gambling seem to be the pure games of chance played at the casinos that are now spreading like wildfire through once staid American communities. An article in *The New York Times* of September 25, 1995, datelined Davenport, Iowa, reports that gambling is the fastest-growing industry in the United States, "a $40 billion business that draws more customers than baseball parks or movie theaters."[8] The *Times* cites a University of Illinois professor who estimates that state governments pay three dollars in costs to social agencies and the criminal justice system for every dollar of revenue they take in from the casinos—a calculus that Adam Smith might have predicted.

Iowa, for example, which did not even have a lottery until 1985, had ten big casinos by 1995, plus a horse track and a dog track with 24-hour slot machines. The article states that "nearly nine out of ten

Iowans say they gamble," with 5.4% of them reporting that they have a gambling problem, up from 1.7% five years earlier. This in a state where a Catholic priest went to jail in the 1970s on charges of running a bingo game. *Al zahr* in its purest form is apparently still with us.

Games of chance must be distinguished from games in which skill makes a difference. The principles at work in roulette, dice, and slot machines are identical, but they explain only part of what is involved in poker, betting on the horses, and backgammon. With one group of games the outcome is determined by fate; with the other group, choice comes into play. The odds—the probability of winning—are all you need to know for betting in a game of chance, but you need far more information to predict who will win and who will lose when the outcome depends on skill as well as luck. There are cardplayers and racetrack bettors who are genuine professionals, but no one makes a successful profession out of shooting craps.

Many observers consider the stock market itself little more than a gambling casino. Is winning in the stock market the result of skill combined with luck, or is it just the result of a lucky gamble? We shall return to this question in Chapter 12.

Losing streaks and winning streaks occur frequently in games of chance, as they do in real life. Gamblers respond to these events in asymmetric fashion: they appeal to the law of averages to bring losing streaks to a speedy end. And they appeal to that same law of averages to suspend itself so that winning streaks will go on and on. The law of averages hears neither appeal. The last sequence of throws of the dice conveys absolutely no information about what the next throw will bring. Cards, coins, dice, and roulette wheels have no memory.

Gamblers may think they are betting on red or seven or four-of-a-kind, but *in reality they are betting on the clock.* The loser wants a short run to look like a long run, so that the odds will prevail. The winner wants a long run to look like a short run, so that the odds will be suspended. Far away from the gaming tables, the managers of insurance companies conduct their affairs in the same fashion. They set their premiums to cover the losses they will sustain in the long run; but when earthquakes and fires and hurricanes all happen at about the same time, the short run can be very painful. Unlike gamblers, insurance companies carry capital and put aside reserves to tide them over during the inevitable sequences of short runs of bad luck.

Time is the dominant factor in gambling. Risk and time are opposite sides of the same coin, for if there were no tomorrow there would be no risk. Time transforms risk, and the nature of risk is shaped by the time horizon: the future is the playing field.

Time matters most when decisions are irreversible. And yet many irreversible decisions must be made on the basis of incomplete information. Irreversibility dominates decisions ranging all the way from taking the subway instead of a taxi, to building an automobile factory in Brazil, to changing jobs, to declaring war.

If we buy a stock today, we can always sell it tomorrow. But what do we do after the croupier at the roulette table cries, "No more bets!" or after a poker bet is doubled? There is no going back. Should we refrain from acting in the hope that the passage of time will make luck or the probabilities turn in our favor?

Hamlet complained that too much hesitation in the face of uncertain outcomes is bad because "the native hue of resolution is sicklied o'er with the pale cast of thought . . . and enterprises of great pith and moment . . . lose the name of action." Yet once we act, we forfeit the option of waiting until new information comes along. As a result, not-acting has value. The more uncertain the outcome, the greater may be the value of procrastination. Hamlet had it wrong: he who hesitates is halfway home.

To explain the beginning of everything, Greek mythology drew on a giant game of craps to explain what modern scientists call the Big Bang. Three brothers rolled dice for the universe, with Zeus winning the heavens, Poseidon the seas, and Hades, the loser, going to hell as master of the underworld.

Probability theory seems a subject made to order for the Greeks, given their zest for gambling, their skill as mathematicians, their mastery of logic, and their obsession with proof. Yet, though the most civilized of all the ancients, they never ventured into that fascinating world. Their failure to do so is astonishing because the Greeks had the only recorded civilization up to that point untrammeled by a dominating priesthood that claimed a monopoly on the lines of communication with the powers of mystery. Civilization as we know it might have progressed at a much faster pace if the Greeks had anticipated what their intellectual progeny—the men of the Renaissance—were to discover some thousand years later.

Despite the emphasis that the Greeks placed on theory, they had little interest in applying it to any kind of technology that would have changed their views of the manageability of the future. When Archimedes invented the lever, he claimed that he could move the earth if only he could find a place to stand. But apparently he gave no thought to changing it. The daily life of the Greeks, and their standard of living, were much the same as the way that their forebears had subsisted for thousands of years. They hunted, fished, grew crops, bore children, and used architectural techniques that were only variations on themes developed much earlier in the Tigris-Euphrates valley and in Egypt.

Genuflection before the winds was the only form of risk management that caught their attention: their poets and dramatists sing repeatedly of their dependence on the winds, and beloved children were sacrificed to appease the winds. Most important, the Greeks lacked a numbering system that would have enabled them to *calculate* instead of just recording the results of their activities.[9]

I do not mean to suggest that the Greeks gave no thought to the nature of probability. The ancient Greek word ΕΙΚΟΣ (*eikos*), which meant plausible or probable, had the same sense as the modern concept of probability: "to be expected with some degree of certainty." Socrates defines ΕΙΚΟΣ as "likeness to truth."[10]

Socrates' definition reveals a subtle point of great importance. *Likeness to truth is not the same thing as truth.* Truth to the Greeks was only what could be proved by logic and axioms. Their insistence on proof set truth in direct contrast to empirical experimentation. For example, in *Phaedo*, Simmias points out to Socrates that "the proposition that the soul is in harmony has not been demonstrated at all but rests only on probability." Aristotle complains about philosophers who, ". . . while they speak plausibly, . . .do not speak what is true." Elsewhere, Socrates anticipates Aristotle when he declares that a "mathematician who argues from probabilities in geometry is not worth an ace."[11] For another thousand years, *thinking* about games and *playing* them remained separate activities.

Shmuel Sambursky, a distinguished Israeli historian and philosopher of science, provides the only convincing thesis I could find to explain why the Greeks failed to take the strategic step of developing a quantitative approach to probability.[12] With their sharp distinction between truth and probability, Sambursky contends in a paper written in 1956, the Greeks could not conceive of any kind of solid structure or harmony in the messy nature of day-to-day existence. Although Aristotle suggested that people should make decisions on the basis of "desire and reasoning directed to some end," he offered no guidance to the likelihood of a successful outcome. Greek dramas tell tale after tale of the helplessness of human beings in the grasp of impersonal fates. When the Greeks wanted a prediction of what tomorrow might bring, they turned to the oracles instead of consulting their wisest philosophers.

The Greeks believed that order is to be found only in the skies, where the planets and stars regularly appear in their appointed places with an unmatched regularity. To this harmonious performance, the Greeks paid deep respect, and their mathematicians studied it intensely. But the perfection of the heavens served only to highlight the disarray of life on earth. Moreover, the predictability of the firmament contrasted sharply with the behavior of the fickle, foolish gods who dwelt on high.

The old Talmudic Jewish philosophers may have come a bit closer to quantifying risk. But here, too, we find no indication that they followed up on their reasoning by developing a methodical approach to risk. Sambursky cites a passage in the Talmud, *Kethuboth 9q*, where the philosopher explains that a man may divorce his wife for adultery without any penalty, but not if he claims that the adultery occurred before marriage.[13]

"It is a double doubt," declares the Talmud. If it is established (method unspecified) that the bride came to the marriage bed no longer a virgin, one side of the double doubt is whether the man responsible was the prospective groom himself—whether the event occurred "under him . . . or not under him." As to the second side of the doubt, the argument continues: "And if you say that it was under him, there

is doubt whether it was by violence or by her free will." Each side of
the double doubt is given a 50–50 chance. With impressive statistical
sophistication, the philosophers conclude that there is only one chance
in four ($1/2 \times 1/2$) that the woman committed adultery before marriage. Therefore, the husband cannot divorce her on those grounds.

One is tempted to assume that the lapse of time between the invention of the astragalus and the invention of the laws of probability was
nothing more than a historical accident. The Greeks and the Talmudic
scholars were so maddeningly close to the analysis that Pascal and
Fermat would undertake centuries later that only a slight push would
have moved them on to the next step.

That the push did not occur was not an accident. Before a society
could incorporate the concept of risk into its culture, change would have
to come, not in views of the present, but in attitudes about the future.

Up to the time of the Renaissance, people perceived the future as
little more than a matter of luck or the result of random variations, and
most of their decisions were driven by instinct. When the conditions of
life are so closely linked to nature, not much is left to human control.
As long as the demands of survival limit people to the basic functions of
bearing children, growing crops, hunting, fishing, and providing shelter, they are simply unable to conceive of circumstances in which they
might be able to influence the outcomes of their decisions. A penny
saved is not a penny earned unless the future is something more than a
black hole.

Over the centuries, at least until the Crusades, most people met
with few surprises as they ambled along from day to day. Nestled in a
stable social structure, they gave little heed to the wars that swept across
the land, to the occasions when bad rulers succeeded good ones, and
even to the permutations of religions. Weather was the most apparent
variable. As the Egyptologist Henri Frankfort has remarked, "The past
and the future—far from being a matter of concern—were wholly
implicit in the present."[14]

Despite the persistence of this attitude toward the future, civilization made great strides over the centuries. Clearly the absence of modern views about risk was no obstacle. At the same time, the advance of

civilization was not in itself a sufficient condition to motivate curious people to explore the possibilities of scientific forecasting.

As Christianity spread across the western world, the will of a single God emerged as the orienting guide to the future, replacing the miscellany of deities people had worshiped since the beginning of time. This brought a major shift in perception: the future of life on earth remained a mystery, but it was now prescribed by a power whose intentions and standards were clear to all who took the time to learn them.

As contemplation of the future became a matter of moral behavior and faith, the future no longer appeared quite as inscrutable as it had. Nevertheless, it was still not susceptible to any sort of mathematical expectation. The early Christians limited their prophecies to what would happen in the afterlife, no matter how fervidly they beseeched God to influence worldly events in their favor.

Yet the search for a better life on earth persisted. By the year 1000, Christians were sailing great distances, meeting new peoples, and encountering new ideas. Then came the Crusades—a seismic culture shock. Westerners collided with an Arab empire that had been launched at Mohammed's urging and that stretched as far eastward as India. Christians, with faith in the future, met Arabs who had achieved an intellectual sophistication far greater than that of the interlopers who had come to dislodge them from the holy sites.

The Arabs, through their invasion of India, had become familiar with the Hindu numbering system, which enabled them to incorporate eastern intellectual advances into their own scholarship, scientific research, and experimentation. The results were momentous, first for the Arabs and then for the West.*

In the hands of the Arabs, the Hindu numbers would transform mathematics and measurement in astronomy, navigation, and commerce. New methods of calculation gradually replaced the abacus,

---

*Peter Kinder has pointed out to me a great historical irony in all this. The Vikings and other Norsemen who laid waste to Roman civilization and destroyed the repositories of learning in the ninth century reappear in history as the Normans who brought back to the West the achievements of Arabic learning in the twelfth century.

which for centuries had been the only tool for doing arithmetic every-where from the Mayans in the western hemisphere, across Europe, to India and the Orient. The word *abacus* derives from the Greek word *abax*, which means sand-tray. Within the trays, columns of pebbles were laid out on the sand.[15] The word *calculate* stems from *calculus*, the Latin word for pebble.

Over the next five hundred years, as the new numbering system took the place of the simple abacus, writing replaced movable counters in making calculations. Written computation fostered abstract thinking, which opened the way to areas of mathematics never conceived of in the past. Now sea voyages could be longer, time-keeping more accu-rate, architecture more ambitious, and production methods more elab-orate. The modern world would be quite different if we still measured and counted with I, V, X, L, C, D, and M—or with the Greek or Hebrew letters that stood for numbers.

But Arabic numbers were not enough to induce Europeans to explore the radical concept of replacing randomness with systematic probability and its implicit suggestion that the future might be pre-dictable and even controllable to some degree. That advance had to await the realization that human beings are not totally helpless in the hands of fate, nor is their worldly destiny always determined by God.

The Renaissance and the Protestant Reformation would set the scene for the mastery of risk. As mysticism yielded to science and logic after 1300 AD, Greek and Roman architectural forms began to replace Gothic forms, church windows were opened to the light, and sculptures showed men and women standing firmly on the ground instead posing as stylized figures with neither muscle nor weight. The ideas that pro-pelled changes in the arts also contributed to the Protestant Reformation and weakened the dominance of the Catholic Church.

The Reformation meant more than just a change in humanity's rela-tionship with God. By eliminating the confessional, it warned people that henceforth they would have to walk on their own two feet and would have to take responsibility for the consequences of their decisions.

But if men and women were not at the mercy of impersonal deities and random chance, they could no longer remain passive in the face of an unknown future. They had no choice but to begin making decisions over a far wider range of circumstances and over far longer periods of time than ever before. The concepts of thrift and abstinence that characterize the Protestant ethic evidenced the growing importance of the future relative to the present. With this opening up of choices and decisions, people gradually recognized that the future offered opportunity as well as danger, that it was open-ended and full of promise. The 1500s and 1600s were a time of geographical exploration, confrontation with new lands and new societies, and experimentation in art, poetic forms, science, architecture, and mathematics. The new sense of opportunity led to a dramatic acceleration in the growth of trade and commerce, which served as a powerful stimulus to change and exploration. Columbus was not conducting a Caribbean cruise: he was seeking a new trade route to the Indies. The prospect of getting rich is highly motivating, and few people get rich without taking a gamble.

There is more to that blunt statement than meets the eye. Trade is a mutually beneficial process, a transaction in which both parties perceive themselves as wealthier than they were before. What a radical idea! Up to that point, people who got rich had done so largely by exploitation or by plundering another's wealth. Although Europeans continued to plunder across the seas, at home the accumulation of wealth was open to the many rather than the few. The newly rich were now the smart, the adventuresome, the innovators—most of them businessmen—instead of just the hereditary princes and their minions.

Trade is also a risky business. As the growth of trade transformed the principles of gambling into the creation of wealth, the inevitable result was capitalism, the epitome of risk-taking. But capitalism could not have flourished without two new activities that had been unnecessary so long as the future was a matter of chance or of God's will. The first was bookkeeping, a humble activity but one that encouraged the dissemination of the new techniques of numbering and counting. The other was forecasting, a much less humble and far more challenging activity that links risk-taking with direct payoffs.

You do not plan to ship goods across the ocean, or to assemble merchandise for sale, or to borrow money without first trying to determine what the future may hold in store. Ensuring that the materials you order are delivered on time, seeing to it that the items you plan to sell are produced on schedule, and getting your sales facilities in place all must be planned before that moment when the customers show up and

2

As Easy as I, II, III

Without numbers, there are no odds and no probabilities; without odds and probabilities, the only way to deal with risk is to appeal to the gods and the fates. Without numbers, risk is wholly a matter of gut.

We live in a world of numbers and calculations, from the clock we squint at when we wake up, to the television channel we switch off at bedtime. As the day proceeds, we count the measures of coffee we put into the coffeemaker, pay the housekeeper, consult yesterday's stock prices, dial a friend's telephone number, check the amount of gas in the car and the speed on the speedometer, press the elevator button in our office building, and open the office door with our number on it. And the day has hardly started!

It is hard for us to imagine a time without numbers. Yet if we were able to spirit a well-educated man from the year 1000 to the present, he probably would not recognize the number zero and would surely flunk third-grade arithmetic; few people from the year 1500 would fare much better.

The story of numbers in the West begins in 1202, when the cathedral of Chartres was nearing completion and King John was finishing his third year on the throne of England. In that year, a book titled *Liber Abaci*, or *Book of the Abacus*, appeared in Italy. The fifteen chapters of the book were entirely handwritten; almost three hundred years would pass before the invention of printing. The author, Leonardo Pisano, was only 27 years old but a very lucky man: his book would receive the endorsement of the Holy Roman Emperor, Frederick II. No author could have done much better than that.[1]

Leonardo Pisano was known for most of his life as Fibonacci, the name by which he is known today. His father's first name was Bonacio, and Fibonacci is a contraction of son-of-Bonacio. Bonacio means "simpleton" and Fibonacci means "blockhead." Bonacio must have been something less than a simpleton, however, for he represented Pisa as consul in a number of different cities, and his son Leonardo was certainly no blockhead.

Fibonacci was inspired to write *Liber Abaci* on a visit to Bugia, a thriving Algerian city where his father was serving as Pisan consul. While Fibonacci was there, an Arab mathematician revealed to him the wonders of the Hindu-Arabic numbering system that Arab mathematicians had introduced to the West during the Crusades to the Holy Land. When Fibonacci saw all the calculations that this system made possible—calculations that could not possibly be managed with Roman letter-numerals—he set about learning everything he could about it. To study with the leading Arab mathematicians living around the Mediterranean, he set off on a trip that took him to Egypt, Syria, Greece, Sicily, and Provence.

The result was a book that is extraordinary by any standard. *Liber Abaci* made people aware of a whole new world in which numbers could be substituted for the Hebrew, Greek, and Roman systems that used letters for counting and calculating. The book rapidly attracted a following among mathematicians, both in Italy and across Europe.

Liber Abaci is far more than a primer for reading and writing with the new numerals. Fibonacci begins with instructions on how to determine from the number of digits in a numeral whether it is a unit, or a multiple of ten, or a multiple of 100, and so on. Later chapters exhibit a higher level of sophistication. There we find calculations using whole numbers and fractions, rules of proportion, extraction of square roots and roots of higher orders, and even solutions for linear and quadratic equations.

Ingenious and original as Fibonacci's exercises were, if the book had dealt only with theory it would probably not have attracted much attention beyond a small circle of mathematical cognoscenti. It commanded an enthusiastic following, however, because Fibonacci filled it with practical applications. For example, he described and illustrated many innovations that the new numbers made possible in commercial bookkeeping, such as figuring profit margins, money-changing, conversions of weights and measures, and—though usury was still prohibited in many places—he even included calculations of interest payments.

Liber Abaci provided just the kind of stimulation that a man as brilliant and creative as the Emperor Frederick would be sure to enjoy. Though Frederick, who ruled from 1211 to 1250, exhibited cruelty and an obsession with earthly power, he was genuinely interested in science, the arts, and the philosophy of government. In Sicily, he destroyed all the private garrisons and feudal castles, taxed the clergy, and banned them from civil office. He also set up an expert bureaucracy, abolished internal tolls, removed all regulations inhibiting imports, and shut down the state monopolies.

Frederick tolerated no rivals. Unlike his grandfather, Frederick Barbarossa, who was humbled by the Pope at the Battle of Legnano in 1176, this Frederick reveled in his endless battles with the papacy. His intransigence brought him not just one excommunication, but two. On the second occasion, Pope Gregory IX called for Frederick to be deposed, characterizing him as a heretic, rake, and anti-Christ. Frederick responded with a savage attack on papal territory; meanwhile his fleet captured a large delegation of prelates on their way to Rome to join the synod that had been called to remove him from power.

Frederick surrounded himself with the leading intellectuals of his age, inviting many of them to join him in Palermo. He built some of Sicily's most beautiful castles, and in 1224 he founded a university to train public servants—the first European university to enjoy a royal charter.

Frederick was fascinated with *Liber Abaci*. Some time in the 1220s, while on a visit to Pisa, he invited Fibonacci to appear before him. In the course of the interview, Fibonacci solved problems in algebra and cubic equations put to him by one of Frederick's many scientists-in-residence. Fibonacci subsequently wrote a book prompted by this meeting, *Liber Quadratorum,* or *The Book of Squares*, which he dedicated to the Emperor.

Fibonacci is best known for a short passage in *Liber Abaci* that led to something of a mathematical miracle. The passage concerns the problem of how many rabbits will be born in the course of a year from an original pair of rabbits, assuming that every month each pair produces another pair and that rabbits begin to breed when they are two months old. Fibonacci discovered that the original pair of rabbits would have spawned a total of 233 pairs of offspring in the course of a year.

He discovered something else, much more interesting. He had assumed that the original pair would not breed until the second month and then would produce another pair every month. By the fourth month, their first two offspring would begin breeding. After the process got started, the total number of pairs of rabbits at the end of each month would be as follows: 1, 2, 3, 5, 8, 13, 21, 34, 55, 89, 144, 233. Each successive number is the sum of the two preceding numbers. If the rabbits kept going for a hundred months, the total number pairs would be 354,224,848,179,261,915,075.

The Fibonacci series is a lot more than a source of amusement. Divide any of the Fibonacci numbers by the next higher number. After 3, the answer is always 0.625. After 89, the answer is always 0.618; after higher numbers, more decimal places can be filled in.* Divide any number by its preceding number. After 2, the answer is always 1.6. After 144, the answer is always 1.618.

The Greeks knew this proportion and called it "the golden mean." The golden mean defines the proportions of the Parthenon, the shape of playing cards and credit cards, and the proportions of the General Assembly Building at the United Nations in New York. The horizontal member of most Christian crosses separates the vertical member by just about the same ratio: the length above the crosspiece is 61.8% of the length below it. The golden mean also appears throughout nature—in flower patterns, the leaves of an artichoke, and the leaf stubs on a palm tree. It is also the ratio of the length of the human body above the navel to its length below the navel (in normally proportioned people, that is). The length of each successive bone in our fingers, from tip to hand, also bears this ratio.†

In one of its more romantic manifestations, the Fibonacci ratio defines the proportions and shape of a beautiful spiral. The accompanying illustrations demonstrate how the spiral develops from a series of

---

*One of those odd quirks that numbers can produce reveals that you can derive 0.618 if you take the square root of 5, which is 2.24, subtract 1, and then divide by 2; this result is the algebraic proof of Fibonacci's sequence of numbers.

†In technical terms, the formula for the Fibonacci ratio is as follows: the ratio of the smaller part to the larger part equals the ratio of the larger part to the whole.

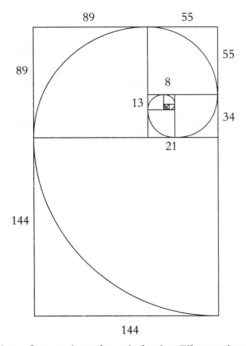

Construction of an equiangular spiral using Fibonacci proportions.
Begin with a 1-unit square, attach another 1-unit square, then a 2-unit square then a 2-unit square where it fits, followed by a 3-unit square where it fits and, continuing in the same direction, attach squares of 5, 8, 13, 21, and 34 units and so on.

(Reproduced with permission from Fascinating Fibonaccis, *by Trudy Hammel Garland; copyright 1987 by Dale Seymour Publications, P.O. Box 10888, Palo Alto, CA 94303.)*

squares whose successive relative dimensions are determined by the
Fibonacci series. The process begins with two small squares of equal size.
It then progresses to an adjacent square twice the size of the first two,
then to a square three times the size of the first two, then to five times,
and so on. Note that the sequence produces a series of rectangles with
the proportions of the golden mean. Then quarter-circle arcs connect
the opposite corners of the squares, starting with the smallest squares
and proceeding in sequence.

This familiar-looking spiral appears in the shape of certain galaxies,
in a ram's horn, in many seashells, and in the coil of the ocean waves that
surfers ride. The structure maintains its form without change as it is
made larger and larger and regardless of the size of the initial square with
which the process is launched: form is independent of growth. The
journalist William Hoffer has remarked, "The great golden spiral seems
to be nature's way of building quantity without sacrificing quality."[2]

Some people believe that the Fibonacci numbers can be used to make
a wide variety of predictions, especially predictions about the stock market; such predictions work just often enough to keep the enthusiasm
going. The Fibonacci sequence is so fascinating that there is even an
American Fibonacci Association, located at Santa Clara University in
California, which has published thousands of pages of research on the
subject since 1962.

Fibonacci's *Liber Abaci* was a spectacular first step in making measurement the key factor in the taming of risk. But society was not yet
prepared to attach numbers to risk. In Fibonacci's day, most people still
thought that risk stemmed from the capriciousness of nature. People
would have to learn to recognize man-made risks and acquire the
courage to do battle with the fates before they would accept the techniques of taming risk. That acceptance was still at least two hundred
years in the future.

We can appreciate the full measure of Fibonacci's achievement
only by looking back to the era before he explained how to tell the difference between 10 and 100. Yet even there we shall discover some
remarkable innovators.

Primitive people like the Neanderthals knew how to tally, but they had few things that required tallying. They marked the passage of days on a stone or a log and kept track of the number of animals they killed. The sun kept time for them, and five minutes or a half-hour either way hardly mattered.

The first systematic efforts to measure and count were undertaken some ten thousand years before the birth of Christ.[3] It was then that humans settled down to grow food in the valleys washed by such great rivers as the Tigris and the Euphrates, the Nile, the Indus, the Yangtse, the Mississippi, and the Amazon. The rivers soon became highways for trade and travel, eventually leading the more venturesome people to the oceans and seas into which the rivers emptied. To travelers ranging over longer and longer distances, calendar time, navigation, and geography mattered a great deal and these factors required ever more precise computations.

Priests were the first astronomers, and from astronomy came mathematics. When people recognized that nicks on stones and sticks no longer sufficed, they began to group numbers into tens or twenties, which were easy to count on fingers and toes.

Although the Egyptians became experts in astronomy and in predicting the times when the Nile would flood or withdraw, managing or influencing the future probably never entered their minds. Change was not part of their mental processes, which were dominated by habit, seasonality, and respect for the past.

About 450 BC, the Greeks devised an alphabetic numbering system that used the 24 letters of the Greek alphabet and three letters that subsequently became obsolete. Each number from 1 to 9 had its own letter, and the multiples of ten each had a letter. For example, the symbol "pi" comes from the first letter of the Greek word "penta," which represented 5; delta, the first letter of "deca," the word for 10, represented 10; alpha, the first letter of the alphabet, represented 1, and rho represented 100. Thus, 115 was written rho–deca–penta, or $\rho\delta\pi$. The Hebrews, although Bemitic rather than Indo-European, used the same kind of cipher-alphabet system.[4]

Handy as these letter–numbers were in helping people to build stronger structures, travel longer distances, and keep more accurate time, the system had serious limitations. You could use letters only with great difficulty—and almost never in your head—for adding or subtracting or multiplying or dividing. These substitutes for numbers provided nothing more than a means of recording the *results* of calculations performed by other methods, most often on a counting frame or abacus. The abacus—the oldest counting device in history—ruled the world of mathematics until the Hindu-Arabic numbering system arrived on the scene between about 1000 and 1200 AD.

The abacus works by specifying an upper limit for the number of counters in each column; in adding, as the furthest right column fills up, the excess counters move one column to the left, and so on. Our concepts of "borrow one" or "carry over three" date back to the abacus.[5]

Despite the limitations of these early forms of mathematics, they made possible great advances in knowledge, particularly in geometry—the language of shape—and its many applications in astronomy, navigation, and mechanics. Here the most impressive advances were made by the Greeks and by their colleagues in Alexandria. Only the Bible has appeared in more editions and printings than Euclid's most famous book, *Elements*.

Still, the greatest contribution of the Greeks was not in scientific innovation. After all, the temple priests of Egypt and Babylonia had learned a good bit about geometry long before Euclid came along. Even the famous theorem of Pythagoras—the square of the hypotenuse of a right triangle is equal to the sum of the square of the other two sides—was in use in the Tigris-Euphrates valley as early as 2000 BC.

The unique quality of the Greek spirit was the insistence on *proof.* "Why?" mattered more to them than "What?" The Greeks were able to reframe the ultimate questions because theirs was the first civilization in history to be free of the intellectual straitjacket imposed by an all-powerful priesthood. This same set of attitudes led the Greeks to become the world's first tourists and colonizers as they made the Mediterranean basin their private preserve.

More worldly as a consequence, the Greeks refused to accept at face value the rules of thumb that older societies passed on to them. They were not interested in samples; their goal was to find concepts that would apply everywhere, in every case. For example, mere measurement would confirm that the square of the hypotenuse of a right triangle is equal to the sum of the squares of the other two sides. But the Greeks asked why that should be so, in all right triangles, great and small, without a single exception to the rule. Proof is what Euclidean geometry is all about. And proof, not calculation, would dominate the theory of mathematics forever after.

This radical break with the analytical methodologies of other civilizations makes us wonder again why it was that the Greeks failed to discover the laws of probability, and calculus, and even simple algebra. Perhaps, despite all they achieved, it was because they had to depend on a clumsy numbering system based on their alphabet. The Romans suffered from the same handicap. As simple a number as 9 required two letters: IX. The Romans could not write 32 as III II, because people would have no way of knowing whether it meant 32, 302, 3020, or some larger combination of 3, 2, and 0. Calculations based on such a system were impossible.

But the discovery of a superior numbering system would not occur until about 500 AD, when the Hindus developed the numbering system we use today. Who contrived this miraculous invention, and what circumstances led to its spread throughout the Indian subcontinent, remain mysteries. The Arabs encountered the new numbers for the first time some ninety years after Mohammed established Islam as a proselytizing religion in 622 and his followers, united into a powerful nation, swept into India and beyond.

The new system of numbering had a galvanizing effect on intellectual activity in lands to the west. Baghdad, already a great center of learning, emerged as a hub of mathematical research and activity, and the Caliph retained Jewish scholars to translate the works of such pioneers of mathematics as Ptolemy and Euclid. The major works of mathematics were soon circulating throughout the Arab empire and by the ninth and tenth centuries were in use as far west as Spain.

Actually, one westerner had suggested a numbering system at least two centuries earlier than the Hindus. About 250 AD, an Alexandrian mathematician named Diophantus wrote a treatise setting forth the advantages of a system of true numbers to replace letters substituting for numbers.[6]

Not much is known about Diophantus, but the little we do know is amusing. According to Herbert Warren Turnbull, a historian of mathematics, a Greek epigram about Diophantus states that "his boyhood lasted 1/6th of his life; his beard grew after 1/12th more; he married after 1/7th more, and his son was born five years later; the son lived to half his father's age, and the father died four years after his son." How old was Diophantus when he died?[7] Algebra enthusiasts will find the answer at the end of this chapter.

Diophantus carried the idea of symbolic algebra—the use of symbols to stand for numbers—a long way, but he could not quite make it all the way. He comments on "the impossible solution of the absurd equation $4 = 4x + 20$."[8] Impossible? Absurd? The equation requires x to be a negative number: -4. Without the concept of zero, which Diophantus lacked, a negative number is a logical impossibility.

Diophantus's remarkable innovations seem to have been ignored. Almost a millennium and a half passed before anyone took note of his work. At last his achievements received their due: his treatise played a central role in the flowering of algebra in the seventeenth century. The algebraic equations we are all familiar with today—equations like $a + bx = c$—are known as Diophantine equations.

The centerpiece of the Hindu-Arabic system was the invention of zero—*sunya* as the Indians called it, and *cifr* as it became in Arabic.[9] The term has come down to us as "cipher," which means empty and refers to the empty column in the abacus or counting frame.*

The concept of zero was difficult to grasp for people who had used counting only to keep track of the number of animals killed or the number of days passed or the number of units traveled. Zero had nothing to do with what counting was for in that sense. As the twentieth-century English philosopher Alfred North Whitehead put it,

---

*The Arabic term survives even in Russian, where it appears as *tsifra*, which is the word for number.

The point about zero is that we do not need to use it in the operations of daily life. No one goes out to buy zero fish. It is in a way the most civilized of all the cardinals, and its use is only forced on us by the needs of cultivated modes of thought.[10]

Whitehead's phrase "cultivated modes of thought" suggests that the concept of zero unleashed something more profound than just an enhanced method of counting and calculating. As Diophantus had sensed, a proper numbering system would enable mathematics to develop into a science of the abstract as well as a technique for measurement. Zero blew out the limits to ideas and to progress.

Zero revolutionized the old numbering system in two ways. First, it meant that people could use only ten digits, from zero to nine, to perform every conceivable calculation and to write any conceivable number. Second, it meant that a sequence of numbers like 1, 10, 100 would indicate that the next number in the sequence would be 1000. Zero makes the whole structure of the numbering system immediately visible and clear. Try that with the Roman numerals I, X, and C, or with V, L, and D—what is the next number in those sequences?

The earliest known work in Arabic arithmetic was written by al-Khowârizmî, a mathematician who lived around 825, some four hundred years before Fibonacci.[11] Although few beneficiaries of his work are likely to have heard of him, most of us know of him indirectly. Try saying "al-Khowârizmî" fast. That's where we get the word "algorithm," which means rules for computing.[12] It was al-Khowârizmî who was the first mathematician to establish rules for adding, subtracting, multiplying, and dividing with the new Hindu numerals. In another treatise, *Hisâb al-jabr w'almuqâbalah,* or "Science of transposition and cancellation," he specifies the process for manipulating algebraic equations. The word *al-jabr* thus gives us our word *algebra,* the science of equations.[13]

One of the most important, surely the most famous, early mathematician was Omar Khayyam, who lived from about 1050 to about 1130 and was the author of the collection of poems known as the *Rubaiyat.*[14] His haunting sequence of 75 four-line poems (the word

Rubaiyat defines the poetic form) was translated in Victorian times by the English poet Edward Fitzgerald. This slim volume has more to do with the delights of drinking wine and taking advantage of the transitory nature of life than with science or mathematics. Indeed, in number XXVII, Omar Khayyam writes:

> Myself when young did eagerly frequent
> Doctor and Saint, and heard great Argument
> About it and about; but evermore
> Came out by the same Door as in I went.

According to Fitzgerald, Omar Khayyam was educated along with two friends, both as bright as he: Nizam al Mulk and Hasan al Sabbah. One day Hasan proposed that, since at least one of the three would attain wealth and power, they should vow that "to whomsoever this fortune falls, he shall share it equally with the rest, and preserve no preeminence for himself." They all took the oath, and in time Nizam became vizier to the sultan. His two friends sought him out and claimed their due, which he granted as promised.

Hasan demanded and received a place in the government, but, dissatisfied with his advancement, left to become head of a sect of fanatics who spread terror throughout the Mohammedan world. Many years later, Hasan would end up assassinating his old friend Nizam.

Omar Khayyam asked for neither title nor office. "The greatest boon you can confer on me," he said to Nizam, "is to let me live in a corner under the shadow of your fortune, to spread wide the advantages of science and pray for your long life and prosperity." Although the sultan loved Omar Khayyam and showered favors on him, "Omar's epicurean audacity of thought and speech caused him to be regarded askance in his own time and country."

Omar Khayyam used the new numbering system to develop a language of calculation that went beyond the efforts of al-Khowârizmî and served as a basis for the more complicated language of algebra. In addition, Omar Khayyam used technical mathematical observations to reform the calendar and to devise a triangular rearrangement of numbers that facilitated the figuring of squares, cubes, and higher powers of mathematics; this triangle formed the basis of concepts developed by the seventeenth-century French mathematician Blaise Pascal, one of the fathers of the theory of choice, chance, and probability.

The impressive achievements of the Arabs suggest once again that an idea can go so far and still stop short of a logical conclusion. Why, given their advanced mathematical ideas, did the Arabs not proceed to probability theory and risk management? The answer, I believe, has to do with their view of life. Who determines our future: the fates, the gods, or ourselves? The idea of risk management emerges only when people believe that they are to some degree free agents. Like the Greeks and the early Christians, the fatalistic Muslims were not yet ready to take the leap.

By the year 1000, the new numbering system was being popularized by Moorish universities in Spain and elsewhere and by the Saracens in Sicily. A Sicilian coin, issued by the Normans and dated "1134 Annoy Domini," is the first known example of the system in actual use. Still, the new numbers were not widely used until the thirteenth century.

Despite Emperor Frederick's patronage of Fibonacci's book and the book's widespread distribution across Europe, introduction of the Hindu-Arabic numbering system provoked intense and bitter resistance up to the early 1500s. Here, for once, we can explain the delay. Two factors were at work.

Part of the resistance stemmed from the inertial forces that oppose any change in matters hallowed by centuries of use. Learning radically new methods never finds an easy welcome.

The second factor was based on more solid ground: it was easier to commit fraud with the new numbers than with the old. Turning a 0 into a 6 or a 9 was temptingly easy, and a 1 could be readily converted into a 4, 6, 7, or 9 (one reason Europeans write 7 as 7̶). Although the new numbers had gained their first foothold in Italy, where education levels were high, Florence issued an edict in 1229 that forbade bankers from using the "infidel" symbols. As a result, many people who wanted to learn the new system had to disguise themselves as Moslems in order to do so.[15]

The invention of printing with movable type in the middle of the fifteenth century was the catalyst that finally overcame opposition to the full use of the new numbers. Now the fraudulent alterations were no longer possible. Now the ridiculous complications of using Roman numerals became clear to everyone. The breakthrough gave a great lift to commercial transactions. Now al-Khowârizmî's multiplication tables became something that all school children have had to learn forever after. Finally, with the first inklings of the laws of probability, gambling took on a whole new dimension.

The algebraic solution to the epigram about Diophantus is as follows. If x was his age when he died, then:

$$x = \frac{x}{6} + \frac{x}{12} + \frac{x}{7} + 5 + \frac{x}{2} + 4.$$

Diophantus lived to be 84 years old.

1200–1700: A THOUSAND
OUTSTANDING FACTS

3

The Renaissance Gambler

Piero della Francesca, who painted the picture of the Virgin that appears on the following page ("The Brera Madonna"), lived from about 1420 to 1492, more than two hundred years after Fibonacci. His dates place him at the center of the Italian Renaissance, and his work epitomizes the break between the new spirit of the fifteenth century and the spirit of the Middle Ages.

Della Francesca's figures, even that of the Virgin herself, represent human beings. They have no halos, they stand solidly on the ground, they are portraits of individuals, and they occupy their own three-dimensional space. Although they are presumably there to receive the Virgin and the Christ Child, most of them seem to be directing their attention to other matters. The Gothic use of shadows in architectural space to create mystery has disappeared; here the shadows serve to emphasize the weight of the structure and the delineation of space that frames the figures.

The egg seems to be hanging over the Virgin's head. More careful study of the painting suggests some uncertainty as to exactly where this heavenly symbol of fertility does hang. And why are these earthly, if pious, men and women so unaware of the strange phenomenon that has appeared above them?

Madonna of Duke Federico Il di Montefeltro. Pinacoteca di Brera, Milan, Italy.

(Reproduction courtesy of Scala/Art Resource, NY.)

Greek philosophy has been turned upside down. Now the mystery is in the heavens. On earth, men and women are free-standing human beings. These people respect representations of divinity but are by no means subservient to it—a message that appears over and over again in the art of the Renaissance. Donatello's charming statue of David was among the first male nude sculptures created since the days of classical Greece and Rome; the great poet-hero of the Old Testament stands confidently before us, unashamed of his pre-adolescent body, Goliath's head at his feet. Brunelleschi's great dome in Florence and the cathedral, with its clearly defined mass and unadorned interior, proclaims that religion has literally been brought down to earth.

The Renaissance was a time of discovery. Columbus set sail in the year Piero died; not long afterward, Copernicus revolutionized humanity's view of the heavens themselves. Copernicus's achievements required a high level of mathematical skill, and during the sixteenth century advances in mathematics were swift and exciting, especially in Italy. Following the introduction of printing from movable type around 1450, many of the classics in mathematics were translated into Italian and published either in Latin or in the vernacular. Mathematicians engaged in spirited public debates over solutions to complex algebraic equations while the crowds cheered on their favorites.

The stimulus for much of this interest dates from 1494, with the publication of a remarkable book written by a Franciscan monk named Luca Paccioli.[1] Paccioli was born about 1445, in Piero della Francesca's hometown of Borgo San Sepulcro. Although Paccioli's family urged the boy to prepare for a career in business, Piero taught him writing, art, and history and urged him to make use of the famous library at the nearby Court of Urbino. There Paccioli's studies laid the foundation for his subsequent fame as a mathematician.

At the age of twenty, Paccioli obtained a position in Venice as tutor to the sons of a rich merchant. He attended public lectures in philosophy and theology and studied mathematics with a private tutor. An apt student, he wrote his first published work in mathematics while in Venice. His Uncle Benedetto, a military officer stationed in Venice, taught Paccioli about architecture as well as military affairs.

In 1470, Paccioli moved to Rome to continue his studies and at the age of 27 he became a Franciscan monk. He continued to move about, however. He taught mathematics in Perugia, Rome, Naples, Pisa, and

Venice before settling down as professor of mathematics in Milan in 1496. Ten years earlier, he had received the title of magister, equivalent to a doctorate.

Paccioli's masterwork, *Summa de arithmetic, geometria et proportionalità* (most serious academic works were still being written in Latin), appeared in 1494. Written in praise of the "very great abstraction and subtlety of mathematics," the *Summa* acknowledges Paccioli's debt to Fibonacci's *Liber Abaci*, written nearly three hundred years earlier. The *Summa* sets out the basic principles of algebra and contains multiplication tables all the way up to 60 × 60—a useful feature at a time when printing was spreading the use of the new numbering system.

One of the book's most durable contributions was its presentation of double-entry bookkeeping. This was not Paccioli's invention, though his treatment of it was the most extensive to date. The notion of double-entry bookkeeping was apparent in Fibonacci's *Liber Abaci* and had shown up in a book published about 1305 by the London branch of an Italian firm. Whatever its source, this revolutionary innovation in accounting methods had significant economic consequences, comparable to the discovery of the steam engine three hundred years later.

While in Milan, Paccioli met Leonardo da Vinci, who became a close friend. Paccioli was enormously impressed with Leonardo's talents and commented on his "invaluable work on spatial motion, percussion, weight and all forces."[2] They must have had much in common, for Paccioli was interested in the interrelationships between mathematics and art. He once observed that "if you say that music satisfies hearing, one of the natural senses . . . [perspective] will do so for sight, which is so much more worthy in that it is the first door of the intellect."

Leonardo had known little about mathematics before meeting Paccioli, though he had an intuitive sense of proportion and geometry. His notebooks are full of drawings made with a straight-edge and a compass, but Paccioli encouraged him to master the concepts he been using intuitively. Martin Kemp, one of Leonardo's biographers, claims that Paccioli "provided the stimulus for a sudden transformation in Leonardo's mathematical ambitions, effecting a reorientation in Leonardo's interest in a way which no other contemporary thinker accomplished." Leonardo in turn supplied complex drawings for Paccioli's other great work, *De Divine Proportione*, which appeared in two handsome manuscripts in 1498. The printed edition came out in 1509.

Leonardo owned a copy of the *Summa* and must have studied it with great care. His notebooks record repeated attempts to understand multiples and fractions as an aid to his use of proportion. At one point, he admonishes himself to "learn the multiplication of the roots from master Luca." Today, Leonardo would barely squeak by in a third-grade arithmetic class.

The fact that a Renaissance genius like da Vinci had so much difficulty with elementary arithmetic is a revealing commentary on the state of mathematical understanding at the end of the fifteenth century. How did mathematicians find their way from here to the first steps of a system to measuring risk and controlling it?

Paccioli himself sensed the power that the miracle of numbers could unleash. In the course of the *Summa*, he poses the following problem:

> A and B are playing a fair game of *balla*. They agree to continue until one has won six rounds. The game actually stops when A has won five and B three. How should the stakes be divided?[3]

This brain-teaser appears repeatedly in the writings of mathematicians during the sixteenth and seventeenth centuries. There are many variations but the question is always the same: How do we divide the stakes in an uncompleted game? The answers differed and prompted heated debates.

The puzzle, which came to be known as the problem of the points, was more significant than it appears. The resolution of how to divide the stakes in an uncompleted game marked the beginning of a systematic analysis of probability—the measure of our confidence that something is going to happen. *It brings us to the threshold of the quantification of risk.*

While we can understand that medieval superstitions imposed a powerful barrier to investigations into the theory of probability, it is interesting to speculate once again about why the Greeks, or even the Romans, had no interest in puzzles like Paccioli's.

The Greeks understood that more things might happen in the future than actually *will* happen. They recognized that the natural sciences are "the science of the probable," to use Plato's terminology.

Aristotle, in *De Caelo* says, "To succeed in many things, or many times, is difficult; for instance, to repeat the same throw ten thousand times with the dice would be impossible, whereas to make it once or twice is comparatively easy."[4]

Simple observation would have confirmed these statements. Yet the Greeks and the Romans played games of chance by rules that make no sense in our own times. This failure is all the more curious, because these games were popular throughout antiquity (the Greeks were already familiar with six-sided dice) and provided a lively laboratory for studying odds and probabilities.

Consider the games played with astragali, the bones used as dice. These objects were oblong, with two narrow faces and two wide faces. The games usually involved throwing four astragali together. The odds of landing on a wide face are obviously higher than the odds of landing on a narrow face. So one would expect the score for landing on a narrow face to be higher than the score for landing on a wide face. But the total scores received for landing on the more difficult narrow faces—1 on one face and 6 on the other—was identical to the scores for the easier wide faces—3 and 4. The "Venus" throw, a play in which each of the four faces—1, 3, 4, 6—appear, earned the most, although equally probable throws of 6, 6, 6, 6 or 1, 1, 1, 1 earned less.[5]

Even though it was common knowledge that long runs of success, or of failure, were less probable than short runs, as Aristotle had pointed out, those expectations were qualitative, not quantitative: ". . . to make it once or twice is comparatively easy."[6] Though people played these games with insatiable enthusiasm, no one appears to have sat down to figure the odds.

In all likelihood the reason was that the Greeks had little interest in experimentation; theory and proof were all that mattered to them. They appear never to have considered the idea of reproducing a certain phenomenon often enough to prove a hypothesis, presumably because they admitted no possibility of regularity in earthly events. Precision was the monopoly of the gods.

By the time of the Renaissance, however, everyone from scientists to explorers and from painters to architects was caught up in investigation, experimentation, and demonstration. Someone who threw a lot of dice would surely be curious about the regularities that turned up over time.

A sixteenth-century physician named Girolamo Cardano was just such a person. Cardano's credentials as a gambling addict alone would justify his appearance in the history of risk, but he demonstrated extraordinary talents in many other areas as well. The surprise is that Cardano is so little known. He is the quintessential Renaissance man.[7]

Cardano was born in Milan about 1500 and died in 1571, a precise contemporary of Benvenuto Cellini. And like Cellini he was one of the first people to leave an autobiography. Cardano called his book *De Vita Propria Liber (The Book Of My Life)* and what a life it was! Actually, Cardano's intellectual curiosity was far stronger than his ego. In his autobiography, for example, he lists the four main achievements of the times in which he lived: the new era of exploration into the two-thirds of the world that the ancients never knew, the invention of firearms and explosives, the invention of the compass, and the invention of printing from movable type.

Cardano was a skinny man, with a long neck, a heavy lower lip, a wart over one eye, and a voice so loud that even his friends complained about it. According to his own account, he suffered from diarrhea, ruptures, kidney trouble, palpitations, even the infection of a nipple. And he boasted, "I was ever hot-tempered, single-minded, and given to women" as well as "cunning, crafty, sarcastic, diligent, impertinent, sad, treacherous, magician and sorcerer, miserable, hateful, lascivious, obscene, lying, obsequious, fond of the prattle of old men."

Cardano was a gambler's gambler. He confessed to "immoderate devotion to table games and dice .... During many years .... I have played not off and on but, as I am ashamed to say, every day." He played everything from dice and cards to chess. He even went so far as to recommend gambling as beneficial "in times of great anxiety and grief .... I found no little solace at playing constantly at dice." He despised kibitzers and knew all about cheating; he warned in particular against players who "smear the cards with soap so that they could slide easily and slip by one another." In his mathematical analysis of the probabilities in dice-throwing, he carefully qualifies his results with ". . . if the die is honest." Still, he lost large sums often enough to conclude that "The greatest advantage from gambling comes from not playing it at all." He was probably the first person in history to write a serious analysis of games of chance.

Cardano was a lot more than a gambler and part-time mathematician. He was the most famous physician of his age, and the Pope and Europe's royal and imperial families eagerly sought his counsel. He had no use for court intrigue, however, and declined their invitations. He provided the first clinical description of the symptoms of typhus, wrote about syphilis, and developed a new way to operate on hernias. Moreover, he recognized that "A man is nothing but his mind; if that be out of order, all's amiss, and if that be well, the rest is at ease." He was an early enthusiast for bathing and showering. When he was invited to Edinburgh in 1552 to treat the Archbishop of Scotland for asthma, he drew on his knowledge of allergy to recommend bedclothes of unspun silk instead of feathers, a pillowcase of linen instead of leather, and the use of an ivory hair comb. Before leaving Milan for Edinburgh, he had contracted for a daily fee of ten gold crowns for his services, but when he departed after about forty days his grateful patient paid him 1,400 crowns and gave him many gifts of great value.

Cardano must have been a busy man. He wrote 131 printed works, claims to have burned 170 more before publication, and left 111 in manuscript form at his death. His writings covered an enormous span of subject matter, including mathematics, astronomy, physics, urine, teeth, the life of the Virgin Mary, Jesus Christ's horoscope, morality, immortality, Nero, music, and dreams. His best seller was *De Subtilitate Rerum* ("On the Subtlety of Things"), a collection of papers that ran to six editions; it dealt with science and philosophy as well as with superstition and strange tales.

He had two sons, both of whom brought him misery. In *De Vita*, Cardano describes Giambattista, the older and his favorite, as "deaf in his right ear [with] small, white, restless eyes. He had two toes on his left foot; the third and fourth counting the great toe, unless I am mistaken, were joined by one membrane. His back was slightly hunched . . . ." Giambattista married a disreputable girl who was unfaithful to him; none of her three children, according to her own admission, had been fathered by her husband. Desperate after three years of hellish marriage, Giambattista ordered his servant to bake a cake with arsenic in it and fed it to his wife, who promptly died. Cardano did everything he could to save his son, but Giambattista confessed to the murder and was beyond rescue. On the way to his beheading, his guards cut off his left hand and tortured him. The younger son, Aldo, robbed his father repeatedly and was in and out of the local jails at least eight times.

Cardano also had a young protégé, Lodovico Ferrari, a brilliant mathematician and for a time Secretary to the Cardinal of Mantua. At the age of 14, Ferrari came to live with Cardano, devoted himself to the older man, and referred to himself as "Cardano's Creation." He argued Cardano's cases in several confrontations with other mathematicians, and some authorities believe that he was responsible for many of the ideas for which Cardano has received credit. But Ferrari provided little solace for the tragedy of Cardano's own sons. A free-spending, free-living man, Ferrari lost all the fingers of his right hand in a barroom brawl and died from poisoning—either by his sister or by her lover—at the age of 43.

Cardano's great book on mathematics, *Ars Magna* (*The Great Art*), appeared in 1545, at the same time Copernicus was publishing his discoveries of the planetary system and Vesalius was producing his treatise on anatomy. The book was published just five years after the first appearance of the symbols "+" and "−" in *Grounde of Artes* by an Englishman named Robert Record. Seventeen years later, an English book called *Whetstone of Witte* introduced the symbol "=" because "noe 2 thynges can be more equalle than a pair of paralleles."[8]

Ars Magna was the first major work of the Renaissance to concentrate on algebra. In it Cardano marches right into the solutions to cubic and quadratic equations and even wrestles with the square roots of negative numbers, unknown concepts before the introduction of the numbering system and still mysterious to many people.[9] Although algebraic notation was primitive and each author chose his own symbols, Cardano did introduce the use of *a*, *b*, *c* that is so familiar to algebra students today. The wonder is that Cardano failed to solve Paccioli's puzzle of the game of *balla*. He did try, but, like other distinguished mathematical contemporaries, he failed at the task.

Cardano's treatise on gambling is titled *Liber de Ludo Aleae* (*Book on Games of Chance*). The word *aleae* refers to games of dice. *Aleatorius*, from the same root, refers to games of chance in general. These words have come down to us in the word aleatory, which describes events whose outcome is uncertain. Thus, the Romans, with their elegant language, have unwittingly linked for us the meanings of gambling and uncertainty.

Liber de Ludo Aleae appears to have been the first serious effort to develop the statistical principles of probablity. Yet the word itself does not appear in the book. Cardano's title and most of his text refer to "chances." The Latin root of probability is a combination of *probare,* which means to test, to prove, or to approve, and *ilis,* which means able to be; it was in this sense of provable or worthy of approval that Cardano might have known the word. The tie between probability and randomness—which is what games of chance are about—did not come into common usage for about a hundred years after *Liber de Ludo Aleae* was published.

According to the Canadian philosopher Ian Hacking, the Latin root of probability suggests something like "worthy of approbation."[10] This was the meaning the word carried for a long time. As an example, Hacking quotes a passage from Daniel Defoe's novel of 1724, *Roxana, or The Fortunate Mistress.* The lady in question, having persuaded a man of means to take care of her, says, "This was the first view I had of living comfortably indeed, and it was a very *probable* way." The meaning here is that she has arrived at a way of life that justifies the esteem of her betters; she was, as Hacking puts it, "a good leg up from her scruffy beginnings."[11]

Hacking cites another example of the changing meaning of probability.[12] Galileo, making explicit use of the word *probabilità,* referred to Copernicus's theory of the earth revolving around the sun as "improbable," because it contradicted what people could see with their own eyes—the sun revolving around the earth. Such a theory was improbable because it did not meet with approval. Less than a century later, using a new (but not yet the newest) meaning, the German scholar Leibniz described the Copernican hypothesis as "incomparably the most probable." For Leibniz, Hacking writes, "probability is determined by evidence and reason."[13] In fact, the German word, *wahrscheinlich,* captures this sense of the concept well: it translates literally into English as "with the appearance of truth."

Probability has always carried this double meaning, one looking into the future, the other interpreting the past, one concerned with our opinions, the other concerned with what we actually know. The distinction will appear repeatedly throughout this book.

In the first sense, probability means the degree of belief or approvability of an opinion—the gut view of probability. Scholars use the term "epistemological" to convey this meaning; epistemological refers to the limits of human knowledge not fully analyzable.

This first concept of probability is much the older of the two; the idea of measuring probability emerged much later. This older sense developed over time from the idea of approbation: how much can we accept of what we know? In Galileo's context, probability was how much we could approve of what we were told. In Leibniz's more modern usage, it was how much credibility we could give the evidence.

The more recent view did not emerge until mathematicians had developed a theoretical understanding of the frequencies of past events. Cardano may have been the first to introduce the statistical side of the theory of probability, but the contemporary meaning of the word during his lifetime still related only to the gut side and had no connection with what he was trying to accomplish in the way of measurement.

Cardano had a sense that he was onto something big. He wrote in his autobiography that *Liber de Ludo Aleae* was among his greatest achievements, claiming that he had "discovered the reason for a thousand astounding facts." Note the words "reason for." The facts in the book about the frequency of outcomes were known to any gambler; the *theory* that explains such frequencies was not. In the book, Cardano issues the theoretician's customary lament: ". . . these facts contribute a great deal to understanding but hardly anything to practical play."

In his autobiography Cardano says that he wrote *Liber de Ludo Aleae* in 1525, when he was still a young man, and rewrote it in 1565. Despite its extraordinary originality, in many ways the book is a mess. Cardano put it together from rough notes, and solutions to problems that appear in one place are followed by solutions that employ entirely different methods in another place. The lack of any systematic use of mathematical symbols complicates matters further. The work was never published during Cardano's lifetime but was found among his manuscripts when he died; it was first published in Basle in 1663. By that time impressive progress in the theory of probability had been made by others who were unaware of Cardano's pathfinding efforts.

Had a century not passed before Cardano's work became available for other mathematicians to build on, his generalizations about probabilities in gambling would have significantly accelerated the advance of mathematics and probability theory. He defined, for the first time, what is now the conventional format for expressing probability as a fraction: the number of favorable outcomes divided by the "circuit"—that is, the total number of possible outcomes. For example, we say the chance of throwing heads is 50/50, heads being one of two equally likely cases. The probability of drawing a queen from a full deck of cards is 1/13, as there are four queens in a deck of 52 cards; the chance of drawing the queen of spades, however, is 1/52, for the deck holds only one queen of spades.

Let us follow Cardano's line of reasoning as he details the probability of each throw in a game of dice.[*] In the following paragraph from Chapter 15 of *Liber de Ludo Aleae*, "On the cast of one die," he is articulating general principles that no one had ever set forth before:

> One-half the total number of faces always represents equality; thus the chances are equal that a given point will turn up in three throws, for the total circuit is completed in six, or again that one of three given points will turn up in one throw. For example, I can as easily throw one, three or five as two, four or six. The wagers there are laid in accordance with this equality if the die is honest.[14]

In carrying this line of argument forward, Cardano calculates the probability of throwing any of two numbers—say, either a 1 or a 2—on a single throw. The answer is one chance out of three, or 33%, because the problem involves two numbers out of a "circuit" of six faces on the die. He also calculates the probability of repeating favorable throws with a single die. The probability of throwing a 1 or a 2 twice in succession is 1/9, which is the square of one chance out of three, or 1/3 multiplied by itself. The probability of throwing a 1 or a 2 three times in succession would be 1/27, or $1/3 \times 1/3 \times 1/3$, while the probability of throwing a 1 or a 2 four times in succession would be 1/3 to the fourth power.

---

[*]Readers who are not interested in the technicalities of this discussion can skip to page 53 without any loss of continuity.

Cardano goes on to figure the probability of throwing a 1 or a 2 with a pair of dice, instead of with a single die. If the probability of throwing a 1 or a 2 with a single die is one out of three, intuition would suggest that throwing a 1 or a 2 with two dice would be twice as great, or 67%. The correct answer is actually five out of nine, or 55.6%. When throwing two dice, there is one chance out of nine that a 1 or a 2 will come up on both dice on the same throw, but the probability of a 1 or a 2 on either die has already been accounted for; hence, we must deduct that one-ninth probability from the 67% that intuition predicts. Thus, $1/3 + 1/3 - 1/9 = 5/9$.

Cardano builds up to games for more dice and more wins more times in succession. Ultimately, his research leads him to generalizations about the laws of chance that convert experimentation into theory.

Cardano took a critical step in his analysis of what happens when we shift from one die to two. Let us walk again through his line of reasoning, but in more detail. Although two dice will have a total of twelve sides, Cardano does not define the probability of throwing a 1 or a 2 with two dice as being limited to only twelve possible outcomes. He recognized that a player might, for example, throw a 3 on one die and a 4 on the other die, but that the player could equally well throw a 4 on the first die and a 3 on the second.

The number of possible combinations that make up the "circuit"—the total number of possible outcomes—adds up to a lot more than the total number of twelve faces found on the two dice. Cardano's recognition of the powerful role of *combinations* of numbers was the most important step he took in developing the laws of probability.

The game of craps provides a useful illustration of the importance of combinations in figuring probabilities. As Cardano demonstrated, throwing a pair of six-sided dice will produce, not eleven (from two to twelve), but thirty-six possible combinations, all the way from snake eyes (two ones) to box cars (double six).

Seven, the key number in craps, is the easiest to throw. It is six times as likely as double-one or double-six and three times as likely as eleven, the other key number. The six different ways to arrive at seven are $6 + 1$, $5 + 2$, $4 + 3$, $3 + 4$, $2 + 5$, and $1 + 6$; note that this pattern is nothing more than the sums of each of three different combinations—5 and 2, 4 and 3, and 1 and 6. Eleven can show up only two ways, because it is the sum of only one combination: $5 + 6$ or $6 + 5$.

There is only one way for each of double-one and double-six to appear. Craps enthusiasts would be wise to memorize this table:

THE PROBABILITY OF EACH SUM
WHEN ROLLING A PAIR OF DICE

Sum	Probability
2	1/36
3	2/36 or 1/18
4	3/36 or 1/12
5	4/36 or 1/9
6	5/36
7	6/36 or 1/6
8	5/36
9	4/36 or 1/9
10	3/36 or 1/12
11	2/36 or 1/18
12	1/36

In backgammon, another game in which the players throw two dice, the numbers on each die may be either added together or considered separately. This means, for example, that, when two dice are thrown, a 5 can appear in fifteen different ways:

5 + 1
5 + 2
5 + 3
5 + 4
5 + 5
5 + 6
1 + 5
2 + 5
3 + 5
4 + 5
6 + 5
1 + 4
4 + 1
2 + 3
3 + 2

The probability of a five-throw is 15/36, or about 42%.[15]

Semantics are important here. As Cardano put it, the *probability of* an outcome is the ratio of favorable outcomes to the total opportunity set. The *odds on* an outcome are the ratio of favorable outcomes to unfavorable outcomes. The odds obviously depend on the probability, but the odds are what matter when you are placing a bet.

If the probability of a five-throw in backgammon is 15 five-throws out of every 36 throws, the odds on a five-throw are 15 to 21. If the probability of throwing a 7 in craps is one out of six throws, the odds on throwing a number other than 7 are 5 to 1. This means that you should bet no more than $1 that 7 will come up on the next throw when the other fellow bets $5 that it won't. The probability of heads coming up on a coin toss are 50/50, or one out of two; since the odds on heads are even, never bet more than your opponent on that game. If the odds on a long-shot at the track are 20–to–1, the theoretical probability of that nag's winning is one out of 21, or 4.8%, not 5%.

In reality, the odds are substantially less than 5%, because, unlike craps, horse racing cannot take place in somebody's living room. Horse races require a track, and the owners of the track and the state that licenses the track all have a priority claim on the betting pool. If you restate the odds on each horse in a race in terms of probabilities—as the 20–to–1 shot has a probability of winning of 4.8%—and add up the probabilities, you will find that the total exceeds 100%. The difference between that total and 100% is a measure of the amount that the owners and the state are skimming off the top.

We will never know whether Cardano wrote *Liber de Ludo Aleae* as a primer on risk management for gamblers or as a theoretical work on the laws of probability. In view of the importance of gambling in his life, the rules of the game must have been a primary inspiration for his work. But we cannot leave it at that. Gambling is an ideal laboratory in which to perform experiments on the quantification of risk. Cardano's intense intellectual curiosity and the complex mathematical principles that he had the temerity to tackle in *Ars Magna* suggest that he must have been in search of more than ways to win at the gaming tables.

Cardano begins *Liber de Ludo Aleae* in an experimental mode but ends with the theoretical concept of combinations. Above its original insights into the role of probability in games of chance, and beyond the mathematical power that Cardano brought to bear on the problems he wanted to solve, *Liber de Ludo Aleae* is the first known effort to put measurement at the service of risk. It was through this process, which Cardano carried out with such success, that risk management evolved. Whatever his motivation, the book is a monumental achievement of originality and mathematical daring.

But the real hero of the story, then, is not Cardano but the times in which he lived. The opportunity to discover what he discovered had existed for thousands of years. And the Hindu-Arabic numbering system had arrived in Europe at least three hundred years before Cardano wrote *Liber de Ludo Aleae*. The missing ingredients were the freedom of thought, the passion for experimentation, and the desire to control the future that were unleashed during the Renaissance.

The last Italian of any importance to wrestle with the matter of probability was Galileo, who was born in 1564, the same year as William Shakespeare. By that time Cardano was already an old man.[16] Like so many of his contemporaries, Galileo liked to experiment and kept an eye on everything that went on around him. He even used his own pulse rate as an aid in measuring time.

One day in 1583, while attending a service in the cathedral in Pisa, Galileo noticed a lamp swaying from the ceiling above him. As the breezes blew through the drafty cathedral, the lamp would swing irregularly, alternating between wide arcs and narrow ones. As he watched, he noted that each swing took precisely the same amount of time, no matter how wide or narrow the arc. The result of this casual observation was the introduction of the pendulum into the manufacture of clocks. Within thirty years, the average timing error was cut from fifteen minutes a day to less than ten seconds. Thus was time married to technology. And that was how Galileo liked to spend his time.

Nearly forty years later, while Galileo was employed as the First and Extraordinary Mathematician of the University of Pisa and Mathematician to His Serenest Highness, Cosimo II, the Grand Duke of Tuscany, he wrote a short essay on gambling "in order to oblige him who has ordered me to produce what occurs to me about the problem."[17] The title of the essay was *Sopra le Scoperte dei Dadi* (*On Playing Dice*). The use of Italian instead of Latin suggests that Galileo had no great relish for a topic that he considered unworthy of serious consideration. He appears to have been performing a disagreeable chore in order to improve the gambling scores of his employer, the Grand Duke.

In the course of the essay, Galileo retraces a good deal of Cardano's work, though Cardano's treatise on gambling would not be published for another forty years. Yet Galileo may well have been aware of Cardano's achievement. Florence Nightingale David, historian and statistician, has suggested that Cardano had thought about these ideas for so long that he must surely have discussed them with friends. Moreover he was a popular lecturer. So mathematicians might very well have been familiar with the contents of *Liber de Ludo Aleae*, even though they had never read it.[18]

Like Cardano, Galileo deals with trials of throwing one or more dice, drawing general conclusions about the frequency of various combinations and types of outcome. Along the way, he suggests that the methodology was something that any mathematician could emulate. Apparently the aleatory concept of probability was so well established by 1623 that Galileo felt there was little more to be discovered.

Yet a great deal remained to be discovered. Ideas about probability and risk were emerging at a rapid pace as interest in the subject spread through France and on to Switzerland, Germany, and England.

France in particular was the scene of a veritable explosion of mathematical innovation during the seventeenth and eighteenth centuries that went far beyond Cardano's empirical dice-tossing experiments. Advances in calculus and algebra led to increasingly abstract concepts that provided the foundation for many practical applications of probability, from insurance and investment to such far-distant subjects as medicine, heredity, the behavior of molecules, the conduct of war, and weather forecasting.

The first step was to devise measurement techniques that could be used to determine what degree of order might be hidden in the uncertain future. Tentative efforts to devise such techniques were under way early in the seventeenth century. In 1619, for example, a Puritan minister named Thomas Gataker published an influential work, *Of the Nature and Use of Lots*, in which he argued that natural law, not divine law, determined the outcome of games of chance.[19] By the end of the seventeenth century, about a hundred years after the death of Cardano and less than fifty years after the death of Galileo, the major problems in probability analysis had been resolved. The next step was to tackle the question of how human beings recognize and respond to the probabilities they confront. This, ultimately, is what risk management and decision-making are all about and where the balance between measurement and gut becomes the focal point of the whole story.

4

The French Connection

Neither Cardano nor Galileo realized that he was on the verge of articulating the most powerful tool of risk management ever to be invented: the laws of probability. Cardano had proceeded from a series of experiments to some important generalizations, but he was interested only in developing a theory of gambling, not a theory of probability. Galileo was not even interested in developing a theory of gambling.

Galileo died in 1642. Twelve years later, three Frenchmen took a great leap forward into probability analysis, an event that is the subject of this chapter. And less than ten years after that, what had been just a rudimentary idea became a fully developed theory that opened the way to significant practical applications. A Dutchman named Huygens published a widely read textbook about probability in 1657 (carefully read and noted by Newton in 1664); at about the same time, Leibniz was thinking about the possibility of applying probability to legal problems; and in 1662 the members of a Paris monastery named Port-Royal produced a pioneering work in philosophy and probability to which they gave the title of *Logic*. In 1660, an Englishman named John Graunt published the results of his effort to generalize demographic data from a statistical sample of mortality records kept by local churches. By the late 1660s, Dutch towns that had traditionally financed themselves by selling annuities were able to put these policies on a sound actuarial footing. By 1700, as we mentioned earlier, the English government was financing its budget deficits through the sale of life annuities.

The story of the three Frenchmen begins with an unlikely trio who saw beyond the gaming tables and fashioned the systematic and theoretical foundations for measuring probability. The first, Blaise Pascal, was a brilliant young dissolute who subsequently became a religious zealot and ended up rejecting the use of reason. The second, Pierre de Fermat, was a successful lawyer for whom mathematics was a sideline. The third member of the group was a nobleman, the Chevalier de Méré, who combined his taste for mathematics with an irresistible urge to play games of chance; his fame rests simply on his having posed the question that set the other two on the road to discovery.

Neither the young dissolute nor the lawyer had any need to experiment in order to confirm their hypotheses. Unlike Cardano, they worked inductively in creating for the first time a *theory* of probability. The theory provided a measure of probability in terms of hard numbers, a climactic break from making decisions on the basis of degrees of belief.

Pascal, who became a celebrated mathematician and occasional philosopher, was born in 1623, just about the time Galileo was putting the finishing touches on *Sopra le Scoperte dei Dadi*. Born in the wake of the religious wars of the sixteenth century, Pascal spent half his life torn between pursuing a career in mathematics and yielding to religious convictions that were essentially anti-intellectual. Although he was a brilliant mathematician and proud of his accomplishments as a "geomaster," his religious passion ultimately came to dominate his life.[1]

Pascal began life as a child prodigy. He was fascinated with shapes and figures and discovered most of Euclidean geometry on his own by drawing diagrams on the tiles of his playroom floor. At the age of 16, he wrote a paper on the mathematics of the cone; the paper was so advanced that even the great Descartes was impressed with it.

This enthusiasm for mathematics was a convenient asset for Pascal's father, who was a mathematician in his own right and earned a comfortable living as a tax collector, a functionary known at the time as a tax farmer. The tax farmer would advance money to the monarch—the equivalent of planting his seeds—and then go about collecting it from the citizenry—the equivalent of gathering in a harvest whose ultimate value, as with all farmers, he hoped would exceed the cost of the seeds.

While Pascal was still in his early teens, he invented and patented a calculating machine to ease the dreary task of adding up M. Pascal's daily accounts. This contraption, with gears and wheels that went forward and backward to add and subtract, was similar to the mechanical calculating machines that served as precursors to today's electronic calculators. The young Pascal managed to multiply and divide on his machine as well and even started work on a method to extract square roots. Unfortunately for the clerks and bookkeepers of the next 250 years, he was unable to market his invention commercially because of prohibitively high production costs.

Recognizing his son's genius, Blaise's father introduced him at the age of 14 into a select weekly discussion group that met at the home of a Jesuit priest named Marin Mersenne, located near the Place Royal in Paris. Abbé Mersenne had made himself the center of the world of science and mathematics during the first half of the 1600s. In addition to bringing major scholars together at his home each week, he reported by mail to all and sundry, in his cramped handwriting, on what was new and significant.[2]

In the absence of learned societies, professional journals, and other means for the exchange of ideas and information, Mersenne made a valuable contribution to the development and dissemination of new scientific theories. The Académie des Sciences in Paris and the Royal Society in London, which were founded about twenty years after Mersenne's death, were direct descendants of Mersenne's activities.

Although Blaise Pascal's early papers in advanced geometry and algebra impressed the high-powered mathematicians he met at Abbé Mersenne's, he soon acquired a competing interest. In 1646, his father fell on the ice and broke his hip; the bonesetters called in to take care of M. Pascal happened to be members of a proselytizing Catholic sect called Jansenists. These people believed that the only path to salvation was through aceticism, sacrifice, and unwavering attachment to the strait and narrow. They preached that a person who fails to reach constantly for ever-higher levels of purity will slip back into immorality. Emotion and faith were all that mattered; reason blocked the way to redemption.

After repairing the hip of Pascal *père*, the Jansenists stayed on for three months to work on the soul of Pascal *fils*, who accepted their doctrine with enthusiasm. Now Blaise abandoned both mathematics and science, along with the pleasures of his earlier life as a man about town.

Religion commanded his full attention. All he could offer by way of explanation was to ask, "Who has placed me here? By whose order and warrant was this place and this time ordained for me? The eternal silence of these infinite spaces leaves me in terror."[3]

The terror became so overwhelming that in 1650, at the age of 27, Pascal succumbed to partial paralysis, difficulty in swallowing, and severe headaches. As a cure, his doctors urged him to rouse himself and resume his pleasure-seeking ways. He lost no time in taking their advice. When his father died, Pascal said to his sister: "Let us not grieve like the pagans who have no hope."[4] In his renewed activities he exceeded even his earlier indulgences and became a regular visitor to the gambling tables of Paris.

Pascal also resumed his researches into mathematics and related subjects. In one of his experiments he proved the existence of vacuums, a controversial issue ever since Aristotle had declared that nature abhors a vacuum. In the course of that experiment he demonstrated that barometric pressure could be measured at varying altitudes with the use of mercury in a tube emptied of all air.

About this time, Pascal became acquainted with the Chevalier de Méré, who prided himself on his skill at mathematics and on his ability to figure the odds at the casinos. In a letter to Pascal some time in the late 1650s, he boasted, "I have discovered in mathematics things so rare that the most learned of ancient times have never thought of them and by which the best mathematicians in Europe have been surprised."[5]

Leibniz himself must have been impressed, for he described the Chevalier as "a man of penetrating mind who was both a gambler and a philosopher." But then Leibniz must have had second thoughts, for he went on to say, "I almost laughed at the airs which the Chevalier de Méré takes on in his letter to Pascal."[6]

Pascal agreed with Leibniz. "M. de Méré," he wrote to a colleague, "has good intelligence but he is not a geometer and this, as you realize, is a great defect."[7] Here Pascal sounds like the academic who takes pleasure in putting down a non-academic. In any case, he underestimated de Méré.[8]

Yet Pascal himself is our source of information about de Méré's intuitive sense of probabilities. The Chevalier bet repeatedly on outcomes with just a narrow margin in his favor, outcomes that his opponents regarded as random results. According to Pascal, de Méré knew that the probability of throwing a 6 with one die rises above 50% with four throws—to 51.77469136%. The Chevalier's strategy was to win a tiny amount on a large number of throws in contrast to betting the chateau on just a few. That strategy also required large amounts of capital, because a 6 might fail to show up for many throws in a row before it appeared in a cluster that would bring its average appearance to over 50%.[9]

De Méré tried a variation on his system by betting that *sonnez*—the term for double-six—had a better than 50% probability of showing up on 24 throws of two dice. He lost enough money on these bets to learn that the probability of double-six was in fact only 49.14% on 24 throws. Had he bet on 25 throws, where the probability of throwing *sonnez* breaks through to 50.55%, he would have ended up a richer man. The history of risk management is written in red as well as in black.

At the time he first met Pascal, the Chevalier was discussing with a number of French mathematicians Paccioli's old problem of the points— how should two players in a game of *balla* share the stakes when they leave the game uncompleted? No one had yet come up with an answer.

Although the problem of the points fascinated Pascal, he was reluctant to explore it on his own. In today's world, this would be the topic for a panel at an annual meeting of one of the learned societies. In Pascal's world, no such forum was available. A little group of scholars might discuss the matter in the intimacy of Abbé Mersenne's home, but the accepted procedure was to start up a private correspondence with other mathematicians who might be able to contribute something to the investigation. In 1654, Pascal turned to Pierre de Carcavi, a member of Abbé Mersenne's group, who put him in touch with Pierre de Fermat, a lawyer in Toulouse.

Pascal could not have approached anyone more competent to help him work out a solution to the problem of the points. Fermat's erudition was awesome.[10] He spoke all the principal European languages and even wrote poetry in some of them, and he was a busy commentator on the literature of the Greeks and Romans. Moreover, he was a mathematician of rare power. He was an independent inventor of analytical geometry, he contributed to the early development of calculus, he did research on the weight of the earth, and he worked on light refraction and optics. In the course of what turned out to be an extended correspondence with Pascal, he made a significant contribution to the theory of probability.

But Fermat's crowning achievement was in the theory of numbers— the analysis of the structure that underlies the relationships of each individual number to all the others. These relationships present countless puzzles, not all of which have been resolved to this very day. The Greeks, for example, discovered what they called perfect numbers, numbers that are the sum of all their divisors other than themselves, like $6 = 1 + 2 + 3$. The next-higher perfect number after 6 is $28 = 1 + 2 + 4 + 7 + 14$. The third perfect number is 496, followed by 8,128. The fifth perfect number is 33,550,336.

Pythagoras discovered what he called amicable numbers, "One who is the other I," numbers whose divisors add up to each other. All the divisors of 284, which are 1, 2, 4, 71, and 142, add up to 220; all the divisors of 220, which are 1, 2, 4, 5, 10, 11, 20, 22, 44, 55, and 110, add up to 284.

No one has yet devised a rule for finding all the perfect numbers or all the amicable numbers that exist, nor has anyone been able to explain all the varying sequences in which they follow one another. Similar difficulties arise with prime numbers, numbers like 1, 3, or 29, that are divisible only by 1 and by themselves. At one point, Fermat believed he might have discovered a formula that would always produce a prime number as its solution, but he warned that he could not prove *theoretically* that the formula would always do so. His formula produced 5, then 17, then 257, and finally 65,537, all of which were prime numbers; the next number to result from his formula was 4,294,967,297.

Fermat is perhaps most famous for propounding what has come to be known as "Fermat's Last Theorem," a note that he scribbled in the margin of his copy of Diophantus's book *Arithmetic*. The notion is simple to describe despite the complexity of its proof.

The Greek mathematician Pythagoras first demonstrated that the square of the longest side of a right triangle, the hypotenuse, is equal to the sum of the squares of the other two sides. Diophantus, an early explorer into the wonders of quadratic equations, had written a similar expression: $x^4 + y^4 + z^4 = u^2$. "Why," asks Fermat, "did not Diophantus seek two [rather than three] fourth powers such that their sum is square? The problem is, in fact impossible, as by my method I am able to prove with all rigor."[11] Fermat observes that Pythagoras was correct that $a^2 + b^2$

$= c^2$, but $a^3 + b^3$ would not be equal to c^3, nor would any integer higher than 2 fit the bill: the Pythagorean theorem works only for squaring.

And then Fermat wrote: "I have a truly marvelous demonstration of this proposition which this margin is too narrow to contain."[12] With this simple comment he left mathematicians dumbfounded for over 350 years as they struggled to find a theoretical justification for what a great deal of empirical experimentation proved to be true. In 1993, an English mathematician named Andrew Wiles claimed that he had solved this puzzle after seven years of work in a Princeton attic. Wiles's results were published in the *Annals of Mathematics* in May 1995, but the mathematicians have continued to squabble over exactly what he had achieved.

Fermat's Last Theorem is more of a curiosity than an insight into how the world works. But the solution that Fermat and Pascal worked out to the problem of the points has long since been paying social dividends as the cornerstone of modern insurance and other forms of risk management.

The solution to the problem of the points begins with the recognition that the player who is ahead when the game stops would have the greater probability of winning if the game were to continue. But how much greater are the leading player's chances? How small are the lagging player's chances? How do these riddles ultimately translate into the science of forecasting?

The 1654 correspondence between Pascal and Fermat on this subject signaled an epochal event in the history of mathematics and the theory of probability.* In response to the Chevalier de Méré's curiosity about the old problem, they constructed a systematic method for analyzing future outcomes. When more things can happen than will happen, Pascal and Fermat give us a procedure for determining the likelihood of each of the possible results—assuming always that the outcomes can be measured mathematically.

They approached the problem from different standpoints. Fermat turned to pure algebra. Pascal was more innovative: he used a geomet-

---

*The full text of this correspondence, translated into English, appears in David, 1962, Appendix 4.

ric format to illuminate the underlying algebraic structure. His methodology is simple and is applicable to a wide variety of problems in probability.

The basic mathematical concept behind this geometric algebra had been recognized long before Fermat and Pascal took it up. Omar Khayyam had considered it some 450 years earlier. In 1303, a Chinese mathematician named Chu Shih-chieh, explicitly denying any originality, approached the problem by means of a device that he called the "Precious Mirror of the Four Elements." Cardano had also mentioned such a device.[13]

Chu's precious mirror has since come to be known as Pascal's Triangle. "Let no one say that I have said nothing new," boasts Pascal in his autobiography. "The arrangement of the subject is new. When we play tennis, we both play with the same ball, but one of us places it better."[14]

$$
\begin{array}{ccccccccccccc}
 & & & & & & 1 & & & & & & \\
 & & & & & 1 & & 1 & & & & & \\
 & & & & 1 & & 2 & & 1 & & & & \\
 & & & 1 & & 3 & & 3 & & 1 & & & \\
 & & 1 & & 4 & & 6 & & 4 & & 1 & & \\
 & 1 & & 5 & & 10 & & 10 & & 5 & & 1 & \\
1 & & 6 & & 15 & & 20 & & 15 & & 6 & & 1 \\
\end{array}
$$

All sorts of patterns greet the eye when we first glance at Pascal's Triangle, but the underlying structure is simple enough: each number is the sum of the two numbers to the right and to the left on the row above.

Probability analysis begins with enumerating the number of different ways a particular event can come about—Cardano's "circuit." That is what the sequence of numbers in each of these expanding rows is designed to provide. The top row shows the probability of an event that cannot fail to happen. Here there is only one possible outcome, with zero uncertainty; it is irrelevant to probability analysis. The next row is the first row that matters. It shows a 50-50 situation: the probability of outcomes like having a boy—or a girl—in a family that is planning to have only one child, or like flipping a head on just one toss of a coin. Add across. With a total of only two possibilities, the result is either one way or the other, a boy or a girl, a head or a tail; the probability of having a boy instead of a girl or of flipping a head instead of a tail is 50%.

The same process applies as we move down the triangle. The third row shows the possible combinations of boys and girls in a family that produces two children. Adding across shows that there are four possible results: one chance of two boys, one chance of two girls, and two chances of one each—a boy followed by a girl or a girl followed by a boy. Now at least one boy (or one girl) appears in three of the four outcomes, setting the probability of at least one boy (or one girl) in a two-child family at 75%; the probability of one boy plus one girl is 50%. The process obviously depends on combinations of numbers in a manner that Cardano had recognized but that had not been published when Pascal took up the subject.

The same line of analysis will produce a solution for the problem of the points. Let us change the setting from Paccioli's game of *balla* to the game of baseball. What is the probability that your team will win the World Series after it has lost the first game? If we assume, as in a game of chance, that the two teams are evenly matched, this problem is identical to the problem of the points tackled by Fermat and Pascal.[15]

As the other team has already won a game, the Series will now be determined by the best of four out of six games instead of four out of seven. How many different sequences of six games are possible, and how many of those victories and losses would result in your team winning the four games it needs for victory? Your team might win the second game, lose the third, and then go on to win the last three. It might lose two in a row and win the next four. Or it might win the necessary four right away, leaving the opponents with only one game to their credit.

Out of six games, how many such combinations of wins and losses are there? The triangle will tell us. All we have to do is find the appropriate row.

Note that the second row of the triangle, the 50-50 row, concerns a family with an only child or a single toss of a coin and adds up to a total of two possible outcomes. The next row shows the distribution of outcomes for a two-child family, or two coin tosses, and adds up to four outcomes, or 2^2. The next row adds up to eight outcomes, or 2^3, and shows what could happen with a three-child family. With six games remaining to settle the outcome of the World Series, we would want to look at the row whose total is 2^6—or two multiplied by itself six times, where there will be 64 possible sequences of wins and losses.[*] The sequence of numbers in that row reads:

$$1 \quad 6 \quad 15 \quad 20 \quad 15 \quad 6 \quad 1$$

Remember that your team still needs four games to win the Series, while the opposing team needs only three. There is just one way your team can win all the games—by winning all the games while the opponents win none; the number 1 at the beginning of the row refers to that possibility. Reading across, the next number is 6. There are six different sequences in which your team (Y) would gain the Series while your opponents (O) win only one more game:

OYYYYY   YOYYYY   YYOYYY   YYYOYY   YYYYOY   YYYYYO

And there are fifteen different sequences in which your team would win four games while your opponents win two.

All the other combinations would produce at least three games for the opposing team and less than the necessary four for yours. This means that there are $1 + 6 + 15 = 22$ combinations in which your team would come out on top after losing the first game, and 42 combinations in which the opposing team would become the champions. As a result, the probability is 22/64—or a tad better than one out of three—that your team will come from behind to win four games before the other team has won three.

The examples reveal something odd. Why would your team play out all six remaining games in sequences where they would have won the Series before playing six games? Or why would they play out all four games when they could win in fewer games?

Although no team in real life would extend play beyond the minimum necessary to determine the championship, a logically complete solution to the problem would be impossible without *all* of the math-

---

[*]Mathematicians will note that what Pascal has really provided here is the binomial expansion, or the coefficients of each successive multiplication of $(a + b)$ by itself. For example, the first row is $(a + b)^0 = 1$, while the fourth row is $(a + b)^3 = 1a^3 + 3a^2b + 3ab^2 + 1b^3$.

ematical possibilities. As Pascal remarked in his correspondence with Fermat, the mathematical laws must dominate the wishes of the players themselves, who are only abstractions of a general principle. He declares that "it is absolutely equal and immaterial to them both whether they let the [match] take its natural course."

The correspondence between Pascal and Fermat must have been an exciting exploration of new intellectual territory for both men. Fermat wrote to Carcavi about Pascal that "I believe him to be capable of solving any problem that he undertakes." In one letter to Fermat, Pascal admitted that "your numerical arrangements ... are far beyond my comprehension." Elsewhere, he also described Fermat as "a man so outstanding in intellect ... in the highest degree of excellence .... [that his works] will make him supreme among the geomasters of Europe."

More than mathematics was involved here for Pascal, who was so deeply involved with religion and morality, and for Fermat the jurist. According to their solutions, there is a matter of *moral right* involved in the division of the stakes in Paccioli's unfinished game of *balla*. Although the players could just as easily split the stakes evenly, that solution would be unacceptable to Pascal and Fermat because it would be unfair to the player who was lucky enough to be ahead when playing ceased.[16]

Pascal is explicit about the moral issues involved and chooses his words with care. In his comments about this work, he points out that "the first thing which we must consider is that the money the players have put into the game no longer belongs to them ... but they have received in return the right to expect that which luck will bring them, according to the rules upon which they agreed at the outset." In the event that they decide to stop playing before the game is over, they will reenter into their original ownership rights of the money they have put into the pot. At that point, "the rule determining that which will belong to them will be proportional to that which they had the right to expect from fortune .... [T]his just distribution is known as the division." The principles of probability theory determine the division, because they determine the just distribution of the stakes.

Seen in these terms, the Pascal–Fermat solution is clearly colored by the notion of risk management, even though they were not thinking explicitly in those terms. Only the foolhardy take risks when the rules are unclear, whether it be *balla*, buying IBM stock, building a factory, or submitting to an appendectomy.

But beyond the moral question, the solutions proposed by Pascal and Fermat lead to precise generalizations and rules for calculating probabilities, including cases involving more than two players, two teams, two genders, two dice, or coins with two sides. Their achievement enabled them to push the limits of theoretical analysis far beyond Cardano's demonstration that two dice of six sides each (or two throws of one die) would produce 6^2 combinations or that three dice would produce 6^3 combinations.

The last letter of the series is dated October 27, 1654. Less than a month later, Pascal underwent some kind of mystical experience. He sewed a description of the event into his coat so that he could wear it next to his heart, claiming "Renunciation, total and sweet." He abandoned mathematics and physics, swore off high living, dropped his old friends, sold all his possessions except for his religious books, and, a short while later, took up residence in the monastery of Port-Royal in Paris.

Yet traces of the old Blaise Pascal lingered on. He established the first commercial bus line in Paris, with all the profits going to the monastery of Port-Royal.

In July 1660, Pascal took a trip to Clermont-Ferrand, not far from Fermat's residence in Toulouse. Fermat proposed a meeting "to embrace you and talk to you for a few days," suggesting a location halfway between the two cities; he claimed bad health as an excuse for not wanting to travel the full distance. Pascal wrote back in August:

> I can scarcely remember that there is such a thing as Geometry [i.e., mathematics]. I recognize Geometry to be so useless that I can find little difference between a man who is a geometrician and a clever craftsman. Although I call it the best craft in the world it is, after all, nothing else but a craft . . . . It is quite possible I shall never think of it again.[17]

Pascal put together his thoughts about life and religion while he was at Port-Royal and published them under the title *Pensées*.[18] In the course of his work on that book, he filled two pieces of paper on both sides with what Ian Hacking describes as "handwriting going in all directions . . . full of erasures, corrections, and seeming afterthoughts." This fragment has come to be known as Pascal's Wager (*le pari de Pascal*), which asks, "God is, or he is not. Which way should we incline? Reason cannot answer."

Here, drawing on his work in analyzing the probable outcomes of the game of *balla*, Pascal frames the question in terms of a game of chance. He postulates a game that ends at an infinite distance in time. At that moment, a coin is tossed. Which way would you bet—heads (God is) or tails (God is not)?

Hacking asserts that Pascal's line of analysis to answer this question is the beginning of the theory of decision-making. "Decision theory," as Hacking describes it, "is the theory of deciding what to do when it is uncertain what will happen."[19] Making that decision is the essential first step in any effort to manage risk.

Sometimes we make decisions on the basis of past experience, out of experiments we or others have conducted in the course of our lifetime. But we cannot conduct experiments that will prove either the existence or the absence of God. Our only alternative is to explore the future *consequences* of believing in God or rejecting God. Nor can we avert the issue, for by the mere act of living we are forced to play this game.

Pascal explained that belief in God is not a decision. You cannot awaken one morning and declare, "Today I think I will decide to believe in God." You believe or you do not believe. The decision, therefore, is whether to choose to act in a manner that will lead to believing in God, like living with pious people and following a life of "holy water and sacraments." The person who follows these precepts is wagering that God is. The person who cannot be bothered with that kind of thing is wagering that God is not.

The only way to choose between a bet that God exists and a bet that there is no God down that infinite distance of Pascal's coin-tossing game is to decide whether an outcome in which God exists is preferable—more valuable in some sense—than an outcome in which God does not exist, even though the probability may be only 50-50. This insight is what conducts Pascal down the path to a decision—a choice in which the value of the outcome and the likelihood that it may occur will differ because the *consequences* of the two outcomes are different.*

If God is not, whether you lead your life piously or sinfully is immaterial. But suppose that God is. Then if you bet against the existence of God by refusing to live a life of piety and sacraments you run the risk of eternal damnation; the winner of the bet that God exists has the possibility of salvation. As salvation is clearly preferable to eternal damnation, the correct decision is to act on the basis that God is. "Which way should we incline?" The answer was obvious to Pascal.

Pascal produced an interesting by-product when he decided to turn over the profits from his bus line to help support the Port-Royal monastery.[20] In 1662, a group of his associates at the monastery published a work of great importance, *La logique, ou l'art de penser* (*Logic, or the Art of Thinking*), a book that ran to five editions between 1662 and 1668.† Although its authorship was not revealed, the primary—but not the sole—author is believed to have been Antoine Arnauld, a man characterized by Hacking as "perhaps the most brilliant theologian of his time."[21] The book was immediately translated into other languages throughout Europe and was still in use as a textbook in the nineteenth century.

The last part of the book contains four chapters on probability that cover the process of developing a hypothesis from a limited set of facts; today, this process is called statistical inference. Among other matters, these chapters contain a "rule for the proper use of reason in determining when to accept human authority," rules for interpreting miracles, a basis of interpreting historical events, and the application of numerical measures to probability.[22]

The final chapter describes a game in which each of ten players risks one coin in the hope of winning the nine coins of his fellow players. The author then points out that there are "nine degrees of probability

---

*At this point, Pascal anticipates Daniel Bernoulli's epochal breakthrough in decision analysis in 1738, which we explore in detail in Chapter 6.

†The Latin title for this book was *Ars Cogitandi*. See Hacking, 1975, pp. 12 and 24.

of losing a coin for only one of gaining nine."[23] Though the observation is innocuous, the sentence has earned immortality. According to Hacking, this is the first occasion in print "where probability, so called, is measured."[24]

The passage deserves immortality for more reasons than that. The author admits that the games he has described are trivial in character, but he draws an analogy to natural events. For example, the probability of being struck by lightning is tiny but "many people . . . are excessively terrified when they hear thunder."[25] Then he makes a critically important statement: "Fear of harm ought to be proportional not merely to the gravity of the harm, but also to the probability of the event."[26] Here is another major innovation: the idea that both gravity and probability should influence a decision. We could turn this assertion around and state that a decision should involve the strength of our desire for a particular outcome as well as the degree of our belief about the probability of that outcome.

The strength of our desire for something, which came to be known as utility, would soon become more than just the handmaiden of probability. Utility was about to take its place at the center of all theories of decision-making and risk-taking. It will reappear repeatedly in the chapters ahead.

Historians are fond of referring to near-misses—occasions when something of enormous importance almost happened but, for one reason or another, failed to happen. The story of Pascal's Triangle is a striking example of a near-miss. We have seen how to predict the probable number of boys or girls in a multi-child family. We have gone beyond that to predict the probable outcome of a World Series (for evenly matched teams) after part of the Series has been played.

In short, we have been forecasting! Pascal and Fermat held the key to a systematic method for calculating the probabilities of future events. Even though they did not turn it all the way, they inserted the key into the lock. The significance of their pioneering work for business management, for risk management, and, in particular, for insurance was to be seized upon by others—for whom the Port-Royal *Logic* was an important first step. The idea of forecasting economic trends or of using probability to forecast economic losses was too remote for Pascal and Fermat to have recognized what they were missing. It is only with hindsight that we can see how close they came.

The inescapable uncertainty of the future will always prevent us from completely banishing the fates from our hopes and fears, but after 1654 mumbo jumbo would no longer be the forecasting method of choice.

5

The Remarkable Notions of the Remarkable Notions Man

We all have to make decisions on the basis of limited data. One sip, even a sniff, of wine determines whether the whole bottle is drinkable. Courtship with a future spouse is shorter than the lifetime that lies ahead. A few drops of blood may evidence patterns of DNA that will either convict or acquit an accused murderer. Public-opinion pollsters interview 2,000 people to ascertain the entire nation's state of mind. The Dow Jones Industrial Average consists of just thirty stocks, but we use it to measure changes in trillions of dollars of wealth owned by millions of families and thousands of major financial institutions. George Bush needed just a few bites of broccoli to decide that that stuff was not for him.

Most critical decisions would be impossible without sampling. By the time you have drunk a whole bottle of wine, it is a little late to announce that it is or is not drinkable. The doctor cannot draw all your blood before deciding what medicine to prescribe or before checking out your DNA. The president cannot take referendums of 100% of all the voters every month before deciding what the electorate wants—nor can he eat all the broccoli in the world before expressing his distaste for it.

Sampling is essential to risk-taking. We constantly use samples of the present and the past to guess about the future. "On the average" is a familiar phrase. But how reliable is the average to which we refer? How representative is the sample on which we base our judgment? What is "normal," anyway? Statisticians joke about the man with his feet in the oven and his head in the refrigerator: on the average he feels pretty good. The fable about the blind men and the elephant is famous precisely because each man had taken such a tiny sample of the entire animal.

Statistical sampling has had a long history, and twentieth-century techniques are far advanced over the primitive methods of earlier times. The most interesting early use of sampling was conducted by the King of England, or by his appointed proxies, in a ceremony known as the Trial of the Pyx and was well established by 1279 when Edward I proclaimed the procedure to be followed.[1]

The purpose of the trial was to assure that the coinage minted by the Royal Mint met the standards of gold or silver content as defined by the Mint's statement of standards. The strange word "pyx" derives from the Greek word for box and refers to the container that held the coins that were to be sampled. Those coins were selected, presumably at random, from the output of the Mint; at the trial, they would be compared to a plate of the King's gold that had been stored in a thrice-locked treasury room called the Chapel of the Pyx in Westminster Abbey. The procedure permitted a specifically defined variance from the standard, as not every coin could be expected to match precisely the gold to which it was being compared.

A more ambitious and influential effort to use the statistical process of sampling was reported in 1662, eight years after the correspondence between Pascal and Fermat (and the year in which Pascal finally discovered for himself whether God is or God is not). The work in question was a small book published in London and titled *Natural and Political Observations made upon the Bills Of Mortality*. The book contained a compilation of births and deaths in London from 1604 to 1661, along with an extended commentary interpreting the data. In the annals of statistical and sociological research, this little book was a stunning breakthrough, a daring leap into the use of sampling methods and the calculation of probabilities—the raw material of every method of risk management, from insurance and the measurement of environmental risks to the design of the most complex derivatives.

The author, John Graunt, was neither a statistician nor a demographer—at that point there was no such thing as either.[2] Nor was he a mathematician, an actuary, a scientist, a university don, or a politician. Graunt, then 42 years old, had spent his entire adult life as a merchant of "notions," such as buttons and needles.

Graunt must have been a keen businessman. He made enough money to be able to pursue interests less mundane than purveying merchandise that holds clothing together. According to John Aubrey, a contemporary biographer, Graunt was "a very ingenious and studious person . . . [who] rose early in the morning to his Study before shoptime . . . . [V]ery facetious and fluent in his conversation."[3] He became close friends with some of the most distinguished intellectuals of his age, including William Petty, who helped Graunt with some of the complexities of his work with the population statistics.

Petty was a remarkable man. Originally a physician, his career included service as Surveyor of Ireland and Professor of Anatomy and Music. He accumulated a substantial fortune as a profiteer during the wars in Ireland and was the author of a book called *Political Arithmetick*, which has earned him the title of founder of modern economics.[4]

Graunt's book went through at least five editions and attracted a following outside as well as inside England. Petty's review in the Parisian *Journal des Sçavans* in 1666 inspired the French to undertake a similar survey in 1667. And Graunt's achievements attracted sufficient public notice for Charles II to propose him for membership in the newly formed Royal Society. The members of the Society were not exactly enthusiastic over the prospect of admitting a mere tradesman, but the King advised them that, "if they found any more such Tradesmen, they should be sure to admit them all, without any more ado." Graunt made the grade.

The Royal Society owes its origins to a man named John Wilkins (1617--1672), who had formed a select club of brilliant acquaintances that met in his rooms in Wadham College.[5] The club was a clone of

Abbé Mersenne's group in Paris. Wilkins subsequently transformed these informal meetings into the first, and the most distinguished, of the scientific academies that were launched toward the end of the seventeenth century; the French Académie des Sciences was founded shortly after, with the Royal Society as its model.

Wilkins later became Bishop of Chichester, but he is more interesting as an early author of science fiction embellished with references to probability. One of his works carried the entrancing title of *The Discovery of a World in the Moone or a discourse tending to prove that 'tis probable there may be another habitable world in that planet*, published in 1640. Anticipating Jules Verne, Wilkins also worked on designs for a submarine to be sent under the Arctic Ocean.

We do not know what inspired Graunt to undertake his compilation of births and deaths in London, but he admits to having found "much pleasure in deducing so many abstruse, and unexpected inferences out of these poor despised Bills of Mortality . . . . And there is pleasure in doing something new, though never so little."[6] But he had a serious objective, too: "[T]o know how many people there be of each Sex, State, Age, Religious, Trade, Rank, or Degree, &c. by the knowing whereof Trade and Government may be made more certain, and Regular; for, if men know the People as aforesaid, they might know the consumption they would make, so as Trade might not be hoped for where it is impossible."[7] He may very well have invented the concept of market research, and he surely gave the government its first estimate of the number of people available for military service.

Information about births and deaths had long been available in parish churches, and the City of London itself had started keeping weekly tallies from 1603 onward. Additional data were available in Holland, where the towns were financing themselves with life annuities—policies purchased for a lump sum that would pay an income for life to the owner of the policy, and occasionally to survivors. Churches in France also kept records of christenings and deaths.

Hacking reports that Graunt and Petty had no knowledge of Pascal or Huygens, but, "Whether motivated by God, or by gaming, or by commerce, or by the law, the same kind of ideas emerged simultaneously in many minds."[8] Clearly Graunt had chosen a propitious moment for publishing and analyzing important information about the population of England.

Graunt was hardly aware that he was the innovator of sampling theory. In fact, he worked with the complete set of the bills of mortality rather than with a sample. But he reasoned systematically about raw data in ways that no one had ever tried before. The manner in which he analyzed the data laid the foundation for the science of statistics.[9] The word "statistics" is derived from the analysis of quantitative facts about the state. Graunt and Petty may be considered the co-fathers of this important field of study.

Graunt did his work at a time when the primarily agricultural society of England was being transformed into an increasingly sophisticated society with possessions and business ventures across the seas. Hacking points out that so long as taxation was based on land and tillage nobody much cared about how many people there were. For example, William the Conqueror's survey known as the Domesday Book of 1085 included cadasters—registers of ownership and value of real property—but paid no heed to the number of human beings involved.

As more and more people came to live in towns and cities, however, headcounts began to matter. Petty mentions the importance of population statistics in estimating the number of men of military age and the potential for tax revenues. But for Graunt, who appears to have been a tradesman first, at a time of rising prosperity, political considerations were of less interest.

There was another factor at work. Two years before the publication of Graunt's *Observations*, Charles II had been recalled from exile in Holland. With the Restoration in full sway, the English were finally rid of the intellectual repression that the Puritans had imposed on the nation. The death of absolutism and Republicanism led to a new sense of freedom and progress throughout the country. Great wealth was beginning to arrive from the colonies across the Atlantic and from Africa and Asia as well. Isaac Newton, now 28 years old, was leading people to think in new ways about the planet on which they lived. Charles II himself was a free soul, a Merry Monarch who offered no apologies for enjoying the good things of life.

It was time to stand up and look around. John Graunt did, and began counting.

❋

Although Graunt's book offers interesting bits for students of sociology, medicine, political science, and history, its greatest novelty is in its use of sampling. Graunt realized that the statistics available to him represented only a fraction of all the births and deaths that had ever occurred in London, but that failed to deter him from drawing broad conclusions from what he had. His line of analysis is known today as "statistical inference"—inferring a global estimate from a sample of data; subsequent statisticans would figure out how to calculate the probable error between the estimate and the true values. With his ground-breaking effort, Graunt transformed the simple process of gathering information into a powerful, complex instrument for interpreting the world—and the skies—around us.

The raw material that Graunt gathered was contained in "Bills of Mortality" that the City of London had started collecting in 1603. That was only incidentally the year in which Queen Elizabeth died; it was also the year in which London suffered one of the worst infestations of the plague. Accurate knowledge of what was going on in the field of public health was becoming increasingly important.[10]

The bills of mortality revealed the causes of death as well as the number of deaths and also listed the number of children christened each week. The accompanying illustration shows the documents for two weeks in the year 1665.* There were 7,165 deaths from plague in just the one week of September 12–19, and only four of 130 parishes were free of the disease.[11]

Graunt was particularly interested in the causes of death, especially "that extraordinary and grand Casualty" the plague, and in the way people lived under the constant threat of devastating epidemic. For the year 1632, for example, he listed nearly sixty different causes of death, with 628 deaths coming under the heading of "aged." The others range from "affrighted" and "bit with mad dog" (one each) to "worms,"

---

*The information on the quantity of bread a penny could buy provided a standard for estimating the cost of living. In our own times, a package of goods and services is used as the standard.

The Diseases and Casualties this Week.

Abortive	5	French-pox	3
Aged	38	Griping in the Guts	14
Broken legge	1	Head-mould shot	1
Cancer	1	Imposthume	4
Childbed	8	Infants	7
Chrisoms	18	Kingsevill	2
Consumption	56	Overlaid	4
Convulsion	25	Plurisie	1
Dropsie	21	Rickets	4
Drowned at St. Kath. Tower	1	Rising of the Lights	8
Executed	6	Rupture	1
Feaver	34	Scurvy	1
Fistula	1	Spotted Feaver	8
Flox and Small-pox	13	Stilborn	7
Flux	2	Stone	1
Found dead (an Infant) at St. Giles in the Fields	1	Stopping of the Stomach	8
		Strangury	1
		Suddenly	3
		Surfeit	9
		Teeth	17
		Tornus	1
		T.ffick	3
		Ulcer	1
		Wormes	1

Christned { Males — 117, Females — 120, In all — 237 }
Buried { Males — 185, Females — 159, In all — 344 } Plague — 0
Decreased in the Burials this Week — 130   Parishes Infected — 38
Parishes clear of the Plague — ●

The Assize of Bread set forth by order of the Lord Maior and Court of Aldermen; A penny Wheaten Loaf to contain Ten Ounces, and three half-penny White Loaves the like weight.

WEEK OF APRIL 11–18, 1665.

The Diseases and Casualties this Week.

Abortive	5	Jaundies	5
Aged	43	Imposthume	11
Ague	2	Infants	15
Apoplexie	1	Killed by a fall from the Belfry at Alhallows the Great	1
Bleeding	2	Kingsevil	2
Burnt in his Bed by a Candle at St. Giles Cripplegate	1	Lethargy	1
Canker	1	Palsie	1
Childbed	42	Plague	7165
Chrisomes	18	Rickets	17
Consumption	134	Rising of the Lights	11
Convulsion	64	Scowring	5
Cough	2	Scurvy	2
Dropsie	33	Spleen	1
Feaver	309	Spotted Feaver	101
Flox and Small-pox	5	Stilborn	17
Frighted	3	Stone	2
Gout	1	Stopping of the stomach	9
Grief	3	Strangury	1
Griping in the Guts	51	Suddenly	1
		Surfeit	49
		Teeth	121
		Thrush	5
		Timpany	1
		Tissick	11
		Vomiting	3
		Winde	3
		Wormes	15

Christned { Males — 95, Females — 81, In all — 176 }
Buried { Males — 4095, Females — 4202, In all — 8297 } Plague — 7165
Increased in the Burials this Week — 607
Parishes clear of the Plague — 4   Parishes Infected — 128

The Assize of Bread set forth by order of the Lord Maior and Court of Aldermen; A penny Wheaten Loaf to contain Nine Ounces and a half, and three half-penny White Loaves the like weight.

WEEK OF SEPTEMBER 12–19, 1665.

(Reproduction courtesy of Stephen Stigler.)

"quinsie," and "starved at nurse." There were only seven "murthers" in 1632 and just 15 suicides.

In observing that "but few are Murthered . . . whereas in Paris few nights came without their Tragedie," Graunt credits the government and the citizen guard of the City of London. He also credits "the natural, and customary, abhorrence of that inhumane Crime, and all Bloodshed by most Englishmen," remarking that even "Usurpers" during English revolutions executed only a few of their countrymen.

Graunt gives the number of deaths from plague for certain years; one of the worst was in 1603, when 82% of the burials were of plague victims. From 1604 to 1624, he calculated that 229,250 people had died of all diseases and "casualties," about a third of which were from children's diseases. Figuring that children accounted for half the deaths from other diseases, he concluded that "about thirty six per centum of all quick conceptions died before six years old." Fewer than 4,000 died of "outward Griefs, as of Cancers, Fistulaes, Sores, Ulcers, broken and bruised Limbs, Impostumes, King's evil, Loprosie, Scald-head, Swine-pox, Wens, &c."

Graunt suggests that the prevalence of acute and epidemical diseases might give "a measure of the state, and disposition of this Climate, and Air . . . as well as its food." He goes on to observe that few are starved, and that the beggars, "swarming up and down upon this City . . . seem to be most of them healthy and strong." He recommends that the state "keep" them and that they be taught to work "each according to his condition and capacity."

After commenting on the incidence of accidents—most of which he asserts are occupation-related—Graunt refers to "one Casualty in our Bills, of which though there be daily talk, [but] little effect." This casualty is the French-Pox—a kind of syphilis—"gotten for the most part, not so much by the intemperate use of Venery (which rather causes the Gowt) as of many common Women."* Graunt wonders why the records show that so few died of it, as "a great part of men have, at one time or another, had some species of this disease." He concludes that most of the deaths from ulcers and sores were in fact caused

---

*The word "venery" descends from the Middle-French word vener, to hunt (from which also comes the word "venison") and from Venus (from which comes the word "venereal"). A venerable word indeed!

by venereal disease, the recorded diagnoses serving as euphemisms. According to Graunt, a person had to be pretty far gone before the authorities acknowledged the true cause of death: "onely hated persons, and such, whose very Noses were eaten of, were reported . . . to have died of this too frequent Maladie."

Although the bills of mortality provided a rich body of facts, Graunt was well aware of the shortcomings in the data he was working with. Medical diagnosis was uncertain: "For the wisest person in the parish would be able to find out very few distempers from a bare inspection of the dead body," Graunt warned. Moreover, only Church of England christenings were tabulated, which meant that Dissenters and Catholics were excluded.

Graunt's accomplishment was truly impressive. As he put it himself, having found "some Truths, and not commonly believed Opinions, to arise from my Meditations upon these neglected Papers, I proceeded further, to consider what benefit the knowledge of the same would bring to the world." His analysis included a record of the varying incidence of different diseases from year to year, movements of population in and out of London "in times of fever," and the ratio of males to females.

Among his more ambitious efforts, Graunt made the first reasoned estimate of the population of London and pointed out the importance of demographic data for determining whether London's population was rising or falling and whether it "be grown big enough, or too big." He also recognized that an estimate of the total population would help to reveal the likelihood that any individual might succumb to the plague. And he tried several estimating methods in order to check on the reliability of his results.

One of his methods began with the assumption that the number of fertile women was double the number of births, as "such women . . . have scarce more than one child in two years."[12] On average, yearly burials were running about 13,000—about the same as the annual nonplague deaths each year. Noting that births were usually fewer in number than burials, he arbitrarily picked 12,000 as the average number of births, which in turn indicated that there were 24,000 "teeming women." He estimated "family" members, including servants and lodgers, at eight per household, and he estimated that the total number of households was about twice the number of households containing a woman of child-bearing age. Thus, eight members of 48,000 families yielded an estimated 384,000 people for the total population of London. This figure may be too low, but it was probably closer to the mark than the common assumption at the time that two million people were living in London.

Another of Graunt's methods began with an examination of a 1658 map of London and a guess that 54 families lived in each 100 square yards—about 200 persons per acre. That assumption produced an estimate of 11,880 families living within London's walls. The bills of mortality showed that 3,200 of the 13,000 deaths occurred within the walls, a ratio of 1:4. Four times 11,880 produces an estimate of 47,520 families. Might Graunt have been figuring backwards from the estimate produced by his first method? We will never know.

Graunt does not use the word "probability" at any point, but he was apparently well aware of the concept. By coincidence, he echoed the comment in the Port-Royal *Logic* about abnormal fears of thunderstorms:

> Whereas many persons live in great fear and apprehension of some of the more formidable and notorious diseases, I shall set down how many died of each: that the respective numbers, being compared with the total 229,520 [the mortality over twenty years], those persons may the better understand the hazard they are in.

Elsewhere he comments, "Considering that it is esteemed an even lay, whether any man lives ten years longer, I supposed it was the same, that one of any ten might die within one year."[13] No one had ever proposed this problem in this fashion, as a case in probability. Having promised "succinct paragraphs, without any long series of multiloquious deductions," Graunt does not elaborate on his reasoning. But his purpose here was strikingly original. He was attempting to estimate average expected ages at death, data that the bills of mortality did not provide.

Using his assessment that "about thirty six per centum of all quick conceptions died before six years old" and a guess that most people die before 75, Graunt created a table showing the number of survivors from ages 6 to 76 out of a group of 100; for purposes of comparison, the right-hand column of the accompanying table shows the data for the United States as of 1993 for the same age levels.

Age	Graunt	1993
0	100	100
6	64	99
16	40	99
26	25	98
36	16	97
46	10	95
56	6	92
66	3	84
76	1	70

Sources: For Graunt, Hacking, 1975, p. 108; for 1993, "This Is Your Life Table," *American Demographics*, February 1995, p. 1.

No one is quite sure how Graunt concocted his table, but his estimates circulated widely and ultimately turned out to be good guesses. They provided an inspiration for Petty's insistence that the government set up a central statistical office.

Petty himself took a shot at estimating average life expectancy at birth, though complaining that "I have had only a common knife and a clout, instead of the many more helps which such a work requires."[14] Using the word "likelihood" without any apparent need to explain what he was talking about, Petty based his estimate on the information for a single parish in Ireland. In 1674, he reported to the Royal Society that life expectancy at birth was 18; Graunt's estimate had been 16.[15]

The facts Graunt assembled changed people's perceptions of what the country they lived in was really like. In the process, he set forth the agenda for research into the country's social problems and what could be done to make things better.

Graunt's pioneering work suggested the key theoretical concepts that are needed for making decisions under conditions of uncertainty. Sampling, averages, and notions of what is normal make up the structure that would in time house the science of statistical analysis, putting information into the service of decision-making and influencing the degrees of belief we hold about the probabilities of future events.

Some thirty years after the publication of Graunt's *Natural and Political Observations*, another work appeared that was similar to Graunt's but even more important to the history of risk management. The author of this work, Edmund Halley, was a scientist of high repute who was familiar with Graunt's work and was able to carry his analysis further. Without Graunt's first effort, however, the idea of such a study might never have occurred to Halley.

Although Halley was English, the data he used came from the Silesian town of Breslau—Breslaw, as it was spelled in those days— located in the easternmost part of Germany; since the Second World War the town has been part of Poland and is now known as Wrozlaw. The town fathers of Breslaw had a long-standing practice of keeping a meticulous record of annual births and deaths.

In 1690 a local scientist and clergyman named Caspar Naumann went through the Breslaw records with a view to "disproving certain current superstitions with regard to the effect of the phases of the moon and the so-called 'climacteric' years on health." Naumann sent the results of his study to Leibniz, who in turn sent them on to the Royal Society in London.[16]

Naumann's data soon attracted the attention of Halley. Halley was then only 35 years old but already one of England's most distinguished astronomers. Indeed, he was responsible for persuading Isaac Newton in 1684 to publish his *Principia*, the work in which Newton first set forth the laws of gravity. Halley paid all the costs of publication out of his own modest resources, corrected the page proofs, and put his own work aside until the job was done. The historian James Newman conjectures that the *Principia* might never have appeared without Halley's efforts.

Widely recognized as a child genius in astronomy, Halley carried his 24-inch telescope with him when he arrived as an undergraduate at Queen's College, Oxford. He left Oxford without receiving a degree, however, and set off to study the heavens in the southern hemisphere; the results of that study established his reputation before he was even 20 years old. By the age of 22, he was already a member of the Royal Society. Oxford turned him down for a professorship in 1691 because he held "materialistic views" that did not match the religious orthodoxy of Oxford. But the dons relented in 1703 and gave him the job. In 1721, he became Royal Astronomer at Greenwich. Meanwhile, he had received his degree by the King's command.

Halley would live to the age of 86. He appears to have been a jolly man, with an "uncommon degree of sprightliness and vivacity," and had many warm friendships that included Peter the Great of Russia. In 1705, in his pathbreaking work on the orbits of comets, Halley identified a total of 24 comets that had appeared between the years 1337 and 1698. Three seemed to be so similar that he concluded that all three were a single comet that had appeared in 1531, 1607, and 1682. Observations of this comet had been reported as far back as 240 BC. Halley's prediction that the comet would reappear in 1758 electrified the world when the comet arrived right on schedule. Halley's name is celebrated every 76 years as his comet sweeps across the skies.

The Breslaw records were not exactly in Halley's main line of work, but he had promised the Royal Society a series of papers for its newly established scholarly journal, *Transactions*, and he had been scouting around for something unusual to write about. He was aware of certain flaws in Graunt's work, flaws that Graunt himself had acknowledged, and he decided to take the occasion to prepare a paper for *Transactions* on the Breslaw data by trying his hand at the analysis of social rather than heavenly statistics for a change.

Graunt, lacking any reliable figure for the total population of London, had had to estimate it on the basis of fragmentary information. He had numbers and causes of deaths but lacked complete records of the ages at which people had died. Given the constant movement of people into and out of London over the years, the reliability of Graunt's estimate was now open to question.

The data delivered by Leibniz to the Royal Society contained monthly data for Breslaw for the years 1687 through 1691, "seeming to be done," according to Halley, "with all the Exactness and Sincerity possible"; the data included age and sex for all deaths and the number of births each year. Breslaw, he pointed out, was far from the sea, so that the "Confluence of Strangers is but small." Births exceeded the "Funerals" by only a small amount and the population was much more stable than London's. All that was lacking was a number for the total population. Halley was convinced that the figures for mortality and birth were sufficiently accurate for him to come up with a reliable estimate of the total.

He found an average of 1,238 births and 1,174 deaths a year over the five-year period, for an annual excess of about 64, which number, he surmised, "may perhaps be balanced by the Levies for the Emperor's Service in his Wars." Directing his attention to the 1,238 annual births and examining the age distribution of those who died, Halley calculated that "but 692 of the Persons born do survive Six whole Years," a much smaller proportion than Graunt's estimate that 64% of all births survived beyond six years. About a dozen of the deaths in Breslaw, on the other hand, occurred between the ages of 81 and 100. Combining a variety of estimates of the percentage of each age group who die each year, Halley worked back from the age distribution of the people dying annually to a grand estimate of 34,000 for the town's total population.

The next step was to devise a table breaking down the population into an age distribution, "from birth to extream Old Age." This table, Halley asserts, offered manifold uses and gave "a more just Idea of the State and condition of Mankind, than any thing yet extant that I know of." For example, the table provided useful information on how many men were of the right age for military service—9,000—and Halley suggested that this estimate of 9/34ths of the population could "pass for a Rule for other places."

Halley's entire analysis embodies the concept of probability and ultimately moves into risk management. Halley demonstrates that his table "shews the odds" that a "Party" of any given age "does not die in a Year." As an illustration, he offers the 25-year age group, which numbered 567, while the 26-year age group numbered 560. The difference of only 7 between the two age groups meant that the probability that a 25-year-old would die in any one year was 7/567, or odds of 80-to-1 that a 25-year-old would make it to 26. Using the same procedure of subtraction between a later age and a given age, and taking the given age as the base, the table could also show the odds that a man of 40 would live to 47; the answer in this instance worked out to odds of 5 1/2-to-1.

Halley carried the analysis further: "[I]f it be enquired at what number Years, it is an even Lay that a Person of any Age shall die, this Table readily performs it." For instance, there were 531 people aged 30, and half that number is 265. One could then look through the table for the age group numbering 265, which appeared to be between 57 and 58. Hence, it would be "an even Wager that . . . a Man of 30 may reasonably expect to live between 27 and 28 years."

The next level of Halley's analysis was the most important of all. The table could be used to reckon the price of insuring lives at different ages, "it being 100 to 1 that a man of 20 dies not in a year, and but 38 to 1 for a Man of 50 Years of Age." On the basis of the odds of dying in each year, the table furnished the necessary information for calculating the value of annuities. At this point Halley launches into a detailed mathematical analysis of the valuation of annuities, including annuities covering two and three lives as well as one. He offers at the same time to provide a table of logarithms to reduce the "Vulgar Arithmetick" imposed by the mass of necessary calculations.

This was a piece of work that was long overdue. The first record we have of the concept of annuities dates back to 225 AD, when an authoritative set of tables of life expectancies was developed by a leading Roman jurist named Ulpian. Ulpian's tables were the last word for over 1400 years!

Halley's work subsequently inspired important efforts in calculating life expectancies on the Continent, but his own government paid no attention to his life tables at the time. Taking their cue from the Dutch use of annuities as a financing device, the English government had attempted to raise a million pounds by selling annuities that would pay back the original purchase price to the buyer over a period of 14 years—but the contract was the same for everyone, regardless of their age! The result was an extremely costly piece of finance for the government. Yet the policy of selling annuities at the same price to everyone continued in England until 1789. The assumption that the average life expectancy at birth was about 14 years was at least an improvement over earlier assumptions: in 1540, the English government had sold annuities that repaid their purchase price in seven years without regard to the age of the buyer.[17]

After the publication of Halley's life tables in *Transactions* in 1693, a century would pass before governments and insurance companies would take probability-based life expectancies into account. Like his comet, Halley's tables turned out to be more than a flash in the sky that appears once in a lifetime: his manipulation of simple numbers formed the basis on which the life-insurance industry built up the data base it uses today.

One afternoon in 1637, when Graunt was just seventeen years old and Halley had not yet been born, a Cretan scholar named Canopius sat down in his chambers at Balliol College, Oxford, and made himself a cup of strong coffee. Canopius's brew is believed to mark the first time coffee was drunk in England; it proved so popular when it was offered to the public that hundreds of coffee houses were soon in operation all over London.

What does Canopius's coffee have to do with Graunt or Halley or with the concept of risk? Simply that a coffee house was the birthplace of Lloyd's of London, which for more than two centuries was the most famous of all insurance companies.[18] Insurance is a business that is totally dependent on the process of sampling, averages, independence of observations, and the notion of normal that motivated Graunt's research into London's population and Halley's into Breslaw's. The rapid development of the insurance business at about the time Graunt and Halley published their research is no coincidence. It was a sign of the times, when innovations in business and finance were flourishing.

The English word for stockbroker—stock jobber—first appeared around 1688, a hundred years before people started trading stocks around the Buttonwood tree on Wall Street, New York. Corporations of all kinds suddenly appeared on the scene, many with curious names like the Lute-String Company, the Tapestry Company, and the Diving Company. There was even a Royal Academies Company that promised to hire the greatest scholars of the age to teach the 2,000 winners of a huge lottery a subject of their own choosing.

The second half of the seventeenth century was also an era of burgeoning trade. The Dutch were the predominant commercial power of the time, and England was their main rival. Ships arrived daily from colonies and suppliers around the globe to unload a profusion of products that had once been scarce or unknown luxuries—sugar and spice, coffee and tea, raw cotton and fine porcelain. Wealth was no longer something that had to be inherited from preceding generations: now it could be earned, discovered, accumulated, invested—and protected from loss.

Moreover, toward the end of the century the English had to finance the sequence of costly wars with the French that had begun with Louis XIV's abortive invasion of England in May 1692 and ended with the English victory at Blenheim and the signing of the Treaty of Utrecht in 1713. On December 15, 1693, the House of Commons established the English national debt with the issue of the million pounds of annuities mentioned above. In 1849, Thomas Babington Macaulay, the great English historian, characterized that momentous event with these resounding words: "Such was the origin of that debt which has since become the greatest prodigy that ever perplexed the sagacity and confounded the pride of statesmen and philosophers."[19]

This was a time for London to take stock of itself and its role in the world. It was also a time to apply the techniques of financial sophistication demanded by war, a rapidly growing wealthy class, and rising overseas trade. Information from remote areas of the world was now of crucial importance to the domestic economy. With the volume of shipping constantly expanding, there was a lively demand for current information with which to estimate sailing times between destinations, weather patterns, and the risks lurking in unfamiliar seas.

In the absence of mass media, the coffee houses emerged as the primary source of news and rumor. In 1675, Charles II, suspicious as many rulers are of places where the public trades information, shut the coffee houses down, but the uproar was so great that he had to reverse himself sixteen days later. Samuel Pepys frequented a coffee house to get news of the arrival of ships he was interested in; he deemed the news he received there to be more reliable than what he learned at his job at the Admiralty.

The coffee house that Edward Lloyd opened in 1687 near the Thames on Tower Street was a favorite haunt of men from the ships that moored at London's docks. The house was "spacious . . . well-built and inhabited by able tradesmen," according to a contemporary publication. It grew so popular that in 1691 Lloyd moved it to much larger and more luxurious quarters on Lombard Street. Nat Ward, a publican whom Alexander Pope accused of trading vile rhymes for tobacco, reported that the tables in the new house were "very Neat and shined with Rubbing." A staff of five served tea and sherbet as well as coffee.

Lloyd had grown up under Oliver Cromwell and he had lived through plague, fire, the Dutch invasion up the Thames in 1667, and the Glorious Revolution of 1688. He was a lot more than a skilled coffee-house host. Recognizing the value of his customer base and responding to the insistent demand for information, he launched "Lloyd's List" in 1696 and filled it with information on the arrivals and departures of ships and intelligence on conditions abroad and at sea. That information was provided by a network of correspondents in major ports on the Continent and in England. Ship auctions took place regularly on the premises, and Lloyd obligingly furnished the paper and ink needed to record the transactions. One corner was reserved for ships' captains where they could compare notes on the hazards of all the new routes that were opening up—routes that led them farther east, farther south, and farther west than ever before. Lloyd's establishment was open almost around the clock and was always crowded.

Then as now, anyone who was seeking insurance would go to a broker, who would then hawk the risk to the individual risk-takers who gathered in the coffee houses or in the precincts of the Royal Exchange. When a deal was closed, the risk-taker would confirm his agreement to cover the loss in return for a specified premium by writing his name under the terms of the contract; soon these one-man insurance operators came to be known as "underwriters."

The gambling spirit of that prosperous era fostered rapid innovation in the London insurance industry. Underwriters were willing to write insurance policies against almost any kind of risk, including, according to one history, house-breaking, highway robbery, death by gin-drinking, the death of horses, and "assurance of female chastity"—of which all but the last are still insurable.[20] On a more serious basis, the demand for fire insurance had expanded rapidly after the great fire of London in 1666.

Lloyd's coffee house served from the start as the headquarters for marine underwriters, in large part because of its excellent mercantile and shipping connections. "Lloyd's List" was eventually enlarged to provide daily news on stock prices, foreign markets, and high-water times at London Bridge, along with the usual notices of ship arrivals and departures and reports of accidents and sinkings.* This publication was so well known that its correspondents sent their messages to the post office addressed simply "Lloyd's." The government even used "Lloyd's List" to publish the latest news of battles at sea.

In 1720, reputedly succumbing to a bribe of £300,000, King George I consented to the establishment of the Royal Exchange Assurance Corporation and the London Assurance Corporation, the first two insurance companies in England, setting them up "exclusive of all other corporations and societies." Although the granting of this monopoly did prevent the establishment of any other insurance *company*, "private and particular persons" were still allowed to operate as underwriters. In fact, the corporations were constantly in difficulty because of their inability to persuade experienced underwriters to join them.

In 1771, nearly a hundred years after Edward Lloyd opened his coffee house on Tower Street, seventy-nine of the underwriters who did business at Lloyd's subscribed £100 each and joined together in the Society of Lloyd's, an unincorporated group of individual entrepreneurs operating under a self-regulated code of behavior. These were the original Members of Lloyd's; later, members came to be known as "Names." The Names committed all their worldly possessions and all their financial capital to secure their promise to make good on their customers' losses. That commitment was one of the principal reasons for the rapid growth of business underwritten at Lloyd's over the years. And thus did Canopius's cup of coffee lead to the establishment of the most famous insurance company in history.

By the 1770s an insurance industry had emerged in the American colonies as well, though most large policies were still being written in England. Benjamin Franklin had set up a fire-insurance company called First American in 1752; the first life insurance was written by the Presbyterian Ministers' Fund, established in 1759. Then, when the Revolution broke out, the Americans, deprived of Lloyd's services, had no choice but to form more insurance companies of their own. The first company to be owned by stockholders was the Insurance Company of North America in Philadelphia, which wrote policies on

---

*Lloyd's, in short, is the ancestor of the huge Bloomberg business news network of our own time.

fire and marine insurance and issued the first life-insurance policies in America—six-term policies on sea captains.*[21]

Insurance achieved its full development as a commercial concept only in the eighteenth century, but the business of insurance dates back beyond the eighteenth century BC. The Code of Hammurabi, which appeared about 1800 BC, devoted 282 clauses to the subject of "bottomry." Bottomry was a loan or a mortgage taken out by the owner of a ship to finance the ship's voyage. No premium as we know it was paid. If the ship was lost, the loan did not have to be repaid.†️ This early version of marine insurance was still in use up to the Roman era, when underwriting began to make an appearance. The Emperor Claudius (10 BC–AD 54), eager to boost the corn trade, made himself a one-man, premium-free insurance company by taking personal responsibility for storm losses incurred by Roman merchants, not unlike the way governments today provide aid to areas hit by earth-quakes, hurricanes, or floods.

Occupational guilds in both Greece and Rome maintained coop-eratives whose members paid money into a pool that would take care of a family if the head of the household met with premature death. This practice persisted into the time of Edward Lloyd, when "friendly soci-eties" still provided this simple form of life insurance.††

The rise of trade during the Middle Ages accelerated the growth of finance and insurance. Major financial centers grew up in Amsterdam, Augsburg, Antwerp, Frankfurt, Lyons, and Venice; Bruges established a Chamber of Assurance in 1310. Not all of these cities were seaports; most trade still traveled over land. New instruments such as bills of exchange came into use to facilitate the transfer of money from cus-

---

*The trust business in Boston was founded by Nathaniel Bowditch in the 1810s to serve the same market.

†This principle applied to life insurance as well. The debts of a soldier who died in battle were forgiven and did not have to be repaid.

††In the United States it survived into the twentieth century. Here it was known as "indus-trial insurance" and usually covered only funeral expenses. My father-in-law had a little book in which he kept a record of the weekly premiums he paid into such a policy.

tomer to shipper, from lender to borrower and from borrower to lender, and, in huge sums, from the Church's widespread domain to Rome.

Quite aside from financial forms of risk management, merchants learned early on to employ diversification to spread their risks. Antonio, Shakespeare's merchant of Venice, followed this practice:

> My ventures are not in one bottom trusted,
> Nor to one place; nor is my whole estate
> Upon the fortune of this present year;
> Therefore, my merchandise makes me not sad.
> (Act I, Scene 1)

The use of insurance was by no means limited to shipments of goods. Farmers, for example, are so completely dependent on nature that their fortunes are peculiarly vulnerable to unpredictable but devastating disasters such as drought, flood, or pestilence. As these events are essentially independent of one another and hardly under the influence of the farmer, they provide a perfect environment for insurance. In Italy, for example, farmers set up agricultural cooperatives to insure one another against bad weather; farmers in areas with a good growing season would agree to compensate those whose weather had been less favorable. The Monte dei Paschi, which became one of the largest banks in Italy, was established in Siena in 1473 to serve as an intermediary for such arrangements.[22] Similar arrangements exist today in less-developed countries that are heavily dependent on agriculture.[23]

Although these are all cases in which one group agrees to indemnify another group against losses, the insurance process as a whole functions in precisely the same manner. Insurance companies use the premiums paid by people who have not sustained losses to pay off people who have. The same holds true of gambling casinos, which pay off the winners from the pot that is constantly being replenished by the losers. Because of the anonymity provided by the insurance company or the gambling casino that acts as intermediary, the actual exchange is less visible. And yet the most elaborate insurance and gambling schemes are merely variations on the Monte dei Paschi theme.

The underwriters active in Italy during the fourteenth century did not always perform to the satisfaction of their customers, and the complaints are familiar. A Florentine merchant named Francesco di Marco

Rembrandt's Storm on the Sea of Galilee.
(Reproduction courtesy of the Isabella Stewart Gardner Museum, Boston.)

My ventures are not in one bottom trusted,
Nor to one place; nor is my whole estate
Upon the fortune of this present year;
Therefore, my merchandise makes me not sad.
(Act I, Scene 1)

Datini, who did business as far away as Barcelona and Southampton, wrote his wife a letter complaining about his underwriters. "For whom they insure," he wrote, "it is sweet to them to take the monies; but when disaster comes, it is otherwise, and each man draws his rump back and strives not to pay."[24] Francesco knew what he was talking about, for he left four hundred marine insurance policies in his estate when he died.

Activity in the insurance business gained momentum around 1600. The term "policy," which was already in general use by then, comes from the Italian "polizza," which meant a promise or an undertaking. In 1601, Francis Bacon introduced a bill in Parliament to regulate insurance policies, which were "tyme out of mynde an usage amonste merchants, both of this realm and of forraine nacyons."

The profit on an investment in goods that must be shipped over long distances before they reach their market depends on more than just the weather. It also depends on informed judgments about consumer needs, pricing levels, and fashions at the time of the cargo's arrival, to say nothing of the cost of financing the goods until they are delivered, sold, and paid for. As a result, forecasting—long denigrated as a waste of time at best and a sin at worst—became an absolute necessity in the course of the seventeenth century for adventuresome entrepreneurs who were willing to take the risk of shaping the future according to their own design.

Commonplace as it seems today, the development of business forecasting in the late seventeenth century was a major innovation. As long as mathematicians had excluded commercial applications from their theoretical innovations, advances toward a science of risk management had to wait until someone asked new questions, questions that, like Graunt's, required lifting one's nose beyond the confines of *balla* and dice. Even Halley's bold contribution to calculations of life expectancies was to him only a sociological study or a game with arithmetic played out for the amusement of his scientific colleagues; his failure to make any reference to Pascal's theoretical work on probability thirty years earlier is revealing.

An enormous conceptual hurdle had to be overcome before the shift could be made from identifying inexorably determined mathematical odds to estimating the probability of uncertain outcomes, to turn from collecting raw data to deciding what to do with them once they were in hand. The intellectual advances from this point forward are in many ways more astonishing than the advances we have witnessed so far.

Some of the innovators drew their inspiration by looking up at the stars, others by manipulating the concept of probability in ways that Pascal and Fermat had never dreamed of. But the next figure we meet was the most original of all: he directed his attention to the question of wealth. We draw on his answers almost every day of our lives.

1700–1900:
MEASUREMENT
UNLIMITED

6

Considering the Nature of Man

In just a few years the commanding mathematical achievements of Cardano and Pascal had been elevated into domains that neither had dreamed of. First Graunt, Petty, and Halley had applied the concept of probability to the analysis of raw data. At about the same time, the author of the Port-Royal *Logic* had blended measurement and subjective beliefs when he wrote, "Fear of harm ought to be proportional not merely to the gravity of the harm, but also to the probability of the event."

In 1738, the *Papers of the Imperial Academy of Sciences in St. Petersburg* carried an essay with this central theme: "the *value* of an item must not be based on its *price*, but rather on the *utility* that it yields."[1] The paper had originally been presented to the Academy in 1731, with the title *Specimen Theoriae Novae de Mensura Sortis (Exposition of a New Theory on the Measurement of Risk)*; its author was fond of italics, and all three of the italicized words in the above quotation are his.* So are all those in the quotations that follow.

It is pure conjecture on my part that the author of the 1738 article had read the Port-Royal *Logic*, but the intellectual linkage between the

---

*As usual, the essay was published in Latin. The Latin title of the publication in which it appeared was *Commentarii Academiae Scientiarum Imperialis Petropolitanae, Tomus V*.

two is striking. Interest in *Logic* was widespread throughout western Europe during the eighteenth century.

Both authors build their arguments on the proposition that any decision relating to risk involves two distinct and yet inseparable elements: the objective facts and a subjective view about the desirability of what is to be gained, or lost, by the decision. Both objective measurement and subjective degrees of belief are essential; neither is sufficient by itself.

Each author has his preferred approach. The Port-Royal author argues that only the pathologically risk-averse make choices based on the consequences without regard to the probability involved. The author of the *New Theory* argues that only the foolhardy make choices based on the probability of an outcome without regard to its consequences.

The author of the St. Petersburg paper was a Swiss mathematician named Daniel Bernoulli, who was then 38 years old.[2] Although Daniel Bernoulli's name is familiar only to scientists, his paper is one of the most profound documents ever written, not just on the subject of risk but on human behavior as well. Bernoulli's emphasis on the complex relationships between measurement and gut touches on almost every aspect of life.

Daniel Bernoulli was a member of a remarkable family. From the late 1600s to the late 1700s, eight Bernoullis had been recognized as celebrated mathematicians. Those men produced what the historian Eric Bell describes as "a swarm of descendants . . . and of this posterity the majority achieved distinction—sometimes amounting to eminence—in the law, scholarship, literature, the learned professions, administration and the arts. None were failures."[3]

The founding father of this tribe was Nicolaus Bernoulli of Basel, a wealthy merchant whose Protestant forebears had fled from Catholic-dominated Antwerp around 1585. Nicolaus lived a long life, from 1623 to 1708, and had three sons, Jacob, Nicolaus (known as Nicolaus I), and Johann. We shall meet Jacob again shortly, as the discoverer of the Law of Large Numbers in his book *Ars Conjectandi* (*The Art of Conjecture*). Jacob was both a great teacher who attracted students from all over Europe and an acclaimed genius in mathematics, engineering, and astronomy. The Victorian statistician Francis Galton describes him as having "a bilious and melancholic temperament . . . sure but slow."[4] His relationship with his father was so poor that he took as his motto *Invito patre sidera verso*—"I am among the stars in spite of my father."[5]

Galton did not limit his caustic observations to Jacob. Despite the evidence that the Bernoulli family provided in confirmation of Galton's theories of eugenics, he depicts them in his book, *Hereditary Genius* as "mostly quarrelsome and jealous."[6]

These traits seem to have run through the family. Jacob's younger brother and fellow-mathematician Johann, the father of Daniel, is described by James Newman, an anthologist of science, as "violent, abusive . . . and, when necessary, dishonest."*[7] When Daniel won a prize from the French Academy of Sciences for his work on planetary orbits, his father, who coveted the prize for himself, threw him out of the house. Newman reports that Johann lived to be 80 years old, "retaining his powers and meanness to the end."

And then there was the son of the middle brother, Nicolaus I, who is known as Nicolaus II. When Nicolaus II's uncle Jacob died in 1705 after a long illness, leaving *The Art of Conjecture* all but complete, Nicolaus II was asked to edit the work for publication even though he was only 18 at the time. He took eight years to finish the task! In his introduction he confesses to the long delay and to frequent prodding by the publishers, but he offers as an excuse of "my absence on travels" and the fact that "I was too young and inexperienced to know how to complete it."[8]

Perhaps he deserves the benefit of the doubt: he spent those eight years seeking out the opinions of the leading mathematicians of his time, including Isaac Newton. In addition to conducting an active correspondence for the exchange of ideas, he traveled to London and Paris to consult with outstanding scholars in person. And he made a number of contributions to mathematics on his own, including an analysis of the use of conjecture and probability theory in applications of the law.

---

*Newman is not easy to characterize, although his *The World of Mathematics* was a major source for this book. He was a student of philosophy and mathematics who became a highly successful lawyer and public servant. A one-time senior member of the editorial board of *Scientific American*, he was an avid collector of scientific documents of great historical importance. He died in 1966.

To complicate matters further, Daniel Bernoulli had a brother five years older than he, also named Nicolaus; by convention, this Nicolaus is known as Nicolaus III, his grandfather being numberless, his uncle being Nicolaus I, and his elder first cousin being Nicolaus II. It was Nicolaus III, a distinguished scholar himself, who started Daniel off in mathematics when Daniel was only eleven years old. As the oldest son, Nicolaus III had been encouraged by his father to become a mathematician. When he was only eight years old, he was able to speak four languages; he became Doctor of Philosophy at Basel at the age of nineteen; and he was appointed Professor of Mathematics at St. Petersburg in 1725 at the age of thirty. He died of some sort of fever just a year later.

Daniel Bernoulli received an appointment at St. Petersburg in the same year as Nicolaus III and remained there until 1733, when he returned to his hometown of Basel as Professor of Physics and Philosophy. He was among the first of many outstanding scholars whom Peter the Great would invite to Russia in the hope of establishing his new capital as a center of intellectual activity. According to Galton, Daniel was "physician, botanist, and anatomist, writer on hydrodynamics; very precocious."[9] He was also a powerful mathematician and statistician, with a special interest in probability.

Bernoulli was very much a man of his times. The eighteenth century came to embrace rationality in reaction to the passion of the endless religious wars of the past century. As the bloody conflict finally wound down, order and appreciation of classical forms replaced the fervor of the Counter-Reformation and the emotional character of the baroque style in art. A sense of balance and respect for reason were hallmarks of the Enlightenment. It was in this setting that Bernoulli transformed the mysticism of the Fort-Royal *Logic* into a logical argument addressed to rational decision-makers.

Daniel Bernoulli's St. Petersburg paper begins with a paragraph that sets forth the thesis that he aims to attack:

Ever since mathematicians first began to study the measurement of risk, there has been general agreement on the following proposition: *Expected values are computed by multiplying each possible gain by the num-*

ber of ways in which it can occur, and then dividing the sum of these products by the total number of cases.[*10]

Bernoulli finds this hypothesis flawed as a description of how people in real life go about making decisions, because it focuses only on the facts; it ignores the consequences of a probable outcome for a person who has to make a decision when the future is uncertain. Price—and probability—are not enough in determining what something is worth. Although the facts are the same for everyone, "the utility . . . is dependent on the particular circumstances of the person making the estimate . . . . There is no reason to assume that . . . the risks anticipated by each [individual] must be deemed equal in value." To each his own.

The concept of utility is experienced intuitively. It conveys the sense of usefulness, desirability, or satisfaction. The notion that arouses Bernoulli's impatience with mathematicians—"expected value"—is more technical. As Bernoulli points out, expected value equals the sum of the values of each of a number of outcomes multiplied by the probability of each outcome relative to all the other possibilities. On occasion, mathematicians still use the term "mathematical expectation" for expected value.

A coin has two sides, heads and tails, with a 50% chance of landing with one side or the other showing—a coin cannot come up showing both heads and tails at the same time. What is the expected value of a coin toss? We multiply 50% by one for heads and do the same for tails, take the sum—100%—and divide by two. The expected value of betting on a coin toss is 50%. You can expect either heads or tails, with equal likelihood.

What is the expected value of rolling two dice? If we add up the 11 numbers that might come up—2 + 3 + 4 + 5 + 6 + 7 + 8 + 9 + 10 + 11 + 12—the total works out to 77. The expected value of rolling two dice is 77/11, or exactly 7.

Yet these 11 numbers do not have an equal probability of coming up. As Cardano demonstrated, some outcomes are more likely than others when there are 36 different combinations that produce the 11

---

*Daniel's uncle Jacob, who will play a major role in the next chapter, once wrote that "the value of our expectation always signifies something in the middle between the best we can hope for and the worst we can fear." (Hacking, 1975, p. 144.)

outcomes ranging from 2 to 12; two can be produced only by double-one, but four can be produced in three ways, by 3 + 1, by 1 + 3, and by 2 + 2. Cardano's useful table (page 52) lists a number of combinations in which each of the 11 outcomes can occur:

Outcome	Probability	Weighted Probability
2	1/36	$2 \times 1/36 = 0.06$
3	2/36	$3 \times 2/36 = 0.17$
4	3/36	$4 \times 3/36 = 0.33$
5	4/36	$5 \times 4/36 = 0.56$
6	5/36	$6 \times 5/36 = 0.83$
7	6/36	$7 \times 6/36 = 1.17$
8	5/36	$8 \times 5/36 = 1.11$
9	4/36	$9 \times 4/36 = 1.00$
10	3/36	$10 \times 3/36 = 0.83$
11	2/36	$11 \times 2/36 = 0.61$
12	1/36	$12 \times 1/36 = 0.33$
		Total 7.00

The expected value, or the mathematical expectation, of rolling two dice is exactly 7, confirming our calculation of 77/11. Now we can see why a roll of 7 plays such a critical role in the game of craps.

Bernoulli recognizes that such calculations are fine for games of chance but insists that everyday life is quite a different matter. Even when the probabilities are known (an oversimplification that later mathematicians would reject), rational decision-makers will try to maximize expected *utility*—usefulness or satisfaction—rather than expected value. Expected utility is calculated by the same method as that used to calculate expected value but with utility serving as the weighting factor.[11]

For example, Antoine Arnauld, the reputed author of the Port-Royal *Logic*, accused people frightened by thunderstorms of overestimating the small probability of being struck by lightning. He was wrong. It was he who was ignoring something. The facts are the same for everyone, and even people who are terrified at the first rumble of thunder are fully aware that it is highly unlikely that lightning will strike precisely where they are standing. Bernoulli saw the situation more clearly: people with a phobia about being struck by lightning place such a heavy weight on the consequences of that outcome that they tremble even though they know that the odds on being hit are tiny.

Gut rules the measurement. Ask passengers in an airplane during turbulent flying conditions whether each of them has an equal degree of anxiety. Most people know full well that flying in an airplane is far safer than driving in an automobile, but some passengers will keep the flight attendants busy while others will snooze happily regardless of the weather.

And that's a good thing. If everyone valued every risk in precisely the same way, many risky opportunities would be passed up. Venturesome people place high utility on the small probability of huge gains and low utility on the larger probability of loss. Others place little utility on the probability of gain because their paramount goal is to preserve their capital. Where one sees sunshine, the other sees a thunderstorm. Without the venturesome, the world would turn a lot more slowly. Think of what life would be like if everyone were phobic about lightning, flying in airplanes, or investing in start-up companies. We are indeed fortunate that human beings differ in their appetite for risk.

Once Bernoulli has established his basic thesis that people ascribe different values to risk, he introduces a pivotal idea: "[The] *utility resulting from any small increase in wealth will be inversely proportionate to the quantity of goods previously possessed.*" Then he observes, "Considering the nature of man, it seems to me that the foregoing hypothesis is apt to be valid for many people to whom this sort of comparison can be applied."

The hypothesis that utility is inversely related to the quantity of goods previously possessed is one of the great intellectual leaps in the history of ideas. In less than one full printed page, Bernoulli converts the process of calculating probabilities into a procedure for introducing subjective considerations into decisions that have uncertain outcomes.

The brilliance of Bernoulli's formulation lies in his recognition that, while the role of facts is to provide a single answer to expected value (the facts are the same for everyone), the subjective process will produce as many answers as there are human beings involved. But he goes even further than that: he suggests a systematic approach for determining how much each individual desires more over less: the desire is inversely proportionate to the quantity of goods possessed.

For the first time in history Bernoulli is applying measurement to something that *cannot be counted*. He has acted as go-between in the wedding of intuition and measurement. Cardano, Pascal, and Fermat provided a method for figuring the risks in each throw of the dice, but Bernoulli introduces us to the risk-*taker*—the player who chooses how much to bet or whether to bet at all. While probability theory sets up the choices, Bernoulli defines the *motivations* of the person who does the choosing. This is an entirely new area of study and body of theory. Bernoulli laid the intellectual groundwork for much of what was to follow, not just in economics, but in theories about how people make decisions and choices in every aspect of life.

Bernoulli offers in his paper a number of interesting applications to illustrate his theory. The most tantalizing, and the most famous, of them has come to be known as the Petersburg Paradox, which was originally suggested to him by his "most honorable cousin the celebrated Nicolaus Bernoulli"—the dilatory editor of *The Art of Conjecture*.

Nicolaus proposes a game to be played between Peter and Paul, in which Peter tosses a coin and continues to toss it until it comes up heads. Peter will pay Paul one ducat if heads comes up on the first toss, two ducats if heads comes up on the second toss, four ducats on the third, and so on. With each additional throw the number of ducats Peter must pay Paul is doubled.* How much should someone pay Paul—who stands to rake in a sizable sum of money—for the privilege of taking his place in this game?

---

*With the assistance of Richard Sylla and Leora Klapper, the best information I have been able to obtain about the value of ducats in the early 18th century is that one ducat could have purchased the equivalent of about $40 in today's money. Baumol and Baumol, Appendix, provides an approximate confirmation of this estimate. See also McKuster, 1978, and Warren and Pearson, 1993.

The paradox arises because, according to Bernoulli, "The accepted method of calculation [expected value] does, indeed, value Paul's prospects at infinity [but] no one would be willing to purchase [those prospects] at a moderately high price . . . . [A]ny fairly reasonable man would sell his chance, with great pleasure, for twenty ducats."*

Bernoulli undertakes an extended mathematical analysis of the problem, based on his assumption that increases in wealth are inversely related to initial wealth. According to that assumption, the prize Paul might win on the two-hundredth throw would have only an infinitesimal amount of additional utility over what he would receive on the one-hundredth throw; even by the 51st throw, the number of ducats won would already have exceeded 1,000,000,000,000,000. (Measured in dollars, the total national debt of the U.S. government today is only four followed by twelve zeroes.)

Whether it be in ducats or dollars, the evaluation of Paul's expectation has long attracted the attention of leading scholars in mathematics, philosophy, and economics. An English history of mathematics by Isaac Todhunter, published in 1865, makes numerous references to the Petersburg Paradox and discusses some of the solutions that various mathematicians had proposed during the intervening years.[12] Meanwhile, Bernoulli's paper remained in its original Latin until a German translation appeared in 1896. Even more sophisticated, complex mathematical treatments of the Paradox appeared after John Maynard Keynes made a brief reference to it in his *Treatise on Probability*, published in 1921. But it was not until 1954—216 years after its original publication—that the paper by Bernoulli finally appeared in an English translation.

The Petersburg Paradox is more than an academic exercise in the exponents and roots of tossing coins. Consider a great growth company whose prospects are so brilliant that they seem to extend into infinity. Even under the absurd assumption that we could make an accurate forecast of a company's earnings into infinity—we are lucky if we can

---

*Bernoulli's solution to the paradox has been criticized because he fails to consider a game in which the prize would rise at a faster rate than the rate Nicolaus had specified. Nevertheless, unless there is a point where the player has zero interest in any additional wealth, the paradox will ultimately come into play no matter what the rate is.

make an accurate forecast of next quarter's earnings—what is a share of stock in that company worth? An infinite amount?[*]

There have been moments when real, live, hands-on professional investors have entertained dreams as wild as that—moments when the laws of probability are forgotten. In the late 1960s and early 1970s, major institutional portfolio managers became so enamored with the idea of growth in general, and with the so-called "Nifty-Fifty" growth stocks in particular, that they were willing to pay any price at all for the privilege of owning shares in companies like Xerox, Coca-Cola, IBM, and Polaroid. These investment managers defined the risk in the Nifty-Fifty, not as the risk of overpaying, but as the risk of *not owning* them: the growth prospects seemed so certain that the future level of earnings and dividends would, in God's good time, always justify whatever price they paid. They considered the risk of paying too much to be minuscule compared with the risk of buying shares, even at a low price, in companies like Union Carbide or General Motors, whose fortunes were uncertain because of their exposure to business cycles and competition.

This view reached such an extreme point that investors ended up by placing the same total market value on small companies like International Flavors and Fragrances, with sales of only $138 million, as they placed on a less glamorous business like U.S. Steel, with sales of $5 billion. In December 1972, Polaroid was selling for 96 times its 1972 earnings, McDonald's was selling for 80 times, and IFF was selling for 73 times; the Standard & Poor's Index of 500 stocks was selling at an average of 19 times. The dividend yields on the Nifty-Fifty averaged less than half the average yield on the 500 stocks in the S&P Index.

The proof of this particular pudding was surely in the eating, and a bitter mouthful it was. The dazzling prospect of earnings rising up to the sky turned out to be worth a lot less than an infinite amount. By 1976, the price of IFF had fallen 40% but the price of U.S. Steel had more than doubled. Figuring dividends plus price change, the S&P 500 had surpassed its previous peak by the end of 1976, but the Nifty-Fifty did not surpass their 1972 bull-market peak until July 1980. Even worse, an equally weighted portfolio of the Nifty-Fifty lagged the performance of the S&P 500 from 1976 to 1990.

---

[*]A theoretical exploration into this question appears in Durand, 1959, which anticipated the events described in the paragraphs immediately following.

But where is infinity in the world of investing? Jeremy Siegel, a professor at the Wharton School of Business at the University of Pennsylvania, has calculated the performance of the Nifty-Fifty in detail from the end of 1970 to the end of 1993.[13] The equally weighted portfolio of fifty stocks, even if purchased at its December 1972 peak, would have realized a total return by the end of 1993 that was less than one percentage point below the return on the S&P Index. If the same stocks had been bought just two years earlier, in December 1970, the portfolio would have outperformed the S&P by a percentage point per year. The negative gap between cost and market value at the bottom of the 1974 debacle would also have been smaller.

For truly patient individuals who felt most comfortable owning familiar, high-quality companies, most of whose products they encountered in their daily round of shopping, an investment in the Nifty-Fifty would have provided ample utility. The utility of the portfolio would have been much smaller to a less patient investor who had no taste for a fifty-stock portfolio in which five stocks actually lost money over twenty-one years, twenty earned less than could have been earned by rolling over ninety-day Treasury bills, and only eleven outperformed the S&P 500. But, as Bernoulli himself might have put it in a more informal moment, you pays your money and you takes your choice.

Bernoulli introduced another novel idea that economists today consider a driving force in economic growth—human capital. This idea emerged from his definition of wealth as "anything that can contribute to the adequate satisfaction of any sort of want . . . . There is then nobody who can be said to possess nothing at all in this sense unless he starves to death."

What form does most people's wealth take? Bernoulli says that tangible assets and financial claims are less valuable than productive capacity, including even the beggar's talent. He suggests that a man who can earn 10 ducats a year by begging will probably reject an offer of 50 ducats to refrain from begging: after spending the 50 ducats, he would have no way of supporting himself. There must, however, be some amount that he would accept in return for a promise never to beg again. If that amount were, for instance, 100 ducats, "we might say that [the beggar] is possessed of wealth worth one hundred."

Today, we view the idea of human capital—the sum of education, natural talent, training, and experience that comprise the wellspring of future earnings flows—as fundamental to the understanding of major shifts in the global economy. Human capital plays the same role for an employee as plant and equipment play for the employer. Despite the enormous accretions of tangible wealth since 1738, human capital is still by far the largest income-producing asset for the great majority of people. Why else would so many breadwinners spend their hard-earned money on life-insurance premiums?

For Bernoulli, games of chance and abstract problems were merely tools with which to fashion his primary case around the desire for wealth and opportunity. His emphasis was on decision-making rather than on the mathematical intricacies of probability theory. He announces at the outset that his aim is to establish "rules [that] would be set up whereby anyone could estimate his prospects from any risky undertaking in light of one's specific financial circumstances." These words are the grist for the mill of every contemporary financial economist, business manager, and investor. Risk is no longer something to be faced; risk has become a set of opportunities open to choice.

Bernoulli's notion of utility—and his suggestion that the satisfaction derived from a specified increase in wealth would be inversely related to the quantity of goods previously possessed—were sufficiently robust to have a lasting influence on the work of the major thinkers who followed. Utility provided the underpinnings for the Law of Supply and Demand, a striking innovation of Victorian economists that marked the jumping-off point for understanding how markets behave and how buyers and sellers reach agreement on price. Utility was such a powerful concept that over the next two hundred years it formed the foundation for the dominant paradigm that explained human decision-making and theories of choice in areas far beyond financial matters. The theory of games—the innovative twentieth century approach to decision-making in war, politics, and business management—makes utility an integral part of its entire system.

Utility has had an equally profound influence on psychology and philosophy, for Bernoulli set the standard for defining human rationality. For example, people for whom the utility of wealth *rises* as they grow richer are considered by most psychologists—and moralists—as neurotic; greed was not part of Bernoulli's vision, nor is it included in most modern definitions of rationality.

Utility theory requires that a rational person be able to measure utility under all circumstances and to make choices and decisions accordingly—a tall order given the uncertainties we face in the course of a lifetime. The chore is difficult enough even when, as Bernoulli assumed, the facts are the same for everyone. On many occasions the facts are not the same for everyone. Different people have different information; each of us tends to color the information we have in our own fashion. Even the most rational among us will often disagree about what the facts mean.

Modern as Bernoulli may appear, he was very much a man of his times. His concept of human rationality fitted neatly into the intellectual environment of the Enlightenment. This was a time when writers, artists, composers, and political philosophers embraced the classical ideas of order and form and insisted that through the accumulation of knowledge mankind could penetrate the mysteries of life. In 1738, when Bernoulli's paper appeared, Alexander Pope was at the height of his career, studding his poems with classical allusions, warning that "A little learning is a dangerous thing," and proclaiming that "The proper study of mankind is man." Denis Diderot was soon to start work on a 28-volume encyclopedia, and Samuel Johnson was about to fashion the first dictionary of the English language. Voltaire's unromantic viewpoints on society occupied center stage in intellectual circles. By 1750, Haydn had defined the classical form of the symphony and sonata.

The Enlightenment's optimistic philosophy of human capabilities would show up in the Declaration of Independence and would help shape the Constitution of the newly formed United States of America. Carried to its violent extreme, the Enlightenment inspired the citizens of France to lop off the head of Louis XVI and to enthrone Reason on the altar of Notre Dame.

Bernoulli's boldest innovation was the notion that each of us—even the most rational—has a unique set of values and will respond accordingly, but his genius was in recognizing that he had to go further than that. When he formalizes his thesis by asserting that utility is inversely proportionate to the quantity of goods possessed, he opens up a fascinating insight into human behavior and the way we arrive at decisions and choices in the face of risk.

According to Bernoulli, our decisions have a predictable and systematic structure. In a rational world, we would all rather be rich than poor, but the intensity of the desire to become richer is tempered by how rich we already are. Many years ago, one of my investment counsel clients shook his finger at me during our first meeting and warned me: "Remember this, young man, you don't have to make me rich. I am rich already!"

The logical consequence of Bernoulli's insight leads to a new and powerful intuition about taking risk. If the satisfaction to be derived from each successive increase in wealth is smaller than the satisfaction derived from the previous increase in wealth, then the *dis*utility caused by a loss will always exceed the positive utility provided by a gain of equal size. That was my client's message to me.

Think of your wealth as a pile of bricks, with large bricks at the foundation and with the bricks growing smaller and smaller as the height increases. Any brick you remove from the top of the pile will be larger than the next brick you might add to it. The hurt that results from losing a brick is greater than the pleasure that results from gaining a brick.

Bernoulli provides this example: two men, each worth 100 ducats, decide to play a fair game, like tossing coins, in which there is a 50-50 chance of winning or losing, with no house take or any other deduction from the stakes. Each man bets 50 ducats on the throw, which means that each has an equal chance of ending up worth 150 ducats or of ending up worth only 50 ducats.

Would a rational person play such a game? The mathematical expectation of each man's wealth after the game has been played with this 50-50 set of alternatives is precisely 100 ducats (150 + 50 divided by 2), which is just what each player started with. The expected value for each is the same as if they had not decided to play the game in the first place.

Bernoulli's theory of utility reveals an asymmetry that explains why an even-Steven game like this is an unattractive proposition. The 50 ducats that the losing player would drop have greater utility than the 50 ducats that the winner would pocket. Just as with the pile of bricks, losing 50 ducats hurts the loser more than gaining 50 ducats pleases the winner.* In a mathematical sense a zero-sum game is a loser's game when it is valued in terms of utility. The best decision for both is to refuse to play this game.

Bernoulli uses his example to warn gamblers that they will suffer a loss of utility even in a fair game. This depressing result, he points out, is:

> Nature's admonition to avoid the dice altogether . . . . [E]veryone who bets any part of his fortune, however small, on a mathematically fair game of chance acts irrationally . . . . [T]he imprudence of a gambler will be the greater the larger part of his fortune which he exposes to a game of chance.

Most of us would agree with Bernoulli that a fair game is a loser's game in utility terms. We are what psychologists and economists call "risk-averse" or "risk averters." The expression has a precise meaning with profound implications.

Imagine that you were given a choice between a gift of $25 for certain or an opportunity to play a game in which you stood a 50% chance of winning $50 and a 50% chance of winning nothing. The gamble has a mathematical expectation of $25—the same amount as the gift—but that expectation is uncertain. Risk-averse people would choose the gift over the gamble. Different people, however, are risk-averse in different degrees.

You can test your own degree of risk aversion by determining your "certainty equivalent." How high would the mathematical expectation of the game have to go before you would prefer the gamble to the gift? Thirty dollars from a 50% chance of winning $60 and a 50% chance of winning nothing? Then the $30 expectation from the gamble would be the equivalent of the $25 for certain. But perhaps you would take the gamble for an expectation of only $26. You might even discover that at heart you are a *risk-seeker*, willing to play the game even when the mathematical expectation of the payoff is less than the certain return of $25. That would be the case, for example, in a game where the payoff differs from 50-50 so that you would win $40 if you toss tails and zero if you toss heads, for an expected value of only $20. But most of us

---

*This is an oversimplification. The utility of any absolute loss depends on the wealth of the loser. Here the implicit assumption is that the two players have equal wealth.

would prefer a game in which the expected value is something in excess of the $50 in the example. The popularity of lottery games provides an interesting exception to this statement, because the state's skim off the top is so large that most lotteries are egregiously unfair to the players.

A significant principle is at work here. Suppose your stockbroker recommends a mutual fund that invests in a cross section of the smallest stocks listed on the market. Over the past 69 years, the smallest 20% of the stock market has provided an income of capital appreciation plus dividend that has averaged 18% a year. That is a generous rate of return. But volatility in this sector has also been high: two-thirds of the returns have fallen between −23% and +59%; negative returns over twelve-month periods have occurred in almost one out of every three years and have averaged 20%. Thus, the outlook for any given year has been extremely uncertain, regardless of the high average rewards generated by these stocks over the long run.

As an alternative, suppose a different broker recommends a fund that buys and holds the 500 stocks that comprise the Standard & Poor's Composite Index. The average annual return on these stocks over the past 69 years has been about 13%, but two-thirds of the annual returns have fallen within the narrower range of −11% and +36%; negative returns have averaged 13%. Assuming the future will look approximately like the past, but also assuming that you do not have 70 years to find out how well you did, is the higher average expected return on the small-stock fund sufficient to justify its much greater volatility of returns? Which mutual fund would you buy?

Daniel Bernoulli transformed the stage on which the risk-taking drama is played out. His description of how human beings employ both measurement and gut in making decisions when outcomes are uncertain was an impressive achievement. As he himself boasts in his paper, "Since all our propositions harmonize perfectly with experience, it would be wrong to neglect them as abstractions resting upon precarious hypotheses."

A powerful attack some two hundred years later ultimately revealed that Bernoulli's propositions fell short of harmonizing perfectly with experience, in large part because his hypotheses about human rationality were more precarious than he as a man of the Enlightenment might want to believe. Until that attack was launched, however, the concept of utility flourished in the philosophical debate over rationality that prevailed for nearly two hundred years after Bernoulli's paper was published. Bernoulli could hardly have imagined how long his concept of utility would survive—thanks largely to later writers who came upon it on their own, unaware of his pioneering work.

7

The Search for Moral Certainty

One winter night during one of the many German air raids on Moscow in World War II, a distinguished Soviet professor of statistics showed up in his local air-raid shelter. He had never appeared there before. "There are seven million people in Moscow," he used to say. "Why should I expect them to hit me?" His friends were astonished to see him and asked what had happened to change his mind. "Look," he explained, "there are seven million people in Moscow and one elephant. Last night they got the elephant."

This story is a modern version of the thunderstorm phobias analyzed in the Port-Royal *Logic,* but it differs at a critical point from the moral of the example cited there. In this case, the individual involved was keenly aware of the mathematical probability of being hit by a bomb. What the professor's experience really illuminates, therefore, is the dual character that runs throughout everything to do with probability: past frequencies can collide with degrees of belief when risky choices must be made.

The story has more to it than that. It echoes the concerns of Graunt, Petty, and Halley, When complete knowledge of the future—or even of the past—is an impossibility, how representative is the information we have in hand? Which counts for more, the seven million humans or the elephant? How should we evaluate new information and incorporate it into degrees of belief developed from prior information?

Is the theory of probability a mathematical toy or a serious instrument for forecasting?

Probability theory is a serious instrument for forecasting, but the devil, as they say, is in the details—in the quality of information that forms the basis of probability estimates. This chapter describes a sequence of giant steps over the course of the eighteenth century that revolutionized the uses of information and the manner in which probability theory can be applied to decisions and choices in the modern world.

The first person to consider the linkages between probability and the quality of information was another and older Bernoulli, Daniel's uncle Jacob, who lived from 1654 to 1705.[1] Jacob was a child when Pascal and Fermat performed their mathematical feats, and he died when his nephew Daniel was only five years old. Talented like all the Bernoullis, he was a contemporary of Isaac Newton and had sufficient Bernoullian ill temper and hubris to consider himself a rival of that great English scientist.

Merely raising the questions that Jacob raised was an intellectual feat in itself, quite apart from offering answers as well. Jacob undertook this task, he tells us, after having meditated on it for twenty years; he completed his work only when he was approaching the age of 80, shortly before he died in 1705.

Jacob was an exceptionally dour Bernoulli, especially toward the end of his life, though he lived during the bawdy and jolly age that followed the restoration of Charles II in 1660.* One of Jacob's more distinguished contemporaries, for example, was John Arbuthnot, Queen Anne's doctor, a Fellow of the Royal Society, and an amateur mathematician with an interest in probability that he pepped up with a generous supply of off-color examples to illustrate his points. In one of Arbuthnot's papers, he considered the odds on whether "a woman of

---

*He did have sufficient poetry in his soul to request that the beautiful Fibonacci spiral be engraved on his tombstone, claiming that the way it could grow without changing its form was "a symbol of fortitude and constancy in adversity: or even of the resurrection of our flesh." He went on to ask that it be inscribed with the epitaph *"Eadem mutata resurgo"* [However changed it is always the same]. See David, 1962, p. 139.

twenty has her maidenhead" or whether "a town-spark of that age 'has not been clap'd.'"[2]

Jacob Bernoulli had first put the question of how to develop probabilities from sample data in 1703. In a letter to his friend Leibniz, he commented that he found it strange that we know the odds of throwing a seven instead of an eight with a pair of dice, but we do not know the probability that a man of twenty will outlive a man of sixty. Might we not, he asks, find the answer to this question by examining a large number of pairs of men of each age?

In responding to Bernoulli, Leibniz took a dim view of this approach. "[N]ature has established patterns originating in the return of events," he wrote, "but only for the most part. New illnesses flood the human race, so that no matter how many experiments you have done on corpses, you have not thereby imposed a limit on the nature of events so that in the future they could not vary."[3] Although Leibniz wrote this letter in Latin, he put the expression, "but only for the most part" into Greek: ως επι το πολυ. Perhaps this was to emphasize his point that a finite number of experiments such as Jacob suggested would inevitably be too small a sample for an exact calculation of nature's intentions.[*]

Jacob was not deterred by Leibniz's response, but he did change the manner in which he went about solving the problem. Leibniz's admonition in Greek would not be forgotten.

Jacob's effort to uncover probabilities from sample data appears in his *Ars Conjectandi* (*The Art of Conjecture*), the work that his nephew Nicolaus finally published in 1713, eight years after Jacob's death.[4] His interest was in demonstrating where the art of thinking—objective analysis—ends and the art of conjecture begins. In a sense, conjecture is the process of estimating the whole from the parts.

Jacob's analysis begins with the observation that probability theory had reached the point where, to arrive at a hypothesis about the likelihood of an event, "it is necessary only to calculate exactly the number of possible cases, and then to determine how much more likely it is that

---

[*]At a later point in the correspondence with Jacob, Leibniz observed, "It is certain that someone who tried to use modern observations from London and Paris to judge mortality rates of the Fathers before the flood would enormously deviate from the truth." (Hacking, 1975, p. 164.)

one case will occur than another." The difficulty, as Jacob goes on to point out, is that the uses of probability are limited almost exclusively to games of chance. Up to that point, Pascal's achievement had amounted to little more than an intellectual curiosity.

For Jacob, this limitation was extremely serious, as he reveals in a passage that echoes Leibniz's concerns:

> But what mortal . . . could ascertain the number of diseases, counting all possible cases, that afflict the human body . . . and how much more likely one disease is to be fatal than another—plague than dropsy . . . or dropsy than fever—and on that basis make a prediction about the relationship between life and death in future generations?
> . . . [W[ho can pretend to have penetrated so deeply into the nature of the human mind or the wonderful structure of the body that in games which depend . . . on the mental acuteness or physical agility of the players he would venture to predict when this or that player would win or lose?

Jacob is drawing a crucial distinction between reality and abstraction in applying the laws of probability. For example, Paccioli's incomplete game of *balla* and the unfinished hypothetical World Series that we analyzed in the discussion of Pascal's Triangle bear no resemblance to real-world situations. In the real world, the contestants in a game of *balla* or in a World Series have differing "mental acuteness or physical agility," qualities that I ignored in the oversimplified examples of how to use probability to forecast outcomes. Pascal's Triangle can provide only hints about how such real-life games will turn out.

The theory of probability can define the probabilities at the gaming casino or in a lottery—there is no need to spin the roulette wheel or count the lottery tickets to estimate the nature of the outcome—but in real life relevant information is essential. And the bother is that we never have all the information we would like. Nature has established patterns, but only for the most part. Theory, which abstracts from nature, is kinder: we either have the information we need or else we have no need for information. As I quoted Fischer Black as saying in the Introduction, the world looks neater from the precincts of MIT on the Charles River than from the hurly-burly of Wall Street by the Hudson.

In our discussion of Paccioli's hypothetical game of *balla* and our imaginary World Series, the long-term records, the physical capabilities, and the I.Q.s of the players were irrelevant. Even the nature of the game itself was irrelevant. Theory was a complete substitute for information.

Real-life baseball fans, like aficionados of the stock market, assemble reams of statistics precisely because they need that information in order to reach judgments about capabilities among the players and the teams—or the outlook for the earning power of the companies trading on the stock exchange. And even with thousands of facts, the track record of the experts, in both athletics and finance, proves that their estimates of the probabilities of the final outcomes are open to doubt and uncertainty.

Pascal's Triangle and all the early work in probability answered only one question: what is the probability of such-and-such an outcome? The answer to that question has limited value in most cases, because it leaves us with no sense of generality. What do we really know when we reckon that Player A has a 60% chance of winning a particular game of *balla*? Can that likelihood tell us whether he is skillful enough to win 60% of the time against Player B? Victory in one set of games is insufficient to confirm that expectation. How many times do Messrs. A and B have to play before we can be confident that A is the superior player? What does the outcome of this year's World Series tell us about the probability that the winning team is the best team all the time not just in that particular series? What does the high proportion of deaths from lung cancer among smokers signify about the chances that smoking will kill you before your time? What does the death of an elephant reveal about the value of going to an air-raid shelter?

But real-life situations often require us to measure probability in precisely this fashion—from sample to universe. In only rare cases does life replicate games of chance, for which we can determine the probability of an outcome *before* an event even occurs—*a priori*, as Jacob Bernoulli puts it. In most instances, we have to estimate probabilities from what happened *after* the fact—*a posteriori*. The very notion of *a posteriori* implies experimentation and changing degrees of belief. There were seven million people in Moscow, but after one elephant was killed by a Nazi bomb, the professor decided the time had come to go to the air-raid shelter.

❋

Jacob Bernoulli's contribution to the problem of developing probabilities from limited amounts of real-life information was twofold. First, he defined the problem in this fashion before anyone else had even recognized the need for a definition. Second, he suggested a solution that demands only one requirement. We must assume that "under similar conditions, the occurrence (or non-occurrence) of an event in the future will follow the same pattern as was observed in the past."[5]

This is a giant assumption. Jacob may have complained that in real life there are too few cases in which the information is so complete that we can use the simple rules of probability to predict the outcome. But he admits that an estimate of probabilities *after the fact* also is impossible unless we can assume that the past is a reliable guide to the future. The difficulty of that assignment requires no elaboration.

The past, or whatever data we choose to analyze, is only a fragment of reality. That fragmentary quality is crucial in going from data to a generalization. We never have all the information we need (or can afford to acquire) to achieve the same confidence with which we know, beyond a shadow of a doubt, that a die has six sides, each with a different number, or that a European roulette wheel has 37 slots (American wheels have 38 slots), again each with a different number. Reality is a series of connected events, each dependent on another, radically different from games of chance in which the outcome of any single throw has zero influence on the outcome of the next throw. Games of chance reduce everything to a hard number, but in real life we use such measures as "a little," "a lot," or "not too much, please" much more often than we use a precise quantitative measure.

Jacob Bernoulli unwittingly defined the agenda for the remainder of this book. From this point forward, the debate over managing risk will converge on the uses of his three requisite assumptions—full information, independent trials, and the relevance of quantitative valuation. The relevance of these assumptions is critical in determining how successfully we can apply measurement and information to predict the future. Indeed, Jacob's assumptions shape the way we view the past itself: after the fact, can we explain what happened, or must we ascribe the event to just plain luck (which is merely another way of saying we are unable to explain what happened)?

Despite all the obstacles, practicality demands that we assume, some-times explicitly but more often implicitly, that Jacob's necessary condi-tions are met, even when we know full well that reality differs from the ideal case. Our answers may be sloppy, but the methodology developed by Jacob Bernoulli and the other mathematicians mentioned in this chapter provides us with a powerful set of tools for developing proba-bilities of future outcomes on the basis of the limited data provided by the past.

Jacob Bernoulli's theorem for calculating probabilities *a posteriori* is known as the Law of Large Numbers. Contrary to the popular view, this law does not provide a method for validating observed facts, which are only an incomplete representation of the whole truth. Nor does it say that an increasing number of observations will increase the proba-bility that what you see is what you are going to get. The law is not a design for improving the quality of empirical tests: Jacob took Leibniz's advice to heart and rejected his original idea of finding firm answers by means of empirical tests.

Jacob was searching for a different probability. Suppose you toss a coin over and over. The Law of Large Numbers does not tell you that the average of your throws will approach 50% as you increase the num-ber of throws; simple mathematics can tell you that, sparing you the tedious business of tossing the coin over and over. Rather, the law states that increasing the number of throws will correspondingly increase the probability that the ratio of heads thrown to total throws will vary from 50% by less than some stated amount, no matter how small. The word "vary" is what matters. The search is not for the true mean of 50% but for the probability that the error between the observed average and the true average will be less than, say, 2%—in other words, that increasing the number of throws will increase the probability that the observed average will fall within 2% of the true average.

That does not mean that there will be no error after an infinite number of throws; Jacob explicitly excludes that case. Nor does it mean that the errors will of necessity become small enough to ignore. *All the law tells us is that the average of a large number of throws will be more likely than the average of a small number of throws to differ from the true average by less than some stated amount.* And there will always be a possibility that the ob-served result will differ from the true average by a larger amount than the specified bound. Seven million people in Moscow were apparently not enough to satisfy the professor of statistics.

The Law of Large Numbers is not the same thing as the Law of Averages. Mathematics tells us that the probability of heads coming up on any individual coin toss is 50%—but the outcome of each toss is independent of all the others. It is neither influenced by previous tosses nor does it influence future tosses. Consequently, the Law of Large Numbers cannot promise that the probability of heads will rise above 50% on any single toss if the first hundred, or million, tosses happen to come up only 40% heads. There is nothing in the Law of Large Numbers that promises to bail you out when you are caught in a losing streak.

To illustrate his Law of Large Numbers, Jacob hypothesized a jar filled with 3000 white pebbles and 2000 black pebbles, a device that has been a favorite of probability theorists and inventors of mind-twisting mathematical puzzles ever since. He stipulates that we must not know how many pebbles there are of each color. We draw an increasing number of pebbles from the jar, carefully noting the color of each pebble before returning it to the jar. If drawing more and more pebbles can finally give us "moral certainty"—that is, certainty as a practical matter rather than absolute certainty—that the ratio is 3:2, Jacob concludes that "we can determine the number of instances *a posteriori* with almost as great accuracy as if they were know to us *a priori*."[6] His calculations indicate that 25,550 drawings from the jar would suffice to show, with a chance exceeding 1000/1001, that the result would be within 2% of the true ratio of 3:2. That's moral certainty for you.

Jacob does not use the expression "moral certainty" lightly. He derives it from his definition of probability, which he draws from earlier work by Leibniz. "Probability," he declares, "is degree of certainty and differs from absolute certainty as the part differs from the whole."[7]

But Jacob moves beyond Leibniz in considering what "certainty" means. It is our individual judgments of certainty that attract Jacob's attention, and a condition of moral certainty exists when we are *almost* completely certain. When Leibniz introduced the concept, he had defined it as "infinitely probable." Jacob himself is satisfied that 1000/1001 is close enough, but he is willing to be flexible: "It would be useful if the magistrates set up fixed limits for moral certainty."[8]

Jacob is triumphant. Now, he declares, we can make a prediction about any uncertain quantity that will be just as scientific as the predictions made in games of chance. He has elevated probability from the world of theory to the world of reality:

> If, instead of the jar, for instance, we take the atmosphere or the human body, which conceal within themselves a multitude of the most varied processes or diseases, just as the jar conceals the pebbles, then for these also we shall be able to determine by observation how much more frequently one event will occur than another.[9]

Yet Jacob appears to have had trouble with his jar of pebbles. His calculation that 25,550 trials would be necessary to establish moral certainty must have struck him as an intolerably large number; the entire population of his home town of Basel at that time was less than 25,550. We must surmise that he was unable to figure out what to do next, for he ends his book right there. Nothing follows but a wistful comment about the difficulty of finding real-life cases in which all the observations meet the requirement that they be independent of one another:

> If thus all events through all eternity could be repeated, one would find that everything in the world happens from definite causes and according to definite rules, and that we would be forced to assume amongst the most apparently fortuitous things a certain necessity, or, so to say, FATE.[10]

Nevertheless, Jacob's jar of pebbles deserves the immortality it has earned. Those pebbles became the vehicle for the first attempt to measure uncertainty—indeed, to define it—and to calculate the probability that an empirically determined number is close to a true value *even when the true value is an unknown.*

Jacob Bernoulli died in 1705. His nephew Nicolaus—Nicolaus the Slow—continued to work on Uncle Jacob's efforts to derive future probabilities form known observations even while he was inching along toward the completion of *Ars Conjectandi*. Nicolaus's results were published in 1713, the same year in which Jacob's book finally appeared.

Jacob had started with the probability that the error between an observed value and the true value would fall within some specified bound; he then went on to calculate the number of observations needed to raise the probability to that amount. Nicolaus tried to turn his uncle's version of probability around. Taking the number of observations as given, he then calculated the probability that they would fall within the specified bound. He used an example in which he assumed that the ratio of male to female births was 18:17. With, say, a total of 14,000 births, the expected number of male births would be 7,200. He then calculated that the odds are at least 43.58-to-1 that the actual number of male births would fall between 7,200 + 163 and 7,200 − 163, or between 7,363 and 7,037.

In 1718, Nicolaus invited a French mathematician named Abraham de Moivre to join him in his research, but de Moivre turned him down: "I wish I were capable of . . . applying the Doctrine of Chances to *Oeconomical* and *Political* Uses [but] I willingly resign my share of that task to better Hands."[11] Nevertheless, de Moivre's response to Nicolaus reveals that the uses of probability and forecasting had come a long way in just a few years.

De Moivre had been born in 1667—thirteen years after Jacob Bernoulli—as a Protestant in a France that was increasingly hostile to anyone who was not Catholic.[12] In 1685, when de Moivre was 18 years old, King Louis XIV revoked the Edict of Nantes, which had been promulgated under the Protestant-born King Henri IV in 1598 to give Protestants, known as Huguenots, equal political rights with Catholics. After the revocation, exercise of the reformed religion was forbidden, children had to be educated as Catholics, and emigration was prohibited. De Moivre was imprisoned for over two years for his beliefs. Hating France and everything to do with it, he managed to flee to London in 1688, where the Glorious Revolution had just banished the last vestiges of official Catholicism. He never returned to his native country.

De Moivre led a gloomy, frustrating life in England. Despite many efforts, he never managed to land a proper academic position. He supported himself by tutoring in mathematics and by acting as a consultant to gamblers and insurance brokers on applications of probability theory.

For that purpose, he maintained an informal office at Slaughter's Coffee House in St. Martin's Lane, where he went most afternoons after his tutoring chores were over. Although he and Newton were friends, and although he was elected to the Royal Society when he was only thirty, he remained a bitter, introspective, antisocial man. He died in 1754, blind and poverty-stricken, at the age of 87.

In 1725, de Moivre had published a work titled *Annuities upon Lives,* which included an analysis of Halley's tables on life and death in Breslaw. Though the book was primarily a work in mathematics, it suggested important questions related to the puzzles that the Bernoullis were trying to resolve and that de Moivre would later explore in great detail.

Stephen Stigler, a historian of statistics, offers an interesting example of the possibilities raised by de Moivre's work in annuities. Halley's table showed that, of 346 men aged fifty in Breslaw, only 142, or 41%, survived to age seventy. That was only a small sample. To what extent could we use the result to generalize about the life expectancy of men fifty years old? De Moivre could not use these numbers to determine the probability that a man of fifty had a less than 50% chance of dying by age seventy, but he would be able to answer this question: "If the true chance were 1/2, what is the probability a ratio as small as 142/346 or smaller should occur?"

De Moivre's first direct venture into the subject of probability was a work titled *De Mensura Sortis* (literally, *On the Measurement of Lots*). This work was first published in 1711 in an issue of *Philosophical Transactions,* the publication of the Royal Society. In 1718, de Moivre issued a greatly expanded English edition titled *The Doctrine of Chances,* which he dedicated to his good friend Isaac Newton. The book was a great success and went through two further editions in 1738 and 1756. Newton was sufficiently impressed to tell his students on occasion, "Go to Mr. de Moivre; he knows these things better than I do." *De Mensura Sortis* is probably the first work that explicitly defines risk as chance of loss: "The Risk of losing any sum is the reverse of Expectation; and the true measure of it is, the product of the Sum adventured multiplied by the Probability of the Loss."

In 1730, de Moivre finally turned to Nicolaus Bernoulli's project to ascertain how well a sample of facts represented the true universe from which the sample was drawn. He published his complete solution in 1733 and included it in the second and third editions of *Doctrine of*

Chances. He begins by acknowledging that Jacob and Nicolaus Bernoulli "have shewn very great skill . . . . [Y]et some things were farther required." In particular, the approach taken by the Bernoullis appeared "so laborious, and of so great difficulty, that few people have undertaken the task."

The need for 25,550 trials was clearly an obstacle. Even if, as James Newman has suggested, Jacob Bernoulli had been willing to settle for the "immoral certainty" of an even bet—probability of 50/100—that the result would be within 2% of the true ratio of 3:2, 8,400 drawings would be needed. Jacob's selection of a probability of 1000/1001 is in itself a curiosity by today's standards, when most statisticians accept odds of 1 in 20 as sufficient evidence that a result is significant (today's lingo for moral certainty) rather than due to mere chance.

De Moivre's advance in the resolution of these problems ranks among the most important achievements in mathematics. Drawing on both the calculus and on the underlying structure of Pascal's Triangle, known as the binomial theorem, de Moivre demonstrated how a set of random drawings, as in Jacob Bernoulli's jar experiment, would distribute themselves around their average value. For example, assume that you drew a hundred pebbles in succession from Jacob's jar, always returning each pebble drawn, and noted the ratio of white to black. Then assume you made a series of successive drawings, each of a hundred balls. De Moivre would be able to tell you beforehand approximately how many of those ratios would be close to the average ratio of the total number of drawings and how those individual ratios would distribute themselves around the grand average.

De Moivre's distribution is known today as a normal curve, or, because of its resemblance to a bell, as a bell curve. The distribution, when traced out as a curve, shows the largest number of observations clustered in the center, close to the average, or mean, of the total number of observations. The curve then slopes symmetrically downward, with an equal number of observations on either side of the mean, descending steeply at first and then exhibiting a flatter downward slope at each end. In other words, observations far from the mean are less frequent than observations close to the mean.

The shape of de Moivre's curve enabled him to calculate a statistical measure of its dispersion around the mean. This measure, now known as the standard deviation, is critically important in judging whether a set of observations comprises a sufficiently representative sample of the universe of which they are just a part. In a normal distribution, approximately 68% of the observations will fall within one standard deviation of the mean of all the observations, and 95% of them will fall within two standard deviations of the mean.

The standard deviation can tell us whether we are dealing with a case of the head-in-the-oven-feet-in-the-refrigerator, where the average condition of this poor man is meaningless in telling us how he feels. Most of the readings would be far from the average of how he felt around his middle. The standard deviation can also tell us that Jacob's 25,550 draws of pebbles would provide an extremely accurate estimate of the division between the black and white pebbles inside the jar, because relatively few observations would be outliers, far from the average.

De Moivre was impressed with the orderliness that made its appearance as the numbers of random and unconnected observations increased; he ascribed that orderliness to the plans of the Almighty. It conveys the promise that, under the right conditions, measurement can indeed conquer uncertainty and tame risk. Using italics to emphasize the significance of what he had to say, de Moivre summarized his accomplishment: "*[A]tho' Chance produces Irregularities, still the Odds will be infinitely great, that in process of Time, those Irregularities will bear no proportion to recurrency of that Order which naturally results from ORIGINAL DESIGN.*"[13]

De Moivre's gift to mathematics was an instrument that made it possible to evaluate the probability that a given number of observations will fall within some specified bound around a true ratio. That gift has provided many practical applications.

For example, all manufacturers worry that defective products may slip through the assembly line and into the hands of customers. One hundred percent perfection is a practical impossibility in most instances— the world as we know it seems to have an incurable habit of denying us perfection.

Suppose the manager of a pin factory is trying to hold down the number of defective pins to no more than 10 out of every 100,000 produced, or 0.01% or the total.[14] To see how things are going, he takes a random sample of 100,000 pins as they come off the assembly line and finds 12 pins without heads—two more than the average of 10 defectives that he had hoped to achieve. How important is that difference? What is the probability of finding 12 defective pins out of a sample of 100,000 if, *on the average,* the factory would be turning out 10 defective pins out of every 100,000 produced? De Moivre's normal distribution and standard deviation provide the answer.

But that is not the sort of question that people usually want answered. More often, they do not know for certain before the fact how many defective units the factory is going to produce *on the average.* Despite good intentions, the true ratio of defectives could end up higher than 10 per 100,000 on the average. What does that sample of 100,000 pins reveal about the likelihood that the average ratio of defectives will exceed 0.01% of the total? How much more could we learn from a sample of 200,000? What is the probability that the average ratio of defectives will fall between 0.009% and 0.011%? Between .007% and .013%? What is the probability that any single pin I happen to pick up will be defective?

In this scenario, the data are given—10 pins, 12 pins, 1 pin—and the probability is the unknown. Questions put in this manner form the subject matter of what is known as *inverse probability*: with 12 defective pins out of 100,000, what is the probability that the true average ratio of defectives to the total is 0.01%?

One of the most effective treatments of such questions was proposed by a minister named Thomas Bayes, who was born in 1701 and lived in Kent.[15] Bayes was a Nonconformist; he rejected most of the ceremonial rituals that the Church of England had retained from the Catholic Church after their separation in the time of Henry VIII.

Not much is known about Bayes, even though he was a Fellow of the Royal Society. One otherwise dry and impersonal textbook in statistics went so far as to characterize him as "enigmatic."[16] He published nothing in mathematics while he was alive and left only two works that were published after his death but received little attention when they appeared.

Yet one of those papers, *Essay Towards Solving A Problem In The Doctrine Of Chances,* was a strikingly original piece of work that immortalized Bayes among statisticians, economists, and other social scientists. This paper laid the foundation for the modern method of statistical inference, the great issue first posed by Jacob Bernoulli.

When Bayes died in 1761, his will, dated a year earlier, bequeathed the draft of this essay, plus one hundred pounds sterling, to "Richard Price, now I suppose a preacher at Newington Green."[17] It is odd that Bayes was so vague about Richard Price's location, because Price was more than just a preacher in Islington in north London.

Richard Price was a man with high moral standards and a passionate belief in human freedom in general and freedom of religion in particular. He was convinced that freedom was of divine origin and therefore was essential for moral behavior; he declared that it was better to be free and sin than to be someone's slave. In the 1780s, he wrote a book on the American Revolution with the almost endless title of *Observations on the Importance of the American Revolution and the Means of Making it a Benefit to the World* in which he expressed his belief that the Revolution was ordained by God. At some personal risk, he cared for the American prisoners of war who had been transferred to camps in England. Benjamin Franklin was a good friend, and Adam Smith was an acquaintance. Price and Franklin read and criticized some of the draft chapters of *The Wealth of Nations* as Smith was writing it.

One freedom bothered Price: the freedom to borrow. He was deeply concerned about the burgeoning national debt, swollen by the wars against France and by the war against the colonies in North America. He complained that the debt was "funding for eternity" and dubbed it the "Grand National Evil."[18]

But Price was not just a minister and a passionate defender of human freedom. He was also a mathematician whose work in the field of probability was impressive enough to win him membership in the Royal Society.

In 1765, three men from an insurance company named the Equitable Society called on Price for assistance in devising mortality tables on which to base their premiums for life insurance and annuities. After studying the work of Halley and de Moivre, among others, Price published two articles on the subject in *Philosophical Transactions;* his biographer, Carl Cone, reports that Price's hair is alleged to have turned gray in one night of intense concentration on the second of these articles.

Price started by studying records kept in London, but the life expectancies in those records turned out to be well below actual mortality rates.[19] He then turned to the shire of Northampton, where records were more carefully kept than in London. He published the results of his study in 1771 in a book titled *Observations on Reversionary Payments,* which was regarded as the bible on the subject until well into the nineteenth century. This work has earned him the title of the founding father of actuarial science—the complex mathematical work in probability that is performed today in all insurance companies as the basis for calculating premiums.

And yet Price's book contained serious, costly errors, in part because of an inadequate data base that omitted the large number of unregistered births. Moreover, he overestimated death rates at younger ages and underestimated them at later ages, and his estimates of migration into and out of Northampton were flawed. Most serious, he appears to have underestimated life expectancies, with the result that the life-insurance premiums were much higher than they needed to be. The Equitable Society flourished on this error; the British government, using the same tables to determine annuity payments to its pensioners, lost heavily.[20]

Two years later, after Bayes had died, Price sent a copy of Bayes's "very ingenious" paper to a certain John Canton, another member of the Royal Society, with a cover letter that tells us a good deal about Bayes's intentions in writing the paper. In 1764, the Royal Society subsequently published Bayes's essay in *Philosophical Transactions,* but even then his innovative work languished in obscurity for another twenty years.

Here is how Bayes put the problem he was trying to solve:

PROBLEM

Given that the number of times in which an unknown event has happened and failed: *Required* the chance that the probability of its happening in a single trial lies somewhere between any two degrees of probability that can be named.[21]

The problem as set forth here is precisely the inverse of the problem as defined by Jacob Bernoulli some sixty years earlier (page 118). Bayes is asking how we can determine the probability that an event will occur under circumstances where we know nothing about it except that it has occurred a certain number of times and has failed to occur a certain number of other times. In other words, a pin could be either defective or it could be perfect. If we identify ten defective pins out of a sample of a hundred, what is the probability that the *total* output of pins—not just any sample of a hundred—will contain between 9% and 11% defectives?

Price's cover letter to Canton reflects how far the analysis of probability had advanced into the real world of decision-making over just a hundred years. "Every judicious person," Price writes, "will be sensible that the problem now mentioned is by no means a curious speculation in the doctrine of chances, but necessary to be solved in order to [provide] a sure foundation for all our reasonings concerning past facts, and what is likely to be hereafter."[22] He goes on to say that neither Jacob Bernoulli nor de Moivre had posed the question in precisely this fashion, though de Moivre had described the difficulty of reaching his own solution as "the hardest that can be proposed on the subject of chance."

Bayes used an odd format to prove his point, especially for a dissenting minister: a billiard table. A ball is rolled across the table, free to stop anywhere and thereafter to remain at rest. Then a second ball is rolled repeatedly in the same fashion, and a count is taken of the number of times it stops to the right of the first ball. That number is "the number of times in which an unknown event has happened." Failure—the number of times the event does not happen—occurs when the ball lands to the left. The probability of the location of the first ball—a single trial—is to be deduced from the "successes" and "failures" of the second.[23]

The primary application of the Bayesian system is in the use of new information to revise probabilities based on old information, or, in the language of the statisticians, to compare posterior probability with the priors. In the case of the billiard balls, the first ball represents the priors and the continuous revision of estimates as to its location as the second ball is repeatedly thrown represents the posterior probabilities.

This procedure of revising inferences about old information as new information arrives springs from a philosophical viewpoint that makes

Bayes's contribution strikingly modern: in a dynamic world, there is no single answer under conditions of uncertainty. The mathematician A.F.M. Smith has summed it up well: "Any approach to scientific inference which seeks to legitimise *an* answer in response to complex uncertainty is, for me, a totalitarian parody of a would-be rational learning process."[24]

Although the Bayesian system of inference is too complex to recite here in detail, an example of a typical application of Bayesian analysis appears in the appendix to this chapter.

The most exciting feature of all the achievements mentioned in this chapter is the daring idea that uncertainty can be measured. Uncertainty means unknown probabilities; to reverse Hacking's description of certainty, we can say that something is uncertain when our information is correct and an event fails to happen, or when our information is incorrect and an event does happen.

Jacob Bernoulli, Abraham de Moivre, and Thomas Bayes showed how to infer previously unknown probabilities from the empirical facts of reality. These accomplishments are impressive for the sheer mental agility demanded, and audacious for their bold attack on the unknown. When de Moivre invoked *ORIGINAL DESIGN*, he made no secret of his wonderment at his own accomplishments. He liked to turn such phrases; at another point, he writes, "If we blind not ourselves with metaphysical dust we shall be led by a short and obvious way, to the acknowledgment of the great *MAKER* and *GOUVERNOUR* of all."[25]

We are by now well into the eighteenth century, when the Enlightenment identified the search for knowledge as the highest form of human activity. It was a time for scientists to wipe the metaphysical dust from their eyes. There were no longer any inhibitions against exploring the unknown and creating the new. The great advances in the efforts to tame risk in the years before 1800 were to take on added momentum as the new century approached, and the Victorian era would provide further impulse.

APPENDIX: AN EXAMPLE OF THE BAYESIAN SYSTEM OF STATISTICAL INFERENCE IN ACTION

We return to the pin-manufacturing company. The company has two factories, the older of which produces 40% of the total output. This means that a pin picked up at random has a 40% probability of coming from the old factory, whether it is defective or perfect; this is the prior probability. We find that the older factory's defective rate is twice that found in the newer factory. If a customer calls and complains about finding a defective pin, which of the two factories should the manager call?

The prior probability would suggest that the defective pin was most likely to have come from the new plant, which produces 60% of the total. On the other hand, that plant produces only one-third of the company's total of defective pins. When we revise the priors to reflect this additional information, the probability that the new plant made the defective pin turns out to be only 42.8%; there is a 57.2% probability that the older plant is the culprit. This new estimate becomes the posterior probability.

8

The Supreme Law of Unreason

During the last 27 years of his life, which ended at the age of 78 in 1855, Carl Friedrich Gauss slept only once away from his home in Göttingen.[1] Indeed, he had refused professorships and had declined honors from the most distinguished universities in Europe because of his distaste for travel.

Like many mathematicians before and after him, Gauss also was a childhood genius—a fact that displeased his father as much as it seems to have pleased his mother. His father was an uncouth laborer who despised the boy's intellectual precocity and made life as difficult as possible for him. His mother struggled to protect him and to encourage his progress; Gauss remained deeply devoted to her for as long as she lived.

Gauss's biographers supply all the usual stories of mathematical miracles at an age when most people can barely manage to divide 24 by 12. His memory for numbers was so enormous that he carried the logarithmic tables in his head, available on instant recall. At the age of eighteen, he made a discovery about the geometry of a seventeen-sided polygon; nothing like this had happened in mathematics since the days of the great Greek mathematicians 2,000 years earlier. His doctoral thesis, "A New Proof That Every Rational Integer Function of One Variable Can Be Resolved into Real Factors of the First or Second

Degree," is recognized by the cognoscenti as the fundamental theorem of algebra. The concept was not new, but the proof was.

Gauss's fame as a mathematician made him a world-class celebrity. In 1807, as the French army was approaching Göttingen, Napoleon ordered his troops to spare the city because "the greatest mathematician of all times is living there."[2] That was gracious of the Emperor, but fame is a two-sided coin. When the French, flushed with victory, decided to levy punitive fines on the Germans, they demanded 2,000 francs from Gauss. That was the equivalent of $5,000 in today's money and purchasing power—a heavy fine indeed for a university professor.[*] A wealthy friend offered to help out, but Gauss rebuffed him. Before Gauss could say no a second time, the fine was paid for him by a distinguished French mathematician, Marquis Pierre Simon de Laplace (1749–1827). Laplace announced that he did this good deed because he considered Gauss, 29 years his junior, to be "the greatest mathematician in the world,"[3] thereby ranking Gauss a few steps below Napoleon's appraisal. Then an anonymous German admirer sent Gauss 1,000 francs to provide partial repayment to Laplace.

Laplace was a colorful personality who deserves a brief digression here; we shall encounter him again in Chapter 12.

Gauss had been exploring some of the same areas of probability theory that had occupied Laplace's attention for many years. Like Gauss, Laplace had been a child prodigy in mathematics and had been fascinated by astronomy. But as we shall see, the resemblance ended there. Laplace's professional life spanned the French Revolution, the Napoleonic era, and the restoration of the monarchy. It was a time that required unusual footwork for anyone with ambitions to rise to high places. Laplace was indeed ambitious, had nimble footwork, and did rise to high places.[4]

In 1784, the King made Laplace an examiner of the Royal Artillery, a post that paid a handsome salary. But under the Republic, Laplace lost no time in proclaiming his "inextinguishable hatred to royalty."[5] Almost immediately after Napoleon came to power, Laplace announced his enthusiastic support for the new leader, who gave him the portfolio of the Interior and the title of Count; having France's most respected sci-

---

[*]The franc/dollar exchange rate has been remarkably steady over the years at around 5:1. Hence, 2,000 francs was the equivalent of $400 dollars of 1807 purchasing power. A dollar in 1807 bought about twelve times as much as today's dollar.

entist on the staff added respectability to Napoleon's fledgling government. But Napoleon, having decided to give Laplace's job to his own brother, fired Laplace after only six weeks, observing, "He was a worse than mediocre administrator who searched everywhere for subtleties, and brought into the affairs of government the spirit of the infinitely small."[6] So much for academics who approach too close to the seats of power!

Later on, Laplace got his revenge. He had dedicated the 1812 edition of his magisterial *Théorie analytique des probabilités* to "Napoleon the Great," but he deleted that dedication from the 1814 edition. Instead, he linked the shift in the political winds to the subject matter of his treatise: "The fall of empires which aspired to universal dominion," he wrote, "could be predicted with very high probability by one versed in the calculus of chance."[7] Louis XVIII took appropriate note when he assumed the throne: Laplace became a Marquis.

Unlike Laplace, Gauss was reclusive and obsessively secretive. He refrained from publishing a vast quantity of important mathematical research—so much, in fact, that other mathematicians had to rediscover work that he had already completed. Moreover, his published work emphasized results rather than his methodology, often obliging mathematicians to search for the path to his conclusions. Eric Temple Bell, one of Gauss's biographers, believes that mathematics might have been fifty years further along if Gauss had been more forthcoming; "Things buried for years or decades in [his] diary would have made half a dozen great reputations had they been published promptly."[8]

Fame and secretiveness combined to make Gauss an incurable intellectual snob. Although his primary achievement was in the theory of numbers, the same area that had fascinated Fermat, he had little use for Fermat's pioneering work. He brushed off Fermat's Last Theorem, which had stood as a fascinating challenge to mathematicians for over a hundred years, as "An isolated proposition with very little interest for me, because I could easily lay down a multitude of such propositions, which one could neither prove nor dispose of."[9]

This was not an empty boast. In 1801, at the age of 24, Gauss had published *Disquisitiones Arithmeticae*, written in elegant Latin, a trailblazing, historic work in the theory of numbers. Much of the book is obscure to a non-mathematician, but what he wrote was beautiful music to himself.[10] He found "a magical charm" in number theory and enjoyed discovering and then proving the generality of relationships such as this:

$$1 = 1^2$$
$$1 + 3 = 2^2$$
$$1 + 3 + 5 = 3^2$$
$$1 + 3 + 5 + 7 = 4^2$$

Or, in general, that the sum of the first n successive odd numbers is n^2. This would make the sum of the first 100 odd numbers, from 1 to 199, equal to 100^2, or 10,000; and the sum of the numbers from 1 to 999 would be equal to 250,000.

Gauss did deign to demonstrate that his theoretical work had important applications. In 1800, an Italian astronomer discovered a small new planet—technically, an asteroid—that he named Ceres. A year later Gauss set out to calculate its orbit; he had already calculated lunar tables that enabled people to figure out the date of Easter in any year. Gauss was motivated in large part by his desire to win a public reputation. But he also wanted to join his distinguished mathematical ancestors—from Ptolemy to Galileo and Newton—in research into celestial mechanics, quite aside from wishing to outdo the astronomical work of his contemporary and benefactor, Laplace. In any event, this particular problem was enticing in itself, given the paucity of relevant data and the speed with which Ceres rotated around the sun.

After a spell of feverish calculation, he came up with a precisely correct solution and was able to predict the exact location of Ceres at any moment. In the process he had developed enough skill in celestial mechanics to be able to calculate the orbit of a comet in just an hour or two, a task that took other scientists three or four days.

Gauss took special pride in his achievements in astronomy, feeling that he was following in the footsteps of Newton, his great hero. Given his admiration for Newton's discoveries, he grew apoplectic at any reference to the story that the fall of an apple on Newton's head had been the inspiration for discovering the law of gravity. Gauss characterized this fable as:

Silly! A stupid, officious man asked Newton how he discovered the law of gravitation. Seeing that he had to deal with a child intellect, and wanting to get rid of the bore, Newton answered that an apple fell and hit him on the nose. The man went away fully satisfied and completely enlightened.[11]

Gauss took a dim view of humanity in general, deplored the growing popularity of nationalist sentiments and the glories of war, and regarded foreign conquest as "incomprehensible madness." His misanthropic attitudes may have been the reason why he stuck so close to home for so much of his life.[12]

Gauss had no particular interest in risk management as such. But he was attracted to the theoretical issues raised by the work in probability, large numbers, and sampling that Jacob Bernoulli had initiated and that had been carried forward by de Moivre and Bayes. Despite his lack of interest in risk management, his achievements in these areas are at the heart of modern techniques of risk control.

Gauss's earliest attempts to deal with probability appeared in a book titled *Theoria Motus* (*Theory of Motion*), published in 1809, on the motion of heavenly bodies. In the book Gauss explained how to estimate an orbit based on the path that appeared most frequently over many separate observations. When *Theoria Motus* came to Laplace's attention in 1810, he seized upon it with enthusiasm and set about clarifying most of the ambiguities that Gauss had failed to elucidate.

Gauss's most valuable contribution to probability would come about as the result of work in a totally unrelated area, geodesic measurement, the use of the curvature of the earth to improve the accuracy of geographic measurements. Because the earth is round, the distance between two points on the surface differs from the distance between those two points as the crow flies. This variance is irrelevant for distances of a few miles, but it becomes significant for distances greater than about ten miles.

In 1816, Gauss was invited to conduct a geodesic survey of Bavaria and to link it to measurements already completed by others for Denmark and northern Germany. This task was probably little fun for an academic stick-in-the-mud like Gauss. He had to work outdoors on rugged terrain, trying to communicate with civil servants and others he considered beneath him intellectually—including fellow scientists. In the end, the study stretched into 1848 and filled sixteen volumes when the results were published.

Since it is impossible to measure every square inch of the earth's surface, geodesic measurement consists of making estimates based on sample distances within the area under study. As Gauss analyzed the distribution of these estimates, he observed that they varied widely, but, as the estimates increased in number, they seemed to cluster around a central point. That central point was the mean—statistical language for the average—of all the observations; the observations also distributed themselves into a symmetrical array on either side of the mean. The more measurements Gauss took, the clearer the picture became and the more it resembled the bell curve that de Moivre had come up with 83 years earlier.

The linkage between risk and measuring the curvature of the earth is closer than it might appear. Day after day Gauss took one geodesic measurement after another around the hills of Bavaria in an effort to estimate the curvature of the earth, until he had accumulated a great many measurements indeed. Just as we review past experience in making a judgment about the probability that matters will resolve themselves in the future in one direction rather than another, Gauss had to examine the patterns formed by his observations and make a judgment about how the curvature of the earth affected the distances between various points in Bavaria. He was able to determine the accuracy of his observations by seeing how they distributed themselves around the average of the total number of observations.

The questions he tried to answer were just variations on the kinds of question we ask when we are making a risky decision. On the average, how many showers can we expect in New York in April, and what are the odds that we can safely leave our raincoat at home if we go to New York for a week's vacation? If we are going to drive across the country, what is the risk of having an automobile accident in the course of the 3,000-mile trip? What is the risk that the stock market will decline by more than 10% next year?

The structure Gauss developed for answering such questions is now so familiar to us that we seldom stop to consider where it came from. But without that structure, we would have no systematic method for deciding whether or not to take a certain risk or for evaluating the risks we face. We would be unable to determine the accuracy of the information in hand. We would have no way of estimating the probability that an event will occur—rain, the death of a man of 85, a 20% decline in the stock market, a Russian victory in the Davis Cup matches, a Democratic Congress, the failure of seatbelts, or the discovery of an oil well by a wildcatting firm.

The process begins with the bell curve, the main purpose of which is to indicate not accuracy but error. If every estimate we made were a precisely correct measurement of what we were measuring, that would be the end of the story. If every human being, elephant, orchid, and razor-billed auk were precisely like all the others of its species, life on this earth would be very different from what it is. But life is a collection of similarities rather than identities; no single observation is a perfect example of generality. By revealing the normal distribution, the bell curve transforms this jumble into order. Francis Galton, whom we will meet in the next chapter, rhapsodized over the normal distribution:

> [T]he "Law Of Frequency Of Error". . . reigns with serenity and in complete self-effacement amidst the wildest confusion. The huger the mob . . . the more perfect is its sway. It is the supreme law of Unreason. Whenever a large sample of chaotic elements are taken in hand . . . an unsuspected and most beautiful form of regularity proves to have been latent all along.[13]

Most of us first encountered the bell curve during our schooldays. The teacher would mark papers "on the curve" instead of grading them on an absolute basis—this is an A paper, this is a C+ paper. Average students would receive an average grade, such as B– or C+ or 80%. Poorer and better students would receive grades distributed symmetrically around the average grade. Even if all the papers were excellent or all were terrible, the best of the lot would receive an A and the worst a D, with most grades falling in between.

Many natural phenomena, such as the heights of a group of people or the lengths of their middle fingers, fall into a normal distribution.

As Galton suggested, two conditions are necessary for observations to be distributed normally, or symmetrically, around their average. First, there must be as large a number of observations as possible. Second, the observations must be independent, like rolls of the dice. *Order is impossible to find unless disorder is there first.*

People can make serious mistakes by sampling data that are not independent. In 1936, a now-defunct magazine called the *Literary Digest* took a straw vote to predict the outcome of the forthcoming presidential election between Franklin Roosevelt and Alfred Landon. The magazine sent about ten million ballots in the form of returnable postcards to names selected from telephone directories and automobile registrations. A high proportion of the ballots were returned, with 59% favoring Landon and 41% favoring Roosevelt. On Election Day, Landon won 39% of the vote and Roosevelt won 61%. People who had telephones and drove automobiles in the mid-1930s hardly constituted a random sample of American voters: their voting preferences were all conditioned by an environment that the mass of people at that time could not afford.

Observations that are truly independent provide a great deal of useful information about probabilities. Take rolls of the dice as an example.

Each of the six sides of a die has an equal chance of coming up. If we plotted a graph showing the probability that each number would appear on a single toss of a die, we would have a horizontal line set at one-sixth for each of the six sides. That graph would bear absolutely no resemblance to a normal curve, nor would a sample of one throw tell us anything about the die except that it had a particular number imprinted on it. We would be like one of the blind men feeling the elephant.

Now let us throw the die six times and see what happens. (I asked my computer to do this for me, to be certain that the numbers were random.) The first trial of six throws produced four 5s, one 6, and one 4, for an average of exactly 5.0. The second was another hodgepodge, with three 6s, two 4s, and one 2, for an average of 4.7. Not much information there.

After ten trials of six throws each, the averages of the six throws began to cluster around 3.5, which happens to be the average of

1+2+3+4+5+6, or the six faces of the die—and precisely half of the mathematical expectation of throwing two dice. Six of my averages were below 3.5 and four were above. A second set of ten trials was a mixed bag: three of them averaged below 3.0 and four averaged above 4.0; there was one reading each above 4.5 and below 2.5.

The next step in the experiment was to figure the averages of the first ten trials of six throws each. Although each of those ten trials had an unusual distribution, the average of the averages came to 3.48! The average was reassuring, but the standard deviation, at 0.82, was wider than I would have liked.* In other words, seven of the ten trials fell between 3.48 + 0.82 and 3.48 − 0.82, or between 4.30 and 2.66; the rest were further away from the average.

Now I commanded the computer to simulate 256 trials of six throws each. The first 256 trials generated an average almost on target, at 3.49; with the standard deviation now down to 0.69, two-thirds of the trials were between 4.18 and 2.80. Only 10% of the trials averaged below 2.5 or above 4.5, while more than half landed between 3.0 and 4.0.

The computer still whirling, the 256 trials were repeated ten times. When those ten samples of 256 trials each were averaged, the grand average came out to 3.499. (I carry out the result to three decimal places to demonstrate how close I came to exactly 3.5.) But the impressive change was the reduction of the standard deviation to only 0.044. Thus, seven of the ten samples of 256 trials fell between the narrow range of 3.455 and 3.543. Five were below 3.5 and five were above. Close to perfection.

Quantity matters, as Jacob Bernoulli had discovered. This particular version of his insight—the discovery that averages of averages miraculously reduce the dispersion around the grand average—is known as the central limit theorem. This theorem was first set forth by Laplace in 1809, in a work he had completed and published just before he came upon Gauss's *Theoria Motus* in 1810.

Averages of averages reveal something even more interesting. We began the experiment I have just described with a die with, as usual, six faces, each of which had an equal chance of coming up when we threw

---

*The standard deviation was the device that de Moivre discovered for measuring the dispersion of observations around their mean. Approximately two-thirds of the observations (68.26%) will fall within a range of plus or minus one standard deviation around the mean; 95.46% will fall within two standard deviations around the mean.

it. The distribution then was flat, bearing no likeness at all to a normal distribution. As the computer threw the die over and over and over, accumulating a growing number of samples, we gleaned more and more information about the die's characteristics.

Very few of the averages of six throws came out near one or six; many of them fell between two and three or between four and five. This structure is precisely what Cardano worked out for his gambling friends, some 250 years ago, as he groped his way toward the laws of chance. Many throws of a single die will average out at 3.5. Therefore, many throws of two dice will average out at double 3.5, or .7.0. As Cardano demonstrated, the numbers on either side of 7 will appear with uniformly diminishing frequency as we move away from 7 to the limits of 2 and 12.

The normal distribution forms the core of most systems of risk management. The normal distribution is what the insurance business is all about, because a fire in Chicago will not be caused by a fire in Atlanta, and the death of one individual at one moment in one place has no relationship to the death of another individual at another moment in a different place. As insurance companies sample the experience of millions of individuals of different ages and of each gender, life expectancies begin to distribute themselves into a normal curve. Consequently, life insurance companies can come up with reliable estimates of life expectancies for each group. They can estimate not only average life expectancies but also the ranges within which actual experience is likely to vary from year to year. By refining those estimates with additional data, such as medical histories, smoking habits, domicile, and occupational activities, the companies can establish even more accurate estimates of life expectancies.*

On occasion, the normal distribution provides even more important information than just a measure of the reliability of samples. A normal distribution is most unlikely, although not impossible, when the

---

*Richard Price's experience reminds us that the data themselves must be of good quality. Otherwise, GIGO: garbage in, garbage out.

observations are dependent upon one another—that is, when the probability of one event is determined by a preceding event. The observations will fail to distribute themselves symmetrically around the mean.

In such cases, we can profitably reason backwards. If independence is the necessary condition for a normal distribution, we can assume that evidence that distributes itself into a bell curve comes from observations that are independent of one another. Now we can begin to ask some interesting questions.

How closely do changes in the prices of stocks resemble a normal distribution? Some authorities on market behavior insist that stock prices follow a random walk—that they resemble the aimless and unplanned lurches of a drunk trying to grab hold of a lamppost. They believe that stock prices have no more memory than a roulette wheel or a pair of dice, and that each observation is independent of the preceding observation. Today's price move will be whatever it is going to be, regardless of what happened a minute ago, yesterday, the day before, or the day before that.

The best way to determine whether changes in stock prices are in fact independent is to find out whether they fall into a normal distribution. Impressive evidence exists to support the case that changes in stock prices are normally distributed. That should come as no surprise. In capital markets as fluid and as competitive as ours, where each investor is trying to outsmart all the others, new information is rapidly reflected in the price of stocks. If General Motors posts disappointing earnings or if Merck announces a major new drug, stock prices do not stand still while investors contemplate the news. No investor can afford to wait for others to act first. So they tend to act in a pack, immediately moving the price of General Motors or Merck to a level that reflects this new information. *But new information arrives in random fashion.* Consequently, stock prices move in unpredictable ways.

Interesting evidence in support of this view was reported during the 1950s by Harry Roberts, a professor at the University of Chicago.[14] Roberts drew random numbers by computer from a series that had the same average and the same standard deviation as price changes in the stock market. He then drew a chart showing the sequential changes of those random numbers. The results produced patterns that were identical to those that stock-market analysts depend on when they are trying to predict where the market is headed. The real price movements and the computer-generated random numbers were indistinguishable from each other. Perhaps it is true that stock prices have no memory.

The accompanying charts show monthly, quarterly, and annual percentage changes in the Standard & Poor's Index of 500 stocks, the professional investor's favorite index of the stock market. The data run from January 1926 through December 1995, for 840 monthly observations, 280 quarterly observations, and 70 annual observations.*

Although the charts differ from one another, they have two features in common. First, as J.P. Morgan is reputed to have said, "The market will fluctuate." The stock market is a volatile place, where a lot can happen in either direction, upward or downward. Second, more observations fall to the right of zero than to the left: the stock market has gone up, on the average, more than it has gone down.

The normal distribution provides a more rigorous test of the random-walk hypothesis. But one qualification is important. Even if the random walk is a valid description of reality in the stock market—even if changes in stock prices fall into a perfect normal distribution—the mean will be something different from zero. The upward bias should come as no surprise. The wealth of owners of common stocks has risen over the long run as the economy and the revenues and profits of corporations have grown. Since more stock-price movements have been up than down, the average change in stock prices should work out to more than zero.

In fact, the average increase in stock prices (excluding dividend income) was 7.7% a year. The standard deviation was 19.3%; if the future will resemble the past, this means that two-thirds of the time stock prices in any one year are likely to move within a range of +27.0% and −12.1%. Although only 2.5% of the years—one out of forty—are likely to result in price changes greater than +46.4%, there is some comfort in finding that only 2.5% of the years will produce bear markets worse than −31.6%.

Stock prices went up in 47 of the 70 years in this particular sample of history, or in two out of every three years. That still leaves stocks falling in 23 of those years; and in 10 of those 23 years, or nearly half, prices plum-

---

*Readers skilled in statistics will protest that I should have used the lognormal analysis in the discussion that follows. For readers not so skilled, the presentation in this form is much more intelligible and the loss of accuracy struck me as too modest to justify further complexity.

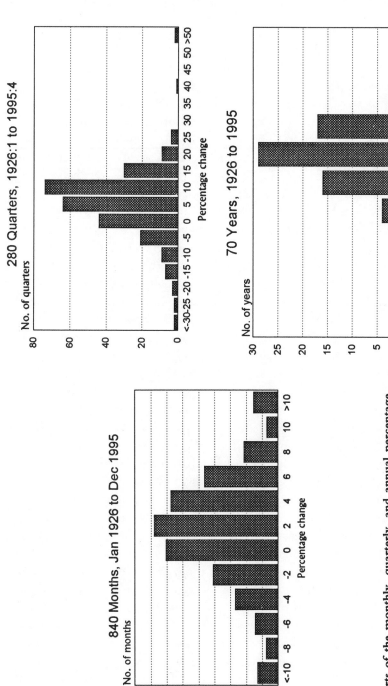

840 Months, Jan 1926 to Dec 1995

280 Quarters, 1926:1 to 1995:4

70 Years, 1926 to 1995

Charts of the monthly, quarterly, and annual percentage price changes in the Standard & Poor's Index of 500 stocks for January 1926 through December 1995.

meted by more than one standard deviation—by more than 12.1%. Indeed, losses in those 22 bad years averaged −15.2%.

Note that the three charts have different scales. The number of observations, shown on the vertical scales, will obviously differ from one another—in any given time span, there are more months than quarters and more quarters than years. The horizontal scales, which measure the range of outcomes, also differ, because stock prices move over a wider span in a year than in a quarter and over a wider span in a quarter than during a month. Each number on the horizontal scale measures price changes between the number to the left and that number.

Let us look first at the 840 monthly changes. The mean monthly change was +0.6%. If we deduct 0.6% from each of the observations in order to correct for the natural upward bias of the stock market over time, the average change becomes +0.00000000000000002%, with 50.6% of the months plus and 49.4% of the months minus. The first quartile observation, 204 below the mid-point, was −2.78%; the third quartile observation, 204 above the mid-point, was +2.91. The symmetry of a normal distribution appears to be almost flawless.

The random character of the monthly changes is also revealed by the small number of runs—of months in which the stock market moved in the same direction as in the preceding month. A movement in the same direction for two months at a time occurred only half the time; runs as long as five months occurred just 9% of the time.

The chart of monthly changes does have a remarkable resemblance to a normal curve. But note the small number of large changes at the edges of the chart. A normal curve would not have those untidy bulges.

Now look at the chart of 280 quarterly observations. This chart also resembles a normal curve. Nevertheless, the dispersion is wide and, once again, those nasty outliers pop up at the extremes. The 1930s had two quarters in which stock prices fell by more than a third—and two quarters in which stock prices rose by nearly 90%! Life has become more peaceful since those woolly days. The quarterly extremes since the end of the Second World War have been in the range of +25% and −25%.

The average quarterly change is +2.0%, but the standard deviation of 12.1% tells us that +2.0% is hardly typical of what we can expect from quarter to quarter. Forty-five percent of the quarters were less than the average of 2.0%, while 55% were above the quarterly average.

The chart of 70 annual observations is the neatest of the three, but the scaling on the horizontal axis of the chart, which is four times the size of the scaling on the quarterly chart, bunches up a lot of large changes.

The differences in scales are not just a technical convenience to make the different time periods comparable to one another on these three charts. The scales tell an important story. An investor who bought and held a portfolio of stocks for 70 years would have come out just fine. An investor who had expected to make a 2% gain each and every three-month period would have been a fool. (Note that I am using the past tense here; we have no assurance that the past record of the stock market will define its future.)

So the stock-market record has produced some kind of resemblance to a random walk, at least on the basis of these 840 monthly observations, because data would not appear to be distributed in this manner around the mean if stock-price changes were not independent of one another—like throws of the dice. After correction for the upward drift, changes were about as likely to be downward as upward; sequential changes of more than a month or so at a time were rare; the volatility ratios across time came remarkably close to what theory stipulates they should have been.

Assuming that we can employ Jacob Bernoulli's constraint that the future will look like the past, we can use this information to calculate the risk that stock prices will move by some stated amount in any one month. The mean monthly price change in the S&P table was 0.6% with a standard deviation of 5.8%. If price changes are randomly distributed, there is a 68% chance that prices in any one month will change by no less than −5.2% or by no more than +6.4%. Suppose we want to know the probability that prices will decline in any one month. The answer works out to 45%—or a little less than half the time. But a decline of more than 10% in any one month has a probability of only 3.5%, which means that it is likely to happen only about once every thirty months; moves of 10% in either direction will show up about once in every fifteen months.

As it happens, 33 of the 840 monthly observations, or about 4% of the total, were more than two standard deviations away from the monthly average of +0.6%—that is, worse than −11% and greater than 12.2%. Although 33 superswings are fewer than we might expect in a perfectly random series of observations, 21 of them were on the downside; chance would put that number at 16 or 17. A market with a built-in long-term upward trend should have even fewer disasters than 16 or 17 over 816 months.

At the extremes, the market is not a random walk. At the extremes, the market is more likely to destroy fortunes than to create them. The stock market is a risky place.

Up to this point, our story has been pretty much about numbers. Mathematicians have held center stage as we studied the innovations of ancient Hindus, Arabs, and Greeks all the way up to Gauss and Laplace in the nineteenth century. Probability rather than uncertainty has been our main theme.

Now the scene is about to shift. Real life is not like Paccioli's game of *balla*, a sequence of independent or unrelated events. The stock market looks a lot like a random walk, but the resemblance is less than perfect. Averages are useful guides on some occasions but misleading on many others. On still other occasions numbers are no help at all and we are obliged to creep into the future guided only by guesses.

This does not mean that numbers are useless in real life. The trick is to develop a sense of when they are relevant and when they are not. So we now have a whole new set of questions to answer.

For instance, which defines the risk of being hit by a bomb, seven million people or one elephant? Which of the following averages should we use to define the stock market's normal performance: the average monthly price change of +0.6% from 1926 to 1995, the piddling average of only +0.1% a month from 1930 to 1940, or the enticing average of +1.0% a month from 1954 to 1964?

In other words, what do we mean by "normal"? How well does any particular average describe normal? How stable, how powerful, is an average as an indicator of behavior? When observations wander away from the average of the past, how likely are they to regress to that average in the future? And if they do regress, do they stop at the average or overshoot it?

What about those rare occasions when the stock market goes up five months in a row? Is it true that everything that goes up must come down? Doth pride always goeth before a fall? What is the likelihood that a company in trouble will bring its affairs into order? Will a manic personality swing over to depression any time soon, and vice versa? When is the drought going to end? Is prosperity just around the corner?

The answers to all these questions depend on the ability to distinguish between normal and abnormal. Much risk-taking rests on the opportunities that develop from deviations from normal. When analysts tell us that their favorite stock is "undervalued," they are saying that an investor can profit by buying the stock now and waiting for its value to return to normal. On the other hand, mental depressions or manic states sometimes last a lifetime. And the economy in 1932 refused to move itself around the corner, even though Mr. Hoover and his advisers were convinced that prodding by the government would only deter it from finding its way back all by itself.

Nobody actually discovered the concept of "normal" any more than anybody actually discovered the concept of "average." But Francis Galton, an amateur scientist in Victorian England, took the foundation that Gauss and his predecessors had created to support the concept of average—the normal distribution—and raised a new structure to help people distinguish between measurable risk and the kind of uncertainty that obliges us to guess what the future will bring.

Galton was not a scientist in search of immutable truths. He was a practical man, enthusiastic about science but still an amateur. Yet his innovations and achievements have had a lasting impact on both mathematics and hands-on decision-making in the everyday world.

9

The Man with the Sprained Brain

Francis Galton (1822–1911) was a social snob who never worked to earn a living, except for a brief stint in a hospital during his early twenties.[1] Yet he was one of the most charming and likable of the many characters mentioned in this account. He was Charles Darwin's first cousin, an occasional inventor, and an avid explorer of parts of Africa where whites had never been seen. He made a seminal contribution to the theory of risk management, but he made that contribution in stubborn pursuit of an evil concept.

Measurement was Galton's hobby—or, rather, obsession. "Wherever you can, count," he would say.[2] He took note of the size of heads, noses, arms, legs, heights, and weights, of the color of eyes, of the sterility of heiresses, of the number of times people fidgeted as they listened to lectures, and of the degree of color change on the faces of spectators at the Derby as they watched the horses run. He classified the degree of attractiveness of girls he passed on the street, pricking a hole in a left-pocket card when a girl was comely and pricking a right-pocket card when she was plain. In his "Beauty Map" of Britain, London girls scored highest; Aberdeen girls scored lowest. He examined 10,000 judges' sentences and observed that most of them occurred at regular intervals of 3, 6, 9, 12, 15, 18, and 24 years, while none appeared at 17 and only a few at 11 or 13. At a cattle exhibition, he tabulated the guesses of 800 visitors as to the weight of an ox and found that the "average *vox populi* was correct to within one percent of the real value."[3]

Galton's Anthropometric Laboratory, which he established in 1884, measured and kept track of the range and character of every possible measurement of the human body, including even finger prints. Finger prints fascinated Galton because, unlike every other part of the body, their configuration never changes as a person grows older. In 1893, he published a 200-page book on the subject that soon led to the widespread use of finger printing by police.

Galton's compulsion to measure was evident even on a trip to Africa in 1849 to hunt big game in what is now Namibia. When he arrived at a village of Hottentots, he discovered "figures that would drive the females of our land desperate—figures that could afford to scoff at Crinoline."[4] One woman in particular caught his attention.[5] As a scientific man, he reported, he was "exceedingly anxious to obtain accurate measurements of her shape." Unable to speak Hottentot and uncertain how to undertake this urgent piece of research, he still managed to achieve his goal:

> Of a sudden my eye fell upon my sextant; the bright thought struck me, and I took a series of observations upon her figure in every direction. . . . [T]his being done, I boldly pulled out my measuring tape, and measured the distance from where I was to the place where she stood, and having thus obtained both base and angles, I worked out the results by trigonometry and logarithms.

Galton was the personification of the Victorian Englishman who strode the earth as though it were his private preserve. On another occasion during his hunting trip to Africa, he grew worried that the local chieftain might attack his camp. Clad in his red hunting coat, cap, and jackboots, he mounted an ox, charged up to the largest hut in the village, and forced the ox's head into the hut. The camp was never attacked.

At another village, he committed a social gaffe by refusing to take part in a ritual in which the host gargles and then spits the liquid into the face of his guest. And when King Nangoro presented him with Princess Chapange for an evening of pleasure, Galton was aghast when she arrived for the occasion "raddled with ochre and butter." "I was dressed in my one well-preserved suit of white linen, so I had her ejected with scant ceremony."

King Nagoro found it hard to believe that there were places in the world inhabited entirely by people with white skins. To him, Galton and his friends were rare migratory animals or some kind of anomaly. One of Galton's companions had to undress repeatedly before the king to prove that he was white all over.

Galton's curiosity was insatiable. When a traveling circus came through Cambridge while he was studying there, he walked straight into the lion's cage, only the fourth person to have done so in that circus's history. He kept himself from falling asleep during his favorite studying hours of 10 p.m. to 2 a.m. with his "Gumption-Reviver machine," a gadget he had invented that kept his head wet with cold water. Later in life, he invented a device for reading under water; he nearly drowned on one occasion when he submerged himself in his bath while enjoying a good book.

As we shall see shortly, Galton's fascination with measurement and his talent for innovation had loathsome consequences. Still he must be credited with a remarkable contribution to statistics and to risk management. As with Cardano, his insistence on testing his ideas through experimentation led to new statistical theory even though a search for new theory was not his primary objective.

Galton moves us into the world of everyday life, where people breathe, sweat, copulate, and ponder their future. We are now far removed from both the gaming tables and the stars, the means chosen by earlier mathematicians to get their theories right. Galton took the theories as he found them and went on to discover what made them tick.

Although Galton never alludes to Jacob Bernoulli, his work reflects Bernoulli's insistence that the study of probability is an essential tool for the analysis of disease, mental acuteness, and physical agility. And he follows in the footsteps of Graunt and Price, whose main interest was the organization of human society rather than the science of nature. What Galton and these other innovators learned along the way led ultimately to the emergence of today's complex instruments for the control and measurement of risk in both business and finance.

Galton grew up in an environment of affluence and lively intellectual activity. His grandfather, Erasmus Darwin, was among the most famous physicians of his time and a man with many interests beyond medicine. He invented a ferry driven by machinery instead of pulled by animals and a lavatory that flushed, experimented with windmills and steam engines, and wrote *The Loves of the Plants*, 2,000 lines of poetry describing in scientific detail the reproductive processes of many different plants. In 1796, when he was 65 years old, Erasmus published a two-volume work called *Zoonomia, or the Theory of Generations*. Although the book went through three editions in seven years, it failed to impress the scientific community because it was rich in theory but poor in facts. Nevertheless, *Zoonomia* bears a striking resemblance to *The Origin of the Species*, published 63 years later by Erasmus's more famous grandson, Charles Darwin.

At the age of four, Galton claimed, he could read any book written in English. He could recite "all the Latin Substantives and adjectives and active verbs besides 52 lines of Latin poetry" and could multiply by 2, 3, 4, 5, 6, 7, 10.[6]

He began to study medicine in Birmingham when he was 16 years old, but described his visits to the wards and the postmortems as "Horror-horror-horror!"[7] After Charles Darwin advised him to "read Mathematics like a house on fire," Galton headed to Cambridge to study math and the classics.[8]

Galton was 22 when his father died, leaving a substantial estate to his seven surviving children. Deciding that he could now do anything he liked, he soon chose to give up formal studies. Inspired by Darwin's voyage to the Galápagos, he made the first of two trips to Africa, sailing up the Nile and then traveling by camel to Khartoum—a total distance of a thousand miles. After his return to England, he idled away four years and then made a second trip to Africa. He wrote a book about Africa in 1853 that gained him membership in the Royal Geographic Society, which awarded him a gold medal, and won him acceptance by the scientific community. In 1856, he was made a fellow of the Royal Society.

His second trip to Africa when he was 27 left Galton "rather used up in health," the result of a combination of physical exhaustion and bouts of depression that were to recur often though briefly throughout his life. He referred to himself on those occasions as someone with a "sprained brain."[9]

Galton was an amateur scientist with a keen interest in heredity but with no interest in business or economics. Yet his studies of "the ideal mean filial type," "the parental type," and "the average ancestral type" led him to a statistical discovery that is essential to forecasting and to risk management.

The study of heredity has to do with the transmission of key characteristics such as intelligence, eye color, size, and behavior from generation to generation. It takes note of the outliers—individuals whose characteristics do not conform to the norm—but it pays more attention to the tendency of all members of a species to look pretty much the same. Hidden within that tendency toward homogeniety—the tendency of the average to dominate—is a powerful statistical tool that relates to many aspects of risk management.

Galton's primary goal was to understand how talent persists through generation after generation in certain families, including the Darwin family—and, not incidentally, the Bernoulli family. Galton had hoped to see that persistence of talent in his own progeny, but he and his wife were childless, as were both of his brothers and one of his sisters. Most of all, he sought to identify "natures preeminently noble" among members of the families he classified as the most highly talented.

In 1883, he labeled this field of study "eugenics," a word whose Greek root means good or well. The adoption of the term a half-century later by the Nazis was associated with the extermination of millions of human beings whom they identified as utterly without talent, or any kind of worth.

Whether Galton should be charged with responsibility for that evil outcome has been the subject of spirited debate. There is nothing about the man to suggest that he would have condoned such barbaric behavior. For him, the good society was a society that had an obligation to help and educate "highly gifted" individuals, regardless of their wealth, social class, or racial background. He proposed inviting and welcoming "emigrants and refugees from other lands" to Britain and encouraging their descendants to become citizens. Yet at the same time he seems to have been looking for ways to limit the reproduction of people who were less talented or ill; he suggests that the good society would also be a society "where the weak could find a welcome and a refuge in celibate monasteries or sisterhoods."[10]

Regardless of the uses to which others put Galton's work in eugenics, its significance extends far beyond the parochial questions he addressed directly. In brief, it gave further credibility to the truism that variety is the spice of life. When Enobarbus paid homage to Cleopatra, he remarked, "Age cannot wither her, nor custom stale her infinite variety." Though always the same woman, she was alternately lover, friend, cool, hot, temptress, enemy, submissive, and demanding. One person can be many.

We can recognize as an individual every one of 5.5 billion people alive today. Countless maples grow in the forests of Vermont, each of which is different from all the other maples, but none of which could be mistaken for a birch or a hemlock. General Electric and Biogen are both stocks listed on the New York Stock Exchange, but each is influenced by entirely different kinds of risk.

Which of the many guises of Cleopatra, of the billions of human beings alive today, of the maples, birches, and hemlocks in Vermont, or of the stocks listed on the New York Stock Exchange is the prototypical exemplar of its class? How much do the members of each class differ from one another? How much does a child in Uganda differ from an old woman in Stockholm? Are the variations systematic or merely the results of random influences? Again, what do we mean by normal anyway?

In searching for the answers to such questions, Galton makes little mention of early mathematicians and ignores social statisticians like Graunt. He does, however, cite at great length a set of empirical studies carried out in the 1820s and 1830s by a Belgian scientist named Lambert Adolphe Jacques Quetelet. Quetelet was twenty years older than Galton, a dogged investigator into social conditions, and as obsessed with measurement as Galton himself.[11]

Quetelet was only 23 years old when he received the first doctorate of science to be awarded by the new University of Ghent. By that time, he had already studied art, written poetry, and co-authored an opera.

He was also what the historian of statistics Stephen Stigler calls "an entrepreneur of science as well as a scientist."[12] He helped found several statistical associations, including the Royal Statistical Society of London and the International Statistical Congress, and for many years he was regional correspondent for the Belgian government's statistical bureau. Around 1820, he became leader of a movement to found a new observatory in Belgium, even though his knowledge of astronomy at the time was scant. Once the observatory was established, he persuaded the government to fund a three-month stay in Paris so that he could study astronomy and meteorology and learn how to run an observatory.

During his time in Paris, he met many of the leading French astronomers and mathematicians, from whom he learned a good bit about probability. He may even have met Laplace, who was then 74 years old and about to produce the final volume of his masterpiece, *Mécanique céleste*. Quetelet was fascinated by the subject of probability. He subsequently wrote three books on the subject, the last in 1853. He also put what he learned about it to good—and practical—use.

Although Quetelet continued to work at the Royal Observatory in Brussels after he returned from Paris in 1820, he also carried on research relating to French population statistics and started to plan for the approaching census of 1829. In 1827, he published a monograph titled "Researches on population, births, deaths, prisons, and poor houses, etc. in the Kingdom of the Low Countries," in which he criticized the procedures used in gathering and analyzing social statistics. Quetelet was eager to apply a method that Laplace had developed back in the 1780s to estimate France's population. Laplace's method called for taking a random sample from a diversified group of thirty *départements* and using the sample as the basis for estimating the total population.

A colleague soon persuaded Quetelet to abandon that approach. The problem was that the officials in charge of the French census would have no way of knowing how representative their sample might be. Each locality had certain customs and conventions that influenced the birth rate. Furthermore, as Halley and Price had discovered, the representative quality of a survey even in a small area could be affected by movements of the population. Unlike Enobarbus, Quetelet found too much variety in the French sociological structure for anyone to generalize on the basis of a limited sample. A complete census of France was decided upon.

This experience led Quetelet to begin using social measurement in a search to explain why such differences exist among people and places—whence the variety that adds the spice? If the differences were random, the data would look about the same each time a sample was taken; if the differences were systematic, each sample would look different from the others.

This idea set Quetelet off on a measurement spree, which Stigler describes as follows:

> He examined birth and death rates by month and city, by temperature, and by time of day. . . . He investigated mortality by age, by profession, by locality, by season, in prisons, and in hospitals. He considered . . . height, weight, growth rate, and strength . . . [and developed] statistics on drunkenness, insanity, suicides, and crime.[13]

The result was *A Treatise on Man and the Development of His Faculties*, which was first published in French in 1835 and subsequently translated into English. The French expression Quetelet chose for "faculties" was *"physique social."* This work established Quetelet's reputation. The author of a three-part review of it in a leading scholarly journal remarked, "We consider the appearance of these volumes as forming an epoch in the literary history of civilization."[14]

The book consisted of more than just dry statistics and plodding text. Quetelet gave it a hero who lives to this very day: *l'homme moyen,* or the average man. This invention captured the public imagination and added to Quetelet's growing fame.

Quetelet aimed to define the characteristics of the *average* man (or woman in some instances), who then became the model of the particular group from which he was drawn, be it criminals, drunks, soldiers, or dead people. Quetelet even speculated that "If an individual at any epoch of society possessed all the qualities of the average man, he would represent all that is great, good, or beautiful."[15]

Not everyone agreed. One of the harshest critics of Quetelet's book was Antoine-Augustin Cournot, a famous mathematician and economist, and an authority on probability. Unless we observe the rules of probability, Cournot maintained, "we cannot get a clear idea of the precision of measurements made in the sciences of observation . . . or of the conditions leading to the success of commercial enterprises."[16] Cournot ridiculed the concept of the average man. An average of all the sides of a bunch of right triangles, he argued, would not be a right triangle, and a totally average man would not be a man but some kind of monstrosity.

Quetelet was undeterred. He was convinced that he could identify the average man for any age, occupation, location, or ethnic origin. Moreover, he claimed that he could find a method to predict why a given individual belonged in one group rather than in another. This was a novel step, for no one up to that point had dared to use mathematics and statistics to separate cause and effect. "[E]ffects are proportional to causes," he wrote, and then went on to italicize these words: "*The greater the number of individuals observed, the more do peculiarities, whether physical or moral, become effaced, and allow the general facts to predominate, by which society exists and is preserved.*"[17] By 1836, Quetelet had expanded these notions into a book on the application of probability to the "moral and political sciences."

Quetelet's study of causes and effects makes for fascinating reading. For example, he carried out an extended analysis of the factors that influence rates of conviction among people accused of crimes. An average of 61.4% of all people accused were convicted, but the probability was less than 50% that they would be convicted for crimes against persons while it was over 60% that they would be convicted for crimes against property. The probability of conviction was less than 61.4% if the accused was a woman older than thirty who voluntarily appeared to stand trial instead of running away and who was literate and well educated. Quetelet also sought to determine whether deviations from the 61.4% average were significant or random: he sought moral certainty in the trials of the immoral.

Quetelet saw bell curves everywhere he looked. In almost every instance, the "errors," or deviations from the average, obediently distributed themselves according to the predictions of Laplace and Gauss—in normal fashion, falling symmetrically along both sides of the average. That beautifully balanced array, with the peak at the average, was what convinced Quetelet of the validity of his beloved average man. It lay behind all the inferences he developed from his statistical investigations.

In one experiment, for example, Quetelet took chest measurements on 5,738 Scottish soldiers. He concocted a normal distribution for the group and then compared the actual result with the theoretical result. The fit was almost perfect.[18]

It had already been demonstrated that Gaussian normal distributions are typical throughout nature; now they appeared to be rooted in the social structures and the physical attributes of human beings. Thus, Quetelet concluded that the close fit to a normal distribution for the Scottish soldiers signified that the deviations around the average were random rather than the result of any systematic differences within the group. The group, in other words, was essentially homogeneous, and the average Scottish soldier was fully representative of all Scottish soldiers. Cleopatra was a woman before all else.

One of Quetelet's studies, however, revealed a less than perfect fit with the normal distribution. His analysis of the heights of 100,000 French conscripts revealed that too many of them fell in the shortest class for the distribution to be normal. Since being too short was an excuse for exemption from service, Quetelet asserted that the measurements must have been distorted by fraud in order to accommodate draft-dodgers.

Cournot's remark that the average man would be some sort of monstrosity reflected his misgivings about applying probability theory to social as opposed to natural data. Human beings, he argued, lend themselves to a bewildering variety of classifications. Quetelet believed that a normally distributed set of human measurements implied only random differences among the sample of people he was examining. But Cournot suspected that the differences might not be random. Consider, for example, how one might classify the number of male births in any one year: by age of parents, by geographical location, by days of the week, by ethnic origin, by weight, by time in gestation, by color of eyes, or by length of middle fingers, just to name a few possibilities. How, then, could you state with any confidence which baby was the *average* baby? Cournot claimed that it would be impossible to determine which data were significant and which were nothing more than the result of chance: "[T]he same size deviation [from the average] may lead to many different judgments."[19] What Cournot did not mention, but what modern statisticians know well, is that most human measurements reflect differences in nutrition, which means that they tend to reflect differences in social status as well.

Today, statisticians refer to the practice that stirred Cournot's misgivings as "data mining." They say that if you torture the data long enough, the numbers will prove anything you want. Cournot felt that

Quetelet was on dangerous ground in drawing such broad generalizations from a limited number of observations. A second set of observations drawn from a group of the same size could just as likely turn up a different pattern from the first.

There is no doubt that Quetelet's infatuation with the normal distribution led him to claim more than he should have. Nevertheless, his analysis was hugely influential at the time. A famous mathematician and economist of a later age, Francis Ysidro Edgeworth, coined the term "Quetelismus" to describe the growing popularity of discovering normal distributions in places where they did not exist or that failed to meet the conditions that identify genuine normal distributions.[20]

When Galton first came upon Quetelet's work in 1863, he was deeply impressed. "An Average is but a solitary fact," he wrote, "whereas if a single other fact be added to it, an entire Normal Scheme, which nearly corresponds to the observed one, starts potentially into existence. Some people hate the very name of statistics, but I find them full of beauty and interest."[21]

Galton was enthralled by Quetelet's finding that "the very curious theoretical law of the deviation from the average"—the normal distribution—was ubiquitous, especially in such measurements as body height and chest measurements.[22] Galton himself had found bell curves in the record of 7,634 grades in mathematics for Cambridge students taking their final exam for honors in mathematics, ranging from highest to "one can hardly say what depth."[23] He found similar statistical patterns in exam grades among the applicants for admission to the Royal Military College at Sandhurst.

The aspect of the bell curve that impressed Galton most was its indication that certain data belonged together and could be analyzed as a relatively homogeneous entity. The opposite would then also be true: absence of the normal distribution would suggest "dissimilar systems." Galton was emphatic: "This presumption is never found to be belied."[24]

But it was differences, not homogeneity, that Galton was pursuing—Cleopatra, not the woman. In developing his new field of study, eugenics, he searched for differences even within groups whose measurable features seemed to fall into a normal distribution. His objective was to classify people by "natural ability," by which he meant

> . . . those qualities of intellect and disposition, which urge and qualify a man to perform acts that lead to reputation. . . . I mean a nature which, when left to itself, will, urged by an inherent stimulus, climb the path that leads to eminence, and has strength to reach the summit. . . . [M]en who achieve eminence, and those who are naturally capable, are, to a large extent, identical."[25]

Galton began with the facts. During the years 1866 to 1869, he collected masses of evidence to prove that talent and eminence are hereditary attributes. He then summarized his findings in his most important work, *Hereditary Genius* (which includes an appendix on Quetelet's work, as well as Galton's own caustic appraisal of the typical prickly Bernoulli personality). The book begins with an estimate of the proportion of the general population that Galton believed he could classify as "eminent." On the basis of obituaries in the *London Times* and in a biographical handbook, he calculated that eminence occurred among English people past middle age in a ratio of one to every 4,000, or about 5,000 people in Britain at that time.

Although Galton said that he did not care to occupy himself with people whose gifts fell below average, he did estimate the number of "idiots and imbeciles" among Britain's twenty million inhabitants as 50,000, or one in 400, making them about ten times as prevalent as his eminent citizens.[26] But it was the eminent ones he cared about. "I am sure," he concluded, that no one "can doubt the existence of grand human animals, of natures preeminently noble, of individuals born to be kings of men."[27] Galton did not ignore "very powerful women" but decided that, "happy perhaps for the repose of the other sex, such gifted women are rare."[28]

Galton was convinced that if height and chest circumference matched Quetelet's hypotheses, the same should be true of head size, brain weight, and nerve fibers—and to mental capacity as well. He demonstrated how well Quetelet's findings agreed with his own estimates of the range of Britons from eminence at one end to idiocy at the other. He arrived at "the undeniable, but unexpected conclusion, that eminently gifted men are raised as much above mediocrity as idiots are depressed below it."[29]

But beyond all that, Galton wanted to prove that heredity *alone* was the source of special talents, not "the nursery, the school, the university, [or] professional careers."[30] And heredity did seem to matter, at least within the parameters that Galton laid out. He found, for example, that a ratio of one out of nine close relatives of 286 judges were father, son, or brother to another judge, a ratio far greater than in the general population. Even better, he found that many relatives of judges were also admirals, generals, novelists, poets, and physicians.* (Galton explicitly excluded clergymen from among the eminent). He was disappointed to note that his "finger marks" failed to distinguish between eminent men and "congenital idiots."[31]

Yet Galton discovered that eminence does not last long; as physicists would put it, eminence has a short half life. He found that only 36% of the sons of eminent men were themselves eminent; even worse, only 9% of their grandsons made the grade. He attempted to explain why eminent families tend to die out by citing their apparent habit of marrying heiresses. Why blame them? Because heiresses must come from infertile families, he argued; if they had had a large number of siblings with whom to share the family wealth, they would not have inherited enough to be classified as heiresses. This was a surprising suggestion, in view of the comfort in which Galton lived after sharing his father's estate with six other siblings.

After reading *Hereditary Genius*, Charles Darwin told Galton, "I do not think I ever in my life read anything more interesting and original . . . a memorable work."[32] Darwin suggested that he go on with his analysis of the statistics of heredity, but Galton needed little encouragement. He was now well on his way to developing the science of eugenics and was eager to discover and preserve what he considered to be the

---

*Galton would surely have classified Cardano as eminent, but what would he have thought of Cardano's disastrous progeny? Gauss, also an eminent man, scored better. He produced five surviving children, of whom one was a distinguished engineer and two of whom emigrated to the United States to run successful businesses (but also to escape from their father's domineering influence); one of them was also a brilliant linguist, a gambler, and a skillful mathematician as well.

best of humanity. He wanted the best people to have more offspring and the lowly to exercise restraint.

But the law of the deviation from the mean stood stubbornly in his way. Somehow he had to explain differences *within* the normal distribution. He realized that the only way he could do so was to figure out why the data arranged themselves into a bell curve in the first place. That search led him to an extraordinary discovery that influences most of the decisions we make today, both small and large.

Galton reported the first step in an article published in 1875, in which he suggested that the omnipresent symmetrical distribution around the mean might be the result of influences that are themselves arrayed according to a normal distribution, ranging from conditions that are most infrequent to conditions that are most frequent and then down to a set of opposite kinds of influences that again are less frequent. Even within each kind of influence, Galton hypothesized, there would be a similar range from least powerful to most powerful and then down again to least powerful. The core of his argument was that "moderate" influences occur much more often than extreme influences, both good and bad.

Galton demonstrated this idea with a gadget he called the Quincunx to the Royal Society around 1874.[33] The Quincunx looked a lot like an up-ended pinball machine. It had a narrow neck like an hour-glass, with about twenty pins stuck into the neck area. At the bottom, where the Quincunx was at its widest, was a row of little compartments. When shot were dropped through the neck, they hit the pins at random and tended to distribute themselves among the compartments in classic Gaussian fashion—most of them piled up in the middle, with smaller numbers on either side, and so on in diminishing numbers.

In 1877, in conjunction with his reading of a major paper titled "Typical Laws of Heredity," Galton introduced a new model of the Quincunx. (We do not know whether he actually built one). This model contained a set of compartments part way down, into which the shot fell and arrayed themselves as they had in the bottom compartments in the first model. When any one of these midway compartments was opened, the shot that had landed in it fell into the bottom compartments where they arrayed themselves—you guessed it—in the usual normal distribution.

The discovery was momentous. Every group, no matter how small and no matter how distinct from some other group, tends to array itself in accordance with the normal distribution, with most of the observations landing in the center, or, to use the more familiar expression, on the average. When all the groups are merged into one, as Quincunx I demonstrated, the shot also array themselves into a normal distribution. The grand normal, therefore, is an average of the averages of the small subgroups.

Quincunx II provided a mechanical version of an idea that Galton had discovered in the course of an experiment proposed by Darwin in 1875. That experiment did not involve dice, stars, or even human beings. It was sweet peas—or peas in the pod. Sweet peas are hardy and prolific, with little tendency to cross-fertilize. The peas in each pod are essentially uniform in size. After weighing and measuring thousands of sweet peas, Galton sent ten specimens of each of seven different weights to nine friends, including Darwin, throughout the British Isles, with instructions to plant them under carefully specified conditions.

After analyzing the results, Galton reported that the offspring of the seven different groups had arrayed themselves, by weight, precisely as the Quincunx would have predicted. The offspring of each individual set of specimens were normally distributed, and the offspring of each of the seven major groups were normally distributed as well. This powerful result, he claimed, was not the consequence of "*petty* influences in various combinations" (Galton's italics). Rather, "[T]he processes of heredity . . . [were] not petty influences, but very important ones."[34] Since few individuals within a group of humans are eminent, few of their offspring will be eminent; and since most people are average, their offspring will be average. Mediocrity always outnumbers talent. The sequence of small-large-small distributions among the sweet peas— according to the normal distribution—confirmed for Galton the dominance of parentage in determining the character of offspring.

The experiment revealed something else, as the accompanying table of diameters of the parent peas and their offspring shows.

DIAMETER OF PARENT SEEDS AND OFFSPRING[35]
(IN HUNDREDTHS OF AN INCH)

Parent	15	16	17	18	19	20	21
Mean diameter of filial	15.4	15.7	16.0	16.3	16.6	17.0	17.3

Note that the spread of diameters among the parents was wider than the dispersion among the offspring. The average diameter of the parents was 0.18 inches within a range of 0.15 to 0.21 inches, or 0.03 on either side of the mean. The average diameter of the offspring was 0.163 inches within a range of 0.154 to 0.173 inches, or only about 0.01 inches on either side of the mean. The offspring had an overall distribution that was tighter than the distribution of the parents.

This experiment led Galton to propound a general principle that has come to be known as regression, or reversion, to the mean: "Reversion," he wrote, "is the tendency of the ideal mean filial type to depart from the parental type, reverting to what may be roughly and perhaps fairly described as the average ancestral type."[36] If this narrowing process were not at work—if large peas produced ever-larger offspring and if small peas produced ever-smaller offspring—the world would consist of nothing but midgets and giants. Nature would become freakier and freakier with every generation, going completely haywire or running out to extremes we cannot even conceive of.

Galton summarized the results in one of his most eloquent and dramatic paragraphs:

> The child inherits partly from his parents, partly from his ancestry.
> . . . [T]he further his genealogy goes back, the more numerous and
> varied will his ancestry become, until they cease to differ from any
> equally numerous sample taken at haphazard from the race at large.
> . . . This law tells heavily against the full hereditary transmission of
> any gift. . . . The law is even-handed; it levies the same succession-
> tax on the transmission of badness as well as of goodness. If it dis-
> courages the extravagant expectations of gifted parents that their
> children will inherit all their powers, it no less discountenances
> extravagant fears that they will inherit all their weaknesses and dis-
> eases.[37]

This was bad news for Galton, no matter how elegantly he articulated it, but it spurred him on in his efforts to promote eugenics. The obvious solution was to maximize the influence of "the average ancestral type" by restricting the production of offspring at the low end of the scale, thereby reducing the left-hand portion of the normal distribution.

Galton found further confirmation of regression to the mean in an experiment that he reported in 1885, on the occasion of his election to the presidency of the British Association for the Advancement of Science. For this experiment, he had gathered an enormous amount of data on humans, data that he had received in response to a public appeal backed by an offer of cash. He ended up with observations for 928 adult children born of 205 pairs of parents.

Galton's focus in this case was on height, or, in the language of his times, stature. His goal was similar to that in the sweet-pea experiment, which was to see how a particular attribute was passed along by heredity from parents to children. In order to analyze the observations, he had to adjust for the difference in height between men and women; he multiplied the female's height in each case by 1.08, summed the heights of the two parents, and divided by two. He referred to the resulting entities as "mid-parents." He also had to make sure that there was no systematic tendency for tall men to marry tall women and for short men to marry short women; his calculations were "close enough" for him to assume that there were no such tendencies.[38]

The results were stunning, as the accompanying table reveals. The diagonal structure of the numbers from lower left to upper right tells us at once that taller parents had taller children and vice versa—heredity matters. The clusters of larger numbers toward the center reveal that each height group among the children was normally distributed and that each set of children from each parental height group also was normally distributed. Finally, compare the furthest right-hand column to the furthest left-hand column. ("Median" means that half the group were taller and half were shorter than the number shown.) The mid-parents with heights of 68.5 inches and up all had children whose median heights were below the height of the mid-parents; the mid-parents who were shorter than 68.5 inches all had children who tended to be taller than they were. Just like the sweet peas.

The consistency of normal distributions and the appearance of regression to the mean enabled Galton to calculate the mathematics of the process, such as the rate at which the tallest parents tend to produce children that are tall relative to their peers but shorter relative to their parents. When a professional mathematician confirmed his results, Galton wrote, "I never felt such a glow of loyalty and respect towards the sovereignty and magnificent sway of mathematical analysis."[39]

Galton's line of analysis led ultimately to the concept of correlation, which is a measurement of how closely any two series vary relative to

CROSS-TABULATION OF 928 ADULT CHILDREN BORN OF 205 MIDPARENTS, SORTED BY THEIR HEIGHT AND THEIR MIDPARENT'S HEIGHT

Height of Mid-parents (inches)	Height of the Adult Child														Total No. of Adult Children	Total No. of Mid-parents	Medians
	<61.7	62.2	63.2	64.2	65.2	66.2	67.2	68.2	69.2	70.2	71.2	72.2	73.2	>75.7			
>73.0	—	—	—	—	—	—	—	—	—	—	—	1	3	—	4	5	—
72.5	—	—	—	—	—	—	—	1	2	1	2	7	2	4	19	6	72.2
71.5	—	—	—	—	1	3	4	3	5	10	4	9	2	2	43	11	69.9
70.5	1	—	1	—	1	1	3	12	18	14	7	4	3	3	68	22	69.5
69.5	—	—	1	16	4	17	27	20	33	25	20	11	4	5	183	41	68.9
68.5	1	—	7	11	16	25	31	34	48	21	18	4	3	—	219	49	68.2
67.5	—	3	5	14	15	36	38	28	38	19	11	4	—	—	211	33	67.6
66.5	—	3	3	5	2	17	17	14	13	4	—	—	—	—	78	20	67.2
65.5	1	—	9	5	7	11	11	7	7	5	2	1	—	—	66	12	66.7
64.5	1	1	4	4	1	5	5	—	2	—	—	—	—	—	23	5	65.8
<64.0	1	—	2	4	1	2	2	1	1	—	—	—	—	—	14	1	—
Totals	5	7	21	59	48	117	138	120	167	99	64	41	17	14	928	205	—
Medians	—	—	66.3	67.8	67.9	67.7	67.9	68.3	68.5	69.0	70.0	—	—	—	—	—	—

(From Francis Galton, 1886, "Regression Toward Mediocrity in Hereditary Stature," Journal of the Anthropological Institute, Vol. 15, pp. 246–263.)

one another, whether it be size of parent and child, rainfall and crops, inflation and interest rates, or the stock prices of General Motors and Biogen.

Karl Pearson, Galton's principal biographer and an outstanding mathematician himself, observed that Galton had created "a revolution in our scientific ideas [that] has modified our philosophy of science and even of life itself."[40] Pearson did not exaggerate: regression to the mean is dynamite. Galton transformed the notion of probability from a static concept based on randomness and the Law of Large Numbers into a dynamic process in which the successors to the outliers are predestined to join the crowd at the center. Change and motion from the outer limits toward the center are constant, inevitable, foreseeable. Given the imperatives of this process, no outcome other than the normal distribution is conceivable. The driving force is always toward the average, toward the restoration of normality, toward Quetelet's *homme moyen*.

Regression to the mean motivates almost every variety of risk-taking and forecasting. It is at the root of homilies like "What goes up must come down," "Pride goeth before a fall," and "From shirtsleeves to shirtsleeves in three generations." Joseph had this preordained sequence of events in mind when he predicted to Pharaoh that seven years of famine would follow seven years of plenty. It is what J.P. Morgan meant when he observed that "the market will fluctuate." It is the credo to which so-called contrarian investors pay obeisance: when they say that a certain stock is "overvalued" or "undervalued," they mean that fear or greed has encouraged the crowd to drive the stock's price away from an intrinsic value to which it is certain to return. It is what motivates the gambler's dream that a long string of losses is bound to give way to a long string of winnings. It is what my doctor means when he predicts that "tincture of time" will cure my complaints. And it is what Herbert Hoover thought was going to happen in 1931, when he promised that prosperity was just around the corner—unhappily for him and for everyone else, the mean was not where he expected it to be.

Francis Galton was a proud man, but he never suffered a fall. His many achievements were widely recognized. He ended a long, full life as a widower traveling and writing in the company of a much younger female relative. He never allowed his fascination with numbers and facts to blind him to the wonders of nature, and he delighted in diversity:

> It is difficult to understand why statisticians commonly limit their inquiries to Averages, and do not revel in more comprehensive views. Their souls seem as dull to the charm of variety as that of the native of one of our flat English counties, whose retrospect of Switzerland was that, if its mountains could be thrown into its lakes, two nuisances would be got rid of at once.[41]

10

Peapods and Perils

Regression to the mean provides many decision-making systems with their philosophical underpinnings. And for good reason. There are few occasions in life when the large are likely to become infinitely large or when the small are likely to become infinitely small. Trees never reach the sky. When we are tempted—as we so often are—to extrapolate past trends into the future, we should remember Galton's peapods.

Yet if regression to the mean follows such a constant pattern, why is forecasting such a frustrating activity? Why can't we all be as prescient as Joseph in his dealings with Pharaoh? The simplest answer is that the forces at work in nature are not the same as the forces at work in the human psyche. The accuracy of most forecasts depends on decisions being made by people rather than by Mother Nature. Mother Nature, with all her vagaries, is a lot more dependable than a group of human beings trying to make up their minds about something.

There are three reasons why regression to the mean can be such a frustrating guide to decision-making. First, it sometimes proceeds at so slow a pace that a shock will disrupt the process. Second, the regression may be so strong that matters do not come to rest once they reach the mean. Rather, they fluctuate around the mean, with repeated, irregular deviations on either side. Finally, the mean itself may be unstable, so that yesterday's normality may be supplanted today by a new normality that we know nothing about. It is perilous in the extreme to assume that prosperity is just around the corner simply because it always has been just around the corner.

Regression to the mean is most slavishly followed on the stock market. Wall Street folklore is full of such catch phrases as "Buy low and sell high," "You never get poor taking a profit," and "The bulls get something and the bears get something but the hogs get nothing." All are variations on a simple theme: if you bet that today's normality will extend indefinitely into the future, you will get rich sooner and face a smaller risk of going broke than if you run with the crowd. Yet many investors violate this advice every day because they are emotionally incapable of buying low or selling high. Impelled by greed and fear, they run with the crowd instead of thinking for themselves.

It is not all that easy to keep the peapods in mind. Since we never know exactly what is going to happen tomorrow, it is easier to assume that the future will resemble the present than to admit that it may bring some unknown change. A stock that has been going up for a while somehow seems a better buy than a stock that has been heading for the cellar. We assume that a rising price signifies that the company is flourishing and that a falling price signifies that the company is in trouble. Why stick your neck out?

Professionals are just as likely as amateurs to try to play it safe. For example, in December 1994, analysts at the brokerage firm of Sanford C. Bernstein & Co. found that professionals who tend to forecast a higher-than-average growth rate for a company consistently overestimate the actual results, while pessimists consistently underestimate them.* "[O]n average," the analysts reported, "expectations are not met."[1]

The consequences are clear: stocks with rosy forecasts climb to unreal heights while stocks with dismal forecasts drop to unreal lows. Then regression to the mean takes over. The more realistic and stout-hearted investors buy as others rush to sell, and sell as others rush to buy. The payoff comes when the actual earnings surprise those who followed the trend.

---

*I am not related to Sanford Bernstein, by the way.

History tells us of many legendary investors who made fortunes by betting on regression to the mean, by buying low and selling high. Among them are Bernard Baruch, Benjamin Graham, and Warren Buffett. That contrarian position is confirmed by a wealth of academic research.

But the few who made it big by copping the bets of the crowd receive all the attention. We hear little about those investors who tried the same thing and failed, either because they acted too soon or not at all, or because the mean to which they expected stock prices to regress was not the mean to which they actually did regress.

Consider those investors who had the temerity to buy stocks in early 1930, right after the Great Crash, when prices had fallen about 50% from their previous highs. Prices proceeded to fall another 80% before they finally hit bottom in the fall of 1932. Or consider the cautious investors who sold out in early 1955, when the Dow Jones Industrials had finally regained their old 1929 highs and had tripled over the preceding six years. Just nine years later, prices were double both their 1929 and their 1955 highs. In both cases, the anticipated return to "normal" failed to take place: normal had shifted to a new location.

In discussing the issue of whether regression to the mean governs the behavior of the stock market, we are really asking whether stock prices are predictable, and if so under what conditions. No investor can decide what risks to take before answering that question.

There is some evidence that the prices of certain stocks rise "too high" and fall "too low." In 1985 at the annual meeting of the American Finance Association, economists Richard Thaler and Werner DeBondt presented a paper titled, "Does the Stock Market Overreact?"[2] To test whether extreme movements of stock prices in one direction provoke regression to the mean and are subsequently followed by extreme movements in the other direction, they studied the three-year returns of over a thousand stocks from January 1926 to December 1982. They classified the stocks that had gone up by more or had fallen by less than the market average in each three-year period as "winners," and the stocks that had gone up by less or had fallen by more than the market average as "losers." They then calculated the average performance of each group over the subsequent three years.

Their findings were unequivocal: "Over the last half-century, loser portfolios . . . outperform the market by, on average, 19.6% thirty-six months after portfolio formation. Winner portfolios, on the other hand, earn [produce returns] about 5.0% less than the market."[3]

Although DeBondt and Thaler's test methods have been subjected to some criticism, their findings have been confirmed by other analysts using different methods. When investors overreact to new information and ignore long-term trends, regression to the mean turns the average winner into a loser and the average loser into a winner. This reversal tends to develop with some delay, which is what creates the profitable opportunity: we could really say that first the market overreacts to short-term news and then underreacts while awaiting new short-term news of a different character.[4]

The reason is simple enough. Stock prices in general follow changes in company fortunes. Investors who focus excessively on the short run are ignoring a mountain of evidence demonstrating that most surges in earnings are unsustainable. On the other hand, companies that encounter problems do not let matters slide indefinitely. Managers will set to work making the hard decisions to put their company back on track—or will find themselves out of a job, replaced by others more zealous.

Regression to the mean decrees that it could not be otherwise. If the winners kept on winning and the losers kept on losing, our economy would consist of a shrinking handful of giant monopolies and virtually no small companies at all. The once-admired monopolies in Japan and Korea are now going through the opposite process, as regression to the mean in the form of irresistible waves of imports is gradually weakening their economic power.

The track records of professional investment managers are also subject to regression to the mean. There is a strong probability that the hot manager of today will be the cold manager of tomorrow, or at least the day after tomorrow, and vice versa. This does not mean that successful managers will inevitably lose their touch or that managers with poor records will ultimately see the light—though that does tend to happen. Often investment managers lose ground simply because no one style of management stays in fashion forever.

Earlier, in the discussion of the Petersburg Paradox, we noted the difficulty investors had in valuing stocks that seemed to have infinite payoffs (page 107). It was inevitable that the investors' unlimited optimism would ultimately lift the price of those growth stocks to unrealistic levels. When regression to the mean sent the stocks crashing, even the best manager of growth-stock portfolios could not help but look foolish. A similar fad took over small stock investing in the late 1970s, when academic research demonstrated that small stocks had been the most successful long-run investment despite their greater risk. By 1983, regression to the mean had once more set in, and small stocks underperformed for years afterward. This time, even the best manager of small-stock investment could not help but look foolish.

In 1994, *Morningstar*, the leading publication on the performance of mutual funds, published the accompanying table, which shows how various types of funds had fared over the five years ending March 1989 and the five years ending March 1994:[5]

Objective	5 Years to March 1989	5 Years to March 1994
International stocks	20.6%	9.4%
Income	14.3%	11.2%
Growth and income	14.2%	11.9%
Growth	13.3%	13.9%
Small company	10.3%	15.9%
Aggressive growth	8.9%	16.1%
Average	13.6%	13.1%

This is a spectacular demonstration of regression to the mean at work. The average performance in both periods was almost identical, but the swings in results from the first period to the second were enormous. The three groups that did better than average in the first period did worse than average in the second; the three groups that did worse than average in the first period did better than average in the second.

This impressive evidence of regression to the mean might provide some valuable advice to investors who are constantly switching managers. It suggests that the wisest strategy is to dismiss the manager with the best recent track record and to transfer one's assets to the manager who has been doing the worst; this strategy is no different from selling stocks that have risen furthest and buying stocks that have fallen furthest. If that contrarian strategy is hard to follow, there is another way to accomplish the same thing. Go ahead and follow your natural instincts. Fire the lagging manager and add to the holdings of the winning manager, but *wait two years before doing it.*

What about the stock market as a whole? Are the popular averages, like the Dow Jones Industrials and the Standard & Poor's Composite of 500 stocks, predictable?

The charts in Chapter 8 (page 147) show that market performance over periods of a year or more does not look much like a normal distribution, but that performance by the month and by the quarter does, though not precisely. Quetelet would interpret that evidence as proof that stock-price movements in the short run are independent—that today's changes tell us nothing about what tomorrow's prices will be. The stock market is unpredictable. The notion of the random walk was evoked to explain why this should be so.

But what about the longer view? After all, most investors, even impatient ones, stay in the market for more than a month, a quarter, or a year. Even though the contents of their portfolios change over time, serious investors tend to keep their money in the stock market for many years, even decades. Does the long run in the stock market really differ from the short run?

If the random-walk view is correct, today's stock prices embody all relevant information. The only thing that would make them change is the availability of new information. Since we have no way of knowing what that new information might be, there is no mean for stock prices to regress to. In other words, there is no such thing as a *temporary* stock price—that is, a price that sits in limbo before moving to some other point. That is also why changes are unpredictable.

But there are two other possibilities. If the DeBondt-Thaler hypothesis of overreaction to recent news applies to the market as a whole and not just to individual stocks, regression to the mean in the performance of the major market averages should become visible as longer-term real-ities make themselves felt. If, on the other hand, investors are more fearful in some economic environments than in others—say, 1932 or 1974 in contrast to 1968 or 1986—stock prices would fall so long as investors are afraid and would rise again as circumstances change and justify a more hopeful view of the future.

Both possibilities argue for ignoring short-term volatility and holding on for the long pull. No matter how the market moves along the way, returns to investors should average out around some kind of long-term normal. If that is the case, the stock market may be a risky place for a matter of months or even for a couple of years, but the risk of losing anything substantial over a period of five years or longer should be small.

Impressive support for this viewpoint appeared in a monograph published in 1995 by the Association for Investment Management & Research—the organization to which most investment professionals belong—and written by two Baylor University professors, William Reichenstein and Dovalee Dorsett.[6] On the basis of extensive research, they conclude that bad periods in the market are *predictably* followed by good periods, and vice versa. This finding is a direct contradiction of the random-walk view, which denies that changes in stock prices are predictable. Stock prices, like the peapods, have shown no tendency to head off indefinitely in one direction or the other.

Mathematics tells us that the variance—a measure of how observations tend to distribute themselves around their average level—of a series of random numbers should increase precisely as the length of the series grows. Observations over three-year periods should show triple the variance of observations over one year, and observations over a decade should show ten times the variance of annual observations. If, on the other hand, the numbers are not random, because regression to the mean is at work; the mathematics works out so that the ratio of the change variance to the time period will be less than one.*

---

*Opposite tendencies are apparent in the historical record of interest rates, which reflect "aversion" to the mean. A trend once in place has a higher probability of continuing than reversing. Over two-year periods, the variance of the yield on 90-day Treasury bills is 2.2 times annual data; over eight-year periods, the variance is nearly 32 times the annual data; for longer-term interest rates, the pattern is similar but muted.

Reichenstein and Dorsett studied the S&P 500 from 1926 to 1993 and found that the variance of three-year returns was only 2.7 times the variance of annual returns; the variance of eight-year returns was only 5.6 times the variance of annual returns. When they assembled realistic portfolios containing a mixture of stocks and bonds, the ratios of variance to time period were even smaller than for portfolios consisting only of stocks.

Clearly, long-run volatility in the stock market is less than it would be if the extremes had any chance of taking over. *In the end, and after their flings, investors listen to Galton rather than dancing along behind the Pied Piper.*

This finding has profound implications for long-term investors, because it means that uncertainty about rates of return over the long run is much smaller than in the short run. Reichenstein and Dorsett provide a wealth of historical data and projections of future possibilities, but the following passage suggests their principal findings (based on results after adjustment for inflation):[7]

> For a one-year holding period, there is a five percent chance that investors in the stock market will lose at least 25% of their money, and a five percent chance that they will make more than 40%. Over thirty years, on the other hand, there is only a five percent chance that a 100% stock portfolio will grow by less than 20% and a five percent chance that owners of this portfolio could end up over fifty times richer than where they started.
>
> Over time, the difference between the returns on risky securities and conservative investments widens dramatically. Over twenty years, there is only a five percent chance that a portfolio consisting only of long-term corporate bonds would much more than quadruple while there is a fifty percent chance that a 100% equity portfolio would grow at least eightfold.

Yet, this painstaking research gives us no easy prescription for getting rich. We all find it difficult to hang in through thin as well as thick. *And Reichenstein and Dorsett tell us only what happened between 1926 and 1993.* Tempting as long-term investing appears in light of their calculations, their analysis is 100% hindsight. Worse, even small differences in annual returns over many years produce big differences in the investor's wealth at the end of the long-run.

The overreaction to new information that DeBondt and Thaler reported in the behavior of stock prices was the result of the human tendency to overweight recent evidence and to lose sight of the long run. After all, we know a lot more about what is happening right now than we can ever know about what will happen at some uncertain date in the future.

Nevertheless, overemphasizing the present can distort reality and lead to unwise decisions and faulty assessments. For example, some observers have deplored what they allege to be a slowdown in productivity growth in the United States over the past quarter-century. Actually, the record over that period is far better than they would lead us to believe. Awareness of regression to the mean would correct the faulty view of the pessimists.

In 1986, Princeton economist William Baumol published an enlightening study of long-run trends in productivity. His data came from 72 countries and reached back to 1870.[8] The study focused on what Baumol calls the process of convergence. According to this process, the countries with the lowest levels of productivity in 1870 have had the highest rates of improvement over the years, while the most productive countries in 1870 have exhibited the slowest rates of improvement—the peapods at work again, in other words. The differences in growth rates have slowly but surely narrowed the gap in productivity between the most backward and the most advanced nations as each group has regressed toward the mean.

Over the 110 years covered by Baumol's analysis, the difference between the most productive nation and the least productive nation converged from a ratio of 8:1 to a ratio of only 2:1. Baumol points out, ". . . what is striking is the apparent implication that *only one variable*, a country's 1870 GDP per work-hour, . . . matters to any substantial degree."[9] The factors that economists usually identify as contributing to growth in productivity—free markets, a high propensity to save and invest, and "sound" economic policies—seem to have been largely irrelevant. "Whatever its behavior," Baumol concludes, each nation was "fated to land close to its predestined position."[10] Here is a worldwide phenomenon that exactly replicates Galton's small-scale experiments.

Assessments of the performance of the United States change radically when appraised from this perspective. As the nation with the highest GDP per work-hour among industrial countries since the turn of the century, the relatively slow rate of growth in productivity in the United States in recent years should come as no surprise. Each successive technological miracle counts for less as the base from which we measure gets bigger. In fact, Baumol's data show that the U.S. growth rate in productivity has been "just middling" for the better part of a century, not merely for the past couple of decades. Between 1899 and 1913 it was already slower than the growth rates of Sweden, France, Germany, Italy, and Japan.

Although Japan has had the highest long-run growth rate of all the developed economies, except during the Second World War, Baumol points out that it had the lowest level of output per worker in 1870 and still ranks behind the United States. But the process of convergence proceeds inexorably, as technology advances, as education spreads, and as increasing size facilitates economies of scale.

Baumol suggests that dissatisfaction with the U.S. record since the late 1960s is the result of myopia on the part of commentators who overemphasize recent performance and ignore long-term trends. He points out that the huge jump in U.S. levels of productivity from about 1950 to 1970 was not our preordained destiny, even for a nation as technologically oriented as the United States. Seen in a longer perspective, that leap was only an aberration that roughly offset the sharp decline from historical growth rates suffered during the 1930s and the Second World War.

Even though the subject matter is entirely different, Baumol's main conclusions echo DeBondt and Thaler:

> We cannot understand current phenomena . . . without systematic examination of earlier events which affect the present and will continue to exercise profound effects tomorrow. . . . [T]he long run is important because it is not sensible for economists and policymakers to attempt to discern long-run trends and their outcomes from the flow of short-run developments, which may be dominated by transient conditions.[11]

Sometimes the long run sets in too late to bail us out, even when regression to the mean is at work. In a famous passage, the great English economist John Maynard Keynes once remarked:

> In the long run, we are all dead. Economists set themselves too easy, too useless a task if in the tempestuous seasons they can only tell us that when the storm is long past the ocean will be flat.[12]

But we are obliged to live in the short run. The business at hand is to stay afloat and we dare not wait for the day the ocean will be flat. Even then its flatness may be only an interlude of unknown duration between tempests.

Dependence on reversion to the mean for forecasting the future tends to be perilous when the mean itself is in flux. The Reichenstein-Dorsettt projections assume that the future will look like the past, but there is no natural law that says it always will. If global warming indeed lies ahead, a long string of hot years will not necessarily be followed by a long string of cold years. If a person becomes psychotic instead of just neurotic, depression may be permanent rather than intermittent. If humans succeed in destroying the environment, floods may fail to follow droughts.

If nature sometimes fails to regress to the mean, human activities, unlike sweet peas, will surely experience discontinuities, and no risk-management system will work very well. Galton recognized that possibility and warned, "An Average is but a solitary fact, whereas if a single other fact be added to it, an entire Normal Scheme, which nearly corresponds to the observed one, starts potentially into existence."[13]

Early in this book we commented on the stability of the daily lives of most people century after century. Since the onset of the industrial revolution about two hundred years ago, so many "single other facts" have been added to the "Average" that defining the "Normal Scheme" has become increasingly difficult. When discontinuities threaten, it is perilous to base decisions on established trends that have always seemed to make perfect sense but suddenly do not.

Here are two examples of how people can be duped by overreliance on regression to the mean.

In 1930, when President Hoover declared that "Prosperity is just around the corner," he was not trying to fool the public with a sound-

bite or a spin. He meant what he said. After all, history had always supported that view. Depressions had come, but they had always gone.*
Except for the period of the First World War, business activity had
fallen in only seven years from 1869 until 1929. The single two-year
setback during those years was 1907–1908, from a very high point; the
average annual decline in real GDP was a modest 1.6%, and that
included one decline of 5.5%.

But production fell in 1930 by 9.3% and in 1931 by 8.6%. At the
very bottom, in June 1932, GDP was 55% below its 1929 peak, even
lower than it had been at the low point of the short-lived depression of
1920. Sixty years of history had suddenly become irrelevant. The trouble stemmed in part from the loss of youthful dynamism over the long
period of industrial development; even during the boom of the 1920s,
economic growth was below the long-term trend defined by the years
from 1870 to 1918. The weakening of forward momentum, combined
with a sequence of policy errors here and abroad and the shock of the
stock market crash in October 1929, drove prosperity away from the
corner it was presumably around.

The second example: In 1959, exactly thirty years after the Great
Crash, an event took place that made absolutely no sense in the light of
history. Up to the late 1950s, investors had received a higher income
from owning stocks than from owning bonds. Every time the yields got
close, the dividend yield on common stocks moved back up over the
bond yield. Stock prices fell, so that a dollar invested in stocks brought
more income than it had brought previously.

That seemed as it should be. After all, stocks are riskier than bonds.
Bonds are *contracts* that specify precisely when the borrower must repay
the principal of the debt and provide the schedule of interest payments.
If borrowers default on a bond contract, they end up in bankruptcy,
their credit ruined, and their assets under the control of creditors.

With stocks, however, the shareholders' claim on the company's
assets has no substance until after the company's creditors have been satisfied. Stocks are perpetuities: they have no terminal date on which the

---

*They called depressions "panics" in those days; "depression" was a euphemism coined for
the occasion. Later, "recession" became the accepted euphemism. One can only speculate
on how deep a recession would have to be before the experts would decide to call it a
"depression."

assets of the company must be distributed to the owners. Moreover, stock dividends are paid at the pleasure of the board of directors; the company has no obligation ever to pay dividends to the stockholders. Total dividends paid by publicly held companies were cut on nineteen occasions between 1871 and 1929; they were slashed by more than 50% from 1929 to 1933 and by about 40% in 1938.

So it is no wonder that investors bought stocks only when they yielded a higher income than bonds. And no wonder that stock prices fell every time the income from stocks came close to the income from bonds.

Until 1959, that is. At that point, stock prices were soaring and bond prices were falling. This meant that the ratio of bond interest to bond prices was shooting up and the ratio of stock dividends to stock prices was declining. The old relationship between bonds and stocks vanished, opening up a gap so huge that ultimately bonds were yielding more than stocks by an even greater margin than when stocks had yielded more than bonds.

The cause of this reversal could not have been trivial. Inflation was the main factor that distinguished the present from the past. From 1800 to 1940, the cost of living had risen an average of only 0.2% a year and had actually declined on 69 occasions. In 1940 the cost-of-living index was only 28% higher than it had been 140 years earlier. Under such conditions, owning assets valued at a fixed number of dollars was a delight; owning assets with no fixed dollar value was highly risky.

The Second World War and its aftermath changed all that. From 1941 to 1959, inflation averaged 4.0% a year, with the cost-of-living index rising every year but one. The relentlessly rising price level transformed bonds from a financial instrument that had appeared inviolate into an extremely risky investment. By 1959, the price of the 2 1/2% bonds the Treasury had issued in 1945 had fallen from $1,000 to $820—and that $820 bought only half as much as in 1949!

Meanwhile, stock dividends took off on a rapid climb, tripling between 1945 and 1959, with only one year of decline—and even that a mere 2%. No longer did investors perceive stocks as a risky asset whose price and income moved unpredictably. The price paid for today's dividend appeared increasingly irrelevant. What mattered was the rising stream of dividends that the future would bring. Over time, those dividends could be expected to exceed the interest payments from bonds, with a commensurate rise in the capital value of the stocks. The smart move was to buy stocks at a premium because of the opportunities for growth and inflation hedging they provided, and to pass up bonds with their fixed-dollar yield.

Although the contours of this new world were visible well before 1959, the old relationships in the capital markets tended to persist as long as people with memories of the old days continued to be the main investors. For example, my partners, veterans of the Great Crash, kept assuring me that the seeming trend was nothing but an aberration. They promised me that matters would revert to normal in just a few months, that stock prices would fall and bond prices would rally.

I am still waiting. The fact that something so unthinkable could occur has had a lasting impact on my view of life and on investing in particular. It continues to color my attitude toward the future and has left me skeptical about the wisdom of extrapolating from the past.

How much reliance, then, can we place on regression to the mean in judging what the future will bring? What are we to make of a concept that has great power under some conditions but leads to disaster under others?

Keynes admitted that "as living and moving beings, we are forced to act . . . [even when]our existing knowledge does not provide a sufficient basis for a calculated mathematical expectation."[14] With rules of thumb, experience, instinct, and conventions—in other words, gut— we manage to stumble from the present into the future. The expression "conventional wisdom," first used by John Kenneth Galbraith, often carries a pejorative sense, as though what most of us believe is inevitably wrong. But without conventional wisdom, we could make no long-run decisions and would have trouble finding our way from day to day.

The trick is to be flexible enough to recognize that regression to the mean is only a tool; it is not a religion with immutable dogma and ceremonies. Used to make mechanical extrapolations of the past, as

President Hoover or my older associates used it, regression to the mean is little more than mumbo-jumbo. Never depend upon it to come into play without constantly questioning the relevance of the assumptions that support the procedure. Francis Galton spoke wisely when he urged us to "revel in more comprehensive views" than the average.

11

The Fabric of Felicity

U p to now, our story has focused on theories about probability and on ingenious ways of measuring it: Pascal's Triangle, Jacob Bernoulli's search for moral certainty in his jar of black and white balls, Bayes's billiard table, Gauss's bell curve, and Galton's Quincunx. Even Daniel Bernoulli, delving for perhaps the first time into the psychology of choice, was confident that what he called utility could be measured.

Now we turn to an exploration of a different sort: Which risks should we take, which risks should we hedge, what information is relevant? How confidently do we hold our beliefs about the future? In short, how do we introduce *management* into dealing with risk?

Under conditions of uncertainty, both rationality and measurement are essential to decision-making. Rational people process information objectively: whatever errors they make in forecasting the future are random errors rather than the result of a stubborn bias toward either optimism or pessimism. They respond to new information on the basis of a clearly defined set of preferences. They know what they want, and they use the information in ways that support their preferences.

Preference means liking one thing better than another: tradeoff is implicit in the concept. That is a useful idea, but a method of measuring preferences would make it more palpable.

That was what Daniel Bernoulli had in mind when he wrote his remarkable paper in 1738, boasting, "It would be wrong to neglect [his ideas] as abstractions resting upon precarious hypotheses." Bernoulli introduced utility as the unit for measuring preferences—for calculating how much we like one thing more than another. The world is full of desirable things, he said, but the amount that people are willing to pay for them differs from one person to another. And the more we have of something, the less we are willing to pay to get more.[1]

Bernoulli's concept of utility was an impressive innovation, but his handling of it was one-dimensional. Today, we recognize that the desire to keep up with the Joneses may lead us to want more and more even when, by any objective standard of measurement, we already have enough. Moreover, Bernoulli built his case on a game in which Paul wins the first time Peter's coin comes up heads, but *Paul loses nothing when Peter's coin comes up tails*. The word "loss" does not appear in Bernoulli's paper, nor did it appear in works on utility theory for another two hundred years. Once it had appeared, however, utility theory became the paradigm of choice in defining how much risk people will take in the hope of achieving some desired but uncertain gain.

Still, the power of Bernoulli's concept of utility is evident in the way his insights into "the nature of man" continue to resonate. Every advance in decision-making theory and in risk evaluation owes something to his efforts to provide definition, quantification, and guides to rational decisions.

One might expect, as a result, that the history of utility theory and decision-making would be dominated by Bernoullians, especially since Daniel Bernoulli was such a well-known scientist. Yet such is not the case: most later developments in utility theory were new discoveries rather than extensions of Bernoulli's original formulations.

Was the fact that Bernoulli wrote in Latin a problem? Kenneth Arrow has pointed out that Bernoulli's paper on a new theory of measuring risk was not translated into German until 1896, and that the first English translation appeared in an American scholarly journal as late as 1954. Yet Latin was still in common usage in mathematics well into the nineteenth century; and the use of Latin by Gauss was surely no barrier to the attention that his ideas commanded. Still, Bernoulli's choice of Latin may help explain why his accomplishments have received greater notice from mathematicians than from economists and students of human behavior.

Arrow suggests a more substantive issue. Bernoulli dealt with utility in terms of numbers, whereas later writers preferred to think of it as a preference-setter: saying "I like this better than that" is not the same as saying "This is worth x utils to me."

Utility theory was rediscovered toward the end of the eighteenth century by Jeremy Bentham, a popular English philosopher who lived from 1748 to 1832. You can still see him on special occasions at University College, London, where, under the terms of his will, his mummified body sits in a glass case with a wax head to replace the original and with his hat between his feet.

His major work, *The Principles of Morals and Legislation,* published in 1789, was fully in the spirit of the Enlightenment:

> Nature has placed mankind under the governance of two sovereign masters, *pain* and *pleasure*. It is for them alone to point out what we ought to do, as well as to determine what we shall do. . . . The *principle of utility* recognizes this subjection, and assumes it for the foundation of that system, the object of which is to rear the fabric of felicity by the hands of reason and law.[2]

Bentham then explains what he means by utility: ". . . that property in any object, whereby it tends to produce benefit, advantage, pleasure, good, or happiness . . . . when the tendency it has to augment the happiness of the community is greater than any it has to diminish it."

Here Bentham was talking about life in general. But the economists of the nineteenth century fastened onto utility as a tool for discovering how prices result from interactive decisions by buyers and sellers. That detour led directly to the law of supply and demand.

According to the mainstream economists of the nineteenth century, the future stands still while buyers and sellers contemplate the opportunities open to them. The focus was on whether one opportunity was superior to another. The possibility of loss was not a consideration. Consequently the distractions of uncertainty and the business cycle did not appear in the script. Instead, these economists spent their time analyzing the psychological and subjective factors that motivate people to pay such-and-such an amount for a loaf of bread or for a bottle of port—or for a tenth bottle of port. The idea that someone might not have the money to buy even one bottle of port was unthinkable. Alfred Marshall, the pre-eminent economist of the Victorian age, once remarked, "No one should have an occupation which tends to make him anything less than a gentleman."[3]

William Stanley Jevons, a card-carrying Benthamite with a fondness for mathematics, was one of the prime contributors to this body of thought. Born in Liverpool in 1837, he grew up wanting to be a scientist. Financial difficulties, however, prompted him to take a job as assayer in the Royal Mint in Sydney, Australia, a gold-rush boom town with a population rapidly approaching 100,000. Jevons returned to London ten years later to study economics and spent most of his life there as Professor of Political Economy at University College; he was the first economist since William Petty to be elected to the Royal Society. Despite his academic title, Jevons was among the first to suggest dropping the word "political" from the phrase "political economy." In so doing, he revealed the level of abstraction toward which the discipline was moving.

Nevertheless, his masterwork, published in 1871, was titled *The Theory of Political Economy*.[4] Jevons opens his analysis by declaring that *"value depends entirely upon utility."* He goes on to say, "[W]e have only to trace out carefully the natural laws of the variation of utility, as depending upon the quantity of a commodity in our possession, in order to arrive at a satisfactory theory of exchange."

Here we have a restatement of Bernoulli's pivotal assertion that utility varies with the quantity of a commodity already in one's possession. Later in the book Jevons qualifies this generalization with a statement typical of a proper Victorian gentleman: "the more refined and intellectual our needs become, the less they are capable of satiety."

Jevons was confident that he had solved the question of value, claiming that the ability to express everything in quantitative terms had made irrelevant the vague generalities that had characterized economics up to that point. He brushed off the problem of uncertainty by announcing that we need simply apply the probabilities learned from past experience and observation: "The test of correct estimation of probabilities is that the calculations agree with the fact on the average. . . . We make calculations of this kind more or less accurately in all the ordinary affairs of life."

Jevons takes many pages to describe earlier efforts to introduce mathematics into economics, though he makes no mention of Bernoulli. He leaves no doubt, however, about what he himself has achieved:

> Previous to the time of Pascal, who would have thought of measuring doubt and belief? Who would have conceived that the investigation of petty games of chance would have led to the creation of perhaps the most sublime branch of mathematical science—the theory of probabilities?
>
> Now there can be no doubt that pleasure, pain, labour, utility, value, wealth, money, capital, etc. are all notions admitting of quantity; nay, the whole of our actions in industry and trade certainly depend upon comparing quantities of advantage and disadvantage.

Jevons's pride in his achievements reflects the enthusiasm for measurement that characterized the Victorian era. Over time, more and more aspects of life succumbed to quantification. The explosion of scientific research in the service of the industrial revolution added a powerful impulse to that trend.

The first systematic population census in Britain had been carried out as early as 1801, and the insurance industry's use of statistics had grown more and more sophisticated throughout the century. Many right-thinking men and women turned to sociological measurement in the hope of relieving the ills of industrialization. They set out to improve life in the slums and to combat crime, illiteracy, and drunkenness among the newly poor.

Some of the suggestions for applying the measurement of utility to society were less than practical, however. Francis Edgeworth, a contemporary of Jevons and an innovative mathematical economist, went as far as to propose the development of a "hedonimeter." As late as the mid-1920s Frank Ramsay, a brilliant young Cambridge mathematician, was exploring the possibility of creating a "psychogalvanometer."

Some Victorians protested that the rush toward measurement smacked of materialism. In 1860, when Florence Nightingale, after consulting with Galton and others, offered to fund a chair in applied statistics at Oxford, her offer was flatly refused. Maurice Kendall, a great statistician and a historian of statistics, observed that "[I]t seems that our senior universities were still whispering from their towers the last enchantments of the Middle Ages. . . [A]fter thirty years of effort Florence gave it up."*[5]

But the movement to bring the social sciences to the same degree of quantification as the natural sciences grew stronger and stronger as time passed. The vocabulary of the natural sciences gradually found its way into economics. Jevons refers to the "mechanics" of utility and self-interest, for example. Concepts like equilibrium, momentum, pressure, and functions crossed from one field to the other. Today, people in the world of finance use terms like financial engineering, neural networks, and genetic algorithms.

One other aspect of Jevons's work as an economist deserves mention. As a man trained in the natural sciences, he could not avoid taking note of what was right in front of his face—the economy did fluctuate. In 1873, just two years after the publication of *The Theory of Political Economy,* a great economic boom that had lasted for over twenty years in Europe and the United States came to an end. Business activity fell steadily for three years, and recovery was slow to come. Industrial production in the United States in 1878 was only 6% higher than it had been in 1872. Over the next 23 years, the prices of U.S. goods and services fell almost uninterruptedly by some 40%, creating much hardship throughout western Europe and North America.

Did this devastating experience cause Jevons to question whether the economic system might be inherently stable at optimal levels of output and employment, as Ricardo and his followers had promised? Not in the least. Instead, he came up with a theory of business cycles based on the influence of sunspots on weather, of weather on harvests, and of harvests on prices, wages, and the level of employment. For Jevons, the trouble with the economy was in heaven and earth, not in its philosophy.

Theories of how people make decisions and choices seem to have become detached from everyday life in the real world. Yet those theo-

---

*Florence Nightingale was described by Edward Cook, one of her biographers, as a "passionate statistician." A compulsive collector of data in the tradition of Galton, she was also an enthusiastic admirer of the work of Quetelet, which inspired her pioneering work in medical and other social statistics. See Kendall and Plackett, 1977, pp. 310–327.

ries prevailed for nearly a hundred years. Even well into the Great Depression, the notion persisted that economic fluctuations were accidents of some kind rather than events inherent in an economic system driven by risk-taking. Hoover's promise in 1930 that prosperity was just around the corner reflected his belief that the Great Crash had been caused by a passing aberration rather than by some structural fault. In 1931, Keynes himself still exhibited the optimism of his Victorian upbringing when he expressed his ". . . profound conviction that the Economic Problem . . . is nothing but a frightful muddle, a transitory and an *unnecessary* muddle."[6] The italics are his.

1900–1960:
CLOUDS OF VAGUENESS
AND THE DEMAND
FOR PRECISION

12

The Measure of Our Ignorance

O ur confidence in measurement often fails, and we reject it. "Last night they got the elephant." Our favorite explanation for such an event is to ascribe it to luck, good or bad as the case may be.

If everything is a matter of luck, risk management is a meaningless exercise. Invoking luck obscures truth, because it separates an event from its cause.

When we say that someone has fallen on bad luck, we relieve that person of any responsibility for what has happened. When we say that someone has had good luck, we deny that person credit for the effort that might have led to the happy outcome. But how sure can we be? Was it fate or choice that decided the outcome?

Until we can distinguish between an event that is truly random and an event that is the result of cause and effect, we will never know whether what we see is what we'll get, nor how we got what we got. When we take a risk, we are betting on an outcome that will result from a decision we have made, though we do not know for certain what the outcome will be. *The essence of risk management lies in maximizing the areas where we have some control over the outcome while minimizing the areas where we have absolutely no control over the outcome and the linkage between effect and cause is hidden from us.*

Just what do we mean by luck? Laplace was convinced that there is no such thing as luck—or hazard as he called it. In his *Essai philosophique sur les probabilités*, he declared:

> Present events are connected with preceding ones by a tie based upon the evident principle that a thing cannot occur without a cause that produces it. . . . All events, even those which on account of their insignificance do not seem to follow the great laws of nature, are a result of it just as necessarily as the revolutions of the sun.[1]

This statement echoes an observation by Jacob Bernoulli that if all events throughout eternity could be repeated, we would find that every one of them occurred in response to "definite causes" and that even the events that seemed most fortuitous were the result of "a certain necessity, or, so to say, FATE." We can also hear de Moivre, submitting to the power of *ORIGINAL DESIGN*. Laplace, surmising that there was a "vast intelligence" capable of understanding all causes and effects, obliterated the very idea of uncertainty. In the spirit of his time, he predicted that human beings would achieve that same level of intelligence, citing the advances already made in astronomy, mechanics, geometry, and gravity. He ascribed those advances to "the tendency, peculiar to the human race [that] renders it superior to animals; and their progress in this respect distinguishes nations and ages and constitutes their true glory."[2]

Laplace admitted that it is sometimes hard to find a cause where there seems to be none, but he also warns against the tendency to assign a particular cause to an outcome when in fact only the laws of probability are at work. He offers this example: "On a table, we see the letters arranged in this order, CONSTANTINOPLE, and we judge that this arrangement is not the result of chance. [Yet] if this word were not employed in any language we should not suspect it came from any particular cause."[3] If the letters happened to be BZUXRQVICPRGAB, we would not give the sequence of letters a second thought, even though the odds on BZUXRQVICPRGAB's showing up in a random drawing are precisely the same as the odds on CONSTANTINOPLE's showing up. We would be surprised if we drew the number 1,000 out of a bottle containing 1,000 numbers; yet the probability of drawing 457 is also only one in a thousand. "The more extraordinary the event," Laplace concludes, "the greater the need of it being supported by strong proofs."[4]

In the month of October 1987, the stock market fell by more than 20%. That was only the fourth time since 1926 that the market had dropped by more than 20% in a single month. But the 1987 crash came out of nowhere. There is no agreement on what caused it, though theories abound. It could not have occurred without a cause, and yet that cause is obscure. Despite its extraordinary character, no one could come up with "strong proofs" of its origins.

Another French mathematician, born about a century after Laplace, gave further emphasis to the concept of cause and effect and to the importance of information in decision-making. Jules-Henri Poincaré, (1854–1912) was, according to James Newman,

> . . . a French savant who looked alarmingly like a French savant. He was short and plump, carried an enormous head set off by a thick spade beard and splendid mustache, was myopic, stooped, distraught in speech, absent-minded and wore pince-nez glasses attached to a black silk ribbon.[5]

Poincaré was another mathematician in the long line of child prodigies that we have met along the way. He grew up to be the leading French mathematician of his time.

Nevertheless, Poincaré made the great mistake of underestimating the accomplishments of a student named Louis Bachelier, who earned a degree in 1900 at the Sorbonne with a dissertation titled "The Theory of Speculation."[6] Poincaré, in his review of the thesis, observed that "M. Bachelier has evidenced an original and precise mind [but] the subject is somewhat remote from those our other candidates are in the habit of treating." The thesis was awarded *"mention honorable,"* rather than the highest award of *"mention très honorable,"* which was essential for anyone hoping to find a decent job in the academic community. Bachelier never found such a job.

Bachelier's thesis came to light only by accident more than fifty years after he wrote it. Young as he was at the time, the mathematics he developed to explain the pricing of options on French government bonds anticipated by five years Einstein's discovery of the motion of electrons—which, in turn, provided the basis for the theory of the random walk in finance. Moreover, his description of the process of speculation anticipated many of the theories observed in financial markets today. "*Mention honorable*"!

The central idea of Bachelier's thesis was this: "The mathematical expectation of the speculator is zero." The ideas that flowed from that startling statement are now evident in everything from trading strategies and the use of derivative instruments to the most sophisticated techniques of portfolio management. Bachelier knew that he was onto something big, despite the indifference he was accorded. "It is evident," he wrote, "that the present theory solves the majority of problems in the study of speculation by the calculus of probability."

But we must return to Poincaré, Bachelier's nemesis. Like Laplace, Poincaré believed that everything has a cause, though mere mortals are incapable of divining all the causes of all the events that occur. "A mind infinitely powerful, infinitely well-informed about the laws of nature, could have foreseen [all events] from the beginning of the centuries. If such a mind existed, we could not play with it at any game of chance, for we would lose."[7]

To dramatize the power of cause-and-effect, Poincaré suggests what the world would be like without it. He cites a fantasy imagined by Camile Flammarion, a contemporary French astronomer, in which an observer travels into space at a velocity greater than the speed of light:

> [F]or him time would have changed sign [from positive to negative].
> History would be turned about, and Waterloo would precede
> Austerlitz. . . . [A]ll would seem to him to come out of a sort of chaos
> in unstable equilibrium. All nature would appear to him delivered
> over to chance.[8]

But in a cause-and-effect world, if we know the causes we can predict the effects. So "what is chance for the ignorant is not chance for the scientist. Chance is only the measure of our ignorance."[9]

But then Poincaré asks whether that definition of chance is totally satisfactory. After all, we can invoke the laws of probability to make predictions. We never know which team is going to win the World Series, but Pascal's Triangle demonstrates that a team that loses the first game has a probability of 22/64 of winning four games before their opponents have won three more. There is one chance in six that the roll of a single die will come up 3. The weatherman predicts today that the probability of rain tomorrow is 30%. Bachelier demonstrates that the odds that the price of a stock will move up on the next trade are precisely 50%. Poincaré points out that the director of a life insurance company is ignorant of the time when each of his policyholders will die, but "he relies upon the calculus of probabilities and on the law of great numbers, and he is not deceived, since he distributes dividends to his stockholders."[10]

Poincaré also points out that some events that appear to be fortuitous are not; instead, their causes stem from minute disturbances. A cone perfectly balanced on its apex will topple over if there is the least defect in symmetry; and even if there is no defect, the cone will topple in response to "a very slight tremor, a breath of air." That is why, Poincaré explained, meteorologists have such limited success in predicting the weather:

> Many persons find it quite natural to pray for rain or shine when they would think it ridiculous to pray for an eclipse. . . . [O]ne-tenth of a degree at any point, and the cyclone bursts here and not there, and spreads its ravages over countries it would have spared. This we could have foreseen if we had known that tenth of a degree, but . . . all seems due to the agency of chance.[11]

Even spins of a roulette wheel and throws of dice will vary in response to slight differences in the energy that puts them in motion. Unable to observe such tiny differences, we assume that the outcomes they produce are random, unpredictable. As Poincaré observes about roulette, "This is why my heart throbs and I hope everything from luck."[12]

Chaos theory, a more recent development, is based on a similar premise. According to this theory, much of what looks like chaos is in truth the product of an underlying order, in which insignificant perturbations are often the cause of predestined crashes and long-lived bull markets. *The New York Times* of July 10, 1994, reported a fanciful application of chaos theory by a Berkeley computer scientist named James

Crutchfield, who "estimated that the gravitational pull of an electron, randomly shifting position at the edge of the Milky Way, can change the outcome of a billiard game on Earth."

Laplace and Poincaré recognized that we sometimes have too little information to apply the laws of probability. Once, at a professional investment conference, a friend passed me a note that read as follows:

The information you have is not the information you want.
The information you want is not the information you need.
The information you need is not the information you can obtain.
The information you can obtain costs more than you want to pay.

We can assemble big pieces of information and little pieces, but we can never get all the pieces together. We never know for sure how good our sample is. That uncertainty is what makes arriving at judgments so difficult and acting on them so risky. We cannot even be 100% certain that the sun will rise tomorrow morning: the ancients who predicted that event were themselves working with a limited sample of the history of the universe.

When information is lacking, we have to fall back on inductive reasoning and try to guess the odds. John Maynard Keynes, in a treatise on probability, concluded that in the end statistical concepts are often useless: "There is a relation between the evidence and the event considered, but it is not necessarily measurable."[13]

Inductive reasoning leads us to some curious conclusions as we try to cope with the uncertainties we face and the risks we take. Some of the most impressive research on this phenomenon has been done by Nobel Laureate Kenneth Arrow. Arrow was born at the end of the First World War and grew up in New York City at a time when the city was the scene of spirited intellectual activity and controversy. He attended public school and City College and went on to teach at Harvard and Stanford. He now occupies two emeritus professorships at Stanford, one in operations research and one in economics.

Early on, Arrow became convinced that most people overestimate the amount of information that is available to them. The failure of economists to comprehend the causes of the Great Depression at the time demonstrated to him that their knowledge of the economy was "very limited." His experience as an Air Force weather forecaster during the Second World War "added the news that the natural world was also unpredictable."[14] Here is a more extended version of the passage from which I quoted in the Introduction:

> To me our knowledge of the way things work, in society or in nature, comes trailing clouds of vagueness. Vast ills have followed a belief in certainty, whether historical inevitability, grand diplomatic designs, or extreme views on economic policy. When developing policy with wide effects for an individual or society, caution is needed because we cannot predict the consequences."[15]

One incident that occurred while Arrow was forecasting the weather illustrates both uncertainty and the human unwillingness to accept it. Some officers had been assigned the task of forecasting the weather a month ahead, but Arrow and his statisticians found that their long-range forecasts were no better than numbers pulled out of a hat. The forecasters agreed and asked their superiors to be relieved of this duty. The reply was: "The Commanding General is well aware that the forecasts are no good. However, he needs them for planning purposes."[16]

In an essay on risk, Arrow asks why most of us gamble now and then and why we regularly pay premiums to an insurance company. The mathematical probabilities indicate that we will lose money in both instances. In the case of gambling, it is statistically impossible to expect—though possible to achieve—more than a break-even, because the house edge tilts the odds against us. In the case of insurance, the premiums we pay exceed the statistical odds that our house will burn down or that our jewelry will be stolen.

Why do we enter into these losing propositions? We gamble because we are willing to accept the large probability of a small loss in the hope that the small probability of scoring a large gain will work in our favor; for most people, in any case, gambling is more entertainment than risk. We buy insurance because we cannot afford to take the risk of losing our home to fire—or our life before our time. That is, we prefer a gamble that has 100% odds on a small loss (the premium we must pay) but a small chance of a large gain (if catastrophe strikes) to a gamble with a certain small gain (saving the cost of the insurance premium) but with uncertain but potentially ruinous consequences for us or our family.

Arrow won his Nobel Prize in part as a result of his speculations about an imaginary insurance company or other risk-sharing institution that would insure against any loss of any kind and of any magnitude, in what he describes as a "complete market." The world, he concluded, would be a better place if we could insure against every future possibility. Then people would be more willing to engage in risk-taking, without which economic progress is impossible.

Often we are unable to conduct enough trials or take enough samples to employ the laws of probability in making decisions. We decide on the basis of ten tosses of the coin instead of a hundred. Consequently, in the absence of insurance, just about any outcome seems to be a matter of luck. Insurance, by combining the risks of many people, enables each individual to enjoy the advantages provided by the Law of Large Numbers.

In practice, insurance is available only when the Law of Large Numbers is observed. The law requires that the risks insured must be both large in number and independent of one another, like successive deals in a game of poker.

"Independent" means several things: it means that the cause of a fire, for example, must be independent of the actions of the policyholder. It also means that the risks insured must not be interrelated, like the probable movement of any one stock at a time when the whole stock market is taking a nose dive, or the destruction caused by a war. Finally, it means that insurance will be available only when there is a rational way to calculate the odds of loss, a restriction that rules out insurance that a new dress style will be a smashing success or that the nation will be at war at some point in the next ten years.

Consequently, the number of risks that can be insured against is far smaller than the number of risks we take in the course of a lifetime. We often face the possibility that we will make the wrong choice and end up regretting it. The premium we pay the insurance company is only one of many certain costs we incur in order to avoid the possibility of a larger, uncertain loss, and we go to great lengths to protect ourselves from the consequences of being wrong. Keynes once asked, "[Why] should anyone outside a lunatic asylum wish to hold money as a store of wealth?" His answer: "The possession of actual money lulls our disquietude; and the premium we require to make us part with money is the measure of our disquietude."[17]

In business, we seal a deal by signing a contract or by shaking hands. These formalities prescribe our future behavior even if conditions change in such a way that we wish we had made different arrangements. At the same time, they protect us from being harmed by the people on the other side of the deal. Firms that produce goods with volatile prices, such as wheat or gold, protect themselves from loss by entering into commodity futures contracts, which enable them to sell their output even before they have produced it. They pass up the possibility of selling later at a higher price in order to avoid uncertainty about the price they will receive.

In 1971, Kenneth Arrow, in association with fellow economist Frank Hahn, pointed up the relationships between money, contracts, and uncertainty. Contracts would not be written in money terms "if we consider an economy without a past or a future."[18] But the past and the future are to the economy what woof and warp are to a fabric. We make no decision without reference to a past that we understand with some degree of certainty and to a future about which we have no certain knowledge. Contracts and liquidity protect us from unwelcome consequences even when we are coping with Arrow's clouds of vagueness.

Some people guard against uncertain outcomes in other ways. They call a limousine service to avoid the uncertainty of riding in a taxi or taking public transportation. They have burglar alarm systems installed in their homes. Reducing uncertainty is a costly business.

Arrow's idea of a "complete market" was based on his sense of the value of human life. "The basic element in my view of the good society," he wrote, "is the centrality of others. . . . These principles imply a general commitment to freedom. . . . Improving economic status and opportunity . . . is a basic component of increasing freedom."[19] But the fear of loss sometimes constrains our choices. That is why Arrow applauds insurance and risk-sharing devices like commodity futures contracts and public markets for stocks and bonds. Such facilities encourage investors to hold diversified portfolios instead of putting all their eggs in one basket.

Arrow warns, however, that a society in which no one fears the consequences of risk-taking may provide fertile ground for antisocial behavior. For example, the availability of deposit insurance to the depositors of savings and loan associations in the 1980s gave the owners a chance to win big if things went right and to lose little if things went wrong. When things finally went wrong, the taxpayers had to pay. Wherever insurance can be had, moral hazard—the temptation to cheat—will be present.*

There is a huge gap between Laplace and Poincaré on the one hand and Arrow and his contemporaries on the other. After the catastrophe of the First World War, the dream vanished that some day human beings would know everything they needed to know and that certainty would replace uncertainty. Instead, the explosion of knowledge over the years has served only to make life more uncertain and the world more difficult to understand.

Seen in this light, Arrow is the most modern of the characters in our story so far. Arrow's focus is not on how probability works or how observations regress to the mean. Rather, he focuses on how we make decisions under conditions of uncertainty and how we live with the decisions we have made. He has brought us to the point where we can take a more systematic look at how people tread the path between risks to be faced and risks to be taken. The authors of the Port-Royal *Logic* and Daniel Bernoulli both sensed what lines of analysis in the field of risk might lie ahead, but Arrow is the father of the concept of risk management as an explicit form of practical art.

The recognition of risk management as a practical art rests on a simple cliché with the most profound consequences: when our world was

---

*It is conceivable, however, that the opposite might occur. Risk often serves as a stimulant. Without risk, a society might turn passive in the face of the future.

created, nobody remembered to include certainty. *We are never certain; we are always ignorant to some degree.* Much of the information we have is either incorrect or incomplete.

Suppose a stranger invites you to bet on coin-tossing. She assures you that the coin she hands you can be trusted. How do you know whether she is telling the truth? You decide to test the coin by tossing it ten times before you agree to play.

When it comes up eight heads and two tails, you say it must be loaded. The stranger hands you a statistics book, which says that this lop-sided result may occur about one out of every nine times in tests of ten tosses each.

Though chastened, you invoke the teachings of Jacob Bernoulli and request sufficient time to give the coin a hundred tosses. It comes up heads eighty times! The statistics book tells you that the probability of getting eighty heads in a hundred tosses is so slight that you will have to count the number of zeroes following the decimal point. The probability is about one in a billion.

Yet you are still not 100% certain that the coin is loaded. Nor will you ever be 100% certain, even if you were to go on tossing it for a hundred years. One chance in a billion ought to be enough to convince you that this is a dangerous partner to play games with, but the possibility remains that you are doing the woman an injustice. Socrates said that likeness to truth is not truth, and Jacob Bernoulli insisted that moral certainty is less than certainty.

Under conditions of uncertainty, the choice is not between rejecting a hypothesis and accepting it, but between reject and not–reject. You can decide that the probability that you are wrong is so small that you should not reject the hypothesis. You can decide that the probability that you are wrong is so large that you *should* reject the hypothesis. But with any probability short of zero that you are wrong—certainty rather than uncertainty—you cannot *accept* a hypothesis.

This powerful notion separates most valid scientific research from hokum. To be valid, hypotheses must be subject to falsification—that is, they must be testable in such fashion that the alternative between reject and not–reject is clear and specific and that the probability is measurable. The statement "He is a nice man" is too vague to be testable. The statement "That man does not eat chocolate after every meal" is falsifiable in the sense that we can gather evidence to show whether the man has or has not eaten chocolate after every meal in the past. If the evidence covers only a week, the probability that we could reject the hypothesis (we doubt that he does not eat chocolate after every meal) will be higher than if the evidence covers a year. The result of the test will be not–reject if no evidence of regular consumption of chocolate is available. But even if the lack of evidence extends over a long period of time, we cannot say with certainty that the man will never start eating chocolate after every meal in the future. Unless we have spent every single minute of his life with him, we could never be certain that he has not eaten chocolate regularly in the past.

Criminal trials provide a useful example of this principle. Under our system of law, criminal defendants do not have to prove their innocence; there is no such thing as a *verdict of innocence*. Instead, the hypothesis to be established is that the defendant is guilty, and the prosecution's job is to persuade the members of jury that they should not reject the hypothesis of guilt. The goal of the defense is simply to persuade the jury that sufficient doubt surrounds the prosecution's case to justify rejecting that hypothesis. That is why the verdict delivered by juries is either "guilty" or "not guilty."

The jury room is not the only place where the testing of a hypothesis leads to intense debate over the degree of uncertainty that would justify rejecting it. That degree of uncertainty is not prescribed. In the end, we must arrive at a subjective decision on how much uncertainty is acceptable before we make up our minds.

For example, managers of mutual funds face two kinds of risk. The first is the obvious risk of poor performance. The second is the risk of failing to measure up to some benchmark that is known to potential investors.

The accompanying chart[20] shows the total annual pretax rate of return (dividends paid plus price change) from 1983 through 1995 to a stockholder in the American Mutual Fund, one of the oldest and largest equity mutual funds in the business. The American Mutual performance is plotted as a line with dots, and the performance of the Standard & Poor's Composite Index of 500 Stocks is represented by the bars.

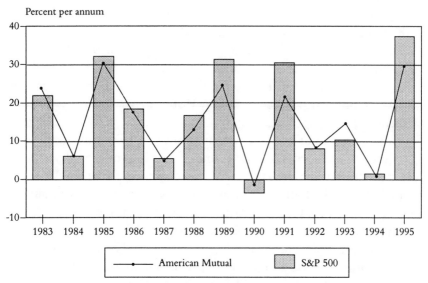

Percent per annum

Total rates of return, 1983–1995, American Mutual vs. S&P 500.

Although American Mutual tracks the S&P 500 closely, it had higher returns in only three out of the thirteen years—in 1983 and 1993, when American Mutual rose by more, and in 1990, when it fell by less. In ten years, American Mutual did about the same as or earned less than the S&P.

Was this just a string of bad luck, or do the managers of American Mutual lack the skill to outperform an unmanaged conglomeration of 500 stocks? Note that, since American Mutual is less volatile than the S&P, its performance was likely to lag in the twelve out of thirteen years in which the market was rising. The Fund's performance might look a lot better in years when the market was declining or not moving up or down.

Nevertheless, when we put these data through a mathematical stress test to determine the significance of these results, we find that American Mutual's managers probably did lack skill.[21] There is only a 20% probability that the results were due to chance. To put it differently, if we ran this test over five other thirteen-year periods, we would expect American Mutual to underperform the S&P 500 in four of the periods.

Many observers would disagree, insisting that twelve years is too small a sample to support so broad a generalization. Moreover, a 20%

probability is not small, though less than 50%. The current convention
in the world of finance is that we should be 95% certain that something
is "statistically significant" (the modern equivalent of moral certainty)
before we accept what the numbers indicate. Jacob Bernoulli said that
1,000 chances out of 1,001 were required for one to be morally certain;
we require only one chance in twenty that what we observe is a matter
of chance.

But if we cannot be 95% certain of anything like this on the basis
of only twelve observations, how many observations would we need?
Another stress test reveals that we would need to track American
Mutual against the S&P 500 for about thirty years before we could be
95% certain that underperformance of this magnitude was not just a
matter of luck. As that test is a practical impossibility, the best judgment
is that the American Mutual managers deserve the benefit of the doubt;
their performance was acceptable under the circumstances.

The next chart shows a different picture. Here we see the relative
performance of a small, aggressive fund called AIM Constellation. This
fund was a lot more volatile during these years than either the S&P
Index or American Mutual. Note that the vertical scale in this chart is
twice the height of the vertical scale in the preceding chart. AIM had a

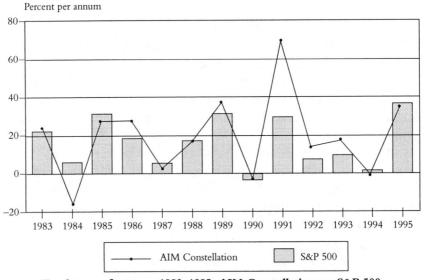

Total rates of returns, 1983–1995, AIM Constellation vs. S&P 500.

disastrous year in 1984, but in five other years it outperformed the S&P 500 by a wide margin. The average annual return for AIM over the thirteen years was 19.8% as compared with 16.7% for the S&P 500 and 15.0% for American Mutual.

Is this record the result of luck or skill? Despite the wide spread in returns between AIM and the S&P 500, the greater volatility of AIM makes this a tough question to answer. In addition, AIM did not track the S&P 500 as faithfully as American Mutual did: AIM went down one year when the S&P 500 was rising, and it earned as much in 1986, as in 1985, as the S&P was earning less. The pattern is so irregular that we would have a hard time predicting this fund's performance even if we were smart enough to predict the returns on the S&P 500.

Because of the high volatility and low correlation, our mathematical stress test reveals that luck played a significant role in the AIM case just as in the American Mutual case. Indeed, we would need a track record exceeding a century before we could be 95% certain that these AIM results were *not* the product of luck! In risk-management terms, there is a suggestion here that the AIM managers may have taken excessive risk in their efforts to beat the market.

Many anti-smokers worry about second-hand smoke and support efforts to making smoking in public places illegal. How great is the risk that you will develop lung cancer when someone lights up a cigarette at the next table in a restaurant or in the next seat on an airplane? Should you accept the risk, or should you insist that the cigarette be extinguished immediately?

In January 1993, the Environmental Protection Administration issued a 510-page report carrying the ominous title *Respiratory Health Effects of Passive Smoking: Lung Cancer and Other Disorders.*[22] A year later, Carol Browner, the EPA Administrator, appeared before a congressional committee and urged it to approve the Smoke-Free Environment Act, which establishes a complex set of regulations designed to prohibit smoking in public buildings. Browner stated that she based her recommendation on the report's conclusion that environmental tobacco smoke, or ETS, is "a known human lung carcinogen."[23]

How much is "known" about ETS? What is the risk of developing lung cancer when someone else is doing the smoking?

There is only one way even to approach certainty in answering these questions: Check every single person who was ever exposed to ETS at any moment since people started smoking tobacco hundreds of years ago. Even then, a demonstrated association between ETS and lung cancer would not be *proof* that ETS was the cause of the cancer.

The practical impossibility of conducting tests on everybody or everything over the entire span of history in every location leaves all scientific research results uncertain. What looks like a strong association may be nothing more than the luck of the draw, in which case a different set of samples from a different time period or from a different locale, or even a different set of subjects from the same period and the same locale, might have produced contrary findings.

There is only one thing we know for certain: an association (not a cause-and-effect) between ETS and lung cancer has a probability that is some percentage short of 100%. The difference between 100% and the indicated probability reflects the likelihood that the ETS has nothing whatsoever to do with causing lung cancer and that similar evidence would not necessarily show up in another sample. The risk of coming down with lung cancer from ETS boils down to a set of odds, just as in a game of chance.

Most studies like the EPA analysis compare the result when one group of people is exposed to something, good or bad, with the result from a "control" group that is not exposed to the same influences. Most new drugs are tested by giving one group the drug in question and comparing their response with the response of a group that has been given a placebo.

In the passive smoking case, the analysis focused on the incidence of lung cancer among non-smoking women living with men who smoked. The data were then compared with the incidence of disease among the control group of non-smoking women living with non-smoking companions. The ratio of the responses of the exposed group to the responses of the control group is called the *test statistic*. The absolute size of the test statistic and the degree of uncertainty surrounding it form the basis for deciding whether to take action of some kind. In other words, the test statistic helps the observer to distinguish between CONSTANTINOPLE and BZUXRQVICPRGAB and cases with more meaningful results. Because of all the uncertainties involved, the ultimate decision is often more a matter of gut than of measurement, just as it is in deciding whether a coin is fair or loaded.

Epidemiologists—the statisticians of health—observe the same convention as that used to measure the performance of investment managers. They usually define a result as statistically significant if there is no more than a 5% probability that an outcome was the result of chance.

The results of the EPA study of passive smoking were not nearly as strong as the results of the much larger number of earlier studies of active smoking. Even though the risk of contracting lung cancer seemed to correlate well with the amount of exposure—how heavily the male companion smoked—the disease rates among women exposed to ETS averaged only 1.19 times higher than among women who lived with non-smokers. Furthermore, this modest test statistic was based on just thirty studies, of which six showed no effect from ETS. Since many of those studies covered small samples, only nine of them were statistically significant.[24] None of the eleven studies conducted in the United States met that criterion, but seven of those studies covered fewer than forty-five cases.[25]

In the end, admitting that "EPA has never claimed that minimal exposure to secondhand smoke poses a huge individual cancer risk,"[26] the agency estimated that "approximately 3,000 American nonsmokers die each year from lung cancer caused by secondhand smoke."[27] That conclusion prompted Congress to pass the Smoke-Free Environment Act, with its numerous regulations on public facilities.

We have reached the point in the story where uncertainty, and its handmaiden luck, have moved to center stage. The setting has changed, in large part because in the 75 years or so since the end of the First World War the world has faced nearly all the risks of the old days and many new risks as well.

The demand for risk management has risen along with the growing number of risks. No one was more sensitive to this trend than Frank Knight and John Maynard Keynes, whose pioneering work we review in the next chapter. Although both are now dead—their most important writings predate Arrow's—almost all the figures we shall meet from now on are, like Arrow, still alive. They are testimony to how young the ideas of risk management are.

The concepts we shall encounter in the chapter ahead never occurred to the mathematicians and philosophers of the past, who were too busy establishing the laws of probability to tackle the mysteries of uncertainty.

13

The Radically Distinct Notion

Francis Galton died in 1911 and Henri Poincaré died the following year. Their passing marked the end of the grand age of measurement, an era that reached back five centuries to Paccioli's game of *balla*. For it was his problem of the points (page 43) that had launched the long march to defining the future in terms of the laws of probability. None of the great mathematicians and philosophers of the past whom we have met so far doubted that they had the tools they needed to determine what the future held. It was only the facts that demanded attention.

I do not mean to imply that Galton and Poincaré finished the task: the principles of risk management are still evolving. But their deaths occurred—and their understanding of risk climaxed—on the eve of one of the great watersheds of history, the First World War.

The optimism of the Victorians was snuffed out by the senseless destruction of human life on the battlefields, the uneasy peace that followed, and the goblins let loose by the Russian revolution. Never again would people accept Robert Browning's assurance that "God's in his heaven:/All's right with the world." Never again would economists insist that fluctuations in the economy were a theoretical impossibility. Never again would science appear so unreservedly benign, nor would religion and family institutions be so unthinkingly accepted in the western world.

World War I put an end to all that. Radical transformations in art, literature, and music produced abstract and often shocking forms that stood in disturbing contrast to the comfortable modes of the nineteenth century. When Albert Einstein demonstrated that an imperfection lurked below the surface of Euclidean geometry, and when Sigmund Freud declared that irrationality is the natural condition of humanity, both men became celebrities overnight.

Up to this point, the classical economists had defined economics as a riskless system that always produced optimal results. Stability, they promised, was guaranteed. If people decided to save more and spend less, the interest rate would fall, thereby encouraging investment or discouraging saving enough to bring matters back into balance. If business managers decided to expand their firms rapidly but households failed to save enough for them to borrow what they needed for expansion, the interest rate would rise to set matters right. Such an economy would never suffer involuntary unemployment or disappointing profits, except perhaps during brief periods of adjustment. Although individual firms and investors took risks, the economy as a whole was risk-free.

Such convictions died hard, even in the face of the economic problems that emerged in the wake of the war. But a few voices were raised proclaiming that the world was no longer what once it had seemed. Writing in 1921, the University of Chicago economist Frank Knight uttered strange words for a man of his profession: "There is much question as to how far the world is intelligible at all. . . . It is only in the very special and crucial cases that anything like a mathematical study can be made."[1] During the depths of the Great Depression, John Maynard Keynes echoed Knight's pessimism:

> We are faced at every turn with the problems of Organic Unity, of Discreteness, of Discontinuity—the whole is not equal to the sum of the parts, comparisons of quantity fail us, small changes produce large effects, and the assumptions of a uniform and homogeneous continuum are not satisfied.[2]

In 1936, in his masterwork, *The General Theory of Employment, Interest and Money*, Keynes flatly rejected Jevon's faith in the universal applicability of measurement: "[Most of our decisions] to do something positive . . . can only be taken as a result of animal spirits . . . and not as the outcome of a weighted average of quantitative benefits multiplied by quantitative probabilities."[3]

Faced with the tensions of the postwar years, only the most naive theorist could pretend that all problems could be solved through the rational application of differential calculus and the laws of probability with well-ordered preferences. Mathematicians and philosophers had to admit that reality encompassed entire sets of circumstances that people had never contemplated before. The distribution of odds no longer followed the distribution Pascal had defined. It violated the symmetry of the bell curve and was regressing to means that were far more unstable than what Galton had specified.

Researchers sought for ways of conducting a systematic analysis of the unexpected. Before the war they had concentrated on the inputs that went into decision-making. Now they recognized that the decision is only the beginning. The devil is in the consequences of our decisions, not in the decisions themselves. As Robert Dixon, an Australian economist, has remarked, "Uncertainty is present in the decision-making process, not so much because there is a future as that there is, and will be, a past. . . . We are prisoners of the future because we will be ensnared by our past."[4] That ultimate realist, Omar Khayyam, had had the same thought nearly a thousand years before:

> The Moving Finger writes; and having writ,
> Moves on: nor all your Piety nor Wit
> Shall lure it back to cancel half a Line,
> Nor all your Tears wash out a Word of it.

What do you do when a decision leads to a result that was not even contemplated in your set of probabilities? Or when low-probability outcomes seem to occur more frequently than they should? Don't the patterns of the past always reveal the path to the future?

Knight and Keynes, the first two to confront such questions in a serious fashion, were both noisy nonconformists, but, together, they defined risk as it has come to be understood today.

❋

Frank Knight was born on a farm in White Oak Township, Illinois, in 1885, the oldest of eleven children.[5] Though he lacked a high-school diploma, he attended two tiny colleges, perhaps the best he could afford in view of his family's poverty. The first was American University (which had no connection to the university with the same name in Washington, D.C.); this college emphasized *temperance* above all else and even taught "the principles of political economy in regard to the use of intoxicating liquors." In its national advertising it urged "parents to send their hard-to-handle boys to American University for disciplining." The second college was Milligan. On Knight's graduation, the president of the college described him as "the best student I have had . . . best read student . . . [with] practical business capacity as well as technical knowledge."

Knight claimed that the reason he became an economist was that plowing was too hard on his feet. Before turning to economics he did graduate work in philosophy at Cornell; he switched to economics after a professor declared, "Stop talking so much, or leave the philosophy department!" But it was not just the overuse of his high, squeaky voice that got him into trouble; one of his philosophy professors predicted, "He will destroy the true philosophic spirit wherever he touches it." Knight was an incurable cynic about human nature. A more sympathetic professor once told him, "You came out of a malodorous environment where every man with a mind doubts everything."

Knight began teaching economics at the University of Iowa in 1919 and moved to the University of Chicago in 1928. He was still teaching there when he died in 1972 at the age of 87; "It beats working for a living," he once remarked. His lectures were often ill prepared, delivered in a rambling, country-boy manner, and larded with heavy-handed humor.

Despite his early exposure to religion and his continuing study of religion throughout his life, Knight was an implacable enemy of everything to do with organized forms of religion. In his presidential address to the American Economic Association in 1950, he likened the pope to Hitler and Stalin. He once said that religion was responsible for his bad sleeping habits: "It's that damned religion. I just can't get it out of my mind."

An irascible, dedicated, honest man, he took a dim view of people who took themselves too seriously. He claimed that economic theory was not at all obscure or complicated, but that most people had a vested interest in refusing to recognize what was "insultingly obvious." Noting a quotation by Lord Kelvin chiseled in stone on the social science building at Chicago—"[W]hen you cannot measure it . . . your knowledge is of a meager and unsatisfactory kind"—Knight sarcastically interpreted it to mean, "Oh, well, if you cannot measure, measure anyhow."[6]

Knight's cynicism and concern for moral values made it hard for him to come to terms with the selfishness, and frequently the violence, of capitalism. He despised the self-interest that motivates both buyers and sellers in the marketplace, even though he believed that only self-interest explains how the system works. Yet he stuck with capitalism, because he considered the alternatives unacceptable.

Knight had no interest in working up empirical proofs of his theories. He harbored too many doubts about the rationality and consistency of human beings to believe that measuring their behavior would produce anything of value. His bitterest sarcasm was reserved for what he saw as "the near pre-emption of [economics] by people who take a point of view which seems to me untenable, and in fact shallow, namely the transfer into the human sciences of the concepts and products of the sciences of nature."

The attitude reflected in this remark is evident in Knight's doctoral dissertation, which was completed at Cornell in 1916 and published as a book in 1921. *Risk, Uncertainty and Profit* is the first work of any importance, and in any field of study, that deals explicitly with decision-making under conditions of uncertainty.

Knight builds his analysis on the distinction between risk and uncertainty:

> Uncertainty must be taken in a sense radically distinct from the familiar notion of Risk, from which it has never been properly separated. . . . It will appear that a *measurable* uncertainty, or "risk" proper . . . is so far different from an *unmeasurable* one that it is not in effect an uncertainty at all.[7]

Knight's emphasis on uncertainty decoupled him from the predominant economic theory of the time, which emphasized decision-making under conditions of perfect certainty or under the established laws of probability—an emphasis that lingers on in certain areas of economic theory today. Knight spoke of the failure of the probability calculus to, in Arrow's words, "reflect the tentative, creative nature of the human mind in the face of the unknown."[8] Clearly Knight was a creature of the twentieth century.

The element of surprise, Knight argued, is common in a system where so many decisions depend on forecasts of the future. His main complaint against classical economics with its emphasis on so-called perfect competition arose from its simplifying assumption of "practical omniscience on the part of every member of the competitive system."[9] In classical economics, buyers and sellers, and workers and capitalists, always have all the information they need. In instances where the future is unknown, the laws of probability will determine the outcome. Even Karl Marx, in his dynamic version of classical economics, never makes reference to forecasting. In that version, workers and capitalists are locked in a drama whose plot is clear to everyone and whose dénouement they are powerless to change.

Knight argued that the difficulty of the forecasting process extends far beyond the impossibility of applying mathematical propositions to forecasting the future. Although he makes no explicit reference to Bayes, he was dubious that we can learn much from an empirical evaluation of the frequency of past occurrences. *A priori* reasoning, he insisted, cannot eliminate indeterminateness from the future. In the end, he considered reliance on the frequency of past occurrences extremely hazardous.

Why? Extrapolation of past frequencies is the favored method for arriving at judgments about what lies ahead. The ability to extrapolate from experience is what differentiates adults from children. Experienced people come to recognize that inflation is somehow associated with high interest rates, that moral character is desirable in the choice of whom we play poker with and whom we marry, that cloudy skies frequently presage bad weather, and that driving at high speed along city streets is dangerous.

Business managers regularly extrapolate from the past to the future but often fail to recognize when conditions are beginning to change from poor to better or from better to worse. They tend to identify turning points only after the fact. If they were better at sensing imminent changes, the abrupt shifts in profitability that happen so often would never occur. The prevalence of surprise in the world of business is evidence that uncertainty is more likely to prevail than mathematical probability.

The reason, Knight explains, is this:

> [Any given] "instance" . . . is so entirely unique that there are no others or not a sufficient number to make it possible to tabulate enough like it to form a basis for any inference of value about any real probability in the case we are interested in. *The same obviously applies to the most of conduct and not to business decisions alone.*[10] (Italics are mine.)

Mathematical probabilities relate to large numbers of independent observations of homogeneous events, such as rolls of the dice—in what Knight describes as the "apodeictic certainty" of games of chance.[*][11] But no event is ever identical to an earlier event—or to an event yet to happen. In any case, life is too short for us to assemble the large samples that such analysis requires. We may make statements like "We are 60% certain that profits will be up next year," or "Sixty percent of our products will do better next year." But Knight insisted that the errors in such forecasts "must be radically distinguished from probability or chance. . . . [I]t is meaningless and fatally misleading to speak of the probability, in an objective sense, that a judgment is correct."[12] Knight, like Arrow, had no liking for clouds of vagueness.

Knight's ideas are particularly relevant to financial markets, where all decisions reflect a forecast of the future and where surprise occurs regularly. Louis Bachelier long ago remarked, "Clearly the price considered most likely by the market is the true current price: if the market judged otherwise, it would quote not this price, but another price higher or lower." The consensus forecasts embedded in security prices mean that those prices will not change if the expected happens. The

---

[*]Knight rarely uses such arcane words. "Apodeictic" means incontestable, necessarily true because logically certain.

volatility of stock and bond prices is evidence of the frequency with which the expected fails to happen and investors turn out to be wrong. Volatility is a proxy for uncertainty and must be accommodated in measuring investment risk.

Galton, a Victorian, would have expected prices to be volatile around a stable mean. Knight and Bachelier, neither of them a Victorian, are silent on precisely what central tendency would prevail, if any. We will have more to say about volatility later on.

Knight disliked John Maynard Keynes intensely, as he revealed when, in 1940, the University of Chicago decided to award Keynes an honorary degree. The occasion prompted Knight to write a rambling letter of protest to Jacob Viner, a distinguished member of the Department of Economics at Chicago. Viner, Knight declared, was the person reported to be responsible "more than anyone else" for the decision to honor Keynes and therefore was "the appropriate party to whom to express something of the shock I received from this news."[13]

Knight grumbled that Keynes's work, and the enthusiasm with which it had been greeted by academics and policymakers, had created "one of my most important . . . sources of difficulty in recent years." After crediting Keynes with "a very unusual intelligence, in the sense of ingenuity and dialectical skill," he went on to complain:

> I have come to consider such capacities, directed to false and subversive ends, as one of the most serious dangers in the whole project of education. . . . I regard Mr. Keynes's [views] with respect to money and monetary theory in particular . . . as, figuratively speaking, passing the keys of the citadel out of the window to the Philistines hammering at the gates.

Although most of the free-market economists at Chicago disagreed with Keynes's conviction that the capitalist system needed a frequent dose of government intervention if it was to survive, they did not share Knight's disdain. They deemed it fit to honor Keynes as a brilliant innovator of economic theory.

Knight may simply have been jealous, for he and Keynes shared the same philosophical approach. For example, they both distrusted classical theories based on the laws of mathematical probability or assumptions of certainty as guides to decision-making. And they both despised the "the mean statistical view of life."[14] In an essay written in 1938, titled "My Early Beliefs," Keynes condemns as "flimsily based [and] disastrously mistaken" the assumption of classical economists that human nature is reasonable.[15] He alludes to "deeper and blinder passions" and to the "insane and irrational springs of wickedness in most men." These were hardly the views of a man who was passing the keys of the citadel to the Philistines hammering at the gates.

Knight may have been annoyed that Keynes had carried the distinction between risk and uncertainty much further than he himself had carried it. And he must surely have been angered when he discovered that the sole reference Keynes made to him in *The General Theory of Employment, Interest and Money* was in a footnote that disparages one of his papers on the interest rate as "precisely in the traditional, classical mould," though Keynes also conceded that the paper "contains many interesting and profound observations on the nature of capital."[16] Only this, after Knight's pioneering explorations into risk and uncertainty fifteen years before.

Keynes was from the opposite end of the intellectual and social spectrum from Knight. He was born in 1883 to an affluent, well-known British family, one of whose ancestors had landed with William the Conqueror. As Robert Skidelsky, his most recent biographer, describes him, Keynes was "not just a man of establishments, but part of the élite of each establishment of which he was a member. There was scarcely a time when he did not look down at England, and much of the world, from a great height."[17] Among Keynes's close friends were prime ministers, financiers, philosophers Bertrand Russell and Ludwig Wittgenstein, and artists and writers such as Lytton Strachey, Roger Fry, Duncan Grant, and Virginia Woolf.

Keynes was educated at Eton and Cambridge, where he studied economics, mathematics, and philosophy under leading scholars. He was a superb essayist, as he demonstrated in presenting his controversial ideas and proposals.

Keynes's professional career began with an extended stint at the Treasury, including service in India and intense involvement in Treasury activities during the First World War. He then participated as chief Treasury representative at the Versailles peace negotiations after the war. Finding the treaty so vindictive that he was convinced it would lead to economic turmoil and political instability, he resigned his post to write a book titled *The Economic Consequences of the Peace*. The book soon became a best seller and established Keynes's international reputation.

Keynes subsequently returned to his beloved King's College at Cambridge to teach, write, and serve as the college's bursar and investment officer, all this while serving as chairman—and investment manager—of a major insurance company. He was an active player in the stock market, where his own fortunes fluctuated wildly. (Like many of his most famous contemporaries, he failed to predict the Great Crash of 1929). He also enriched King College's wealth by risk-taking on the Exchange. By 1936, Keynes had built a personal fortune from a modest inheritance into the equivalent of £10,000,000 in today's money.[18] He designed Britain's war financing during the Second World War, negotiated a large loan by the United States to Britain immediately after the war, and wrote much of the Bretton Woods agreements that established the postwar international monetary system.

Ideas came to Keynes in such a rush and in such volume that he often found himself at odds with something he had said or written earlier. That did not disturb him. "When somebody persuades me that I am wrong," he wrote, "I change my mind. What do *you* do?"[19]

In 1921, Keynes completed a book titled *A Treatise on Probability*. He had begun work on it shortly after graduating from Cambridge and had worked on it fitfully for about fifteen years; he even took it with him on his travels abroad, including a trip on horseback through Greece with the painter Duncan Grant. He struggled to convey novel ideas with the clarity he prized. He never quite broke away from his training in philosophy at Cambridge, where, he later reminisced, "'What *exactly* do you mean?' was the phrase most frequently on our lips. If it appeared under cross-examination that you did not mean *exactly* anything, you lay under a strong suspicion of meaning nothing whatever."[20]

A Treatise on Probability is a brilliant exploration of the meaning and applications of probability, much of it a critique of the work of earlier writers, many of whom have made their appearance in the earlier pages of this book. Unlike Knight, Keynes does not distinguish categorically between risk and uncertainty; in less precise fashion, he contrasts what is definable from what is undefinable when we contemplate the future. Like Knight, however, Keynes has little patience with decisions based on the frequency of past occurrences: He felt that Galton's peapod analogy was applicable to nature but irrelevant to human beings. He rejects analyses based on events but welcomes predictions based on propositions. His preferred expression is "degrees of belief—or the *a priori* probabilities, as they used to be called."[21]

Keynes begins the book with an attack on traditional views of probability; many of our old friends are victims, including Gauss, Pascal, Quetelet, and Laplace. He declares that probability theory has little relevance to real-life situations, especially when applied with the "incautious methods and exaggerated claims of the school of Laplace."[22]

An objective probability of some future event does exist—"it is not, that is to say, subject to human caprice"—but our ignorance denies us the certainty of knowing what that probability is; we can only fall back on estimates. "There is little likelihood," Keynes suggests, "of our discovering a method of recognizing particular probabilities, without any assistance whatever from intuition or direct judgment. . . . A proposition is not probable because we think it so."[23]

Keynes suggests that "we pass from the opinions of theorists to the experience of practical men." He pokes fun at the seat-of-the-pants method that most insurance companies use in calculating their premiums. He doubts that two equally intelligent brokers would consistently arrive at the same result: "It is sufficient if the premium he names *exceeds* the probable risk."[24] He cites the odds quoted by Lloyd's on August 23, 1912, on the three-way race for the presidency of the United States; the odds added up to 110%! The reinsurance rates in the insurance market on the *Waratagh*, a ship that disappeared off South Africa, varied from hour to hour as bits of wreckage were discovered and as a rumor spread that under similar circumstances a vessel had stayed afloat, not seriously damaged, for two months before being discovered. Yet the probability that the *Waratagh* had sunk remained constant even while the market's evaluation of that probability fluctuated wildly.

Keynes was scornful of what he refers to as "The Law of Great Numbers." Simply because similar events have been observed repeatedly in the past is a poor excuse for believing that they will probably occur in the future. Rather, our confidence in an outcome should be strengthened only when we can discover "a situation where each new series differs in some significant fashion from the others."[25]

He heaps scorn on the arithmetic mean, "a very inadequate axiom." Instead of adding up a series of observations and then dividing the sum by the total number of observations, "Equal suppositions would have equal consideration, if the . . . estimates had been multiplied together instead of added."[26] Granted, the arithmetic mean is simple to use, but Keynes quotes a French mathematician who had pointed out that nature is not troubled by difficulties of analysis, nor should humanity be so troubled.

Keynes rejects the term "events" as used by his predecessors in probability theory, because it implies that forecasts must depend on the mathematical frequencies of past occurrences. He preferred the term "proposition," which reflects degrees of belief about the probability of *future* events. Bradley Bateman, an economist who teaches at Grinnell College, has observed that probability to Keynes is the basis on which we analyze and evaluate propositions.[27]

If Keynes believed that probability reflects degrees of belief about the future, and that past events are only a modest part of the input, we might conclude that he regarded probability as a subjective concept. Not so. Modern though he is in so many ways, he occasionally revealed his Victorian background. At the time he wrote *A Treatise on Probability*, he believed that all rational people would in time come to recognize the correct probability of a certain outcome and would hold identical degrees of belief. "When once the facts are given which determine our knowledge, what is probable or improbable in these circumstances has been fixed objectively and is independent of our opinion."[28]

Yielding to criticism of this unrealistic view, Keynes later began to focus increasingly on how uncertainty influences decisions and, in turn, the world economy. At one point in the *Treatise* he declares, "Perception of probability, weight, and risk are all highly dependent on judgment," and "the basis of our degrees of belief is part of our human outfit."[29] Charles Lange, a statistician and an old friend, once remarked that he was pleased that "Maynard does not prefer algebra to earth."

Keynes's view of economics ultimately revolves around uncertainty—uncertainty as to how much a family will save or spend, uncertainty as to what portion of its accumulated savings a family will spend in the future (and when it will spend that portion), and, most important, uncertainty as to how much profit any given outlay on capital goods will produce. The decisions business firms make on how much to spend (and when to spend it) on new buildings, new machinery, new technology, and new forms of production constitute a dynamic force in the economy. The fact that those decisions are essentially irreversible, however, makes them extremely risky given the absence of any objective guide to the probability that they will turn out as planned.

As Frank Knight observed fifteen years before Keynes published *The General Theory*, "At the bottom of the uncertainty problem in economics is the forward-looking character of the economic process itself."[30] Because the economic environment is constantly changing, all economic data are specific to their own time period. Consequently they provide only a frail basis for generalizations. Real time matters more than time in the abstract, and samples drawn from the past have little relevance. What was 75% probable yesterday has an unknown probability tomorrow. A system that cannot rely on the frequency distribution of past events is peculiarly vulnerable to surprise and is inherently volatile.

Keynes had no use for a hypothetical economy in which past, present, and future are merged by an impersonal time machine into a single moment. Involuntary unemployment and disappointing profits occur too frequently for an economy to work as the classical economists had assumed it would. If people decide to save more and spend less, consumer spending will fall and investment will decline. The interest rate in any case might fail to fall in response to the higher propensity to save. Keynes argued that interest is a reward for parting with liquidity, not for refraining from consumption. Even if the interest rate does decline, it may not decline enough to encourage business managers to risk investing further capital in an economic environment in which animal spirits are lacking and in which shifting to a new set of decisions is costly. Decisions, once made, create a new environment with no opportunity to replay the old.

Another reason for a decline in investment spending may be that business firms have exhausted all opportunities for earning a profit. Keynes once remarked, "The Middle Ages built cathedrals and sang dirges. . . . [T]wo masses for the dead are twice as good as one; but not so two railways from London to York."[31] That same idea had appeared in a song popular during the Great Depression, "Brother, Can You Spare a Dime?" "Once I built a building, now it's done./Once I built a railroad, made it run."

Keynes and his followers focused on money and contracts to demonstrate that uncertainty rather than mathematical probability is the ruling paradigm in the real world. The desire for liquidity and the urge to cement future arrangements by legally enforceable agreements testify to the dominance of uncertainty in our decision-making. We are no longer willing to accept the guidance that the mathematical frequency of past events might provide.

Keynes rejected theories that ignored uncertainty. The "signal failure of [the classical doctrine] for the purposes of scientific prediction," he observed, "has greatly impaired, in the course of time, the prestige of its practitioners."[32] The classical economists, he charged, had reached a state where they were looked upon as "Candides, who . . . having left this world for the cultivation of their gardens, teach that all is for the best in the best of all possible worlds, provided we will let well alone."[33]

Impatient with Candide-based theories, Keynes proposed a course of action that was diametrically opposed to laissez-faire: a more active role for the government, not just in order to substitute government demand for waning private demand, but to reduce the uncertainties abroad in the economy. We have discovered over time that Keynes's cure has on occasion been worse than the disease and that his analysis has other, less visible, faults. Yet none of that can detract from his primary contribution to economic theory and the understanding of risk.

At the end of the single-paragraph first chapter of *The General Theory*, Keynes wrote: "[T]he characteristics . . . assumed by the classical theory happen not to be those of the economic society in which we actually live, with the result that its teaching is misleading and disastrous if we attempt to apply it to the facts of experience."[34] Given the state of the world in 1936, Keynes could hardly have concluded otherwise. Uncertainty must provide the core of the new economic theory.

In 1937, in response to criticisms of *The General Theory*, Keynes summed up his views:

> By "uncertain" knowledge . . . I do not mean merely to distinguish what is known for certain from what is only probable. The game of roulette is not subject, in this sense, to uncertainty. . . . The sense in which I am using the term is that in which the prospect of a European war is uncertain, or the price of copper and the rate of interest twenty years hence, or the obsolescence of a new invention. . . . About these matters, there is no scientific basis on which to form any calculable probability whatever. We simply do not know![35]

A tremendous idea lies buried in the notion that we simply do not know. Rather than frightening us, Keynes's words bring great news: we are not prisoners of an inevitable future. Uncertainty makes us free.

Consider the alternative. All the thinkers from Pascal to Galton told us that the laws of probability work because we have no control over the next throw of the dice, or where our next error in measurement will occur, or the influence of a static normality to which matters ultimately revert. In this context, everything in life is like Jacob Bernoulli's jar: we are free to pull out any pebble, but we cannot choose its color. As Laplace reminded us, "All events, even those which on account of their insignificance do not seem to follow the great laws of nature, are a result of it just as necessarily as the revolutions of the sun."[36]

This is, in short, a story of the inevitable. Where everything works according to the laws of probability, we are like primitive people—or gamblers—who have no recourse but to recite incantations to their gods. Nothing that we do, no judgment that we make, no response to our animal spirits, is going to have the slightest influence on the final result. It may appear to be a well-ordered world in which the proba-bilities yield to careful mathematical analysis, but each of us might just as well retire to a windowless prison cell—a fate that the flutter of a butterfly's wings billions of years ago may have ordained in any case.

What a bore! But thank goodness, the world of pure probability does not exist except on paper or perhaps as a partial description of nature. It has nothing to do with breathing, sweating, anxious, and creative human beings struggling to find their way out of the darkness.

That is good news, not bad news. Once we understand that we are not obliged to accept the spin of the roulette wheel or the cards we are dealt, we are free souls. Our decisions matter. We can change the world. Keynes's economic prescriptions reveal that as we make deci-sions we *do* change the world.

Whether that change turns out to be for better or for worse is up to us. The spin of the roulette wheel has nothing to do with it.

14

The Man Who Counted Everything Except Calories

W e have just witnessed Frank Knight's determination to elevate uncertainty to a central role in the analysis of risk and decision-making and the energy and eloquence with which Keynes mounted his attack on the assumptions of the classical economists. Yet faith in the reality of rational behavior and in the power of measurement in risk management persisted throughout all the turmoil of the Depression and the Second World War. Theories on these matters now began to move along sharply divergent paths, one traveled by the followers of Keynes ("We simply do not know") and the other by the followers of Jevons ("Pleasure, pain, labour, utility, value, wealth, money, capital, etc. are all notions admitting of quantity.")

During the quarter-century that followed the publication of Keynes's *General Theory*, an important advance in the understanding of risk and uncertainty appeared in the guise of the theory of games of strategy. This was a practical paradigm rooted in the Victorian conviction that measurement is indispensable in interpreting human behavior. The theory focuses on decision-making, but bears little resemblance to the many other theories that originated in games of chance.

Despite its nineteenth-century forebears, game theory represents a dramatic break from earlier efforts to incorporate mathematical inevitability into decision-making. In the utility theories of both Daniel Bernoulli and Jevons, the individual makes choices in isolation, unaware of what others might be doing. In game theory, however, two or more people try to maximize their utility simultaneously, each aware of what the others are about.

Game theory brings a new meaning to uncertainty. Earlier theories accepted uncertainty as a fact of life and did little to identify its source. Game theory says that *the true source of uncertainty lies in the intentions of others.*

From the perspective of game theory, almost every decision we make is the result of a series of negotiations in which we try to reduce uncertainty by trading off what other people want in return for what we want ourselves. Like poker and chess, real life is a game of strategy, combined with contracts and handshakes to protect us from cheaters.

But unlike poker and chess, we can seldom expect to be a "winner" in these games. Choosing the alternative that we judge will bring us the highest payoff tends to be the riskiest decision, because it may provoke the strongest defense from players who stand to lose if we have our way. So we usually settle for compromise alternatives, which may require us to make the best of a bad bargain; game theory uses terms like "maximin" and "minimax" to describe such decisions. Think of seller-buyer, landlord-tenant, husband-wife, lender-borrower, GM-Ford, parent-child, President-Congress, driver-pedestrian, boss-employee, pitcher-batter, soloist-accompanist.

Game theory was invented by John von Neumann (1903–1957), a physicist of immense intellectual accomplishment.[1] Von Neumann was instrumental in the discovery of quantum mechanics in Berlin during the 1920s, and he played a major role in the creation of the first American atomic bomb and, later, the hydrogen bomb. He also invented the digital computer, was an accomplished meteorologist and mathematician, could multiply eight digits by eight digits in his head, and loved telling ribald jokes and reciting off-color limericks. In his work with the military, he preferred admirals to generals because admirals were the heavier drinkers. His biographer Norman Macrae describes him as "excessively polite to everybody except . . . two long-suffering wives," one of whom once remarked, "He can count everything except calories."[2]

A colleague interested in probability analysis once asked von Neumann to define certainty. Von Neumann said first design a house and make sure the living-room floor will not give way. To do that, he suggested, "Calculate the weight of a grand piano with six men huddling over it to sing. Then triple that weight." That will guarantee certainty.

Von Neumann was born in Budapest to a well-to-do, cultured, jolly family. Budapest at the time was the sixth-largest city in Europe, prosperous and growing, with the world's first underground subway. Its literacy rate was over 90%. More than 25% of the population was Jewish, including the von Neumanns, although John von Neumann paid little attention to his Jewishness except as a source of jokes.

He was by no means the only famous product of pre-World War I Budapest. Among his contemporaries were famous physicists like himself—Leo Szilard and Edward Teller—as well as celebrities from the world of entertainment—George Solti, Paul Lukas, Leslie Howard (born Lazlo Steiner), Adolph Zukor, Alexander Korda, and, perhaps most famous of all, ZsaZsa Gabor.

Von Neumann studied in Berlin at a leading scientific institution that had considered Einstein unqualified for a research grant.[3] He went on to Göttingen, where he met such distinguished scientists as Werner Heisenberg, Enrico Fermi, and Robert Oppenheimer. During his first visit to the United States, in 1929, von Neumann fell in love with the country and spent most of his subsequent career, except for extended periods working for the U.S. government, at the Institute for Advanced Study in Princeton. His starting salary at the Institute in 1937 was $10,000, the equivalent of over $100,000 in current purchasing power. When Einstein joined the Institute in 1933, he had asked for a salary of $3,000; he received $16,000.

Von Neumann first presented his theory of games of strategy in a paper that he delivered in 1926, at the age of 23, to the Mathematical Society at the University of Göttingen; the paper appeared in print two years later. Robert Leonard of the University of Quebec, a leading historian of game theory, has surmised that this paper was not so much the product of a "detached moment of inspiration" as an effort by von

Neumann to focus his restless fancy on a subject that had been attract-
ing the attention of German and Hungarian mathematicians for some
time. Apparently the stimulus for the work was primarily mathematical,
with little or nothing to do with decision-making as such.

Although the subject matter of the paper appears to be trivial at first
glance, it is highly complex and mathematical. The subject is a rational
strategy for playing a childhood game called match-penny. Each of two
players turns up a coin at the same moment as the other. If both coins
are heads or if both are tails, player A wins. If different sides come up,
player B wins. When I was a boy, we played a variation of this game in
which my opponent and I took turns shouting either "Odds!" or
"Evens!" as, at an agreed call, we opened our fists to show either one
finger or two.

According to von Neumann, the trick in playing match-penny
against "an at least moderately intelligent opponent" lies not in trying
to guess the intentions of the opponent so much as in not revealing
your own intentions. Certain defeat results from any strategy whose
aim is to win rather than to avoid losing. (Note that dealing with the
possibility of losing appears here for the first time as an integral part of
risk management.) So you should play heads and tails in random fashion, simulating a machine that would systematically reveal each side of
the coin with a probability of 50%. You cannot expect to win by
employing this strategy, but neither can you expect to lose.

If you try to win by showing heads six times out of every ten plays,
your opponent will catch on to your game plan and will win an easy
victory. She will play tails six times out of every ten plays if she wins
when the pennies fail to match; she will play heads six times out of
every ten plays if she wins when the pennies do match.

So the only rational decision *for both players* is to show heads and
tails in random fashion. Then, over the long run, the pennies will
match half the time and will fail to match half the time. Fun for a little
while, but then boring.

The mathematical contribution von Neumann made with this
demonstration was the proof that this was the only outcome that could
emerge from rational decision-making by the two players. It is not the
laws of probability that decree the 50-50 payoff in this game. Rather,
it is the players themselves who *cause* that result. Von Neumann's paper
is explicit about this point:

... [E]ven if the rules of the game do not contain any elements of "hazard" (i.e., no draws from urns) ... dependence on ... the statistical element is such an intrinsic part of the game itself (if not of the world) that there is no need to introduce it artificially.[4]

The attention von Neumann's paper attracted suggests that he had something of mathematical importance to convey. It was only later that he realized that more than mathematics was involved in the theory of games.

In 1938, while he was at the Institute for Advanced Study socializing with Einstein and his friends, von Neumann met the German-born economist Oskar Morgenstern. Morgenstern became an instant acolyte. He took to game theory immediately and told von Neumann he wanted to write an article about it. Though Morgenstern's capability in mathematics was evidently not up to the task, he persuaded von Neumann to collaborate with him on a paper, a collaboration that extended into the war years. The results of their joint efforts was *Theory of Games and Economic Behavior*, the classic work in both game theory and its application to decision-making in economics and business. They completed the 650 pages of their book in 1944, but the wartime paper shortage made Princeton University Press hesitant to publish it. At last a member of the Rockefeller family personally subsidized the publication of the book in 1953.

The economic subject matter was not entirely new to von Neumann. He had had some interest in economics earlier, when he was trying to see how far he could go in using mathematics to develop a model of economic growth. Always the physicist as well as the mathematician, his primary focus was on the notion of equilibrium. "As [economics] deals throughout with quantities," he wrote, "it must be a mathematical science in matter if not in language ... a close analogy to the science of statical mechanics."

Morgenstern was born in Germany in 1902 but grew up and was educated in Vienna. By 1931, he had attained sufficient distinction as an economist to succeed Friedrich von Hayek as director of the prestigious Viennese Institute for Business Cycle Research. Though he was a Christian with a touch of anti-Semitism, he left for the United States in

1938, following the German invasion of Austria, and soon found a position on the economics faculty at Princeton.[5]

Morgenstern did not believe that economics could be used for predicting business activity. Consumers, business managers, and policymakers, he argued, all take such predictions into consideration and alter their decisions and actions accordingly. This response causes the forecasters to change their forecast, prompting the public to react once again. Morgenstern compared this constant feedback to the game played by Sherlock Holmes and Dr. Moriarty in their attempts to outguess each other. Hence, statistical methods in economics are useless except for descriptive purposes, "but the diehards don't seem to be aware of this."[6]

Morgenstern was impatient with the assumption of perfect foresight that dominated nineteenth-century economic theory. No one, he insisted, can know what everybody else is going to do at any given moment: "Unlimited foresight and economic equilibrium are thus irreconcilable with each other."[7] This conclusion drew high praise from Frank Knight and an offer by Knight to translate this paper by Morgenstern from German into English.

Morgenstern appears to have been short on charm. Nobel Laureate Paul Samuelson, the author of the long-run best-selling textbook in economics, once described him as "Napoleonic. . . . [A]lways invoking the authority of some physical scientists or other."[*8] Another contemporary recalls that the Princeton economics department "just hated Oskar."[9] Morgenstern himself complained about the lack of attention his beloved masterpiece received from others. After visiting Harvard in 1945 he noted "none of them" had any interest in game theory.[10] He reported in 1947 that a fellow economist named Röpke said that game theory "was Viennese coffeehouse gossip."[†] When he visited a group of distinguished economists in Rotterdam in 1950, he discovered that they "wanted to know nothing about [game theory] because it disturbs them."

---

*The feeling appears to have been mutual. Morgenstern took a dim view of Samuelson's knowledge of mathematics. Complaining that "[von Neumann] says [Samuelson] has murky ideas about stability," he predicted that "even in thirty years he won't absorb game theory!" See Leonard, 1994, p. 494n.

†Röpke, also a Christian, was far more emphatic than Morgenstern had been about his reasons for leaving Hitler's Germany.

Although an enthusiast for the uses of mathematics in economic analysis—he despised Keynes's nonrigorous treatment of expectations and described *The General Theory* as "simply horrible"—Morgenstern complained constantly about his problems with the advanced material into which von Neumann had lured him.[11] Throughout their collaboration Morgenstern held von Neumann in awe. "He is a mysterious man," Morgenstern wrote on one occasion. "The moment he touches something scientific, he is totally enthusiastic, clear, alive, then he sinks, dreams, talks superficially in a strange mixture. . . . One is presented with the incomprehensible."

The combination of the cool mathematics of game theory and the tensions of economics seemed a natural fit for a mathematician with an enthusiasm for economics and an economist with an enthusiasm for mathematics. But the stimulus to combine the two arose in part from a shared sense that, to use Morgenstern's words, the application of mathematics to economics was "in a lamentable condition."[12]

An imperial motivation was also there—the aspiration to make mathematics the triumphant master in the analysis of society as well as in the analysis of the natural sciences. While that approach would be welcomed by many social scientists today, it was probably the main source of the resistance that game theory encountered when it was first broadly introduced in the late 1940s. Keynes ruled the academic roost at the time, and he rejected any sort of mathematical description of human behavior.

The Theory of Games and Economic Behavior loses no time in advocating the use of the mathematics in economic decision-making. Von Neumann and Morgenstern dismiss as "utterly mistaken" the view that the human and psychological elements of economics stand in the way of mathematical analysis. Recalling the lack of mathematical treatment in physics before the sixteenth century or in chemistry and biology before the eighteenth century, they claim that the outlook for mathematical applications in those fields "at these early periods can hardly have been better than that in economics—*mutatis mutandis*—at present."[13]

Von Neumann and Morgenstern reject the objection that their rigidly mathematical procedures and their emphasis on numerical quantities are unrealistic simply because "the common individual . . . conducts his economic activities in a sphere of considerable haziness."[14] After all, people respond hazily to light and heat, too:

> [I]n order to build a science of physics, these phenomena [heat and light] had to be measured. And subsequently, the individual has come to use the results of such measurements—directly or indirectly—even in his everyday life. The same may obtain in economics at a future date. Once a fuller understanding of human behavior has been achieved with the aid of a theory that makes use of [measurement], the life of the individual may be materially affected. It is, therefore, not an unnecessary digression to study these problems.[15]

The analysis in *The Theory of Games and Economic Behavior* begins with the simple case of an individual who faces a choice between two alternatives, as in the choice between heads and tails in match-penny. But this time von Neumann and Morgenstern go more deeply into the nature of the decision, with the individual making a choice between two combinations of events instead of between two single possibilities.

They take as an example a man who prefers coffee to tea and tea to milk.[16] We ask him this question: "Do you prefer a cup of coffee to a glass that has a 50-50 chance of being filled with tea or milk?" He prefers the cup of coffee.

What happens when we reorder the preferences but ask the same question? This time the man prefers milk over both coffee and tea but still prefers coffee to tea. Now the decision between coffee for certain and a 50-50 chance of getting tea or milk has become less obvious than it was the first time, because now the uncertain outcome contains something he really likes (milk) as well as something he could just as well do without (tea). By varying the probabilities of finding tea or milk and by asking at what point the man is indifferent between the coffee for certain and the 50-50 gamble, we can develop a quantitative estimate—a hard number—to measure by how much he prefers milk to coffee and coffee to tea.

The example becomes more realistic when we translate it into a technique for measuring the utility—the degree of satisfaction—of possessing $1 compared to the utility of possessing a second dollar, for a total of $2. This man's favored outcome must now be $2, which takes the place of milk in the above example; no money takes the place of tea, the least favored outcome, and $1 becomes the middle choice and takes the place of coffee.

Once again we ask our subject to choose between a sure thing and a gamble. But in this case the choice is between $1 versus a gamble that pays either $2 or nothing. We set the odds in the gamble at a 50% chance of $2 and a 50% chance of nothing, giving it a mathematical expectancy of $1. If the man declares that he is indifferent between the $1 certain and the gamble, then he is neutral on the subject of risk at this low level of the gamble. According to the formula proposed by von Neumann and Morgenstern, the probability on the favorite possibility—in this case the $2 outcome—defines how much the subject prefers $1 over zero compared with how much he prefers $2 over zero. Here 50% means that his preference for $1 over zero is half as great as his preference for $2 over zero. Under these circumstances, the utility of $2 is double the utility of $1.

The response might well differ with other people or under other circumstances. Let us see what happens when we increase the amount of money involved and change the probabilities in the gamble. Assume now that this man is indifferent between $100 certain and a gamble with a 67% probability of paying $200 and a 33% probability of coming up zero. The mathematical expectancy of this gamble is $133; in other words, the man's preference for the certain outcome—$100—is now larger than it was when only a couple of dollars were involved. The 67% probability on $200 means that his preference for $100 over zero is two-thirds as great as his preference for $200 over zero: the utility of the first $100 is larger than the utility of the second $100. The utility of the larger sum diminishes as the amount of money at risk increases from single digits to triple digits.

If all this sounds familiar, it is. The reasoning here is precisely the same as in the calculation of the "certainty equivalent," which we derived from Bernoulli's fundamental principle that the utility of increases in wealth will be inversely related to the amount of wealth already possessed (page 105). This is the essence of risk aversion—that is, how far we are willing to go in making decisions that may provoke others to make decisions that will have adverse consequences for us.

This line of analysis puts von Neumann and Morgenstern strictly in the classical mode of rationality, for rational people always understand their preferences clearly, apply them consistently, and lay them out in the fashion described here.

Alan Blinder, a long-time member of the Princeton economics faculty, co-author of a popular economics textbook, and Vice Chairman of the Federal Reserve Board from 1994 to 1996, has provided an interesting example of game theory.[17] The example appeared in a paper published in 1982. The subject was whether coordination is possible, or even desirable, between monetary policy, which involves the control of short-term interest rates and the supply of money, and fiscal policy, which involves the balance between federal government spending and tax revenue.

The players in this game are the monetary authorities of the Federal Reserve System and the politicians who determine the mix between government spending and tax revenues. The Federal Reserve authorities perceive control of inflation as their primary responsibility, which makes them favor economic contraction over economic expansion. They serve long terms—fourteen years for members of the Board, and until retirement age for presidents of the Federal Reserve Banks—so they can act with a good deal of independence from political pressures. The politicians, on the other hand, have to run regularly for election, which leads them to favor economic expansion over economic contraction.

The object of the game is for one player to force the other to make the unpleasant decisions. The Fed would prefer to have tax revenues exceed spending rather than to have the government suffer a budget deficit. A budget surplus would tend to hold inflation in check, thereby protecting the members of the Fed from being seen as the bad guys. The politicians, who worry about being elected, would prefer the Fed to keep interest rates low and the money supply ample. That policy would stimulate business activity and employment and would relieve Congress and the President of the need to incur a budget deficit. Neither side wants to do what the other side wants to do.

Blinder sets up a matrix that shows the preferences of each side in regard to each of three decisions by the other: contract, do nothing, or

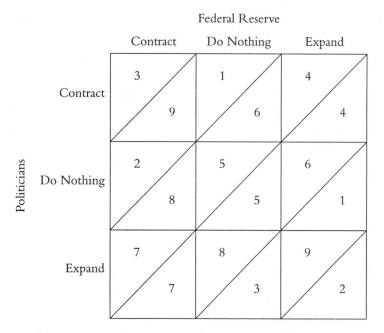

Blinder's payoff matrix.
(Adapted from Alan S. Blinder, 1982, "Issues in the Coordination of Monetary and Fiscal Policies," in Monetary Policy Issues in the 1980s, *Kansas City, Missouri: Federal Reserve Bank of Kansas City, pp. 3–34.)*

expand. The numbers above the diagonal in each square represent the order of preference of the members of the Fed; the numbers below the diagonals represent the order of preference of the politicians.

The highest-ranked preferences of the Fed (1, 2, and 3) appear in the upper left-hand corner of the matrix, where at least one side is contractionary while the other is either supportive or does nothing to rock the boat. The members of the Fed clearly prefer to have the politicians do their job for them. The three highest-ranked preferences of the politicians appear in the lower right-hand corner, where at least one side is expansionary while the other is either supportive or does nothing to rock the boat. The politicians clearly prefer to have the Fed adopt expansionary policies and for the politicians to do nothing. The lowest-ranked preferences of the politicians appear in the left-hand column, while the lowest-ranked preferences of the Fed appear in the bottom row. This is hardly a situation in which much accommodation is likely.

How will the game end? Assuming that the relationship between the Fed and the politicians is such that collaboration and coordination are impossible, the game will end in the lower left-hand corner where monetary policy is contractionary and fiscal policy is expansionary. This is precisely the outcome that emerged in the early Reagan years, when Blinder wrote this paper.

Why this outcome and no other? First, both sides are displaying their character here—an austere Fed and generous politicians. Under our assumption that the Fed cannot persuade the politicians to run a budget surplus and that the politicians cannot persuade the Fed to lower interest rates, neither side has any desire to alter its preferences nor can either dare to be simply neutral.

Look upward and to the right from those two 7s. Note that there is no number below the diagonal (the politicians' preference) looking upward on the left-hand vertical that is lower than 7; there is no number above the diagonal (the Fed's preference) looking horizontally to the right that is lower than 7. As long as the Fed is contractionary and the politicians are expansionary, both sides are making the best of a bad bargain.

That is not the case in the upper right-hand corner, where the Fed's monetary policy is less tight and a budget surplus emerges. Looking left horizontally and above the diagonals, we note that both the choices rank higher than 4: the Fed would rather do nothing or even be contractionary as compared to contributing to a business expansion that might end up in an inflationary situation. The opposite view would prevail among the politicians. Looking downward vertically, we find that both the choices rank higher than 4: the politicians would rather do nothing or run a deficit than follow a policy that cost them their jobs if their constituents lose their jobs as a result.

This outcome is known as a Nash Equilibrium, named after John Nash, another Princetonian and one of the 1994 winners of the Nobel Prize for his contributions to game theory.[18] Under the Nash Equilibrium the outcome, though stable, is less than optimal. Both sides would obviously prefer almost anything to this one. Yet they cannot reach a better bargain unless they drop their adversarial positions and work together on a common policy that would give each a supportive, or at least a neutral, role that would keep them from getting into each other's way. An example of that radically different state of affairs arose in 1994, when Fed policy was contractionary and the politicians were uncharacteristically willing to stand by without interfering.

Blinder's game reveals a keen insight into the way contesting powers in Washington behave toward one another. But it can be generalized into many other situations: Drop the bomb, do nothing, or sue for peace. Cut prices, do nothing, or raise prices. Bet your poker hand on the basis of the probabilities, fold, or bluff.

In Blinder's example, the players know each other's intentions, which is seldom the case. It also fails to include the preferences of consumers, employees, and business managers, all of whom are very much involved in the outcome. When we change the rules by expanding the number of players or by restricting the information available to the players, we have no choice but to resort to higher mathematics. As von Neumann and Morgenstern remarked, ". . . what a complexity of theoretical forms must be expected in social theory."

In August 1993, the Federal Communications Commission decided to auction off wireless communications rights. Two licenses would be issued for each of 51 zones around the country; no bidder could acquire more than one license in any zone. The usual procedure in such auctions is to call for sealed bids and to award the contract to the highest bidders. This time, acting on the advice of Paul Milgrom, a Stanford University professor, the FCC chose to conduct the auction according to game theory, calling it a "Spectrum Auction."

First, all bids would be open, so that each contestant would always know what all the others were doing. Second, there would be successive rounds of bidding until no contestant wanted to raise its bid any higher. Third, between rounds, contestants could switch their bid from one zone to another or could bid simultaneously for licenses in adjoining zones; since there is an economic advantage in having licenses in adjoining zones, a particular license might be worth more to one party than it would be to another. In short, each decision would be based on the known decisions of the other players.

The contestants found that making decisions was no easy matter. Each of them had to guess about the intentions of the others, studying their reputation for aggressiveness, their financial capacity, and their existing licensing structures. On occasion, a properly placed bid by one contestant would clearly signal its intentions to the others, thereby avoiding a cycle of competitive bidding for some particular license. Pacific Telesis, which hired Milgrom as their consultant in the auction, went so far as to take out full-page ads in cities where potential competitors were located to make clear their determination to win no matter what. Some contestants joined together to prevent costly bidding for the same license.

The auction went on for 112 rounds over three months and brought the government $7.7 billion. Although some argued that the government could have raised more money if the FCC had prohibited the alliances, the allocation of licenses in the end probably turned out to be more efficient in terms of the economies of building franchises than it would have been under the traditional procedure.

The motivation to avoid destructive bidding competitions is understandable. The highest bidder in an auction of this kind often suffers what is known as the Winner's Curse—overpaying out of a determination to win. The Winner's Curse does not need a fancy auction—the same curse may be visited on an investor in a hurry to buy a stock on which someone has provided a hot tip. To avoid the curse, trading sometimes takes place on computer screens in a manner that closely resembles the spectrum auction. The players—usually large financial institutions like pension funds or mutual funds—are anonymous, but all bids and offers are displayed on the screen together with reservation prices above which the investor will not buy and below which the seller will not sell.

In January 1995, the publication *Pensions and Investments* reported on another application of game theory in making investments. ANB Investment Management & Trust in Chicago had introduced a strategy explicitly designed to avoid the Winner's Curse. The chief investment officer, Neil Wright, saying he had based the strategy on the Nash Equilibrium, claimed that the Winner's Curse is usually associated with stocks that have abnormally wide price ranges, which "means there is a lot of uncertainty about how the company will do." A wide price range also indicates limited liquidity, which means that a relatively small volume of buying or selling will have a significant impact on the price of the stock. Wright accordingly planned to select his portfolio from stocks with narrow trading ranges, an indication that they are priced around consensus views, with sellers and buyers more or less evenly matched. The assumption is that such stocks can be bought for little more than their consensus valuation.

Von Neumann and Morgenstern based *The Theory of Games and Economic Behavior* on one essential element of behavior: the winnings that will accrue to an individual who maximizes his utility—makes the best of the available tradeoffs within the constraints set by the game theory—will depend upon how much he "can get if he behaves 'rationally.' This 'can get' [the winnings he can expect] is, of course, presumed to be a minimum; he may get more if others make mistakes (behave irrationally)."[19]

This stipulation has posed a major problem for critics, including distinguished behavioral psychologists like Daniel Ellsberg and Richard Thaler, whom we will meet later. In a highly critical paper published in 1991, the historian Philip Mirowski asserted, "All is not well in the House of Game Theory—in every dreamhouse a heartache—and signs of pathology can no longer be ignored."[20] He cites criticisms by Nobel Prize winners Henry Simon, Kenneth Arrow, and Paul Samuelson. He claims that game theory would never have amounted to anything had von Neumann not sold it to the military; he even goes so far as to speculate, "Some laid the blame for the escalation of nuclear weaponry directly at the door of game theory."[21] Indeed, Mirowski claims that Morgenstern was a "godsend" to von Neumann because he proposed economists as an audience for game theory when no one else was interested. Mirowski is scathing about the naiveté and oversimplification of their definitions of "that sadly abused word," rationality, which he describes as "a strange *potage*."[22]

Yet, game theory's assumption of rational behavior, and von Neumann and Morgenstern's dream that such behavior can be measured and expressed in numbers, has unleashed a flood of exciting theories and practical applications. As the examples I have offered make clear, its influence has reached far beyond the military.

During the 1950s and 1960s efforts were renewed to broaden the study of rationality, particularly in economics and finance. Some of the ideas advanced then seem lacking in substance today; in Chapters 16 and 17 we will subject those ideas to critical analysis. But we must understand that, up to about 1970, much of the enthusiasm for rationality, for measurement, and for the use of mathematics in forecasting emerged from the optimism that accompanied the great victories of the Second World War.

The return of peacetime was heralded as an opportunity to apply the lessons learned so painfully during the long years of depression and war. Perhaps the dreams of the Enlightenment and the Victorian age might at last come true for all members of the human race. Keynesian economics was enlisted as a means of controlling the business cycle and promoting full employment. The aim of the Bretton Woods Agreements was to recapture the stability of the nineteenth-century gold standard. The International Monetary Fund and the World Bank were set up to nourish economic progress among disadvantaged people around the world. Meanwhile, the United Nations would keep peace among nations.

In this environment, the Victorian concept of rational behavior regained its former popularity. Measurement always dominates intuition: rational people make choices on the basis of information rather than on the basis of whim, emotion, or habit. Once they have analyzed all the available information, they make decisions in accord with well-defined preferences. They prefer more wealth to less and strive to maximize utility. But they are also risk-averse in the Bernoullian sense that the utility of additional wealth is inversely related to the amount already possessed.

With the concept of rationality so well defined and so broadly accepted in intellectual circles, its transformation into rules for governing risk and maximizing utility was bound to influence the world of investing and managing wealth. The setting was perfect.

The achievements that followed brought Nobel prizes to gifted scholars, and the definitions of risk and the practical applications that emerged from those achievements revolutionized investment management, the structure of markets, the instruments used by investors, and the behavior of the millions of people who keep the system working.

15

The Strange Case of the Anonymous Stockbroker

This chapter deals specifically with how to measure risk when we invest in securities. Impossible as that may sound, quantification of investment risk is a process that is alive, well, and regularly practiced by professionals in today's world of globalized investing. Charles Tschampion, a managing director of the $50 billion General Motors pension fund, recently remarked, "Investment management is not art, not science, it's engineering. . . . We are in the business of managing and engineering financial investment risk." The challenge for GM, according to Tschampion, "is to first not take more risk than we need to generate the return that is offered."[1] A high degree of philosophical and mathematical sophistication lies behind Tschampion's words.

Throughout most of the history of stock markets—about 200 years in the United States and even longer in some European countries—it never occurred to anyone to define risk with a number. Stocks were risky and some were riskier than others, and people let it go at that. Risk was in the gut, not in the numbers. For aggressive investors, the goal was simply to maximize return; the faint-hearted were content with savings accounts and high-grade long-term bonds.

The most authoritative statement on the subject of risk had been issued in 1830 and had been purposefully vague.[2] It appeared in the judge's decision in a lawsuit over the administration of the estate of John McLean of Boston. McLean had died on October 23, 1823, leaving $50,000 in trust for his wife to receive the "profits and income thereof" during her lifetime; on her death, the trustees were to distribute half the remainder to Harvard College and the other half, or "moiety," to Massachusetts General Hospital. When Mrs. McLean died in 1828, the estate was valued at only $29,450. Harvard and the hospital promptly joined in bringing suit against the trustees.

In rendering his decision in the case, Justice Samuel Putnam concluded that the trustees had conducted themselves "honestly and discreetly and carefully, according to the existing circumstances, in the discharge of their trusts." He declared that trustees cannot be held accountable for a loss of capital that was not "owing to their wilful default. . . . If that were otherwise, who would undertake such hazardous responsibility?" He continued with what came to be immortalized as the Prudent Man Rule:

> Do what you will, the capital is at hazard. . . . All that can be required of a trustee to invest, is, that he shall conduct himself faithfully and exercise a sound discretion. He is to observe how men of prudence, discretion, and intelligence manage their own affairs, not in regard to speculation, but in regard to the permanent disposition of their funds, considering the probable income, as well as the probable safety of the capital to be invested.

There the matter rested for 122 years.

In June 1952, the *Journal of Finance*, the leading academic journal in finance published a fourteen-page article titled "Portfolio Selection."[3] Its author was Harry Markowitz, an unknown 25-year-old graduate student at the University of Chicago. That paper was innovative on so many levels, and ultimately so influential both theoretically and in terms of practicality, that it earned Markowitz a Nobel Prize in Economic Science in 1990.

In choosing equity investing as his topic, Markowitz was dealing with a subject that serious journals up to that time had considered too dicey and speculative for sober academic analysis. Even more daring, Markowitz was dealing with the management of the investor's total wealth, the *portfolio*.* His main theme was that a portfolio of securities is entirely different from holdings considered individually.

He had no interest in the foolishness that characterized most stock-market literature, such as lessons from a ballet dancer on how to become a millionaire without really trying, or how to be recognized as a guru among market forecasters.[4] Nor did he make any effort to present his ideas in the simple-minded language typical of most articles about the stock market. At a time when any kind of mathematical treatment was rare in economics, particularly in finance—Jevons and von Neumann had cut a lot less ice up to that point than they had hoped—ten of the fourteen pages that make up Markowitz's article carry equations or complicated graphs.

Markowitz is parsimonious in providing footnotes and bibliography: he makes only three references to other writers in a setting where many academics measured accomplishment by the number of footnotes an author could manage to compile. This failure to credit his intellectual forebears is curious: Markowitz's methodology is a synthesis of the ideas of Pascal, de Moivre, Bayes, Laplace, Gauss, Galton, Daniel Bernoulli, Jevons, and von Neumann and Morgenstern. It draws on probability theory, on sampling, on the bell curve and dispersion around the mean, on regression to the mean, and on utility theory. Markowitz has told me that he knew all these ideas but was not familiar with their authors, though he had invested a good deal of time studying von Neumann and Morgenstern's book on economic behavior and utility.

Markowitz placed himself solidly in the company of those who see human beings as rational decision-makers. His approach reflects the spirit of the early years after the Second World War, when many social scientists set about reviving the Victorian faith in measurement and the belief that the world's problems could be solved.

---

*The word has a Latin root, from *portare*, to carry, and *foglio*, leaf or sheet. *Portfolio* has thus come to mean a collection of paper assets.

Strangely, Markowitz had no interest in equity investment when he first turned his attention to the ideas dealt with in "Portfolio Selection." He knew nothing about the stock market. A self-styled "nerd" as a student, he was working in what was then the relatively young field of linear programming. Linear programming, which happened to be an innovation to which John von Neumann had made significant contributions, is a means of developing mathematical models for minimizing costs while holding outputs constant, or for maximizing outputs while holding costs constant. The technique is essential for dealing with problems like those faced by an airline that aims to keep a limited number of aircraft as busy as possible while flying to as many destinations as possible.

One day, while waiting to see his professor to discuss a topic for his doctoral dissertation, Markowitz struck up a conversation with a stock broker sharing the waiting room who urged him to apply linear programming to the problems investors face in the stock market. Markowitz's professor seconded the broker's suggestion, enthusiastically, though he himself knew so little about the stock market that he could not advise Markowitz on how or where to begin the project. He referred Markowitz to the dean of the business school, who, he hoped, might know something about the subject.

The dean told Markowitz to read John Burr Williams' *The Theory of Investment Value*, an influential book on finance and business management. Williams was a scrappy, impatient man who had launched a successful career as a stock broker in the 1920s but had returned to Harvard as a graduate student in 1932, at the age of thirty, hoping to find out what had caused the Great Depression (he didn't). *The Theory of Investment Value*, published in 1938, was his Ph.D. thesis.

Markowitz dutifully went to the library and sat down to read. The book's very first sentence did the trick for him: "No buyer considers all securities equally attractive at their present market prices . . . on the contrary, he seeks 'the best at the price.'"[5] Many years later, when Markowitz was telling me about his reaction, he recalled, "I was struck with the notion that you should be interested in risk as well as return."

That "notion" seems unremarkable enough in the 1990s, but it attracted little interest in 1952, or, for that matter, for more than two decades after Markowitz's article was published. In those days, judgments about the performance of a security were expressed in terms of how much money the investor made or lost. Risk had nothing to do with it. Then, in the late 1960s, the aggressive, performance-oriented managers of mutual fund portfolios began to be regarded as folk heroes, people like Gerry Tsai of the Manhattan Fund ("What is the Chinaman doing?" was a popular question along Wall Street) and John Hartwell of the Hartwell & Campbell Growth Fund ("[Performance means] seeking to get better than average results over a fairly long period of time—consistently").[6]

It took the crash of 1973–1974 to convince investors that these miracle-workers were just high rollers in a bull market and that they too should be interested in risk as well as return. While the Standard & Poor's 500 fell by 43% from December 1972 to September 1974, the Manhattan Fund lost 60% and the Hartwell & Cambell Fund fell by 55%.

This was a dark time, one marked by a series of ominous events: Watergate, skyrocketing oil prices, the emergence of persistent inflationary forces, the breakdown of the Bretton Woods Agreements, and an assault on the dollar so fierce that its foreign exchange value fell by 50%.

The destruction of wealth in the bear markets of 1973–1974 was awesome, even for investors who had thought they had been investing conservatively. After adjustment for inflation, the loss in equity values from peak to trough amounted to 50%, the worst performance in history other than the decline from 1929 to 1931. Worse, while bondholders in the 1930s actually gained in wealth, long-term Treasury bonds lost 28% in price from 1972 to the bottom in 1974 while inflation was running at 11% a year.

The lessons learned from this debacle persuaded investors that "performance" is a chimera. The capital markets are not accommodating machines that crank out wealth for everyone on demand. Except in limited cases like holding a zero-coupon debt obligation or a fixed-rate certificate of deposit, investors in stocks and bonds have no power over the return they will earn. Even the rate on savings accounts is set at the whim of the bank, which responds to the changing interest rates in the markets themselves. Each investor's return depends on what other investors will pay for assets at some point in the uncertain future, and the behavior of countless other investors is something that no one can control, or even reliably predict.

On the other hand, investors *can* manage the risks that they take. Higher risk should in time produce more wealth, but only for investors who can stand the heat. As these simple truths grew increasingly obvious over the course of the 1970s, Markowitz became a household name among professional investors and their clients.

Markowitz's objective in "Portfolio Selection" was to use the notion of risk to construct portfolios for investors who "consider expected return a desirable thing *and* variance of return an undesirable thing."[7] The italicized "and" that links return and variance is the fulcrum on which Markowitz builds his case.

Markowitz makes no mention of the word "risk" in describing his investment strategy. He simply identifies variance of return as the "undesirable thing" that investors try to minimize. Risk and variance have become synonymous. Von Neumann and Morgenstern had put a number on utility; Markowitz put a number on investment risk.

Variance is a statistical measurement of how widely the returns on an asset swing around their average. The concept is mathematically linked to the standard deviation; in fact, the two are essentially interchangeable. The greater the variance or the standard deviation around the average, the less the average return will signify about what the outcome is likely to be. A high-variance situation lands you back in the head-in-the-oven-feet-in-the-refrigerator syndrome.

Markowitz rejects Williams' premise that investing is a single-minded process in which the investor bets the ranch on what appears to be "the best at the price." Investors diversify their investments, because diversification is their best weapon against variance of return. "Diversification," Markowitz declares, "is both observed and sensible; a rule of behavior which does not imply the superiority of diversification must be rejected both as a hypothesis and as a maxim."

The strategic role of diversification is Markowitz's key insight. As Poincaré had pointed out, the behavior of a system that consists of only a few parts that interact strongly will be unpredictable. With such a system you can make a fortune or lose your shirt with one big bet. In a diversified portfolio, by contrast, some assets will be rising in price even when other assets are falling in price; at the very least, the rates of return among the assets will differ. The use of diversification to reduce volatility appeals to everyone's natural risk-averse preference for certain rather than uncertain outcomes. Most investors choose the lower expected return on a diversified portfolio instead of betting the ranch, even when the riskier bet might have a chance of generating a larger payoff—if it pans out.

Although Markowitz never mentions game theory, there is a close resemblance between diversification and von Neumann's games of strategy. In this case, one player is the investor and the other player is the stock market—a powerful opponent indeed and secretive about its intentions. Playing to win against such an opponent is likely to be a sure recipe for losing. By making the best of a bad bargain—by diversifying instead of striving to make a killing—the investor at least maximizes the probability of survival.

The mathematics of diversification helps to explain its attraction. While the return on a diversified portfolio will be equal to the average of the rates of return on its individual holdings, its volatility will be *less than* the average volatility of its individual holdings. This means that diversification is a kind of free lunch at which you can combine a group of risky securities with high expected returns into a relatively low-risk portfolio, so long as you minimize the covariances, or correlations, among the returns of the individual securities.

Until the 1990s, for example, most Americans regarded foreign securities as too speculative and too difficult to manage to be appropriate investments. So they invested just about all their money at home. That parochial view was costly, as the following calculations demonstrate.

From 1970 to 1993, the Standard & Poor's Index of 500 stocks brought its investors a total of capital appreciation plus income that averaged 11.7% a year. The volatility of the Index's return, as measured by its standard deviation, averaged 15.6% a year; this meant that about two-thirds of the annual returns fell between 11.7% + 15.6%, or 27.3% on the high side, and 11.7% − 15.6%, or −3.9% on the low side.

The major markets outside the United States are usually tracked by an index published by Morgan Stanley & Company that covers Europe, Australia, and the Far East. This index is known as EAFE for short; the regulars in these markets pronounce it "Eee-fuh." EAFE's average annual return for a dollar-based investor from 1970 to 1993 was 14.3% versus S&P's 11.7%, but EAFE was also more volatile. Largely because of Japan, and because foreign market returns are translated back into a dollar that fluctuates in value in the foreign exchange markets, EAFE's standard deviation of 17.5% was over two full percentage points above the volatility of the S&P 500.

EAFE and the U.S. markets do not usually move up and down together, which is why international diversification makes good sense. If an investor's portfolio had held 25% of its assets in EAFE and 75% in the S&P since 1970, its standard deviation of 14.3% would have been *lower than either the S&P or EAFE*, even while it was producing an average return that bettered the S&P 500 alone by an average of 0.6% a year.

An even more dramatic illustration of the power of diversification appears in the accompanying chart, which shows the track record of 13 so-called emerging stock markets in Europe, Latin America, and Asia from January 1992 through June 1994. The average monthly return of each market is plotted on the vertical axis; each market's

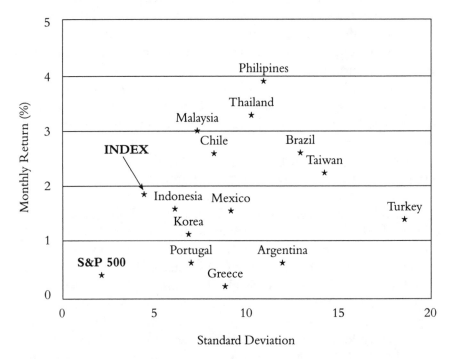

The blessings of diversification. The track records of 13 emerging stock markets compared to the index (average of 13) and the S&P 500 from January 1992 through June 1994. The data are in percentages per month.

monthly standard deviation of return is plotted on the horizontal axis. The chart also shows an equally weighted index of the 13 markets as well as the performance of the S&P 500 over the same time period.

Although many investors think of emerging markets as a homogeneous group, the graph shows that these 13 markets tend to be largely independent of one another. Malaysia, Thailand, and the Philippines had returns of 3% a month or better, but Portugal, Argentina, and Greece were barely in the black. Volatilities ranged from about 6% all the way out to nearly 20% *a month*. There is plenty of heat in this oven.

The lack of correlation, or low covariance, among the markets caused the index to have the lowest standard deviation of any of its 13 components. A simple average of the monthly standard deviations of the twelve markets works out to 10.0%; the actual standard deviation of the diversified portfolio was only 4.7%. Diversification works.

Note that the emerging markets were much riskier than the U.S. stock market over this 18-month period. They were also a lot more profitable, which explains why investors were so enthusiastic about these markets at the time.

The riskiness of these markets came to light just eight months after the end of the time period covered here. Had the analysis been extended to February 1995, it would have included the Mexican debacle at the end of 1994; the Mexican market fell by 60% between June 1994 and February 1995. From January 1992 to February 1995, the average return of the 13 markets was only a little over 1% a month, down from nearly 2% during the time span shown on the chart, while the standard deviation of the index jumped from under 5% to 6% a month; an investor in Mexico and Argentina would have ended up losing money.* The Philipines, the best-performing market, dropped from 4% a month to only 3% a month. Meanwhile, the performance of the S&P 500 showed virtually no change at all.

---

*The standard deviation of the Mexican market alone leapt from 8% to 10% a month (four times the monthly volatility of the S&P 500) to better than 15% a month during the first half of 1995.

By substituting a statistical stand-in for crude intuitions about uncertainty, Markowitz transformed traditional stock-picking into a procedure for selecting what he termed "efficient" portfolios. Efficiency, a term adopted from engineering by economists and statisticians, means maximizing output relative to input, or minimizing input relative to output. Efficient portfolios minimize that "undesirable thing" called variance while simultaneously maximizing that "desirable thing" called getting rich. This process is what prompted Tschampion 30 years later to describe the managers of the General Motors pension fund as "engineers."

Investors will always want to own securities that represent "the best at the price." The expected return of a portfolio made up of such securities will be the mean, or average, of the expectations for each of the individual holdings. But holdings that appear to offer the best returns frequently disappoint while others exceed the investor's fondest hopes. Markowitz assumed that the probabilities of actual portfolio returns above and below the mean expectation will distribute themselves into a nice, symmetrically balanced Gaussian normal curve.

The spread of that curve around the mean, from loss to gain, reflects the variance of the portfolio—with the range of possible outcomes reflecting the likelihood that the portfolio's actual rate of return will differ from its expected rate of return. This is what Markowitz meant when he introduced the concept of variance to measure risk, or the uncertainty of return; the combined approach to risk and return is commonly referred to by professionals and academics as mean/variance optimization. Common stocks have a much wider range of possible results than an obligation of the U.S. Treasury that will come due and pay off in 90 days; the return on the Treasury obligation has almost no uncertainty, because buyers will see their money again so soon.

Markowitz reserved the term "efficient" for portfolios that combine the best holdings at the price with the least of the variance— "optimization" is the technical word. The approach combines two clichés that investors learn early in the game: nothing ventured, nothing gained, but don't put all your eggs in one basket.

It is important to recognize that there is no one efficient portfolio that is more efficient than all others. Thanks to linear programing, Markowitz's method produces a menu of efficient portfolios. Like any menu, this one has two sides: what you want is on one side and the cost of what you want is on the other. The higher the expected return, the greater the risks involved. But each efficient portfolio on the menu will have the highest expected return for any given level of risk or the lowest level of risk for any expected return.

Rational investors will select the portfolio that best suits their taste for either aggressive objectives or defensive objectives. In the tradition of von Neumann and Morgenstern, the system provides a method to maximize each investor's utility. This is the only point in the Markowitz system in which gut matters. All else is measurement.

"Portfolio Selection" revolutionized the profession of investment management by elevating risk to equal importance with expected return. That paper, together with the book by the same name that Markowitz wrote in 1959, provided the groundwork for just about all of the theoretical work in finance that followed. It has also supported a variety of applications over time, ranging from techniques of stock selection and the allocation of portfolios between stocks and bonds to the valuation and management of options and more complex derivative securities.

Despite its importance, critics of "Portfolio Selection" have turned Markowitz's work into a punching bag, attacking from every side the entire set of assumptions that support it. Some of the problems they have raised are more mechanical and technical than substantive and have been overcome. Other problems continue to stir controversy.

The first is whether investors are rational enough in their decision-making to follow the prescription that Markowitz set out for them. If intuition triumphs over measurement in investing, the whole exercise could turn out to be a waste of time and a flawed explanation of why markets behave as they do.

Another criticism questions whether variance is the proper proxy for risk. Here the consequences are less clear. If investors perceive risk as something different from variance, some other measure might serve equally well and still preserve Markowitz's optimizing approach to risk and return. And perhaps not.

Finally, what would happen if Markowitz's assumption that there is a positive relationship between risk and return fails to survive empirical tests? If high returns are systematically available on low-risk securities, or if you land in the soup with securities you thought were low-risk, a retreat to the drawing board will be necessary.

We shall deal here briefly with the technical problems and then at greater length with the question of how well variance serves as a proxy for risk. Investor rationality is so important a matter that we devote Chapters 16 and 17 to it; investors, after all, are just people, although engaged in a particular activity, which means that the whole question of human rationality is involved.

The technical problems arise from Markowitz's assumption that investors will have no difficulty estimating the inputs to his model—expected returns, variances, and the covariances among all the individual holdings. But, as Keynes emphasized in *A Treatise on Probability* and later as well, the use of data from the past is dangerous. And degrees of belief do not always lend themselves to precise measurement, particularly with the precision that the Markowitz approach requires. As a practical matter, most applications of the approach combine past experience with forecasts, though investors recognize that a significant margin of error surrounds the results of such calculations. In addition, the sensitivity of the process to small differences in estimates of the inputs makes the results even more tentative.

The most difficult step is in amassing the calculations required to measure how each individual stock or bond might vary in relation to each other stock or bond. William Baumol, the author of the paper demonstrating how long-term trends in productivity regress to the mean, calculated as late as 1966—fourteen years after the appearance of "Portfolio Selection"—that a single run to select efficient portfolios on the computers of that time would cost from $150 to $350, even assuming that the estimates of the necessary inputs were accurate. A more elaborate search would have run into thousands of dollars.[8]

Markowitz himself was concerned about obstacles to the practical use of his ideas. In cooperation with William Sharpe—a graduate student who later shared the Nobel Prize with him—Markowitz made it possible to skip over the whole problem of calculating covariances among the individual securities. His solution was to estimate how each security varies in relation to the market as a whole, a far simpler matter. This technique subsequently led to Sharpe's development of what has come to be known as the Capital Asset Pricing Model, which analyzes how financial assets would be valued if all investors religiously followed Markowitz's recommendations for building portfolios. CAPM, as it is known, uses the term "beta" to describe the average volatility of individual stocks or other assets relative to the market as a whole over some specific period of time. The AIM Constellation Fund that we looked at in Chapter 12, for example, had a beta of 1.36 during the years 1983 to 1995, which means that AIM tended to move up or down 1.36% every time the S&P 500 moved up or down 1%; it tended to fall 13.6% every time the market dropped 10%, and so on. The more stodgy American Mutual Fund had a beta of only 0.80%, indicating that it was significantly less volatile than the S&P 500.

Another mathematical problem stems from the idea that a portfolio, or the security markets themselves, can be described with only two numbers: expected return and variance. Dependence on just those two numbers is appropriate if, and only if, security returns are normally distributed on a bell curve like Gauss's. No outliers are permitted, and the array of results on either side of the mean must be symmetrically distributed.

When the data are not normally distributed, the variance may fail to reflect 100% of the uncertainties in the portfolio. Nothing is perfect in the real world, so this is indeed a problem. But it is more of a problem to some investors than to others. For many, the data fit the normal distribution closely enough to be a useful guide to portfolio decisions and calculations of risk. For others, such imperfections have become a source of developing new kinds of strategies that will be described later on.

The matter of defining risk in terms of a number is crucial. How can investors decide how much risk to take unless they can ascribe some order of magnitude to the risks they face?

The portfolio managers at BZW Global Investors (formerly Wells Fargo–Nikko Investment Advisors) once built this dilemma into an interesting story. A group of hikers in the wilderness came upon a bridge that would greatly shorten their return to their home base. Noting that the bridge was high, narrow, and rickety, they fitted themselves out with ropes, harnesses, and other safeguards before starting across. When they reached the other side, they found a hungry mountain lion patiently awaiting their arrival.[9]

I have a hunch that Markowitz, with his focus on volatility, would have been taken by surprise by that mountain lion. Kenneth Arrow, a man who thinks about risks in many different dimensions and who understands the difference between the quantifiable and the messy, would be more likely to worry that the mountain lion, or some other peril, might be waiting at the other side of the bridge.

Nevertheless, volatility, or variance, has an intuitive appeal as a proxy for risk. Statistical analysis confirms what intuition suggests: most of the time, an increase in volatility is associated with a decline in the price of the asset.[10] Moreover, our gut tells us that uncertainty should be associated with something whose value jumps around a lot over a wide range. Most assets whose value is given to springing up violently tend to collapse with equal violence. If you were asked to rank the riskiness of shares of the Brazil Fund, shares of General Electric, a U.S. Treasury bond due in thirty years, and a U.S. Treasury bill due in ninety days, the ranking would be obvious. So would the relative volatility of these four securities. The overwhelming importance of volatility is evident in the role it plays in fashioning the risk-hedging instruments known as derivatives: options, swaps, and other instruments tailored to specific investor requirements.

Morningstar, the Chicago-based service that analyzes the performance of mutual funds, has provided an interesting example of how well volatility serves as a proxy for risk.[11] In May 1995, Morningstar reported that mutual funds that invest in bonds and that charge fees (known as 12b-1 fees) to cover their promotional expenses—fees that come out of the shareholders' pockets—had standard deviations that averaged about 10% higher than bond funds that do not charge such fees. Morningstar came to this conclusion: "The true cost of 12b-1 fees, then, at least for bond funds, is not a slightly lower return, but a higher risk investment. . . . [I]t is the logical consequence of moving marketing costs into the investment equation."

Yet there is no strong agreement on what causes volatility to fluctuate or even on what causes it in the first place. We can say that volatility sets in when the unexpected happens. But that is of no help, because, by definition, nobody knows how to predict the unexpected.

On the other hand, not everyone worries about volatility. Even though risk means that more things can happen than will happen—a definition that captures the idea of volatility—that statement specifies no time dimension. Once we introduce the element of time, the linkage between risk and volatility begins to diminish. Time changes risk in many ways, not just in its relation to volatility.

My wife's late aunt, a jolly lady, used to boast that she was my only in-law who never asked me what I thought the market was going to do. The reason, she explained, was this: "I didn't buy in order to sell." If you are not going to sell a stock, what happens to its price is a matter of indifference. For true long-term investors—that small group of people like Warren Buffett who can shut their eyes to short-term fluctuations and who have no doubt that what goes down will come back up—volatility represents opportunity rather than risk, at least to the extent that volatile securities tend to provide higher returns than more placid securities.

Robert Jeffrey, a former manufacturing executive who now manages a substantial family trust, has expressed the same idea in a more formal manner: Volatility fails as a proxy for risk because "volatility per se, be it related to weather, portfolio returns, or the timing of one's morning newspaper delivery, is simply a benign statistical probability factor that tells us nothing about risk until coupled with a consequence."[12] The consequence of volatility to my wife's aunt was nil; the consequence of volatility to an investor who will need to invade capital tomorrow is paramount. Jeffrey sums the matter up in these words: "[T]he real risk in holding a portfolio is that it might not provide its owner, either during the interim or at some terminal date or both, with the *cash* he requires to make essential outlays." (The italics are mine.)

Jeffrey recognized that the risk inherent in different assets has meaning only when it is related to the investor's liabilities. This definition of risk reappears in many different guises, all of them useful. The central idea is that variability should be studied in reference to some benchmark or some minimum rate of return that the investor has to exceed.

In the simplest version of this approach, risk is just the chance of losing money. In that view, a zero nominal return becomes the benchmark as investors try to build portfolios that minimize the probability of negative returns over some time period.

That view is a long way from Markowitz's, as we can see from the following illustration. Consider two investors. One of them invested 100% in the S&P 500 at the beginning of 1955 and held on for forty years. The other invested in a 30-year Treasury bond. In order to maintain the 30-year maturity, this investor sells his original bond (now a 29-year bond) at the end of each year and buys a new 30-year bond.

According to the Markowitz method of measuring risk, the second investor's bond, with an annual standard deviation of 10.4%, was a lot less risky than the first investor's stock portfolio, whose standard deviation worked out to 15.3%. On the other hand, the total return on the stock portfolio (capital appreciation plus income) was much higher than the bond's total return—an annual average of 12.2% as against only 6.1%. The stock portfolio's high return more than compensated for its greater volatility. The probability of a year with a zero return on the stock portfolio was 22%; the bondholder faced a 28% probability of a down year. The stock portfolio returned more than the bond's *average* return in two-thirds of the years in the time period. Which investor took the greater risk?

Or consider those 13 emerging markets I mentioned earlier. From the end of 1989 to February 1994, they were three times as volatile as the S&P 500, but an investor in the package of emerging markets had fewer losing months, was consistently wealthier, and, even after the sharp drop at the end of 1994, ended up three times richer than the investor in the S&P 500. Which was riskier, the S&P 500 or the emerging markets index?

The degree to which a volatile portfolio is risky, in other words, depends on what we are comparing it with. Some investors, and many portfolio managers, do not consider a volatile portfolio risky if its returns have little probability of ending up below a specified benchmark.* That benchmark need not be zero. It can be a moving target, such as the minimum required return for a corporation to keep its pension fund solvent, or the rate of return on some index or model portfolio (like the S&P 500), or the 5% of assets that charitable foundations are mandated to spend each year. Morningstar ranks mutual funds by riskiness in terms of how frequently their returns fall below the return on 90-day Treasury bills.

Yet measuring risk as the probability of falling short of a benchmark in no way invalidates Markowitz's prescription for portfolio manage-

---

*For an extended and informative discussion of these issues, see *The Journal of Investing*, Fall 1994.

ment. Return is still desirable and risk is still undesirable; expected return is to be maximized at the same time that risk is to be minimized; volatility still suggests the probability of falling short. Optimization under these conditions differs little from what Markowitz had in mind. The process holds up even when risk is seen as a multi-dimensional concept that incorporates an asset's sensitivity to unexpected changes in such major economic variables as business activity, inflation, and interest rates, as well as its sensitivity to fluctuations in the market in which it trades.

Risk can be measured in yet another probability-based fashion, this one based exclusively on past experience. Suppose an investor acts as a market-timer, trying to buy before prices rise and sell before prices fall. How much margin of error can a market-timer sustain and still come out ahead of a simple buy-and-hold strategy?

One of the risks of market timing is being out of the market when it has a big upward move. Consider the period from May 26, 1970, to April 29, 1994. Suppose our market-timer was in cash instead of stocks for only the five best days in the market out of that 14-year period of 3,500 trading days. He might feel pretty good at having just about doubled his opening investment (before taxes), until he reckoned how he would have done if he had merely bought in at the beginning and held on without trying anything tricky. Buy-and-hold would have *tripled* his investment. Market timing is a risky strategy!

Risk measurement becomes even more complicated when the parameters are fluid rather than stationary. Volatility itself does not stand still over time. The annual standard deviation of monthly returns on the S&P 500 amounted to 17.7% from the end of 1984 to the end of 1990; over the next four years the standard deviation was only 10.6% a year. Similar abrupt changes have occurred in bond-market volatility. If such variation can develop in broadly diversified indexes, the likelihood is much greater that it will appear in the case of individual stocks and bonds.

The problem does not end there. Few people feel the same about risk every day of their lives. As we grow older, wiser, richer, or poorer, our perception of what risk is and our aversion to taking risk will shift, sometimes in one direction, sometimes in the other. Investors as a group also alter their views about risk, causing significant changes in how they value the future streams of earnings that they expect stocks and long-term bonds to provide.

An ingenious approach to this possibility was developed by Markowitz's student, associate, and fellow Nobel Laureate, William Sharpe. In 1990, Sharpe published a paper that analyzed the relationship between changes in wealth and the willingness of investors to own risky assets.[13] Although, in accordance with the view of Bernoulli and of Jevons, wealthy people are probably more risk-averse than other people, Sharpe hypothesized that *changes* in wealth also influence an investor's aversion to risk. Increases in wealth give people a thicker cushion to absorb losses; losses make the cushion thinner. The consequence is that increases in wealth tend to strengthen the appetite for risk while losses tend to weaken it. Sharpe suggests that these variations in risk aversion explain why bull markets or bear markets tend to run to extremes, but ultimately regression to the mean takes over as contrary investors recognize the overreaction that has occurred and correct the valuation errors that have accumulated.

Despite the criticisms of Markowitz's theory of portfolio selection, his contribution has been immense. It has provided the foundation for the primary theoretical work accomplished since 1952 and has given rise to practical applications that dominate the field of investing. Indeed, diversification has become a veritable religion among investors. Even the attacks on Markowitz have triggered new concepts and new applications that might never have come about without his innovative contributions.

Yet much of what one makes of Markowitz's achievement, and the structure whose foundations he laid, depends on how one feels about the controversial issue of investor rationality. Just as Wall Street was beginning to apply the new theories of investment, the sound of different drummers was heard. The critically important work on rational behavior, most of which dates from the tumultuous early 1970s, provoked a dramatic break with the optimistic views of rationality that had characterized the innovations of the 1950s and 1960s. The stage was set to take up cudgels against the models of Daniel Bernoulli, Jevons, and von Neumann, to say nothing of the central assumptions of traditional economic theory.

The response to this rough assault on hallowed principles of behavior was tentative at first, in part because academics do not always express themselves with clarity, and in part because of the enormous vested interests that had accumulated around the established theories of decision-making and choice. But the gloomy environment of the 1970s provided the impulse that unleashed the power, ingenuity, and common sense that marked the new ideas and ultimately brought them into the forefront of academic research and to the attention of practitioners. Today the journals are full of attacks on concepts of rational behavior and risk aversion.

Daniel Bernoulli had admitted in his paper that there were "exceedingly rare exceptions" to his propositions. He underestimated how frequently human beings stray from the strait and narrow path he laid out for them. Recent research reveals that many of the deviations from established norms of rational behavior are systematic.

There is another possibility. Perhaps people are not nonrational, but the traditional model of rationality may specify a pattern of behavior that captures only in part the way that rational human beings make their decisions. If that is the case, the problem is with the model of rationality rather than with us human beings. If the choices people make are both logical and predictable, even with varying rather than constant preferences, or with preferences that do not suit the strict prescriptions of rationality, behavior can still be modeled by mathematical techniques. Logic can follow a variety of paths in addition to the paths specified in the traditional model.*

A growing volume of research reveals that people yield to inconsistencies, myopia, and other forms of distortion throughout the process of decision-making. That may not matter much when the issue is whether one hits the jackpot on the slot machine or picks a lottery number that makes dreams come true. But the evidence indicates that these flaws are even more apparent in areas where the consequences are more serious.

The word "irrational" may be too strong to apply to such behavior, because irrationality conveys craziness and most people are (perhaps

---

*Jack Benny had a routine on a Sunday radio show in which he remained silent when confronted by a mugger demanding "Your money or your life." After a long pause, the mugger cried, "Come on!" "I'm thinking it over," Benny predictably responded.

DEGREES OF BELIEF: EXPLORING UNCERTAINTY

16

The Failure of
Invariance

All of us think of ourselves as rational beings even in times of crisis, applying the laws of probability in cool and calculated fashion to the choices that confront us. We like to believe we are above-average in skills, intelligence, farsightedness, experience, refinement, and leadership. Who admits to being an incompetent driver, a feckless debater, a stupid investor, or a person with an inferior taste in clothes?

Yet how realistic are such images? Not everyone can be above average. Furthermore, the most important decisions we make usually occur under complex, confusing, indistinct, or frightening conditions. Not much time to consult the laws of probability. Life is not a game of *balla*. It often comes trailing Kenneth Arrow's clouds of vagueness.

And yet most humans are not utterly irrational beings who take risks without forethought or who hide in a closet when anxiety strikes. As we shall see, the evidence suggests that we reach decisions in accord with an underlying structure that enables us to function predictably and, in most instances, systematically. The issue, rather, is the degree to which the reality in which we make our decisions deviates from the rational decision models of the Bernoullis, Jevons, and von Neumann. Psychologists have spawned a cottage industry to explore the nature and causes of these deviations.

The classical models of rationality—the model on which game theory and most of Markowitz's concepts are based—specifies how people *should* make decisions in the face of risk and what the world would be like if people did in fact behave as specified. Extensive research and experimentation, however, reveal that departures from that model occur more frequently than most of us admit. You will discover yourself in many of the examples that follow.

The most influential research into how people manage risk and uncertainty has been conducted by two Israeli psychologists, Daniel Kahneman and Amos Tversky. Although they now live in the United States—one at Princeton and the other at Stanford—both served in the Israeli armed forces during the 1950s. Kahneman developed a psychological screening system for evaluating Israeli army recruits that is still in use. Tversky served as a paratroop captain and earned a citation for bravery. The two have been collaborating for nearly thirty years and now command an enthusiastic following among both scholars and practitioners in the field of finance and investing, where uncertainty influences every decision.[1]

Kahneman and Tversky call their concept Prospect Theory. After reading about Prospect Theory and discussing it in person with both Kahneman and Tversky, I began to wonder why its name bore no resemblance to its subject matter. I asked Kahneman where the name had come from. "We just wanted a name that people would notice and remember," he said.

Their association began in the mid-1960s when both were junior professors at Hebrew University in Jerusalem. At one of their first meetings, Kahneman told Tversky about an experience he had had while instructing flight instructors on the psychology of training. Referring to studies of pigeon behavior, he was trying to make the point that reward is a more effective teaching tool than punishment. Suddenly one of his students shouted, "With respect, Sir, what you're saying is literally for the birds. . . . My experience contradicts it."[2] The student explained that the trainees he praised for excellent performance almost always did worse on their next flight, while the ones he criticized for poor performance almost always improved.

Kahneman realized that this pattern was exactly what Francis Galton would have predicted. Just as large sweetpeas give birth to smaller sweetpeas, and vice versa, performance in any area is unlikely to go on improving or growing worse indefinitely. We swing back and forth in everything we do, continuously regressing toward what will turn out to be our average performance. The chances are that the quality of a student's next landing will have nothing to do with whether or not someone has told him that his last landing was good or bad.

"Once you become sensitized to it, you see regression everywhere," Kahneman pointed out to Tversky.[3] Whether your children do what they are told to do, whether a basketball player has a hot hand in tonight's game, or whether an investment manager's performance slips during this calendar quarter, their future performance is most likely to reflect regression to the mean regardless of whether they will be punished or rewarded for past performance.

Soon the two men were speculating on the possibility that ignoring regression to the mean was not the only way that people err in forecasting future performance from the facts of the past. A fruitful collaboration developed between them as they proceeded to conduct a series of clever experiments designed to reveal how people make choices when faced with uncertain outcomes.

Prospect Theory discovered behavior patterns that had never been recognized by proponents of rational decision-making. Kahneman and Tversky ascribe these patterns to two human shortcomings. First, emotion often destroys the self-control that is essential to rational decision-making. Second, people are often unable to understand fully what they are dealing with. They experience what psychologists call cognitive difficulties.

The heart of our difficulty is in sampling. As Leibniz reminded Jacob Bernoulli, nature is so varied and so complex that we have a hard time drawing valid generalizations from what we observe. We use shortcuts that lead us to erroneous perceptions, or we interpret small samples as representative of what larger samples would show.

Consequently, we tend to resort to more subjective kinds of measurement: Keynes's "degrees of belief" figure more often in our decision-making than Pascal's Triangle, and gut rules even when we think we are using measurement. Seven million people and one elephant!

We display risk-aversion when we are offered a choice in one setting and then turn into risk-*seekers* when we are offered the same choice in a different setting. We tend to ignore the common components of a problem and concentrate on each part in isolation—one reason why Markowitz's prescription for portfolio-building was so slow to find acceptance. We have trouble recognizing how much information is enough and how much is too much. We pay excessive attention to low-probability events accompanied by high drama and overlook events that happen in routine fashion. We treat costs and uncompensated losses differently, even though their impact on wealth is identical. We start out with a purely rational decision about how to manage our risks and then extrapolate from what may be only a run of good luck. As a result, we forget about regression to the mean, overstay our positions, and end up in trouble.

Here is a question that Kahneman and Tversky use to show how intuitive perceptions mislead us. Ask yourself whether the letter K appears more often as the first or as the third letter of English words. You will probably answer that it appears more often as the first letter. Actually, K appears as the third letter twice as often. Why the error? We find it easier to recall words with a certain letter at the beginning than words with that same letter somewhere else.

The asymmetry between the way we make decisions involving gains and decisions involving losses is one of the most striking findings of Prospect Theory. It is also one of the most useful.

Where significant sums are involved, most people will reject a fair gamble in favor of a certain gain—$100,000 certain is preferable to a 50-50 possibility of $200,000 or nothing. We are risk-averse, in other words.

But what about losses? Kahneman and Tversky's first paper on Prospect Theory, which appeared in 1979, describes an experiment showing that our choices between negative outcomes are mirror images of our choices between positive outcomes.[4] In one of their experiments they first asked the subjects to choose between an 80% chance of winning $4,000 and a 20% chance of winning nothing versus a 100% chance of receiving $3,000. Even though the risky choice has a higher mathematical expectation—$3,200—80% of the subjects chose the

$3,000 certain. These people were risk-averse, just as Bernoulli would have predicted.

Then Kahneman and Tversky offered a choice between taking the risk of an 80% chance of *losing* $4,000 and a 20% chance of breaking even versus a 100% chance of losing $3,000. Now 92% of the respondents chose the gamble, even though its mathematical expectation of a loss of $3,200 was once again larger than the certain loss of $3,000. When the choice involves losses, we are risk-seekers, not risk-averse.

Kahneman and Tversky and many of their colleagues have found that this asymmetrical pattern appears consistently in a wide variety of experiments. On a later occasion, for example, Kahneman and Tversky proposed the following problem.[5] Imagine that a rare disease is breaking out in some community and is expected to kill 600 people. Two different programs are available to deal with the threat. If Program A is adopted, 200 people will be saved; if Program B is adopted, there is a 33% probability that everyone will be saved and a 67% probability that no one will be saved.

Which program would you choose? If most of us are risk-averse, rational people will prefer Plan A's certainty of saving 200 lives over Plan B's gamble, which has the same mathematical expectancy but involves taking the risk of a 67% chance that everyone will die. In the experiment, 72% of the subjects chose the risk-averse response represented by Program A.

Now consider the identical problem posed differently. If Program C is adopted, 400 of the 600 people will die, while Program D entails a 33% probability that nobody will die and a 67% probability that 600 people will die. Note that the first of the two choices is now expressed in terms of 400 deaths rather than 200 survivors, while the second program offers a 33% chance that no one will die. Kahneman and Tversky report that 78% of their subjects were risk-seekers and opted for the gamble: they could not tolerate the prospect of the sure loss of 400 lives.

This behavior, although understandable, is inconsistent with the assumptions of rational behavior. The answer to a question should be the same regardless of the setting in which it is posed. Kahneman and Tversky interpret the evidence produced by these experiments as a demonstration that people are not risk-averse: they are perfectly willing to choose a gamble when they consider it appropriate. But if they are not risk-averse, what are they? "The major driving force is *loss aversion*," writes Tversky (italics added). "It is not so much that people hate uncertainty—but rather, they hate losing."[6] Losses will always loom larger than gains. Indeed, losses that go unresolved—such as the loss of a child or a large insurance claim that never gets settled—are likely to provoke intense, irrational, and abiding risk-aversion.[7]

Tversky offers an interesting speculation on this curious behavior:

> Probably the most significant and pervasive characteristic of the human pleasure machine is that people are much more sensitive to negative than to positive stimuli. . . . [T]hink about how well you feel today, and then try to imagine how much better you *could* feel. . . . [T]here are a few things that would make you feel better, but the number of things that would make you feel worse is unbounded.[8]

One of the insights to emerge from this research is that Bernoulli had it wrong when he declared, "[The] utility resulting from any small increase in wealth will be inversely proportionate to the quantity of goods previously possessed." Bernoulli believed that it is the pre-existing level of wealth that determines the value of a risky opportunity to become richer. Kahneman and Tversky found that the valuation of a risky opportunity appears to depend far more on the reference point from which the possible gain or loss will occur than on the final value of the assets that would result. It is not how rich you are that motivates your decision, but whether that decision will make you richer or poorer. As a consequence, Tversky warns, "our preferences . . . can be manipulated by changes in the reference points."[9]

He cites a survey in which respondents were asked to choose between a policy of high employment and high inflation and a policy of lower employment and lower inflation. When the issue was framed in terms of an unemployment rate of 10% or 5%, the vote was heavily in favor of accepting more inflation to get the unemployment rate down. When the respondents were asked to choose between a labor force that was 90% employed and a labor force that was 95% employed, low inflation appeared to be more important than raising the percentage employed by five points.

Richard Thaler has described an experiment that uses starting wealth to illustrate Tversky's warning.[10] Thaler proposed to a class of students that they had just won $30 and were now offered the following choice: a coin flip where the individual wins $9 on heads and loses $9 on tails versus no coin flip. Seventy percent of the subjects selected the coin flip. Thaler offered his next class the following options: starting wealth of zero and then a coin flip where the individual wins $39 on heads and wins $21 on tails versus $30 for certain. Only 43 percent selected the coin flip.

Thaler describes this result as the "house money" effect. Although the choice of payoffs offered to both classes is identical—regardless of the amount of the starting wealth, the individual will end up with either $39 or $21 versus $30 for sure—people who start out with money in their pockets will choose the gamble, while people who start out with empty pockets will reject the gamble. Bernoulli would have predicted that the decision would be determined by the amounts $39, $30, or $21 whereas the students based their decisions on the reference point, which was $30 in the first case and zero in the second.

Edward Miller, an economics professor with an interest in behavioral matters, reports a variation on these themes. Although Bernoulli uses the expression "any small increase in wealth," he implies that what he has to say is independent of the size of the increase.[11] Miller cites various psychological studies that show significant differences in response, depending on whether the gain is a big one or a small one. Occasional large gains seem to sustain the interest of investors and gamblers for longer periods of time than consistent small winnings. That response is typical of investors who look on investing as a game and who fail to diversify; diversification is boring. Well-informed investors diversify because they do not believe that investing is a form of entertainment.

Kahneman and Tversky use the expression "failure of invariance" to describe inconsistent (not necessarily incorrect) choices when the same problem appears in different frames. Invariance means that if A is preferred to B and B is preferred to C, then rational people will prefer A to C; this feature is the core of von Neumann and Morgenstern's approach to utility. Or, in the case above, if 200 lives saved for certain is the rational decision in the first set, saving 200 lives for certain should be the rational decision in the second set as well.

But research suggests otherwise:

> The failure of invariance is both pervasive and robust. It is as common among sophisticated respondents as among naive ones.... Respondents confronted with their conflicting answers are typically puzzled. Even after rereading the problems, they still wish to be risk averse in the "lives saved" version; they will be risk seeking in the "lives lost" version; and they also wish to obey invariance and give consistent answers to the two versions....
>
> The moral of these results is disturbing. Invariance is normatively essential [what we *should* do], intuitively compelling, and psychologically unfeasible.[12]

The failure of invariance is far more prevalent than most of us realize. The manner in which questions are framed in advertising may persuade people to buy something despite negative consequences that, in a different frame, might persuade them to refrain from buying. Public opinion polls often produce contradictory results when the same question is given different twists.

Kahneman and Tversky describe a situation in which doctors were concerned that they might be influencing patients who had to choose between the life-or-death risks in different forms of treatment.[13] The choice was between radiation and surgery in the treatment of lung cancer. Medical data at this hospital showed that no patients die during radiation but have a shorter life expectancy than patients who survive the risk of surgery; the overall difference in life expectancy was not great enough to provide a clear choice between the two forms of treatment. When the question was put in terms of risk of death during treatment, more than 40% of the choices favored radiation. When the question was put in terms of life expectancy, only about 20% favored radiation.

One of the most familiar manifestations of the failure of invariance is in the old Wall Street saw, "You never get poor by taking a profit." It would follow that cutting your losses is also a good idea, but investors hate to take losses, because, tax considerations aside, a loss taken is an acknowledgment of error. Loss-aversion combined with ego leads investors to gamble by clinging to their mistakes in the fond hope that some day the market will vindicate their judgment and make them whole. Von Neumann would not approve.

The failure of invariance frequently takes the form of what is known as "mental accounting," a process in which we separate the components of the total picture. In so doing we fail to recognize that a decision affecting each component will have an effect on the shape of the whole. Mental accounting is like focusing on the hole instead of the doughnut. It leads to conflicting answers to the same question.

Kahneman and Tversky ask you to imagine that you are on your way to see a Broadway play for which you have bought a ticket that cost $40.[14] When you arrive at the theater, you discover you have lost your ticket. Would you lay out $40 for another one?

Now suppose instead that you plan to buy the ticket when you arrive at the theater. As you step up to the box office, you find that you have $40 less in your pocket than you thought you had when you left home. Would you still buy the ticket?

In both cases, whether you lost the ticket or lost the $40, you would be out a total of $80 if you decided to see the show. You would be out only $40 if you abandoned the show and went home. Kahneman and Tversky found that most people would be reluctant to spend $40 to replace the lost ticket, while about the same number would be perfectly willing to lay out a second $40 to buy the ticket even though they had lost the original $40.

This is a clear case of the failure of invariance. If $80 is more than you want to spend on the theater, you should neither replace the ticket in the first instance nor buy the ticket in the second. If, on the other hand, you are willing to spend $80 on going to the theater, you should be just as willing to replace the lost ticket as you are to spend $40 on the ticket despite the disappearance of the original $40. *There is no difference other than in accounting conventions between a cost and a loss.*

Prospect Theory suggests that the inconsistent responses to these choices result from two separate mental accounts, one for going to the theater, and one for putting the $40 to other uses—next month's lunch money, for example. The theater account was charged $40 when the ticket was purchased, depleting that account. The lost $40 was charged to next month's lunch money, which has nothing to do with the theater account and is off in the future anyway. Consequently, the theater account is still awaiting its $40 charge.

Thaler recounts an amusing real-life example of mental accounting.[15] A professor of finance he knows has a clever strategy to help him deal with minor misfortunes. At the beginning of the year, the professor plans for a generous donation to his favorite charity. Anything untoward that happens in the course of the year—a speeding ticket, replacing a lost possession, an unwanted touch by an impecunious relative—is then charged to the charity account. The system makes the losses painless, because the charity does the paying. The charity receives whatever is left over in the account. Thaler has nominated his friend as the world's first Certified Mental Accountant.

In an interview with a magazine reporter, Kahneman himself confessed that he had succumbed to mental accounting. In his research with Tversky he had found that a loss is less painful when it is just an addition to a larger loss than when it is a free-standing loss: losing a second $100 after having already lost $100 is less painful than losing $100 on totally separate occasions. Keeping this concept in mind when moving into a new home, Kahneman and his wife bought all their furniture within a week after buying the house. If they had looked at the furniture as a separate account, they might have balked at the cost and ended up buying fewer pieces than they needed.[16]

We tend to believe that information is a necessary ingredient to rational decision-making and that the more information we have, the better we can manage the risks we face. Yet psychologists report circumstances in which additional information gets in the way and distorts decisions, leading to failures of invariance and offering opportunities for people in authority to manipulate the kinds of risk that people are willing to take.

Two medical researchers, David Redelmeier and Eldar Shafir, reported in the *Journal of the American Medical Association* on a study designed to reveal how doctors respond as the number of possible options for treatment is increased.[17] Any medical decision is risky—no one can know for certain what the consequences will be. In each of Redelmeier and Shafir's experiments, the introduction of additional options raised the probability that the physicians would choose either the original option or decide to do nothing.

In one experiment, several hundred physicians were asked to prescribe treatment for a 67-year-old man with chronic pain in his right hip. The doctors were given two choices: to prescribe a named medication or to "refer to orthopedics and do not start any new medication"; just about half voted against any medication. When the number of choices was raised from two to three by adding a second medication option, along with "refer to orthopedics," three-quarters of the doctors voted against medication and for "refer to orthopedics."

Tversky believes that "probability judgments are attached not to events but to descriptions of events . . . the judged probability of an event depends upon the explicitness of its description."[18] As a case in point, he describes an experiment in which 120 Stanford graduates were asked to assess the likelihood of various possible causes of death. Each student evaluated one of two different lists of causes; the first listed specific causes of death and the second grouped the causes under a generic heading like "natural causes."

The following table shows some of the estimated probabilities of death developed in this experiment:

	Group I	*Group II*	*Actual*
Heart disease	22		34
Cancer	18		23
Other natural causes	33		35
Total natural causes	73	58	92
Accident	32		5
Homicide	10		1
Other unnatural causes	11		2
Total unnatural causes	53	32	8

These students vastly overestimated the probabilities of violent deaths and underestimated deaths from natural causes. But the striking revelation in the table is that the estimated probability of dying under either set of circumstances was higher when the circumstances were explicit as compared with the cases where the students were asked to estimate only the total from natural or unnatural causes.

In another medical study described by Redelmeier and Tversky, two groups of physicians at Stanford University were surveyed for their diagnosis of a woman experiencing severe abdominal pain.[19] After receiving a detailed description of the symptoms, the first group was asked to decide on the probability that this woman was suffering from ectopic pregnancy, a gastroenteritis problem, or "none of the above." The second group was offered three additional possible diagnoses along with the choices of pregnancy, gastroenteritis, and "none of the above" that had been offered to the first group.

The interesting feature of this experiment was the handling of the "none of the above" option by the second group of doctors. Assuming that the average competence of the doctors in each group was essentially equal, one would expect that that option as presented to the first group would have included the three additional diagnoses with which the second group was presented. In that case, the second group would be expected to assign a probability to the three additional diagnoses plus "none of the above" that was approximately equal to the 50% probability assigned to "none of the above" by the first group.

That is not what happened. The second group of doctors assigned a 69% probability to "none of the above" plus the three additional diagnoses and only 31% to the possibility of pregnancy or gastroenteritis— to which the first group had assigned a 50% probability. Apparently, the greater the number of possibilities, the higher the probabilities assigned to them.

Daniel Ellsberg (the same Ellsberg as the Ellsberg of the Pentagon Papers) published a paper back in 1961 in which he defined a phenomenon he called "ambiguity aversion."[20] Ambiguity aversion means that people prefer to take risks on the basis of known rather than unknown probabilities. Information matters, in other words. For example, Ellsberg offered several groups of people a chance to bet on drawing either a red ball or a black ball from two different urns, each holding 100 balls. Urn 1 held 50 balls of each color; the breakdown in Urn 2 was unknown. Probability theory would suggest that Urn 2 was also split 50-50, for there was no basis for any other distribution. Yet the overwhelming preponderance of the respondents chose to bet on the draw from Urn 1.

Tversky and another colleague, Craig Fox, explored ambiguity aversion more deeply and discovered that matters are more complicated than Ellsberg suggested.[21] They designed a series of experiments to discover whether people's preference for clear over vague probabilities appears in all instances or only in games of chance.

The answer came back loud and clear: people will bet on vague beliefs in situations where they feel especially competent or knowledgeable, but they prefer to bet on chance when they do not. Tversky and Fox concluded that ambiguity aversion "is driven by the feeling of incompetence . . . [and] will be present when subjects evaluate clear and vague prospects jointly, but it will greatly diminish or disappear when they evaluate each prospect in isolation."[22]

People who play dart games, for example, would rather play darts than games of chance, although the probability of success at darts is vague while the probability of success at games of chance is mathematically predetermined. People knowledgeable about politics and ignorant about football prefer betting on political events to betting on games of chance set at the same odds, but they will choose games of chance over sports events under the same conditions.

In a 1992 paper that summarized advances in Prospect Theory, Kahneman and Tversky made the following observation: "Theories of choice are at best approximate and incomplete . . . Choice is a constructive and contingent process. When faced with a complex problem, people . . . use computational shortcuts and editing operations."[23] The evidence in this chapter, which summarizes only a tiny sample of a huge body of literature, reveals repeated patterns of irrationality, inconsistency, and incompetence in the ways human beings arrive at decisions and choices when faced with uncertainty.

Must we then abandon the theories of Bernoulli, Bentham, Jevons, and von Neumann? No. There is no reason to conclude that the frequent absence of rationality, *as originally defined*, must yield the point to Macbeth that life is a story told by an idiot.

The judgment of humanity implicit in Prospect Theory is not necessarily a pessimistic one. Kahneman and Tversky take issue with the assumption that "only rational behavior can survive in a competitive environment, and the fear that any treatment that abandons rationality will be chaotic and intractable." Instead, they report that most people can survive in a competitive environment even while succumbing to the quirks that make their behavior less than rational by Bernoulli's standards. "[P]erhaps more important," Tversky and Kahneman suggest, "the evidence indicates that human choices are orderly, although not always rational in the traditional sense of the word."[24] Thaler adds: "Quasi-rationality is neither fatal nor immediately self-defeating."[25] Since orderly decisions are predictable, there is no basis for the argument that behavior is going to be random and erratic merely because it fails to provide a perfect match with rigid theoretical assumptions.

Thaler makes the same point in another context. If we were always rational in making decisions, we would not need the elaborate mechanisms we employ to bolster our self-control, ranging all the way from dieting resorts, to having our income taxes withheld, to betting a few bucks on the horses but not to the point where we need to take out a second mortgage. We accept the certain loss we incur when buying insurance, which is an explicit recognition of uncertainty. We employ those mechanisms, and they work. Few people end up in either the poorhouse or the nuthouse as a result of their own decision-making.

Still, the true believers in rational behavior raise another question. With so much of this damaging evidence generated in psychology laboratories, in experiments with young students, in hypothetical situations where the penalties for error are minimal, how can we have any confidence that the findings are realistic, reliable, or relevant to the way people behave when they have to make decisions?

The question is an important one. There is a sharp contrast between generalizations based on theory and generalizations based on experiments. De Moivre first conceived of the bell curve by writing equations on a piece of paper, not, like Quetelet, by measuring the dimensions of soldiers. But Galton conceived of regression to the mean—a powerful concept that makes the bell curve operational in many instances—by studying sweetpeas and generational change in human beings; he came up with the theory after looking at the facts.

Alvin Roth, an expert on experimental economics, has observed that Nicholas Bernoulli conducted the first known psychological experiment more than 250 years ago: he proposed the coin-tossing game between Peter and Paul that guided his uncle Daniel to the discovery of utility.[26] Experiments conducted by von Neumann and Morgenstern led them to conclude that the results "are not so good as might be hoped, but their general direction is correct."[27] The progression from experiment to theory has a distinguished and respectable history.

It is not easy to design experiments that overcome the artificiality of the classroom and the tendency of respondents to lie or to harbor disruptive biases—especially when they have little at stake. But we must be impressed by the remarkable consistency evident in the wide variety of experiments that tested the hypothesis of rational choice. Experimental research has developed into a high art.*

Studies of investor behavior in the capital markets reveal that most of what Kahneman and Tversky and their associates hypothesized in the laboratory is played out by the behavior of investors who produce the avalanche of numbers that fill the financial pages of the daily paper. Far away from laboratory of the classroom, this empirical research confirms a great deal of what experimental methods have suggested about decision-making, not just among investors, but among human beings in general.

As we shall see, the analysis will raise another question, a tantalizing one. If people are so dumb, how come more of us smart people don't get rich?

---

*Kahneman has described his introduction to experimentation when one of his professors told the story of a child being offered the choice between a small lollipop today or a larger lollipop tomorrow. The child's response to this simple question correlated with critical aspects of the child's life, such as family income, one or two parents present, and degree of trust.

17

The Theory Police

Investors must expect to lose occasionally on the risks they take. Any other assumption would be foolish. But theory predicts that the expectations of rational investors will be unbiased, to use the technical expression: a rational investor will overestimate part of the time and underestimate part of the time but will not overestimate or underestimate all of the time—or even most of the time. Rational investors are not among the people who always see the glass as either half empty or half full.

Nobody really believes that the real-life facts fit that stylized description of investors always rationally trading off risk and return. Uncertainty is scary. Hard as we try to behave rationally, our emotions often push us to seek shelter from unpleasant surprises. We resort to all sorts of tricks and dodges that lead us to violate the rational prescriptions. As Daniel Kahneman points out, "The failure of the rational model is not in its logic but in the human brain it requires. Who could design a brain that could perform the way this model mandates? Every single one of us would have to know and *understand* everything, completely and at once."[1] Kahneman was not the first to recognize the rigid constraints of the rational model, but he was one of the first to explain the consequences of that rigidity and the manner in which perfectly normal human beings regularly violate it.

If investors have a tendency to violate the rational model, that model may not be a very reliable description of how the capital markets behave. In that case, new measures of investment risk would be in order.

Consider the following scenario. Last week, after weeks of indecision, you finally liquidated your long-standing IBM position at $80 share. This morning you check your paper and discover that IBM is selling at $90. The stock you bought to replace IBM is down a little. How do you react to this disappointing news?

Your first thought might be whether you should tell your spouse about what has happened. Or you might curse yourself for being impatient. You will surely resolve to move more slowly in the future before scrapping a long-term investment, no matter how good an idea it seems. You might even wish that IBM had disappeared from the market the instant you sold it, so that you would never learn how it performed afterward.

The psychologist David Bell has suggested that "decision regret" is the result of focusing on the assets you might have had if you had made the right decision.[2] Bell poses the choice between a lottery that pays $10,000 if you win and nothing if you lose versus $4,000 for certain. If you choose to play the lottery and lose, you tell yourself that you were greedy and were punished by fate, but then you go on about your business. But suppose you choose the $4,000 certain, the more conservative choice, and then find out that the lottery paid off at $10,000. How much would you pay never to learn the outcome?

Decision regret is not limited to the situation in which you sell a stock and then watch it go through the roof. What about all those stocks you never bought, many of which are performing better than the stocks you did buy? Even though everyone knows it is impossible to choose *only* top performers, many investors suffer decision regret over those forgone assets. I believe that this kind of emotional insecurity has a lot more to do with decisions to diversify than all of Harry Markowitz's most elegant intellectual perorations on the subject—the more stocks you own, the greater the chance of holding the big winners!

A similar motivation prompts investors to turn their trading over to active portfolio managers, despite evidence that most of them fail to outperform the major market indexes over the long run. The few who do succeed on occasion tend to show little consistency from year to year; we have already seen how difficult it was to distinguish between luck and skill in the cases of American Mutual and AIM Constellation.* Yet the law of averages predicts that about half the active managers will beat the market this year. Shouldn't *your* manager be among them? *Somebody* is going to win out, after all.

The temptations generated by thoughts of forgone assets are irresistible to some people. Take Barbara Kenworthy, who was manager of a $600 million bond portfolio at Prudential Investment Advisors in May 1995. *The Wall Street Journal* quoted Ms. Kenworthy as saying, "We're all creatures of what burned us most recently."[3] To explain what she meant, the *Journal* commented, "Ms. Kenworthy is plunging into long-term bonds again despite her reckoning that value isn't quite there, because not to invest would be to momentarily lag behind the pack." The reporter, with a sense of the ironic, then remarked, "This is an intriguing time horizon for an investor in 30-year bonds."

Imagine yourself as an investment adviser trying to decide whether to recommend Johnson & Johnson or a start-up biogenetic company to a client. If all goes well, the prospects for the start-up company are dazzling; Johnson & Johnson, though a lot less exciting, is a good value at its current price. And Johnson & Johnson is also a "fine" company with a widely respected management team. What will you do if you make the wrong choice? The day after you recommend the start-up company, its most promising new drug turns out to be a wash-out. Or right after you recommend Johnson & Johnson, another pharmaceutical company issues a new product to compete with its biggest-selling drug. Which outcome will generate less decision regret and make it easier to go on working with a disgruntled client?

Keynes anticipated this question in *The General Theory*. After describing an investor with the courage to be "eccentric, unconventional and rash in the eyes of average opinion," Keynes says that his success "will only confirm the general belief in his rashness; and . . . if his decisions are unsuccessful . . . he will not receive much mercy. Worldly wisdom teaches that it is better for reputation to fail conventionally than to succeed unconventionally."[4]

---

*An excellent review of this matter appears in "The Triumph of Indexing," a booklet published by the Vanguard Group of mutual funds in May 1995. This controversial subject receives more detailed treatment later in this chapter.

Prospect Theory confirms Keynes's conclusion by predicting which decision you will make. First, the absolute performance of the stock you select is relatively unimportant. The start-up company's performance as compared with Johnson & Johnson's performance taken as a reference point is what matters. Second, loss aversion and anxiety will make the joy of winning on the start-up company less than the pain if you lose on it. Johnson & Johnson is an acceptable "long-term" holding even if it often underperforms.

The stocks of good companies are not necessarily good stocks, but you can make life easier by agreeing with your clients that they are. So you advise your client to buy Johnson & Johnson.

I am not making up a story out of whole cloth. An article in *The Wall Street Journal* of August 24, 1995, goes on at length about how professional investment managers have grown leery of investing in financial instruments known as derivatives—the subject of the next chapter—as a result of the widely publicized disasters at Procter & Gamble and in Orange County, California, among others. The article quotes John Carroll, manager of GTE Corporation's $12 billion pension fund: "If you made the right call and used derivatives, you might get a small additional return. But if you make the wrong call, you could wind up unemployed, with a big dent in your credibility as an investor." Andrew Turner, director of research at a leading consulting firm for institutional investors, adds, "Even if you keep your job, you don't want to get labeled as [someone] who got snookered by an investment bank." A major Boston money manager agrees: "If you buy comfortable-looking . . . stocks like Coca Cola, you're taking very little career risk because clients will blame a stupid market if things go wrong."

With Richard Thaler in the vanguard, a group of academic economists have responded to flaws in the rational model by launching a new field of study called "behavioral finance." Behavioral finance analyzes how investors struggle to find their way through the give and take between risk and return, one moment engaging in cool calculation and the next yielding to emotional impulses. The result of this mixture between the rational and not-so-rational is a capital market that itself fails to perform consistently in the way that the theoretical models predict that it will perform.

Meir Statman, a professor in his late forties at the University of Santa Clara, describes behavioral finance as "not a branch of standard finance: it is its replacement with a better model of humanity."[5] We might dub the members of this group the Theory Police, because they are constantly checking to see whether investors are obeying or disobeying the laws of rational behavior as laid down by the Bernoullis, Jevons, von Neumann, Morgenstern, and Markowitz.

Richard Thaler started thinking about these problems in the early 1970s, while working on his doctoral dissertation at the University of Rochester, an institution known for its emphasis on rational theory.[6] His subject was the value of a human life, and he was trying to prove that the correct measure of that value is the amount people would be willing to pay to save a life. After studying risky occupations like mining and logging, he decided to take a break from the demanding statistical modeling he was doing and began to ask people what value they would put on their own lives.

He started by asking two questions. First, how much would you be willing to pay to eliminate a one-in-a-thousand chance of immediate death? And how much would you have to be paid to accept a one-in-a-thousand chance of immediate death? He reports that "the differences between the answers to the two questions were astonishing. A typical answer was 'I wouldn't pay more than $200, but I wouldn't accept an extra risk for $50,000!'" Thaler concluded that "the disparity between buying and selling prices was *very* interesting."

He then decided to make a list of what he called "anomalous behaviors"—behaviors that violated the predictions of standard rational theory. The list included examples of large differences between the prices at which a person would be willing to buy and sell the same item. It also included examples of the failure to recognize sunk costs—money spent that would never be recouped—as with the $40 theater ticket in the previous chapter. Many of the people he questioned would "choose not to choose regret." In 1976, he used the list as the basis for an informal paper that he circulated only to close friends and "to colleagues I wanted to annoy."

Shortly thereafter, while attending a conference on risk, Thaler met two young researchers who had been converted by Kahneman and

Tversky to the idea that so-called anomalous behavior is often really normal behavior, and that adherence to the rules of rational behavior is the exception. One of them later sent Thaler a paper by Kahneman and Tversky called "Judgment Under Uncertainty." After reading it, Thaler remarks, "I could hardly contain myself."[7] A year later, he met Kahneman and Tversky and he was off and running.

Meir Statman began to be interested in nonrational behavior when, as a student of economics, he noted that people reveal a tendency to look at problems in pieces rather than in the aggregate. Even qualified scholars in reputable journals reached faulty conclusions by failing to recognize that the whole is the product of *interaction* among its parts, or what Markowitz called covariances, rather than just a collection of discrete pieces. Statman soon recognized that the distortions caused by mental accounting were by no means limited to the public at large.

Statman cites a case that he found in a journal about a homeowner's choice between a fixed-rate mortgage and a variable-rate mortgage.[8] The paper dealt with the covariance between mortgage payments and the borrower's income and concluded that variable rates were appropriate for people whose income generally keeps pace with inflation and that fixed rates were appropriate for people whose incomes is relatively constant. But Statman noted that the authors ignored the covariance between the value of the house itself and the two variables mentioned; for example, an inflationary rise in the value of the house might make a variable-rate mortgage easy enough to carry regardless of what happened to the homeowner's income.

In 1981, Hersh Shefrin, a colleague of Statman's at Santa Clara University, showed Statman a paper titled "An Economic Theory of Self-Control," which Shefrin had written with Thaler.[9] The paper made the point that people who have trouble exercising self-control deliberately limit their options. People with weight problems, for example, avoid having a cake ready at hand. The paper also noted that people choose to ignore the positive covariance between their mortgage payments and the value of their house as borrowing collateral; they view the house as a "piggy bank" that is not to be touched, even though they always have the option to borrow more against it and, thanks to home equity loans, sometimes do.* After reading this paper, Statman too was off and running.

A year later, Shefrin and Statman collaborated on an illuminating paper on behavioral finance titled "Explaining Investor Preference for Cash Dividends,"[10] which appeared in the *Journal of Financial Economics* in 1984.

Why corporations pay dividends has puzzled economists for a long time. Why do they pay out their assets to stockholders, especially when they themselves are borrowing money at the same time? From 1959 to 1994, nonfinancial corporations in the United States borrowed more than $2 trillion while paying out dividends of $1.8 trillion.[†] They could have avoided nearly 90% of the increase in their indebtedness if they had paid no dividends at all.

From 1959 to 1994, individuals received $2.2 trillion of the dividends distributed by all corporations, financial as well as nonfinancial, and incurred an income-tax liability on every dollar of that money. If corporations had used that money to repurchase outstanding shares in the open market instead of distributing it in dividends, earnings per share would have been larger, the number of outstanding shares would have been smaller, and the price of the shares would have been higher. The remaining stockholders could have enjoyed "home-made" dividends by selling off their appreciated shares to finance their consumption and would have paid the lower tax rate on capital gains that prevailed during most of that period. On balance, stockholders would have been wealthier than they had been.

To explain the puzzle, Shefrin and Statman draw on mental accounting, self-control, decision regret, and loss aversion. In the spirit

---

*In a speech to the National Association of Realtors in May 1995, none other than the Chairman of the Federal Reserve Board, Alan Greenspan, confirmed the piggy bank metaphor: "It is hard to overestimate the importance of house price trends for consumer psyches and behavior. . . . Consumers view their home equity as a cushion or security blanket against the possibility of future hard times." As a consequence of the growth in borrowing in the form of home equity loans, home equity has shrunk from 73% of home value in 1983 to around 55% at this writing, provoking what the July 10, 1995, issue of *Business Week* describes as "a major deterrent to buoyant spending."

†We exclude financial corporations from these calculations to avoid double-counting. Banks and other financial organizations re-lend to the nonfinancial sector most of the money they borrow.

of Adam Smith's "impartial spectactor" and Sigmund Freud's "super-ego," investors resort to these deviations from rational decision-making because they believe that limiting their spending on consumption to the amount of income they receive in the form of dividends is the way to go; financing consumption by selling shares is a no-no.

Shefrin and Statman hypothesize the existence of a split in the human psyche. One side of our personality is an internal planner with a long-term perspective, an authority who insists on decisions that weight the future more heavily than the present. The other side seeks immediate gratification. These two sides are in constant conflict.

The planner can occasionally win the day just by emphasizing the rewards of self-denial. But when the need arises, the planner can always talk about dividends. As the light fixture "hides" the liquor bottle from the alcoholic, dividends "hide" the pool of capital that is available to finance immediate gratification. By repeatedly reciting the lesson that spending dividends is acceptable but that invading principal is sinful, the planner keeps a lid on how much is spent on consumption.

Once that lesson is driven home, however, investors become insistent that the stocks they own pay a reliable dividend and hold out a promise of regular increases. No dividend, no money to spend. No choice. Selling a few shares of stock and the receipt of a dividend are perfect substitutes for financing consumption *in theory*—and selling shares even costs less in taxes—but in a setting of self-control contrivances, they are far from perfect substitutes in practice.

Shefrin and Statman ask the reader to consider two cases. First, you take $600 of dividend income and buy a television set. Second, you sell $600 of stock and use the proceeds to buy a television set. The following week, the company becomes a takeover candidate and the stock zooms. Which case causes you more regret? In theory, you should be indifferent. You could have used the $600 of dividend income to buy more shares of the stock instead of buying the TV. So that was just as costly a decision as your decision to sell the shares to finance the TV. Either way, you are out the appreciation on $600 worth of shares.

But oh, what a horror if dividends are cut! In 1974, when the quadrupling of oil prices forced Consolidated Edison to eliminate its dividend after 89 years of uninterrupted payments, hysteria broke out at the company's annual meeting of stockholders. Typical was one question put to the company chairman, "What are we to do? You don't know when the dividend is coming back. Who is going to pay my rent? I had a husband. Now Con Ed has to be my husband." This shareholder never gave a thought to the possibility that paying dividends out of losses would only weaken the company and might ultimately force it into bankruptcy. What kind of a husband would that be? Selling her shares to pay the rent was not one of the options she allowed herself to consider; the dividend income and the capital were kept in separate pockets as far as she was concerned. As in a good marriage, divorce was inadmissible.

In a discussion of Shefrin and Statman's work, Merton Miller, a Nobel Laureate at the University of Chicago and one of the more formidable defenders of rational theory, made the following observation about investors who do not rely on professional advisers:

> For these investors, stocks are usually more than just the abstract "bundles of returns" of our economic models. Behind each holding may be a story of family business, family quarrels, legacies received, [and] divorce settlements . . . almost totally irrelevant to our theories of portfolio selection. That we abstract from all these stories in building our models is not because the stories are uninteresting but because they may be too interesting and thereby distract us from the pervasive market forces that should be our principal concern.[11]

In Chapter 10, I mentioned a paper titled "Does the Stock Market Overreact?" which Thaler and one of his graduate students, Werner DeBondt, presented at the annual meeting of the American Finance Association in December 1985. There this paper served as an example of regression to the mean. It can also serve as an example of the failure of the theory of rational behavior.

I was a discussant at the session at which Thaler and DeBondt presented their findings, and I began by saying, "At long last, the academic world has caught up with what investors have known all along."[12] Their answer to the question posed by the title was an unqualified "Yes."

As an example of Prospect Theory, Thaler and DeBondt demonstrated that, when new information arrives, investors revise their beliefs, not according to the objective methods set forth by Bayes, but by overweighting the new information and underweighting prior and longer-term information. That is, they weight the probabilities of outcomes on the "distribution of impressions" rather than on an objective calculation based on historical probability distributions. As a consequence, stock prices systematically overshoot so far in either direction that their reversal is predictable regardless of what happens to earnings or dividends or any other objective factor.

The paper provoked criticism from members of the audience who were shocked by this evidence of irrational pricing. The dispute continued over a number of years, focusing primarily on the manner in which Thaler and DeBondt had gathered and tested their data. One problem related to the calendar: an excessive proportion of the profits from selling the winners and buying the losers appeared in the one month of January; the rest of the year appeared to have been about break-even. But different tests by different folks continued to produce conflicting results.

In May 1993, a related paper entitled "Contrarian Investment, Extrapolation, and Risk" appeared under the auspices of the prestigious National Bureau of Economic Research.[13] The three academic authors, Josef Lakonishok, André Shleifer, and Robert Vishny, provided an elaborate statistical analysis which confirmed that so-called "value" stocks—stocks that sell at low prices relative to company earnings, dividends, or assets—tend to outperform more highly valued stocks even after adjustments for volatility and other accepted measures of risk.

The paper was memorable for more than the conclusion it reached, which was not original by any means, nor for the thoroughness and polish of the statistical presentation. Its importance lay in its confirmation of Thaler and DeBondt's behavioral explanation of these kinds of results. In part because of fear of decision regret and in part because of myopia, investors price the stocks of troubled companies too low in the short run when regression to the mean would be likely to restore most of them to good health over the long run. By the same token, companies about which recent information has indicated sharp improvement are overpriced by investors who fail to recognize that matters cannot get better and better indefinitely.

Lakonishok, Shleifer, and Vishny have certainly convinced themselves. In 1995, they launched their own firm to manage money in accordance with their contrarian model.

✸

Thaler never recovered from his early fascination with that "*very interesting*" disparity between prices for which people were willing to buy and sell the identical items. He coined the expression "endowment effect" to describe our tendency to set a higher selling price on what we own (are endowed with) than what we would pay for the identical item if we did not own it.*

In a paper written in 1990 with Daniel Kahneman and another colleague, Jack Knetsch, Thaler reported on a series of classroom experiments designed to test the prevalence of the endowment effect.[14] In one experiment, some of the students were given Cornell coffee mugs and were told they could take them home; they were also shown a range of prices and asked to set the lowest price at which they would consider selling their mug. Other students were asked the highest price they would be willing to pay to buy a mug. The average owner would not sell below $5.25, while the average buyer would not pay more than $2.25. A series of additional experiments provided consistent results.

The endowment effect is a powerful influence on investment decisions. Standard theory predicts that, since rational investors would all agree on investment values, they would all hold identical portfolios of risky assets like stocks. If that portfolio proved too risky for one of the investors, he could combine it with cash, while an investor seeking greater risk could use the portfolio as collateral for borrowings to buy more of the same.

The real world is not like that at all. True, the leading institutional investors do hold many stocks in common because the sheer volume of dollars they must invest limits them to stocks with the highest market values—stocks like General Electric and Exxon. But smaller investors have a much wider range of choice. It is rare indeed to find two of them holding identical portfolios, or even to find significant duplication in holdings. Once something is owned, its owner does not part with it lightly, regardless of what an objective valuation might reveal.

---

*As usual, Shakespeare got there first. In Act 1, Scene 1, lines 168–171 of *Timon of Athens*, the Jeweler says to Timon, "My Lord, tis rated/As those which sell would give; but you well know/Things of like value differing in their owners/Are prized by their masters."

For example, the endowment effect arising from the nationality of the issuing company is a powerful influence on valuation. Even though international diversification of investment portfolios has increased in recent years, Americans still hold mostly shares of American companies and Japanese investors hold mostly shares of Japanese companies. Yet, at this writing, the American stock market is equal to only 35% and the Japanese to only 30% of the world market.

One explanation for this tendency is that it is more costly to obtain information on securities in a foreign market than it is to obtain information on securities in the home market. But that explanation seems insufficient to explain such a great difference in holdings. There must be more compelling reasons why investors are so reluctant to hold securities domiciled in markets that account for 65% to 70% of the investible universe.

A masterful study of the influence of the endowment effect on international investing was carried out in 1989 by Kenneth French, then at the University of Chicago and now at Yale, and James Poterba at MIT.[15] The target of their inquiry was the absence of cross-border ownership between Japanese and American investors. At that time, Japanese investors owned just over 1% of the U.S. stock market, while American investors owned less than 1% of the Tokyo market. A good deal of activity was taking place across the borders; substantial buying and selling of American stocks went on in Japan and of Japanese stocks in the United States. But net purchases on either side were tiny.

The result was a striking distortion of valuations across the markets. French and Poterba's calculations indicated that the small holdings of Japanese stocks by U.S. investors could be justified only if the Americans expected annual real (inflation-adjusted) returns of 8.5% in the United States and 5.1% in Japan. The small holdings of American stocks by Japanese investors could be justified only if the Japanese expected real annual returns of 8.2% in Japan and 3.9% in the United States. Neither taxation nor institutional restrictions were sufficient to explain disparities that would set von Neumann spinning in his grave.*

---

*In Chapter 7 of Thaler, 1987, in fact, Thaler declared that von Neumann-Morgenstern utility had failed in psychological testing. See p. 139.

Nor could theories of rational investor decision-making explain them. The endowment effect must be the answer.*

The evidence presented in this chapter gives only a hint of the diligence of the Theory Police in apprehending people in the act of violating the precepts of rational behavior. The literature on that activity is large, growing, and diverse.

Now we come to the greatest anomaly of all. Even though millions of investors would readily plead guilty to acting in defiance of rationality, the market—where it really counts—act *as though* rationality prevailed.

What does it mean to say "where it really counts"? And, if that is the case, what are the consequences for managing risk?

Keynes provides a precise definition of what it means to say "where it really counts." In a famous passage in *The General Theory of Employment, Interest and Money*, Keynes describes the stock market as, ". . . so to speak, a game of Snap, of Old Maid, of Musical Chairs—a pastime in which he is victor who says *Snap* neither too soon nor too late, who passes the Old Maid to his neighbor before the game is over, who secures a chair for himself when the music stops."[16]

Keynes's metaphor suggests a test to determine whether the market acts as though rationality prevails, where it counts: the prevalence of nonrational behavior should provide endless opportunities for rational investors to say *Snap*, to pass on the Old Maid, or to seize a chair ahead of investors on the run from the Theory Police. If those opportunities do not present themselves, or are too brief to provide an advantage, we might just as well assume that the market is rational even though we recognize that many irrational forces are coursing through it. "Where it counts" means that there are very few opportunities to profit by betting against irrational investors, even though there is so much evidence of their presence in the market. Where it counts, the market's behavior conforms to the rational model.

---

*This bald assertion should be interpreted broadly. Cross-cultural problems and concerns for the health of the home country add to the value of domestic securities and detract from the value of foreign securities.

If all investors went through the identical rational thinking process, expected returns and adjustments for risk would look the same to everyone in possession of the same information at the same moment. In the unlikely event that a few investors succumbed to nonrational behavior, they would end up buying high and selling low as better-informed investors were driving prices back to a rational valuation. Otherwise, prices would change only when new information became available, and new information arrives in random fashion.

That is how a fully rational market would work. No one could outperform the market as a whole. All opportunities would be exploited. At any level of risk, all investors would earn the same rate of return.

In the real world, investors seem to have great difficulty outperforming one another in any convincing or consistent fashion. Today's hero is often tomorrow's blockhead. Over the long run, active investment managers—investors who purport to be stock-pickers and whose portfolios differ in composition from the market as a whole—seem to lag behind market indexes like the S&P 500 or even broader indexes like the Wilshire 5000 or the Russell 3000. Over the past decade, for example, 78% of all actively managed equity funds underperformed the Vanguard Index 500 mutual fund, which tracks the unmanaged S&P 500 Composite; the data for earlier periods are not as clean, but the S&P has been a consistent winner over long periods of time.

There is nothing new about this pattern. In 1933, Alfred Cowles, a wealthy investor and a brilliant amateur scholar, published a study covering a large number of printed financial services as well as every purchase and sale made over four years by twenty leading fire insurance companies. Cowles concluded that the best of a series of random forecasts made by drawing cards from an appropriate deck was just as good as the best of a series of actual forecasts, and that the results achieved by the insurance companies "could have been achieved through a purely random selection of stocks."[17] Today, with large, sophisticated, and well-informed institutional investors dominating market activity, getting ahead of the market and staying there is far more difficult than it was in the past.

If investors are unable to outguess one another with any degree of reliability, perhaps the computer can capitalize on the market's nonrational behavior; machines are immune from such human flaws as the endowment effect, myopia, and decision regret. So far, computer models that instruct the investor to buy when others are frightened and to sell when others are overconfident have produced mixed or irregular results. The investors become either more frightened or more overconfident than the computer model predicts, or else their behavior is outside the patterns the computer can recognize. Yet computerized trading is a fruitful area for further research, as we shall see shortly.

Human investors do turn in outstanding track records from time to time. But even if we ascribe those achievements to skill rather than luck, two problems remain.

First, past performance is a frail guide to the future. In retrospect, the winners are fully visible, but we have no reliable way of identifying *in advance* the investors whose skills will win out in the years ahead. Timing also matters. Even the most successful investors, people like Benjamin Graham and Warren Buffett, have had long periods of underperformance that would make any manager wince. Others zoom to fame on one or two brilliant calls, only to fall flat when their public following grows large. No one knows when their next takeoff will come, if ever.

The fine performance record of unmanaged index funds is vulnerable to the same kinds of criticism, because the guidance provided by past performance is no more reliable here than it is for active managements. Indeed, more dramatically than any other portfolio, the indexes reflect all the fads and nonrational behavior that is going on in the market. Yet a portfolio designed to track one of the major indexes, like the S&P 500, still has clear advantages over actively managed portfolios. Since turnover occurs only when a change is made in the index, transaction costs and capital-gains taxes can be held to a minimum. Furthermore, the fees charged by managers of index funds run about 0.10% of assets; active managers charge many times that, often exceeding 1% of assets. These built-in advantages are due neither to luck nor are they sensitive to some particular time period; they are working for the investor all the time.

The second problem in relying on evidence of superior management skills is that winning strategies tend to have a brief half-life. Capital markets as active and liquid as ours are so intensely competitive that results from testing ideas on past data are difficult to replicate or sustain in real time. Many smart people fail to get rich because people not so smart soon follow in their footsteps and smother the advantage their strategy was designed to create.

Because of the danger that free-riders will hop aboard a successful strategy, it is quite possible that there are investors out there who beat the market consistently beyond the probability of luck but who stubbornly guard their obscurity. Nobel Laureate Paul Samuelson, an eloquent defender of the hypothesis that markets act as though they were rational, has admitted that possibility: "People differ in their heights, pulchritude, and acidity, why not in their P.Q., or performance quotient?" But he goes on to point out that the few people who have high P.Q.s are unlikely to rent their talents "to the Ford Foundation or the local bank trust department. They have too high an I.Q. for that."[18] You will not find them on Wall $treet Week, on the cover of *Time*, or contributing papers to scholarly journals on portfolio theory.

Instead, they are managing private partnerships that limit the number of investors they accept and that mandate seven-figure minimum participations. Since they participate in the capital appreciation as well as receiving a fee, adding other people's money to their own gives them an opportunity to leverage their P.Q.s. It may well be that some of them would qualify as Snap champs.

In Chapter 19 we shall look at what some of these investors are trying to do. Their strategies draw on theoretical and empirical concepts that reach back to the origins of probability and to the Chevalier de Méré himself. But those strategies incorporate a more complex view of market rationality than I have set forth. If there is validity to the notion that risk equals opportunity, this little tribe is showing the way.

Nevertheless, private partnerships are peripheral to the mainstream of the marketplace. Most investors either have too little money to participate, or, like the giant pension funds, they are so big that they cannot allocate a significant portion of their assets to the partnerships. Moreover, the funds may be inhibited by the fear of decision regret in the event that these unconventional investments go sour. In any case, when the largest investors begin to experiment with exotic quantitative concepts, they must be careful not to get in each other's way.

What are the consequences of all this for managing risks? Does the presence of nonrational behavior make investing a riskier activity than it would otherwise be? The answer to that question requires putting it into its historical setting.

Capital markets have always been volatile, because they trade in nothing more than bets on the future, which is full of surprises. Buying shares of stock, which carry no maturity date, is a risky business. The only way investors can liquidate their equity positions is by selling their shares to one another: everyone is at the mercy of everyone else's expectations and buying power. Similar considerations apply to bonds, which return their principal value in cash to their owners but only at some future date.

Such an environment provides a perfect setting for nonrational behavior: uncertainty is scary. If the nonrational actors in the drama overwhelm the rational actors in numbers and in wealth, asset prices are likely to depart far from equilibrium levels and to remain there for extended periods of time. Those periods are often long enough to exhaust the patience of the most rational of investors. Under most circumstances, therefore, the market is more volatile than it would be if everyone signed up for the rational model and left Kahneman and Tversky to find other fields to plow.[19]

Nevertheless, explicit attention to investment risk and to the trade-off between risk and return is a relatively young notion. Harry Markowitz laid out the basic idea for the first time only in 1952, which seems like a long time ago but is really a late-comer in the history of markets. And with a great bull market getting under way in the early 1950s, Markowitz's focus on the risks of portfolio selection attracted little attention at the time. Academic interest speeded up during the 1960s, but it was only after 1974 that practitioners sat up and took notice.

The explanation for this delayed reaction has to do with changes in the volatility of the market. From 1926 to 1945—a period that included the Great Crash, the Depression, and the Second World War—the standard deviation of annual total returns (income plus change in capital values) was 37% a year while returns averaged only about 7% a year. That was really risky business!

Investors brought that memory bank to the capital markets in the late 1940s and on into the 1950s. Once burned, twice shy. A renewal of speculative fever and unbridled optimism was slow to develop despite a mighty bull market that drove the Dow Jones Industrial Average from less than 200 in 1945 to 1,000 by 1966. From 1946 to 1969, despite a handsome return of over 12% a year and a brief outburst of speculative enthusiasm in 1961, the standard deviation of total returns was only one-third of what it had been from 1926 to 1945.

This was the memory that bank investors carried into the 1970s. Who would worry about risk in a market like that? Actually, everyone should have worried. From the end of 1969 to the end of 1975, the return on the S&P 500 was only half what it had been from 1946 to 1969, while the annual standard deviation nearly doubled, to 22%. During 12 of the 24 calendar quarters over this period, an investor in the stock market would have been better off owning Treasury bills.

Professional managers, who by 1969 had pushed client portfolios as high as 70% in common stocks, felt like fools. Their clients took an even harsher view. In the fall of 1974, the maiden issue of *The Journal of Portfolio Management* carried a lead article by a senior officer of Wells Fargo Bank who admitted the bitter truth:

> Professional investment management and its practitioners are inconsistent, unpredictable, and in trouble. . . . Clients are afraid of us, and what our methods might produce in the way of further loss as much or more than they are afraid of stocks. . . . The business badly needs to replace its cottage industry operating methods.[20]

For the first time risk management became the biggest game in town. First came a major emphasis on diversification, not only in stock holdings, but across the entire portfolio, ranging from stocks to bonds to cash assets. Diversification also forced investors to look into new areas and to develop appropriate management techniques. The traditional strategy of buy-and-hold-until-maturity for long-term bonds, for example, was replaced by active, computer-based management of fixed-income assets. Pressures for diversification also led investors to look outside the United States. There they found opportunities for high returns, quite apart from the diversification benefits of international investing.

But even as the search for risk-management techniques was gaining popularity, the 1970s and the 1980s gave rise to new uncertainties that had never been encountered by people whose world view had been shaped by the benign experiences of the postwar era. Calamities struck, including the explosion in oil prices, the constitutional crisis caused by Watergate and the Nixon resignation, the hostage-taking in Teheran, and the disaster at Chernobyl. The cognitive dissonances created by these shocks were similar to those experienced by the Victorians and the Edwardians during the First World War.

Along with financial deregulation and a wild inflationary sleighride, the environment generated volatility in interest rates, foreign exchange rates, and commodity prices that would have been unthinkable during the preceding three decades. Conventional forms of risk management were incapable of dealing with a world so new, so unstable, and so frightening.

These conditions gave rise to a perfect example of Ellsberg's ambiguity aversion. We can calculate probabilities from real-life situations only when similar experiences have occurred often enough to resemble the patterns of games of chance. Going out without an umbrella on a cloudy day is risky, but we have seen enough cloudy days and have listened to enough weather reports to be able to calculate, with some accuracy, the probability of rain. But when events are unique, when the shape and color of the clouds have never been seen before, ambiguity takes over and risk premiums skyrocket. You either stay home or take the umbrella whenever you go out, no matter how inconvenient. That is what happened in the 1970s, when the valuations of both stocks and bonds were extremely depressed compared with the valuations that prevailed during the 1960s.

The alternative is to discover methods to mute the impact of the unexpected, to manage the risk of the unknown. Although diversification has never lost its importance, professional investors recognized some time ago that it was both inadequate as a risk-management technique and too primitive for the new environment of volatility and uncertainty.

Fortuitously perhaps, impressive technological innovation coincided with the urgent demand for novel methods of risk control. Computers were introduced into investment management just as concerns about risk were escalating. Their novelty and extraordinary power added to the sense of alienation, but at the same time computers greatly expanded the capacity to manipulate data and to execute complex strategies.

If, as Prospect Theory suggested, investors had met the enemy and it was them, now the search was on for protective measures that made more sense than decision regret or myopia or the endowment effect. A new age of risk management was about to open, with concepts, techniques, and methodologies that made use of the financial system but whose customers were spread well beyond the parochial precincts of the capital markets.

The decisive step from superstition to the supercomputer was about to be taken.

18

The Fantastic System of Side Bets

D erivatives are the most sophisticated of financial instruments, the most intricate, the most arcane, even the most risky. Very 1990s, and to many people a dirty word.

Here is what *Time* magazine had to say in an April 1994 cover story:

> [T]his fantastic system of side bets is not based on old-fashioned human hunches but on calculations designed and monitored by computer wizards using abstruse mathematical formulas . . . developed by so-called quants, short for quantitative analysts.

We have just looked at the fantastic system of side bets based on old-fashioned human hunches. Now we turn to the fantastic system concocted by the quants.

Despite the mystery that has grown up about these instruments in recent years, there is nothing particularly modern about them. Derivatives go back so far in time that they have no identifiable inventors: no Cardano, Bernoulli, Graunt, or Gauss. The use of derivatives arose from the need to reduce uncertainty, and surely there is nothing new about that.

Derivatives are financial instruments that have no value of their own. That may sound weird, but it is the secret of what they are all about. They are called derivatives because they derive their value from the value of some other asset, which is precisely why they serve so well to hedge the risk of unexpected price fluctuations. They hedge the risk in owning things like bushels of wheat, French francs, government bonds, and common stocks—in short any asset whose price is volatile.

Frank Knight once remarked, "Every act of production is a speculation in the relative value of money and the good produced."[1] Derivatives cannot reduce the risks that go with owning volatile assets, but they can determine who takes on the speculation and who avoids it.

Today's derivatives differ from their predecessors only in certain respects: they are valued mathematically instead of by seat-of-the-pants methods, the risks they are asked to respond to are more complex, they are designed and managed by computers, and they are put to novel purposes. None of these features is the root cause of the dramatic growth in the use of derivatives or the headlines they have grabbed.

Derivatives have value only in an environment of volatility; their proliferation is a commentary on our times. Over the past twenty years or so, volatility and uncertainty have emerged in areas long characterized by stability. Until the early 1970s, exchange rates were legally fixed, the price of oil varied over a narrow range, and the overall price level rose by no more than 3% or 4% a year. The abrupt appearance of new risks in areas so long considered stable has triggered a search for novel and more effective tools of risk management. Derivatives are symptomatic of the state of the economy and of the financial markets, not the cause of the volatility that is the focus of so much concern.

Derivatives come in two flavors: as futures (contracts for future delivery at specified prices), and as options that give one side the opportunity to buy from or sell to the other side at a prearranged price. Sophisticated as they may appear in the fancy dress in which we see them today, their role in the management of risk probably originated centuries ago down on the farm. The particulars may have changed over time, but the farmer's fundamental need for controlling risk has not. Farmers cannot tolerate volatility, because they are perennially in debt. Their huge investments in land and equipment and in inventories of seed and fertilizer make bank financing unavoidable. Before the farmer sees any money coming his way, he has to pay for his inputs, plant his crop, and then, constantly fearful of flood, drought, and blight, wait months until harvest time. His great uncertainty is what the price will be when he is finally in a position to deliver his crop to the market. If the price he receives is below his cost of production, he might be unable to pay his debts and might lose everything.

The farmer is helpless before the risks of weather and insects, but he can at least escape the uncertainty of what his selling price will be. He can do that by selling his crop when he plants it, promising future delivery to the buyer at a prearranged price. He may miss out on some profit if prices rise, but the futures contract will protect him from catastrophe if prices fall. He has passed along the risk of lower prices to someone else.

That someone else is often a food processor who faces the opposite risk—he will gain if the prices of his inputs fall while the crop is still in the ground, but he will be in trouble if prices rise and boost the cost of his raw materials. By taking on the farmer's contract, the processor lets the farmer assume the risk that agricultural prices might rise. This transaction, involving supposedly risky contracts for both parties, actually *lowers* total risk in the economy.

On occasion, the other side of the deal is a speculator—someone who is willing to take over uncertainty from others out of a conviction about how matters will turn out. In theory at least, speculators in commodities will make money over the long run because there are so many people whose financial survival is vulnerable to the risks of volatility. As a result, volatility tends to be underpriced, especially in the commodity markets, and the producer's loss aversion gives the speculator a built-in advantage. This phenomen goes under the strange name of "backwardation."

In the twelfth century, sellers at medieval trade fairs signed contracts, called *lettres de faire*, promising future delivery of the items they sold. In the 1600s, Japanese feudal lords sold their rice for future delivery in a market called *cho-ai-mai* under contracts that protected them from bad weather or warfare. For many years, in markets such as metals, foreign exchange, agricultural products, and, more recently, stocks and bonds, the use of contracts for future delivery has been a common means of protection against the risks of volatile prices. Futures contracts for commodities like wheat, pork bellies, and copper have been trading on the Chicago Board of Trade since 1865.

Options also have a long history. In Book I of *Politics*, Aristotle described an option as "a financial device which involves a principle of universal application." Much of the famous Dutch tulip bubble of the seventeenth century involved trading in options on tulips rather than in the tulips themselves, trading that was in many ways as sophisticated as anything that goes on in our own times. Tulip dealers bought options known as *calls* when they wanted the assurance that they could increase their inventories when prices were rising; these options gave the dealer the right, but not the obligation, to call on the other side to deliver tulips at a prearranged price. Growers seeking protection against falling prices would buy options known as *puts* that gave them the right to put, or sell, to the other side at a prearranged price. The other side of these options—the sellers—assumed these risks in return for premiums paid by the buyers of the options, premiums that would presumably compensate sellers of calls for taking the risk that prices would rise and to compensate sellers of puts for taking the risk that prices would fall.

Incidentally, recent research has punched a hole in the tales of the notorious mania for tulips in seventeenth-century Holland, supposedly fueled by the use of options. Actually, it seems, options gave more people an opportunity to participate in a market that had previously been closed to them. The opprobrium attached to options during the so-called tulip bubble was in fact cultivated by vested interests who resented the intrusion of interlopers onto their turf.[2]

In the United States, options appeared early on. Brokers were trading put and call options on stocks as early as the 1790s, not long after the famous Buttonwood Tree Agreement established what was to become the New York Stock Exchange.

An ingenious risk-management contract was issued on June 1, 1863, when the Confederate States of America, hard up for credit and desperate for money, issued the "7 Per Cent Cotton Loan." The loan had some unusual provisions that gave it the look of a derivative instrument.[3]

The principal amount was not repayable in Confederate dollars nor was it repayable at the Confederate capitol in Richmond, Virginia. Instead, it was set at "3 Millions Sterling Or 75 Millions Francs" and it was repayable in forty semiannual installments in Paris, London,

Amsterdam, or Frankfurt, at the option of the bondholder—who was given the additional option of taking payment in cotton rather than money, at the rate of sixpence sterling per pound, "at any time not later than six months after the ratification of a Treaty of Peace between the belligerents."

The embattled Confederate government was using a sophisticated form of risk management to tempt English and French investors to lend them urgently needed foreign exchange to finance their armament purchases abroad. At the same time, it was building up a foreign constituency with a vested interest in the Confederacy's survival. The risk of devaluation of the Confederate dollar was covered by the option of repayment in British or French money.* The option of collecting the debt in cotton was a hedge against inflation and was sweetened by offering cotton at sixpence when the prevailing price in Europe was 24 pence. Furthermore, as the obligation was convertible "at any time" into cotton, this option was something of a hedge against the fortunes of war for those lenders nimble enough to pick up their cotton before the Confederate States collapsed.

The Confederate States were the sellers of these options: they took on uncertain liabilities because they had no choice in the matter. A promise to repay the loan in Confederate dollars would have been laughed out of the credit markets or would have necessitated an intolerable double-digit interest rate. The premium the Confederates received in return from the lenders who acquired these options was a reduction in the interest rate on the loan: 7% was only about a percentage point more than the U.S. government was paying for long-term money at that time. The introduction of the options made this a transaction in which *uncertainty itself was an integral part*.

The history of these bonds is interesting. The subscription books were opened in March 1863, but, in keeping with the conventions of the times, the proceeds were not to be received by September. The bonds sold above their offering price for a brief period after the March offering, but then the price broke sharply as stories began to circulate about Jefferson Davis's connection with some repudiated bonds in

---

*The bond even offered protection against the possibility that one pound sterling might subsequently buy more or less than 25 francs. The French went off gold in 1870, at which time one pound sterling could buy substantially more than 25 francs.

Mississippi. Concerned that subscribers would reneg on the payments due in September, the Confederate Treasury went into the market to support the price by buying up some £1.4 million of the £3 million issued. The Confederates met the payments due in September 1863 and the two semiannual payments in 1864, but that was the end. Only about £370,000 par value was ever redeemed in cotton.

Many people are willing but unwitting buyers of options. Anyone who has ever taken out a mortgage with a prepayment privilege owns an option. Here it is the borrower—the homeowner—rather than the lender who has the option to determine the conditions of repayment. What is the price of that option? The interest rate the borrower pays to the bank is higher than it would be without the prepayment option. If mortgage rates fall, the homeowner will prepay the old mortgage and take out a new one at a lower rate, leaving the banker with the loss of a high-interest loan replaced by a low-interest loan. This option is such a conventional feature, often a mandated feature, of home mortgages today that most homeowners are not even aware that they are paying extra for the privilege—and neither are most of the bankers!*

There is more than meets the eye in the design of the cotton bond, the farmer's futures contracts, the tulip options, and mortgage prepayment privileges. Most business and financial transactions are a bet in which the buyer hopes to be buying low and the seller hopes to be selling high. One side is always doomed to disappointment. Risk-management products are different. They exist, not necessarily because someone is seeking a profit, but because there is a demand for instruments that transfer risk from a risk-averse party to someone willing to bear risk. In the case of the cotton loan, the Confederacy took on a foreign-exchange risk and even the risk of victory itself in order to save the difference between 7% and the interest that would have been demanded without the options; it may even have received money that would not have been forthcoming under other conditions. The lenders—the buyers of the Confederate bonds—acquired options that

---

*This is an oversimplification to make the basic point. Most individual home mortgages are packaged with other mortgages and sold off in the open market to a wide variety of investors. In effect, the bankers have traded off the risks of prepayment to a market more willing to bear that risk; these mortgage-backed securities are complex, volatile, and much too risky for amateur investors to play around with.

reduced their risk sufficiently to compensate for the lower interest rate or for the possibility that the Confederates would lose the war. By trading uncertainty, both parties were winners.

What is an option worth? How did the traders in tulip options decide how much to pay for a call or a put, and why did those values change over time? How did the lenders to the Confederates decide that the options to receive payment in sterling or francs or cotton were sufficient to hedge the risks they took in making the loans? How much extra is the homeowner with a prepayment privilege paying the mortgage banker?

The answers to these questions may become clearer if we look at an example of an actively traded option on a stock. On June 6, 1995, when AT&T stock was selling at 50, there was an option outstanding on AT&T stock that gave the owner the right to buy one share of stock at 50 1/4 until October 15, 1995. The stock was selling for less than 50 1/4—the "strike price"; if the stock remained below the strike price for the duration of the option, the option would be worthless and its owner would lose the entire premium paid for it. Yet that premium is all that the buyer of the option had at risk and all that the seller of the option could hope to gain. If AT&T stock rose above the strike price before October 15 by an amount greater than the option premium, the option would generate a profit. In fact, the potential profit on the option would be limitless.

The option on AT&T stock was selling for $2.50 on June 6, 1995. Why $2.50?

Resolving Paccioli's unfinished game of *balla* was kid stuff compared to this! We can only wonder whether two quants like Pascal and Fermat could have come up with an answer—and why they did not even try. The Dutch tulip mania, a striking example of what happens when "old-fashioned human hunches" take over, had occurred only twenty years before Pascal and Fermat first laid out the principles of probability theory; the memory of it must still have been vivid when they began their historic deliberations. Perhaps they ignored the challenge of valuing an option because the key to the puzzle is in the price of uncertainty, a concept that seems more appropriate to our own times than it may have seemed to theirs.

The first effort to use mathematics rather than intuition in valuing an option was made by Louis Bachelier back in 1900. In the 1950s and 1960s, a few more people tried their hands at it, including Paul Samuelson.

The puzzle was finally solved in the late 1960s by an odd three-some, none of whom was yet thirty years old when their collaboration began.[4] Fischer Black was a physicist-mathematician with a doctorate from Harvard who had never taken a course in economics or finance. He soon found his scientific academic studies too abstract for his taste and went to work at the Boston-based management consulting firm of Arthur D. Little. Myron Scholes had a fresh Ph.D. in finance from the Graduate School of Business at the University of Chicago, to which he had fled to escape his family's publishing enterprise; he had just joined the MIT faculty. Robert C. Merton, whose first published paper was titled "The 'Motionless' Motion of Swift's Flying Island," had received a B.S. degree in mathematical engineering at Columbia but was teaching economics at MIT as an assistant to Samuelson and was as yet without a Ph.D.

Black died in 1995 at the age of 57. He was a cool man of few words; his presidential address to the American Economic Association in 1985 had a one-word-one-syllable title—"Noise"—and took less than fifteen minutes to deliver. Scholes is dark, intense, and voluble. Merton is friendly and irrepressible. All three have been brilliant innovators in finance, beyond their contribution to option theory.

The story begins in 1965, when Black made friends with a colleague named Jack Treynor; Treynor was just starting on a path that would lead him to become a theoretical powerhouse in the field of finance. At the time, he was studying economics on the side under the guidance of Franco Modigliani of the MIT faculty, who would later earn a Nobel Prize in economics. When Treynor showed Black his early work on a model to explain how the markets trade off risk and return, Black was fascinated. A passionate believer in free markets, Black decided to apply Treynor's ideas to the valuation of options, and, to help himself along, he took Treynor's advice to join a Thursday evening finance workshop at MIT.

Three years later, Black was still staring at equations that refused to produce an answer. Treynor's analysis of how market fluctuations influence the valuation of individual securities simply did not fit the bill. At that point, Black recalls, "Myron Scholes and I started working together." They had met each other at the Thursday evening workshops, where Black discovered that Scholes had been frustrated in taking the same approach to the same problem. The more they worked together over their equations, the clearer it seemed that the answer had nothing to do with Treynor's models of risk and reward.

In the spring of 1970, Scholes told Merton about the troubles he and Black were having. The problem appealed to Merton immediately. He soon resolved their dilemma by pointing out that they were on the right track for reasons they themselves had failed to recognize. The model was soon completed.

Despite its complex algebraic appearance, the basic ideas behind the model are easy to understand. The value of an option depends on four elements: time, prices, interest rates, and volatility. These elements apply to puts as well as to calls; in what follows, I explain how they work in terms of a call option, which gives the owner the right to buy the stock at a specified price.

The first element is the period of time until the option is due to expire; when the time to expiration is long, the option will be worth more than when the time is short. The second element is the spread between the current price of the stock and the price specified in the option contract at which the owner can buy or sell the stock—this is known as the strike price; the option will be worth more when the actual price is above the strike price than when it is below the strike price. Third, the value also depends on the interest the buyer can earn on his money while waiting to exercise the option as well as the income the seller can receive on the underlying asset over the same time period. But what really matters is the fourth element: the expected volatility of the underlying asset, such as the AT&T stock in the example above, where AT&T was selling for 50 and the owner of the option had the right to buy it at 50 1/4 any time between June 6 and October 15, 1995.

The probability that the price of AT&T stock might go up—or down—is irrelevant. The only thing that matters is how far the stock price might move, not the direction in which it moves. The notion that the direction of price change is irrelevant to the valuation of an option is so counterintuitive that it explains in part why Black and Scholes took so long to come up with the answer they were seeking—

even when it was right in front of them. But it unlocks the puzzle because of the asymmetric nature of the option itself: the investor's potential loss is limited to the premium, while the potential profit is unlimited.

If AT&T stock goes to 45, or 40, or even to 20 during the life of the option, the owner of the option still stands to lose no more than $2.50. Between 50 1/4 and 52 3/4, the owner will gain less than $2.50. Above 52 3/4, the potential profit is infinite—at least in theory. With all the variables cranked in, the Black-Scholes model indicates that the AT&T option was worth about $2.50 in June 1995 because investors expected AT&T stock to vary within a range of about 10%, or five points, in each direction during the four months the option would be in existence.

Volatility is always the key determinant. By way of contrast to AT&T, consider the stock of software leader Microsoft. On the same day that AT&T stock was at 50 and its option was selling for $2.50, Microsoft stock was selling at 83 1/8, and an option to buy a share of Microsoft within four months at 90 was trading for $4.50. The price of this option was 80% above the price of the AT&T option, although Microsoft stock was selling at only about 60% above AT&T. The price of Microsoft stock was nearly seven points away from the strike price, compared with the mere quarter of a point difference in the case of AT&T. The market clearly expected Microsoft to be more volatile than AT&T. According to the Black-Scholes model, the market expected Microsoft to be exactly twice as volatile as AT&T over the following four months.

Microsoft stock is a lot riskier than AT&T stock. In 1995, AT&T had revenues of nearly $90 billion, 2.3 million shareholders, a customer in just about every household and every business in the nation, a weakened but still powerful monopolistic position in its industry, and a long history of uninterrupted dividend payments. Microsoft stock had been available to the public only since 1982, its revenues at the time were just $6 billion, it had a much narrower customer base than AT&T, it had brilliant competitors straining to break its hold on the software industry, and it had never paid a dividend.

Option traders understand such differences. Anything that makes a stock move at all is what matters, because stocks that tend to drop fast also tend to rise fast. Buyers of options are looking for action; investors who sell options like stocks that stand still. If Microsoft goes to 100 and the owner of the option exercises his right to "call" the stock at 90 from the seller of the option, the seller is going to be out ten points. But if Microsoft hangs in around 83, at which it was trading when the transaction took place, the seller of the option would walk away with the entire premium of $4.50. By the same token, the right to prepay a home mortgage is worth a lot more when interest rates are jumping around than when they are stable.

Options bear a strong family resemblance to insurance policies and are often bought and sold for the same reasons. Indeed, if insurance policies were converted into marketable securities, they would be priced in the marketplace exactly as options are priced. During the time period covered by the premium payment, the buyer of an insurance policy has the right to put something to the insurance company at a prearranged price—his burned-down house, destroyed car, medical bills, even his dead body—in return for which the insurance company is obliged to pay over to him the agreed-upon value of the loss he has sustained. If the house does not burn down, if the car never has an accident, if the policyholder enjoys perfect health, and if he lives beyond his life expectancy, he will be out the premiums he has paid and collects nothing. The premium itself will depend on the degree of uncertainty surrounding each outcome—the structure of the house, the age of the car (and its drivers), the policyholder's medical history, and whether the man is a coal miner or a computer operator. The derivatives we call options, by expanding the variety of risks that can be insured, help to create Kenneth Arrow's ideal world where all risks are insurable.

Derivatives are not transactions in shares of stock or interest rates, in human lives, in houses vulnerable to fire, or in home mortgages. *The product in derivative transactions is uncertainty itself.* That is why options on Microsoft cost more than options on AT&T, why earthquake insurance is more expensive in California than in Maine, why the lenders to the Confederate States were able to extract such onerous terms, and why bankers worry about a decline in mortgage rates.

Black and Scholes set down their ideas about option valuation in an article that they mailed in October 1970 to *The Journal of Political*

Economy, a prestigious journal published by Chicago University. The editors promptly rejected the paper, claiming that Black and Scholes had put too much finance into it and too little economics.* Harvard's *Review of Economics and Statistics* was equally prompt in returning the paper. Neither publication even bothered to have a referee review it. The paper finally saw the light of day in the May/June 1973 issue of *The Journal of Political Economy,* but only after two influential members of the Chicago faculty had interceded. The article turned out to be one of the most influential pieces of research ever published in the field of economics or finance.

In one of those strange coincidences in which events seem to happen in bunches, the Chicago Board Options Exchange opened for business in April 1973, just one month before the Black-Scholes paper appeared in print. That exchange, more familiarly known as the CBOE, began its operations in the smoking lounge of the Chicago Board of Trade, the established center for trading in commodities. The CBOE, for the first time, provided traders in stock options with standardized contracts and with market-makers who gave the options liquidity by standing ready to buy or sell them on demand. The CBOE also promised strict regulation of trading practices as well as prompt, public reporting of all transactions.

On the first day of trading, 911 options changed hands on 16 individual stock issues. By 1978, daily volume had climbed to an average of 100,000 contracts. By mid-1995, a million stock options were changing hands daily. Another 300,000 options were trading on four other exchanges around the country. With each option representing a hundred shares of stock, activity in the option markets is significant relative to the volume on the stock exchanges themselves.

The CBOE now boasts one of the most technologically sophisticated trading centers in the world. It consists of a spacious trading floor, a basement with an acre and a half of computers, enough wiring to reach twice around the Equator, and a telephone system that could service a city of 50,000.

---

*Black suspected that something more unpleasant was involved: that his lack of proper warpaint in the form of a degree in economics excluded him from the tribal membership that the editors considered essential for an appearance in the *JPE.*

There was a second coincidence. At the very time the Black-Scholes article appeared in *The Journal of Political Economy* and the CBOE started trading, the hand-held electronic calculator appeared on the scene. Within six months of the publication of the Black-Scholes model, Texas Instruments placed a half-page ad in *The Wall Street Journal* that proclaimed, "Now you can find the Black-Scholes value using our . . . calculator." Before long, options traders were using technical expressions right out of the Black-Scholes article, such as hedge ratios, deltas, and stochastic differential equations. The world of risk management had vaulted into a new era.

In September 1976, Hayne Leland, a 35-year-old finance professor at Berkeley, had a sleepless night worrying about his family's finances. As Leland tells the story, "Lifestyles were in danger, and it was time for invention."[5]

Necessity is the mother of invention: Leland had a brainstorm. He would singlehandedly overcome the intense risk aversion that dominated the capital markets in the wake of the debacle of simultaneous crashes in both the bond market and the stock market in 1973–1974. He set about developing a system that would insure investment portfolios against loss in the same way that an insurance company protects a policyholder from loss when an accident occurs. Insured investors could then take on the risk of carrying a large proportion—perhaps even all—of their wealth in stocks. Like any option holder, they would have unlimited upside and a downside limited to nothing more than an insurance premium. Sugarplums began to dance in Leland's head.

By dawn, he was convinced that he had the whole thing figured out. "Eureka!" he shouted. "Now I know how to do it." But after he got up and faced the day, he was beset by a host of theoretical and mechanical difficulties. He went immediately to the office of his friend Mark Rubinstein, a Berkeley colleague who Leland knew could be trusted with his secret. Rubinstein was not only a keen theoretician and a serious scholar; he had had experience trading options on the floor of the Pacific Stock Exchange.

Groggy but manic, Leland laid out his scheme. Rubinstein's first reaction was, "I'm surprised I never thought of that myself." He became an eager collaborator, to the point where the two men, at this very first meeting, agreed to form a company to market their product, which would be called, naturally, portfolio insurance.

As Leland described it, portfolio insurance would mimic the performance of a portfolio that owns a put option—the right to sell an asset to someone else at a stated price over a specific period of time. Suppose an investor buys 100 shares of AT&T at 50 and simultaneously buys a put on AT&T with an exercise price of 45. No matter how low AT&T may fall, this investor cannot lose more than five points. If AT&T drops to 42 before the option expires, the investor could put the stock to the seller of the option, receive $4500, and go into the market and buy back the stock at a cost of only $4,200. The put under these circumstances would have a value of $300. Net, the investor could lose no more than $500.

Leland's notion was to replicate the performance of a put option by what he called a dynamically programmed system that would instruct a client to sell stocks and increase the cash position as stock prices fell. By the time the stocks hit the floor that the client has designated—45 in the AT&T example—the portfolio would be 100% cash and could suffer no further loss. If the stocks went back up, the portfolio would reinvest the cash on a similar schedule. If stocks never declined at all below the starting price, the portfolio would enjoy all the appreciation. Just as with a plain-vanilla put option, details of the dynamic program would depend on the distance from the starting point to the floor, the time period involved, and the expected volatility of the portfolio.

The distance between the starting point and the floor was comparable to the deductible on an insurance policy: this much loss the policyholder would have to cover. The cost of the policy would be in its step-by-step character. As the market began to fall, the portfolio would gradually liquidate but would still hold some stock. As the market began to rise, the portfolio would start buying but would still be carrying some cash. The result would be a portfolio that underperformed slightly in both directions; that underperformance constituted the premium. The more volatile the market, the greater the underperformance premium, just as the premiums on conventional insurance policies depend on the uncertainty of what is insured.

Two years later after that fateful meeting, Leland and Rubinstein were ready to go, convinced that they had cleared away all the snags.

They had had many adventures along the way, including a catastrophic error in computer programming that had led them to believe for a time that the whole idea was impossible. Rubinstein started playing the system with his own money and was so successful at it that he was written up in *Fortune* magazine. Marketing began in earnest in 1979, but the concept turned out to be hard for two academics to sell. They brought on John O'Brien, a professional marketer and an expert in portfolio theory; O'Brien landed their first client in the fall of 1980. Before long, the demand for portfolio insurance was so intense that major competitors entered the field, notably the leading portfolio-management group at Wells Fargo Bank in San Francisco. By 1987, some $60 billion dollars in equity assets were covered by portfolio insurance, most of it on behalf of large pension funds.

Implementation was difficult at first, because handling simultaneous orders to buy or sell several hundred stocks was complicated and costly. In addition, active portfolio managers of pension funds resented having some outsider give them orders, with little or no warning, to add to or sell off parts of their portfolios.

These problems were resolved when the market for futures contracts on the S&P 500 opened up in 1983. These contracts are much like the farmer's contract described earlier, in that they promise delivery at a specified date and at a prearranged price. But there are two important differences. The other side of the S&P 500 futures contract is an organized, regulated exchange, not an individual or a business firm; this has long been the case with futures contracts on commodities as well. But unlike tangible commodities, the 500 stocks in the S&P index are not literally deliverable when the contract matures. Instead, the owner of the contract makes a cash settlement based on the variation in the index between the signing of the contract and its maturity. Investors must put up cash with the exchange each day to cover these variations, so that all contracts are fully collateralized at all times; that is how the exchange is in the position to take the other side when an investor wants to buy or sell a futures contract on the index.

The S&P futures have another attraction. They give an investor an effective and inexpensive method of buying or selling a proxy for the market as a whole, in preference to trying to unload or load up on a large number of securities in a limited period of time. The investor's underlying portfolio, and any managers of that portfolio, remain undisturbed. The index futures greatly simplified the mechanics of carrying out portfolio insurance programs.

To the clients who signed up, portfolio insurance appeared to be the ideal form of risk management that all investors dream about—a chance to get rich without any risk of loss. Its operation differed in only one way from an actual put option and in only one way from a true insurance policy.

But those differences were enormous and ultimately turned out to be critical. A put option is a contract: the seller of the AT&T put option is legally bound to buy if the owner of the option puts the stock. Put options on the CBOE require the seller to post cash collateral to be certain that the potential buyer is protected. Insurance companies also sign contracts obliging them to make good in the event of a claim of loss, and they set aside reserves to cover this eventuality.

Where does the necessary cash come from to reliquify insured portfolios when stock prices are falling? From the stock market itself—all the other investors to whom the insured investors will want to sell their stocks. But no reserves or collateral exist to guarantee that the liquidity will be there when called upon. The market had no legal obligation to bail out Leland and Rubinstein's clients and other insured portfolios against loss. Those other investors were not even aware of the role they were expected to play. Leland's brainstorm assumed that the buyers would be there, but he had no way to guarantee that they would actually show up when called upon to do their duty.

The chickens that Leland and Rubinstein hatched in their laboratory came home to roost on Monday, October 19, 1987. The preceding week had been a disaster. The Dow Jones Industrials had fallen by 250 points, or about 10%, with nearly half the drop occurring on Friday. A huge overhang of sell orders had then built up over the weekend, waiting to be executed at Monday's opening. The market dropped 100 points by noon, nearly another 200 points in the next two hours, and almost 300 points in the final hour and a quarter. Meanwhile, as the managers of insured portfolios struggled to carry out their programed sales, they were contributing to the waves of selling that overwhelmed the market.

When the dust had settled, the owners of the insured portfolios were in better shape than many other investors. They had all done some selling during the bad week that preceded October 19, and most of them got out either at or only slightly below their designated floors. But the selling took place at prices far lower than anticipated. The dynamic programs that drove portfolio insurance underestimated the market's volatility and overestimated its liquidity. What happened was like a life insurance policy with a variable-rate instead of a fixed-rate premium, in which the company has the right to raise its premium as the insured's body temperature rises, degree by degree, increasing the probability of early demise. The cost of portfolio insurance in that feverish market turned out to be much higher than paper calculations had predicted.

The unhappy experience with portfolio insurance did nothing to quell the growing appetite for risk-management products, even though portfolio insurance itself virtually vanished from the scene. During the 1970s and 1980s, volatility seemed to be breaking out all over, even in places where it had been either absent or muted. Volatility erupted in the foreign exchange markets after the dollar was cut free from gold in 1981 and allowed to fluctuate freely; volatility overwhelmed the normally serene bond market during the wild swings in interest rates from 1979 to the mid-1980s; and volatility shot up in commodity markets during the huge jumps in oil prices in 1973 and again in 1978.

These unexpected outbreaks of volatility soon littered the corporate landscape with a growing number of dead carcasses, providing grim warnings to executives that a fundamental change in the economic environment was taking place. For example, Laker Airlines, a fabulously successful upstart in transatlantic travel, ended up in bankruptcy after ordering new McDonnell-Douglas aircraft in response to soaring demand; with most of its revenues in pounds and with the foreign exchange value of the dollar climbing higher and higher, Laker found it impossible to earn enough to pay off the dollar obligations on their DC-10s. Reputable savings and loan associations went under as the interest rates they had to pay their depositors mounted while the income they received on their fixed-rate mortgage loans never budged. Continental Airlines succumbed when oil prices went through the roof during the Gulf War.

As a consequence, a new kind of customer appeared in the financial markets: the corporation seeking to transfer the new risks in exchange rates, interest rates, and commodity prices to someone better equipped to carry them. The corporation was responding as Kahneman and Tversky would have predicted, but with an added flourish. As we might have expected, the pain of potential losses loomed larger than the satisfaction from potential gains, so that risk aversion influenced strategic decisions. But when volatility exploded in areas where it had never been much of a concern, corporate managers, like the farmers of yesteryear, began to worry about the very survival of their companies, not just about a sequence of earnings that was more irregular than they or their stockholders might have liked.

Even though corporations could execute hedges in the liquid and active markets for options and futures—which now included interest rate and foreign exchange contracts as well as commodities and stock indexes—these contracts were expressly designed to appeal to as many investors as possible. The risk-management needs of most corporations are too specific in terms of both coverage and time spans to find ready customers in the public markets.

Wall Street has always been a hothouse of financial innovation, and brokerage houses are quick to jump into the breach when a new demand for their talents arises. Major banks, insurance companies, and investment banking firms with worldwide business connections lost no time in establishing new units of specialized traders and financial engineers to design tailor-made risk-management products for corporate customers, some related to interest rates, some to currencies, and some to the prices of raw materials. Before long, the value of the underlying assets involved in these contracts—referred to as the "notional value"—was in the trillions of dollars, amounts that at first stunned and frightened people who were unaware of how the contracts actually worked.

Although approximately two hundred firms are in this business today, it is highly concentrated among the giants. In 1995, commercial banks alone held derivatives with a notional value of $18 trillion, of which $14 trillion was accounted for by just six institutions: Chemical, Citibank, Morgan, Bankers Trust, Bank of America, and Chase.[6]

Almost all of these arrangements function like the cash settlement conditions of the futures contracts, as described above. Each side is obliged to pay to the other only the *changes* in the underlying values, not the far larger notional amounts. When the same institution or the same corporation has a variety of contracts in effect with a counterparty, payments frequently net out the impact of the entire set of contracts instead of treating each contract as a separate deal. As a result, the functional liabilities are far smaller than the staggering magnitudes of the notional values. According to a survey conducted during 1995 by the Bank for International Settlements, the notional value of all derivatives outstanding around the world, excluding derivatives traded in organized exchanges, amounted to $41 trillion, but if every party obligated to pay reneged on their payments, the loss to their creditors would run to only $1.7 trillion, or 4.3% of the notional value.[7]

These new products are in essence combinations of conventional options or futures contracts, but, in their most sophisticated versions, they incorporate all the risk-management inventions I have described, from Pascal's Triangle to Gauss's normal distribution, from Galton's regression to the mean to Markowitz's emphasis on covariance, and from Jacob Bernoulli's ideas on sampling to Arrow's search for universal insurance. The responsibility of pricing such complex arrangements goes well beyond what Black, Scholes, and Merton had so painstakingly worked out. Indeed, all three men ultimately showed up in Wall Street to help in designing and valuing these new risk-management products.

But who takes the other side of contracts that come into existence precisely because they are too specific in their coverage to trade in the public markets? Who would be in a position to play the role of speculator and assume the volatility that the corporations were so urgently trying to shed? Few of the counterparties to these tailor-made corporate deals are speculators.

In some instances, the counterparty is another company with opposite requirements. For example, an oil company seeking protection from a fall in the price of oil could accommodate an airline seeking protection from a rising oil price. A French company needing dollars for a U.S. subsidiary could assume the franc obligations of an American company with a French subsidiary, while the American company took care of the obligations of the dollar requirements of the French subsidiary.

But perfect matches are hard to find. In the majority of instances, the bank or the dealer who originated the deal assumes the role of counterparty in exchange for a fee or spread for executing it. These banks and dealers are stand-ins for an insurance company: they can afford to take on the volatility that corporations are trying so hard to avoid because, unlike their customers, they can diversify their exposure by servicing a large number of customers with different needs. If their books become unbalanced, they can go into the public markets and use the options and futures contracts trading there to hedge their positions, at least in part. Combined with the risk-reducing features of diversification, the ingenuity of the financial markets has transformed the patterns of volatility in the modern age into risks that are far more manageable for business corporations than would have been the case under any other conditions.

In 1994, a few of these apparently sound, sane, rational, and efficient risk-management arrangements suddenly blew up, causing enormous losses among the customers that the risk-management dealers were supposedly sheltering from disaster. The surprise was not just in the events themselves; the real shocker was in the prestige and high reputation of the victims, which included such giants as Procter & Gamble, Gibson Greetings, and the German Metallgesellschaft AG.[8]

There is no inherent reason why a hedging instrument should wreak havoc on its owner. On the contrary, significant losses on a hedge should mean that the company's primary bet is simultaneously providing a big payoff. If an oil company loses on a hedge against a decline in the price of oil, it must be making a large profit on the higher price that caused the loss in the hedging contract; if an airline loses on a hedge against a rise in the price of oil, it must be because the price has fallen and lowered its operating costs.

These disasters in derivative deals among big-name companies occurred for the simple reason that corporate executives ended up adding to their exposure to volatility rather than limiting it. They turned the company's treasury into a profit center. They treated low-probability events as being impossible. When given a choice between a certain loss and a gamble, they chose the gamble. They ignored the most fundamental principle of investment theory: *you cannot expect to make large profits without taking the risk of large losses.*

In deep trouble in a series of derivative transactions with Bankers Trust, Gibson Greetings provided a perfect example of prospect theory in action. Bankers Trust told the treasurer at one point in 1994 that Gibson's losses stood at $17.5 million, but, according to the treasurer, Bankers Trust also told him the losses could be "potentially without limit."[9] Gibson promptly signed a new arrangement that capped the loss at $27.5 million but, if everything worked exactly right, could reduce the loss to only $3 million. Prospect theory predicts that people with losses will gamble in preference to accepting a sure loss. Gibson could have liquidated out at $17.5 million for certain but chose the gamble instead. As a director of another company described what happens in such situations, "It's a lot like gambling. You get in deep. And you think 'I'll get out of it with this one last trade.'" But Gibson did not get out of it on one last trade. As the loss column headed toward $20.7 million, Gibson called it quits: it sued Bankers Trust for having violated a "fiduciary relationship."

Procter & Gamble, as described by Carol Loomis, a reporter for *Fortune* magazine, was being "chewed up [during 1994] by derivatives that incorporated astounding leverage and confounding complexity." These derivatives also were created by Bankers Trust, whose full-page ads in business and financial publications proclaimed, "Risk wears many disguises. Helping you see beneath its surface is the strength of Bankers Trust."

Procter & Gamble's management dutifully followed Gibson in acting out prospect theory. Whether Raymond Mains, the corporate treasurer, was doing a good job was not determined by the absolute level of interest rates that the company paid to borrow money; the company judged his performance on a what-have-you-done-for-us-lately basis. In other words, they looked only at how much less Mains was paying compared with what money had cost them the year before. The heat in that oven was hot. In a sarcastic comment on the company's disaster, Nobel Laureate Merton Miller joked, "You know Procter & Gamble? Procter is the widow and Gamble is the orphan."

The deal that triggered all the trouble was extremely complicated in detail—fun in the negotiating, like analyzing a case at Harvard Business School. It was signed in the fall of 1993, following four years in which short-term interest rates declined almost without interruption from about 10% to less than 3%; the deal revealed P&G's belief that, after such an extended decline, a significant increase in interest rates was so unlikely as to be impossible. Clearly, nobody in the executive offices had read Galton—regression to the mean appears to have been unknown to them.

They bet the ranch on what would have been no more than a modest saving if interest rates had remained stable or had fallen further. The deal involved a notional amount of $200 million in the form of a five-year loan from Bankers to P&G, but the *maximum* interest saving to the company compared with what it would have paid in a straight commercial-paper borrowing would have been $7.5 million over the life of the loan. According to the *Fortune* article, if things went wrong instead of right—if interest rates rose instead of continuing to fall—the exposure would put the company into the position of "covering the risks of interest rate earthquakes."

On February 4, 1994, only four months after the deal was signed, the Federal Reserve startled the markets by raising short-term interest rates. As Loomis reported, "With remarkable fury, these quakes then occurred." It is obvious that the P&G executives had never heard of Kahneman and Tversky either, for on February 14, already showing losses, the company entered into yet another contract, this one for $94 million over 4 1/4 years, that had them betting once again that interest rates would fall.

Interest rates did not fall. The interest rate on commercial paper had climbed from 3 1/4% in February to 6 1/2% in December while the prime rate moved from 6% to 8 1/2%. It was a catastrophe for P&G. Under the initial contract, they were left with a commitment to pay Bankers Trust 14 1/2 percentage points in interest until late 1998 and, under the second contract, to pay 16.4 percentage points in interest over the same period.

Bankers Trust is being sued here, too, and has received no payments from P&G at this writing. Mr. Mains is no longer with the company.

What are we to make of all this? Are derivatives a suicidal invention of the devil or the last word in risk management?* Bad enough that fine

*The literature on derivatives is massive, but I especially recommend the Fall 1994 issue of the *Journal of Applied Corporate Finance*, which is entirely devoted to the subject, and Smithson and Smith's book on managing risk (Smithson and Smith, 1995).

companies like Procter & Gamble and Gibson Greetings can get into trouble, but is the entire financial system at risk because so many people are trying to shed risks and slough them off onto someone else? How well can the someone else manage that responsibility? In a more fundamental sense, as the twentieth century draws to a close, what does the immense popularity of derivatives tell us about society's view of risk and the uncertain future that lies ahead? I shall postpone my response to that last question to the next, and final, chapter.

James Morgan, a columnist for the *Financial Times*, once remarked, "A derivative is like a razor. You can use it to shave yourself. . . . Or you can use it to commit suicide."[10] Users of derivatives have that choice. They do not have to use derivatives to commit suicide.

Precisely who persuaded whom to do what in the case of Procter & Gamble and the other companies remains obscure, but the cause of the disasters is clear enough: they took the risk of volatility instead of hedging it. They made the stability of their cash flows, and thereby the integrity of their long-term future, hostages to the accuracy of their interest-rate forecasts. While Bankers Trust and the other dealers in derivatives were managing their books on the basis of Pascal's Triangle, Gauss's bell curves, and Markowitz's covariances, the corporate risk-takers were relying on Keynesian degrees of belief. This was not the place to bet the corporate ranch or to act out failures of invariance.

Speculators who think they know what the future holds always risk being wrong and losing out. The long history of finance is cluttered with stories of fortunes lost on big bets. No one needed derivatives in order to go broke in a hurry. No one need go broke any faster just because derivatives have become a widely used financial instrument in our times. The instrument is the messenger; the investor is the message.

The losses at a few corporations in 1994 made banner headlines but posed no threat to anyone else. But suppose the errors had run in the other direction—that is, suppose the corporation had had huge winnings instead of losses. Would the counterparties to these transactions have been able to pay? The counterparties to most of the big tailor-made derivatives contracts are major money-center banks and top-tier investment bankers and insurance companies. The big players all made a lot less money in 1994, the year of surprises, than they had made in 1993, but *none of them was at any point in trouble*. Bankers Trust, for example, reported that losses "were all within our capital limits and we knew the extent of our exposures all the time. . . . The risk control processes worked fine."

The financial solvency of these institutions supports the financial solvency of the world economic system itself. Every single day, they are involved in millions of transactions involving trillions of dollars in a complex set of arrangements whose smooth functioning is essential. The margin for error is miniscule. Poor controls over the size and diversification of exposures are intolerable when the underlying volatility of the derivatives is so high and when so much is at stake beyond the fortunes of any single institution.

Everyone is aware of the dangers inherent in this situation, from the management of each institution on up to the governmental regulatory agencies that supervise the system. So-called "systemic risk" has become a parlor word in those circles and is the focus of attention at central banks and ministries of finance around the world. The measurement of the overall risk exposure in the system has been progressing in both comprehensiveness and sophistication.*

But there is only a fine line between guaranteeing absolute safety and stifling the development of financial innovations that, properly handled, could reduce the volatility of corporate cash flows. Corporations that shelter their cash flows from volatility can afford to take greater internal risks in the form of higher levels of investment or expenditures on research and development. Financial institutions themselves are vulnerable to volatility in interest rates and exchange rates; to the extent that they can hedge that volatility, they can extend more credit to a wider universe of deserving borrowers.

---

*In July 1995, the Federal Reserve Board, the Treasury Department, and the FDIC requested comments on a proposal to revise their requirements for commercial bank risk controls on transactions involving foreign exchange, commodities, and trading in debt and equity instruments. The document runs to 130 single-spaced pages. The so-called Basle Committee, consisting of representatives of central bankers from major economies, has issued the authoritative framework for the supervision of derivatives activities of banks and securities firms; it was published as a Federal Reserve press release on May 16, 1995.

Society stands to benefit from such an environment. In November 1994, Alan Greenspan, Chairman of the Federal Reserve Board, declared:

> There are some who would argue that the role of the bank supervisor is to minimize or even eliminate bank failure; but this view is mistaken, in my judgment. The willingness to take risk is essential to the growth of a free market economy. . . . [I]f all savers and their financial intermediaries invested only in risk-free assets, the potential for business growth would never be realized.[11]

19

Awaiting the Wildness

T he great statistician Maurice Kendall once wrote, "Humanity did not take control of society out of the realm of Divine Providence . . . to put it at the mercy of the laws of chance."[1] As we look ahead toward the new millennium, what are the prospects that we can finish that job, that we can hope to bring more risks under control and make progress at the same time?

The answer must focus on Leibniz's admonition of 1703, which is as pertinent today as it was when he sent it off to Jacob Bernoulli: "Nature has established patterns originating in the return of events, but only for the most part." As I pointed out in the Introduction, that qualification is the key to the whole story. Without it, there would be no risk, for everything would be predictable. Without it, there would be no change, for every event would be identical to a previous event. Without it, life would have no mystery.

The effort to comprehend the meaning of nature's tendency to repeat itself, but only imperfectly, is what motivated the heroes of this book. But despite the many ingenious tools they created to attack the puzzle, much remains unsolved. Discontinuities, irregularities, and volatilities seem to be proliferating rather than diminishing. In the world of finance, new instruments turn up at a bewildering pace, new markets are growing faster than old markets, and global interdependence makes risk management increasingly complex. Economic insecurity, especially in the job market, makes daily headlines. The environment, health, personal safety, and even the planet Earth itself appear to be under attack from enemies never before encountered.

The goal of wresting society from the mercy of the laws of chance continues to elude us. Why?

For Leibniz, the difficulty in generalizing from samples of information arises from nature's complexity, not from its waywardness. He believed that there is too much going on for us to figure it all out by studying a set of finite experiments, but, like most of his contemporaries, he was convinced that there was an underlying order to the whole process, ordained by the Almighty. The missing part to which he alluded with "only for the most part" was not random but an invisible element of the whole structure.

Three hundred years later, Albert Einstein struck the same note. In a famous comment that appeared in a letter to his fellow-physicist Max Born, Einstein declared, "You believe in a God who plays with dice, and I in complete law and order in a world which objectively exists."[2]

Bernoulli and Einstein may be correct that God does not play with dice, but, for better or for worse and in spite of all our efforts, human beings do not enjoy complete knowledge of the laws that define the order of the objectively existing world.

Bernoulli and Einstein were scientists concerned with the behavior of the natural world, but human beings must contend with the behavior of something beyond the patterns of nature: themselves. Indeed, as civilization has pushed forward, nature's vagaries have mattered less and the decisions of people have mattered more.

Yet the growing interdependence of humanity was not a concern to any of the innovators in this story until we come to Knight and Keynes in the twentieth century. Most of these men lived in the late Renaissance, the Enlightenment, or the Victorian age, and so they thought about probability in terms of nature and visualized human beings as acting with the same degree of regularity and predictability as they found in nature.

Behavior was simply not part of their deliberations. Their emphasis was on games of chance, disease, and life expectancies, whose outcomes are ordained by nature, not by human decisions. Human beings were always assumed to be rational (Daniel Bernoulli describes rationality as "the nature of man"), which simplifies matters because it makes human behavior as predictable as nature's—perhaps more so. This view led to the introduction of terminology from the natural sciences to explain both economic and social phenomena. The process of quantifying subjective matters like preferences and risk aversion was taken for granted and above dispute. In all their examples, no decision by any single individual had any influence on the welfare of any other individual.

The break comes with Knight and Keynes, both writing in the aftermath of the First World War. Their "radically distinct notion" of uncertainty had nothing whatsoever to do with nature or with the debate between Einstein and Born. Uncertainty is a consequence of the irrationalities that Knight and Keynes perceived in *human nature*, which means that the analysis of decision and choice would no longer be limited to human beings in isolated environments like Robinson Crusoe's. Even von Neumann, with his passionate belief in rationality, analyzes risky decisions in a world where the decisions of each individual have an impact on others, and where each individual must consider the probable responses of others to his or her own decisions. From there, it is only a short distance to Kahneman and Tversky's inquiries into the failure of invariance and the behavioral investigations of the Theory Police.

Although the solutions to much of the mystery that Leibniz perceived in nature were well in hand by the twentieth century, we are still trying to understand the even more tantalizing mystery of how human beings make choices and respond to risk. Echoing Leibniz, G.K. Chesterton, a novelist and essayist rather than a scientist, has described the modern view this way:

> The real trouble with this world of ours is not that it is an unreasonable world, nor even that it is a reasonable one. The commonest kind of trouble is that it is nearly reasonable, but not quite. Life is not an illogicality; yet it is a trap for logicians. It looks just a little more mathematical and regular than it is; its exactitude is obvious, but its inexactitude is hidden; its wildness lies in wait.[3]

In such a world, are probability, regression to the mean, and diversification useless? Is it even possible to adapt the powerful tools that interpret the variations of nature to the search for the roots of inexactitude? Will wildness always lie in wait?

Proponents of chaos theory, a relatively new alternative to the ideas of Pascal and others, claim to have revealed the hidden source of inexactitude. According to chaos theorists, it springs from a phenomenon called "nonlinearity." Nonlinearity means that results are not proportionate to the cause. But chaos theory also joins with Laplace, Poincaré, and Einstein in insisting that *all results have a cause*—like the balanced cone that topples over in response to "a very slight tremor."

Students of chaos theory reject the symmetry of the bell curve as a description of reality. They hold in contempt linear statistical systems in which, for example, the magnitude of an expected reward is assumed to be consistent with the magnitude of the risks taken to achieve it, or, in general, where results achieved bear a systematic relationship to efforts expended. Consequently, they reject conventional theories of probability, finance, and economics. To them, Pascal's Arithmetic Triangle is a toy for children, Francis Galton was a fool, and Quetelet's beloved bell curve is a caricature of reality.

Dimitris Chorafas, an articulate commentator on chaos theory, describes chaos as ". . . a time evolution with sensitive dependence on initial conditions."[4] The most popular example of this concept is the flutter of a butterfly's wings in Hawaii that is the ultimate cause of a hurricane in the Caribbean. According to Chorafas, chaos theorists see the world "in a state of vitality. . . characterized by turbulence and volatility."[5] This is a world in which deviations from the norm do not cluster symmetrically on either side of the average, as Gauss's normal distribution predicts; it is a craggy world in which Galton's regression to the mean makes no sense, because the mean is always in a state of flux. The idea of a norm does not exist in chaos theory.

Chaos theory carries Poincaré's notion of the ubiquitous nature of cause and effect to its logical extreme by rejecting the concept of discontinuity. What appears to be discontinuity is not an abrupt break with the past but the logical consequence of preceding events. In a world of chaos, wildness is always waiting to show itself.

Making chaos theory operational is something else again. According to Chorafas, "The signature of a chaotic time series . . . is that prediction accuracy falls off with the increasing passage of time." This view leaves the practitioners of chaos theory caught up in a world of minutiae, in which all the signals are tiny and everything else is mere noise.

As forecasters in financial markets who focus on volatility, practitioners of chaos theory have accumulated immense quantities of transactions data that have enabled them, with some success, to predict changes in security prices and exchange rates, as well as variations in risk, within the near future.[6] They have even discovered that roulette wheels do not produce completely random results, though the advantage bestowed by that discovery is too small to make any gambler rich.

So far, the accomplishments of the theory appear modest compared to its claims. Its practitioners have managed to cup the butterfly in their hands, but they have not yet traced all the airflows impelled by the flutterings of its wings. But they are trying.

In recent years, other sophisticated innovations to foretell the future have surfaced, with strange names like genetic algorithms and neural networks.[7] These methods focus largely on the nature of volatility; their implementation stretches the capability of the most high-powered computers.

The objective of genetic algorithms is to replicate the manner in which genes are passed from one generation to the next. The genes that survive create the models that form the most durable and effective offspring.* Neural networks are designed to simulate the behavior of the human brain by sifting out from the experiences programed into them those inferences that will be most useful in dealing with the next experience. Practitioners of this procedure have uncovered behavior patterns in one system that they can use to predict outcomes in entirely different systems, the theory being that all complex systems like democracy, the path of technological development, and the stock market share common patterns and responses.[8]

---

*al-Khowârizmî, the mathematician whose name furnished the root of the word "algorithm," would surely be astonished to see the offspring of what he launched nearly 1200 years ago.

These models provide important insights into the complexity of reality, but there is no proof of cause and effect in the recognition of patterns that precede the arrival of other patterns in financial markets or in the spin of a roulette wheel. Socrates and Aristotle would be as skeptical about chaos theory and neural networks as the theorists of those approaches are about conventional approaches.

Likeness to truth is not the same as truth. Without any theoretical structure to explain why patterns seem to repeat themselves across time or across systems, these innovations provide little assurance that today's signals will trigger tomorrow's events. We are left with only the subtle sequences of data that the enormous power of the computer can reveal. Thus, forecasting tools based on nonlinear models or on computer gymnastics are subject to many of the same hurdles that stand in the way of conventional probability theory: the raw material of the model is the data of the past.

The past seldom obliges by revealing to us when wildness will break out in the future. Wars, depressions, stock-market booms and crashes, and ethnic massacres come and go, but they always seem to arrive as surprises. After the fact, however, when we study the history of what happened, the source of the wildness appears to be so obvious to us that we have a hard time understanding how people on the scene were oblivious to what lay in wait for them.

Surprise is endemic above all in the world of finance. In the late 1950s, for example, a relationship sanctified by over eighty years of experience suddenly came apart when investors discovered that a thousand dollars invested in low-risk, high-grade bonds would, for the first time in history, produce more income than a thousand dollars invested in risky common stocks.* In the early 1970s, long-term interest rates

---

*From 1871 to 1958, stock yields exceeded bond yields by an average of about 1.3 percentage points, with only three transitory reversals, the last in 1929. In an article in *Fortune* magazine for March 1959 Gilbert Burke declared, "It has been practically an article of faith in the U.S. that good stocks must yield more income than good bonds, and that when they do not, their prices will promptly fall." (See *Bank Credit Analyst*, 1995.) There is reason to believe that stocks yielded more than bonds even before 1871, which is the starting point for reliable stock market data. Since 1958, bond yields have exceeded stock yields by an average of 3.5 percentage points.

rose above 5% for the first time since the Civil War and have dared to *remain* above 5% ever since.

Given the remarkable stability of the key relationships between bond yields and stocks yields, and the trendless history of long-term interest rates over so many years, no one ever dreamed of anything different. Nor did people have any reason for doing so before the development of contracyclical monetary and fiscal policy and before they had experienced a price level that only went up instead of rising on some occasions and falling on others. In other words, these paradigm shifts may not have been unpredictable, but they were unthinkable.

If these events were unpredictable, how can we expect the elaborate quantitative devices of risk management to predict them? How can we program into the computer concepts that we cannot program into ourselves, that are even beyond our imagination?

We cannot enter data about the future into the computer because such data are inaccessible to us. So we pour in data from the past to fuel the decision-making mechanisms created by our models, be they linear or nonlinear. But therein lies the logician's trap: past data from real life constitute a sequence of events rather than a set of independent observations, which is what the laws of probability demand. History provides us with only one sample of the economy and the capital markets, not with thousands of separate and randomly distributed numbers. Even though many economic and financial variables fall into distributions that approximate a bell curve, the picture is never perfect. Once again, resemblance to truth is not the same as truth. It is in those outliers and imperfections that the wildness lurks.

Finally, the science of risk management sometimes creates new risks even as it brings old risks under control. Our faith in risk management encourages us to take risks we would not otherwise take. On most counts, that is beneficial, but we must be wary of adding to the amount of risk in the system. Research reveals that seatbelts encourage drivers to drive more aggressively. Consequently, the number of accidents rises even though the seriousness of injury in any one accident declines.* Derivative financial instruments designed as hedges have tempted investors to transform them into speculative vehicles with sleigh-rides for payoffs and involving risks that no corporate risk manager should

---

*For an extensive analysis of such cases, see Adams, 1995.

contemplate. The introduction of portfolio insurance in the late 1970s encouraged a higher level of equity exposure than had prevailed before. In the same fashion, conservative institutional investors tend to use broad diversification to justify higher exposure to risk in untested areas—but diversification is not a guarantee against loss, only against losing everything at once.

⊛

Nothing is more soothing or more persuasive than the computer screen, with its imposing arrays of numbers, glowing colors, and elegantly structured graphs. As we stare at the passing show, we become so absorbed that we tend to forget that the computer only answers questions; it does not ask them. Whenever we ignore that truth, the computer supports us in our conceptual errors. Those who live only by the numbers may find that the computer has simply replaced the oracles to whom people resorted in ancient times for guidance in risk management and decision-making.

At the same time, we must avoid rejecting numbers when they show more promise of accuracy than intuition and hunch, where, as Kahneman and Tversky have demonstrated, inconsistency and myopia so often prevail. G.B. Airy, one of many brilliant mathematicians who have served as director of Britain's Royal Observatory, wrote in 1849, "I am a devoted admirer of theory, hypothesis, formula, and every other emanation of pure intellect which keeps erring man straight among the stumbling-blocks and quagmires of matter-of-fact observations."[9]

The central theme of this whole story is that the quantitative achievements of the heroes we have met shaped the trajectory of progress over the past 450 years. In engineering, medicine, science, finance, business, and even in government, decisions that touch everyone's life are now made in accordance with disciplined procedures that far outperform the seat-of-the-pants methods of the past. Many catastrophic errors of judgment are thus either avoided, or else their consequences are muted.

Cardano the Renaissance gambler, followed by Pascal the geometer and Fermat the lawyer, the monks of Port-Royal and the ministers of Newington, the notions man and the man with the sprained brain, Daniel Bernoulli and his uncle Jacob, secretive Gauss and voluble

Quetelet, von Neumann the playful and Morgenstern the ponderous, the religious de Moivre and the agnostic Knight, pithy Black and loquacious Scholes, Kenneth Arrow and Harry Markowitz—all of them have transformed the perception of risk from chance of loss into opportunity for gain, from FATE and ORIGINAL DESIGN to sophisticated, probability-based forecasts of the future, and from helplessness to choice.

Opposed though he was to mechanical applications of the laws of probability and the quantification of uncertainty, Keynes recognized that this body of thought had profound implications for humanity:

> The importance of probability can only be derived from the judgment that it is *rational* to be guided by it in action; and a practical dependence on it can only be justified by a judgment that in action we *ought* to act to take some account of it.
>
> It is for this reason that probability is to us the "guide of life," since to us, as Locke says, "in the greatest part of our concernment, God has afforded only the Twilight, as I may so say, of Probability, suitable, I presume, to that state of Mediocrity and Probationership He has been pleased to place us in here."[10]

Notes

INTRODUCTION

1. Quoted in Keynes, 1921, frontispiece to Chapter XXVIII.
2. Personal conversation.
3. Arrow, 1992, p. 46.

CHAPTER 1

1. Quoted in Ignatin and Smith, 1976, p. 80. The quotation is from Book I, Chapter X, of *The Wealth of Nations*.
2. Keynes, 1936, p. 159.
3. *Ibid.*, p. 150.
4. This entire paragraph is from Bolen, 1976.
5. Excellent background on all this may be found in David, 1962, pp. 2–21.
6. See David, 1962, p. 34.
7. Hayano, 1982.
8. Johnson, 1995.
9. See David, p. 2.
10. Sambursky, 1956, p. 36.
11. *Ibid.*, p. 37.
12. *Ibid.*, pp. 36–40.
13. Rabinovitch, 1969.
14. Frankfort, 1956; quoted in Heilbroner, 1995, p. 23. See also David, 1962, pp. 21–26.
15. See Eves, 1983, p. 136.

CHAPTER 2

1. Most of the background and biographical material on Fibonacci comes from the *Encyclopedia Brittanica*; Eves, 1983, p. 161; Hogben, 1968, p. 250; and Garland, 1987.

2. Two stimulating commentaries on the Fibonacci numbers are Garland, 1987, and Hoffer, 1975. The examples here are drawn from those two sources.

3. The background material presented here comes primarily from Hogben, 1968, Chapter I.

4. See Hogben, 1968, p. 35; also Eves, 1983, Chapter I.

5. See Hogben, 1968, p. 36 and pp. 246–250.

6. The background material on Diophantus is from Turnbull, 1951, p. 113.

7. *Ibid.*, p. 110.

8. *Ibid.*, p. 111.

9. See Hogben, 1968, pp. 244–246.

10. From Newman, 1988a, p. 433.

11. The background material on al-Khowârizmî is primarily from Muir, 1961, and Hogben, 1968.

12. Hogben, 1968, p. 243.

13. See Hogben, 1968, Chapter VI, for an extended and stimulating discussion of the development of algebra and the uses of zero.

14. The background material on Omar Khayyam is from Fitzgerald.

15. Hogben, 1968, p. 245.

CHAPTER 3

1. The background material on Paccioli comes primarily from David, 1962, pp. 36–39, and Kemp, 1981, pp. 146–148.

2. The material on Paccioli and Leonardo is from Kemp, 1981, pp. 248–250.

3. David, 1962, p. 37.

4. Sambursky, 1956.

5. *Ibid.*

6. *Ibid.*

7. The background material on Cardano and the quotations are primarily from Ore, 1953, and Morley, 1854, with some quotes from Cardan, 1930.

8. David, 1962, p. 61.

9. See Sarton, 1957, pp. 29–32; also Muir, 1961, pp. 35–38.

10. Hacking, 1975, p. 18. The complete discussion, which runs through Chapter 3, "Opinion," is well worth careful study.

11. Hacking, 1975, p. 22.

12. *Ibid.*, p. 26.

13. *Ibid.*, p. 44.

14. David, 1962, p. 58.

15. Kogelman and Heller, 1986, pp. 164–165.

16. The background material on Galileo is primarily from David, 1962, Chapter 7, pp. 61–69.

17. David, 1962, p. 65.

18. *Ibid.*, p. 13.

19. Stigler, 1988.

CHAPTER 4

1. The background material on Pascal is from Muir, 1961, pp. 77–100; David, 1962, pp. 34–79; and Hacking, 1975, pp. 55–70.

2. See David, 1962, p. 74.

3. Muir, 1961, p. 90.

4. *Ibid.*, p. 93.

5. *Ibid.*, p. 94.

6. *Ibid.*, p. 95.

7. David, 1961, p. 69; see also Appendix 4.

8. See Huff, 1959, pp. 63–69.

9. See Hogben, 1968, p. 551; see also Hacking, 1975, pp. 58–59.

10. See David, 1962, pp. 71–75.

11. Turnbull, 1951, p. 130.

12. *Ibid.*, p. 131.

13. See Hogben, 1968, pp. 277–279; see also David, 1962, p. 34.

14. Turnbull, 1951, p. 131; also Eves, 1984, p. 6.

15. I am grateful to Stanley Kogelman for helping me work out these examples.

16. This point, and the quotation from Pascal that follows, are from Guilbaud, 1968; the translation is mine.

17. David, 1962, p. 252.

18. All the material that follows is from Hacking, 1975, Chapter 8, "The Great Decision," pp. 63–70.

19. Hacking, p. 62.

20. The material about the Port-Royal monastery is from Hacking, 1975, pp. 73–77.

21. *Ibid.*, p. 25.

22. *Ibid.*, p. 74.

23. *Ibid.*, p. 77.

24. *Ibid.*, p. 77.

25. *Ibid.*, p. 77.

26. *Ibid.*, p. 77.

CHAPTER 5

1. I am grateful to Stigler (1977) for this description and to Stephen Stigler personally for drawing the Trial of the Pyx to my attention.

2. The background material on Graunt is from Muir, 1961; David, 1962; and Newman, 1988g. (Direct quotations from *Natural and Political Obligations* are primarily from Newman.)

3. Newman, 1988g, p. 1394.

4. The background material on Petty is from Hacking, 1975, pp. 102–105.

5. The material about Wilkins and the Royal Society is from Hacking, 1975, pp. 169–171.

6. Graunt, p. 1401.

7. *Ibid.*, p. 1401.

8. Hacking, 1975, p. 103.

9. I am grateful to Stephen Stigler for making this point clear to me.

10. See Hacking, 1975, pp. 103–105.

11. The illustration is from Stigler, 1996.

12. David, 1962, p. 107. An extended explanation of Graunt's calculations and estimating procedure appears on pp. 107–109.

13. Hacking, 1975, p. 107.

14. *Ibid.*, p. 110.

15. See discussion in Hacking, 1975, pp. 105–110.

16. The background material on Naumann and Halley and the quotations from Halley are primarily from Newman, 1988g, pp. 1393–1396 and 1414–1432.

17. See discussion in Hacking, 1975, pp. 111–121.

18. The material that follows on the history of insurance in general and Lloyd's in particular is from Flower and Jones, 1974; also Hodgson, 1984.

19. Macaulay, 1848, p. 494. For Macaulay's full and fascinating story of the English national debt, see the entire chapter that runs from p. 487 to p. 498.

20. Flower and Jones, 1974.

21. American Academy of Actuaries, 1994, and Moorehead, 1989.

22. Interesting background material on the role of the Monte dei Paschi may be found in Chichilnisky and Heal, 1993.

23. See, in particular, Townsend, 1995, and Besley, 1995.

24. Flower and Jones, 1974, p. 13.

CHAPTER 6

1. Bernoulli, Daniel, 1738.

2. The background material on the Bernoulli family is from Newman, 1988f.

3. Bell, 1965, p. 131.

4. Newman, 1988f, p. 759.

5. *Ibid.*

6. *Ibid.*

7. *Ibid.*

8. This story and the quotes are from David, 1962, pp. 133–135.

9. Stigler, 1993.

10. All Bernoulli quotations are from Bernoulli, 1738.

11. An extended and lucid example of expected utilities and risk may be found in Bodie, Kane, and Marcus, 1992, Chapter 7, pp. 183–209. See also Kritzman, 1995, Chapter 3, pp. 21–32.

12. Todhunter, 1949. See also Bassett, 1987, and the list of references therein.

13. Siegel, 1994, Chapter 8, pp. 95–104.

CHAPTER 7

1. Background material on Jacob Bernoulli is from Newman, 1988f.

2. Hacking, 1975, p. 166; see also Kendall, 1974.

3. *Gesammelte Werke* (ed. Pertz and Gerhardt), Halle 1855, vol. 3, pp. 71–97. I am grateful to Marta Steele and Doris Bullard for the translation into English. Chapter XXX of Keynes, 1921, has an illuminating discussion of this exchange between Leibniz and Bernoulli.

4. An excellent analysis of *Ars Conjectandi* may be found in David, 1962, pp. 133–139 and in Stigler, 1986, pp. 63–78.

5. Bernoulli, Jacob, 1713, p. 1430.

6. *Ibid.*, p. 1431.

7. Hacking, 1975, p. 145.

8. *Ibid.*, p. 146.

9. *Ibid.*, p. 163.

10. David, 1962, p. 137.

11. Stigler, 1986, p. 71. This book was an invaluable source of information for this chapter.

12. The background material on de Moivre is from Stigler, 1986, Chapter 2, and David, 1962, Chapter XV.

13. Stigler, 1986, p. 85.

14. This example is freely adapted from Groebner and Shannon, 1993, Chapter 20.

15. The background material on Bayes is from Stigler, 1986, and Cone, 1952.

16. Groebner and Shannon, 1993, p. 1014.

17. Stigler, 1986, p. 123.

18. Cone, 1952, p. 50.

19. *Ibid.*, p. 41.

20. *Ibid.*, pp. 42–44.

21. Bayes, 1763.

22. Price's letter of transmittal and Bayes's essay are reprinted in Kendall and Plackett, 1977, pp. 134–141.

23. An excellent description of this experiment may be found in Stigler, 1986, pp. 124–130.

24. Smith, 1984. This paper contains an excellent analysis of the Bayesian approach.

25. David, 1962, p. 177.

CHAPTER 8

1. The biographical material on Gauss is primarily from Shaaf, 1964, and from Bell, 1965.

2. Schaaf, 1964, p. 40.

3. Bell, 1965, p. 310.

4. The biographical background on Laplace is from Newman, 1988d, pp. 1291–1299.

5. Newman, 1988d, p. 1297.

6. *Ibid.*, p. 1297.

7. *Ibid.*, p. 1297.

8. Bell, 1965, p. 324.

9. *Ibid.*, p. 307.

10. The following discussion and examples are from Schaaf, 1964, pp. 23–25.

11. Bell, 1965, p. 321.

12. *Ibid.*, p. 331.

13. Quoted in Schaaf, 1964, p. 114.

14. Details on Roberts' experiment may be found in Bernstein, 1992, pp. 98–103.

CHAPTER 9

1. The biographical background on Galton is primarily from Forrest, 1974.

2. Newman, 1988e, p. 1142.

3. *Ibid.*, p. 1143.

4. Kelves, 1985.

5. The details of these African anecdotes, including the quotations, are from Forrest, 1974, pp. 38–57.

6. Forrest, 1974, p. 4.

7. *Ibid.*, p. 12.

8. *Ibid.*, p. 12.

9. Newman, 1988e.

10. Galton, 1869, p. 20. This citation was brought to my attention by Stigler in personal correspondence.

11. The background material on Quetelet is from Keynes, 1921, pp. 334–335, and Stigler, 1986, pp. 161–182 and 206–268.

12. Stigler, 1986, p. 162.

13. *Ibid.*, p. 169.

14. *Ibid.*, p. 170.

15. *Ibid.*, p. 171.

16. An excellent discussion of Cournot's views on probability may be found in Stigler, 1986, pp. 195–201.

17. Stigler, 1986, p. 172.

18. A detailed description of Quetelet's experiment may be found in Galton, 1869, in Newman's abstract, p. 1157.

19. Stigler, 1986, p. 171.

20. *Ibid.*, p. 203.

21. Forrest, 1974, p. 202.

22. Stigler, 1986, p. 268.

23. Forrest, 1974, p. 89.

24. Galton, 1883, p. 49. Also quoted in Stigler, 1986, p. 271.

25. Forrest, 1974, p. 92.

26. *Ibid.*, p. 91.

27. Galton, 1869, from Newman's abstract, p. 1153.

28. Forrest, 1974, p. 201.

29. Galton, 1869, in Newman's abstract, p. 1162.

30. Forrest, 1974, p. 89.

31. *Ibid.*, p. 217.

32. *Ibid.*, p. 217.

33. *Ibid.*, p. 101.

34. A detailed description of the Quincunx, including an illustration and photographs of Galton's original notes, may be found in Stigler, 1986, pp. 275–281.

35. Stigler, 1986, p. 281.

36. Forrest, 1974, p. 189.

37. *Ibid.*, p. 189.

38. *Ibid.*, p. 190.

39. This discussion, including the table that follows, are from Stigler, 1986, pp. 283–290.

40. Stigler, 1986, p. 289.

41. Forrest, 1974, p. 199.

CHAPTER 10

1. Sanford C. Bernstein & Co., 1995.

2. DeBondt and Thaler, 1986.

3. *Ibid.*

4. See Dreman and Berry, 1995.

5. Morningstar Mutual Funds, April 1, 1994.

6. Reichenstein and Dorsett, 1995, pp. 46–47.

7. These conclusions are distilled from Reichenstein and Dorsett, 1995, Table 11, p. 32.

8. Baumol, 1986. For an extended analysis of this process, see Baumol, Nelson, and Wolff, 1994.

9. Baumol, 1986, p. 1077.

10. *Ibid.*, p. 1077.

11. *Ibid.*, p. 1084.

12. Keynes, 1924, p. 88.

13. Forrest, 1974, pp. 201–202.

14. Despite help from others, I have been unable to locate the source of this quotation, which has long been in my files. A similar comment appears in Keynes, 1936, pp. 152–153.

CHAPTER 11

1. Bernoulli, 1738.

2. Jevons quotes these passages in *The Theory of Political Economy.* An abstract appears in Newman, 1988a, pp. 1193–1212, and the quotation in question appears on p. 1197.

3. Quoted in Skidelsky, 1983, p. 47.

4. All the following quotations are from Jevons, 1970.

5. Kendall, 1972, p. 43.

6. Keynes, 1931, p. vii.

CHAPTER 12

1. Laplace, 1814, p. 1301.

2. *Ibid.,* p. 1302.

3. *Ibid.*, p. 1307.

4. *Ibid.*, p. 1308.

5. Newman, 1988b, p. 1353.

6. The story about Louis Bachelier is recounted in more detail in Bernstein, 1992, pp. 19–20

7. Poincaré in Newman, 1988a, p. 1359.

8. *Ibid.*, pp. 1362–1363.

9. *Ibid.*, p. 1359.

10. *Ibid.*, p. 1360.

11. *Ibid.*, p. 1361.

12. *Ibid.*, p. 1362.

13. Keynes, 1921, p.3.

14. Personal correspondence.

15. Arrow, 1992, p. 46.

16. *Ibid.*, p. 47.

17. Keynes, 1937, p. 213.

18. Arrow and Hahn, 1971.

19. Arrow, 1992, p. 45.

20. The data for the two charts that follow are from *Morningstar Mutual Funds*, a bi-weekly publication.

21. This particular stress test is derived from Rubinstein, 1991. Mark Kritzman assisted me in developing this application.

22. EPA, 1992.

23. *Ibid.,* p. 1-1.

24. *Ibid.*, p. 1-8.

25. *Ibid.,* Table 5-2.

26. *Ibid.*, 1994, p. 3.

27. *Ibid.,* 1992, p. 1-1.

CHAPTER 13

1. Knight, 1921, p. 209.

2. Keynes, 1933, in Moggridge, 1972, Vol. X, p. 262.

3. Keynes, 1936, p. 161.

4. Dixon, 1986, p. 587.

5. Most of the background material on Knight was generously supplied to me by Donald Dewey and is drawn from Dewey, 1987; Dewey, 1990; and personal correspondence.

6. Quoted by Herbert Stein in *Wall Street Journal*, November 1, 1995, p. A14.

7. Knight, 1921, p. 205.

8. Arrow, 1951.

9. Knight, 1921, p. 197.

10. *Ibid.*, p. 226.

11. *Ibid.*, p. 223.

12. *Ibid.*, p. 227.

13. Donald Dewey provided me with the text of this letter.

14. Quoted in Newman, 1988c, p. 1336, which cites the *Times Literary Supplement*, February 23, 1951, p. 111.

15. Keynes, 1971, p. 98.

16. Keynes, 1936, p. 176n.

17. Skidelsky, 1986, p. 1.

18. See Blaug, 1994, p. 1209, for citations on Keynes's personal financial affairs.

19. This quotation appears in Moggridge, Vol. X, p. 440. See also Keynes, 1921, p. 408.

20. Keynes, 1971, p. 88.

21. Keynes, 1933, in Keynes, 1972, pp. 338–339.

22. Keynes, 1921, p. 51.

23. *Ibid.*, pp. 3–4.

24. *Ibid.*, pp. 22–26

25. *Ibid.*, pp. 407.

26. *Ibid.*, pp. 206–209.

27. Bateman, 1987, p. 101.

28. Keynes, 1921, pp. 3–4.

29. *Ibid.*, p. 5.

30. Knight, 1921, p. 237.

31. Keynes, 1936, p. 171.

32. *Ibid.*, p. 33.

33. *Ibid.*, p. 33.

34. *Ibid.*, p. 3.

35. Keynes, 1937.

36. Laplace, 1814, p. 1301.

CHAPTER 14

1. Most of the background material and much of the detail about von Neumann is from Macrae, 1992.

2. *Ibid.,* p. 20.

3. *Ibid.*, p. 87.

4. Quoted in Leonard, 1995, p. 7.

5. Re Morgenstern's anti-Semitism, see Leonard, 1995, Section III.1.

6. *Ibid.*, p. 16.

7. *Ibid.*

8. Leonard, 1994, footnote 3.

9. *Ibid.*, footnote 4.

10. This and the subsequent quotations in this paragraph are from Mirowski, 1991, p. 239.

11. Leonard, 1995, p. 22n.

12. *Ibid.*, p. 22.
13. von Neumann, 1944, p. 3.
14. *Ibid.*, p. 9.
15. *Ibid.*, p. 20.
16. This example is adapted from von Neumann, 1944, Chapter I, Section 3.3, pp. 17–20.
17. Blinder, 1982, esp. pp. 22–24.
18. For an interesting biography of Nash and his contribution to game theory, see Nasar, 1994.
19. von Neumann, 1944, p. 33.
20. Mirowski, 1991, p. 234.
21. *Ibid.*, p. 229.
22. *Ibid.*, pp. 231 and 237.

CHAPTER 15

1. From an address on February 7, 1995, on the subject of investing worldwide.
2. The full text of "The Prudent Man Decision" may be found in *The Journal of Portfolio Management*, Fall 1976, pp. 67–71.
3. A full biographical sketch of Markowitz and a detailed analysis of his 1952 paper appears in Bernstein, 1992, Chapter 2.
4. Darvan, 1994 (reprint).
5. Williams, 1938, p. 1.
6. Kaplan and Welles, 1969, p. 168.
7. All quotations from Markowitz are from Markowitz, 1952.
8. Baumol, 1966.
9. Wells Fargo–Nikko Investment Advisors, *Global Currents*, March 1995, p. 1.
10. See Sorensen, 1995, p. 12.
11. Phillips, 1995.
12. Jeffrey, 1984.
13. Sharpe, 1990, p. 34.
14. Thaler, personal correspondence.

CHAPTER 16

1. A large literature is available on the theories and backgrounds of Kahneman and Tversky, but McKean, 1985, is the most illuminating for lay readers.

2. McKean, 1985, p. 24.

3. *Ibid.*, p. 25

4. Kahneman and Tversky, 1979, p. 268.

5. McKean, 1985, p. 22; see also Kahneman and Tversky, 1984.

6. Tversky, 1990, p. 75. At greater length on this subject, see Kahneman and Tversky, 1979.

7. I am grateful to Dr. Richard Geist of Harvard Medical School for bringing this point to my attention.

8. Tversky, 1990, p. 75.

9. *Ibid.*, p. 75.

10. *Ibid.*, pp. 58–60.

11. Miller, 1995.

12. Kahneman and Tversky, 1984.

13. McKean, 1985, p. 30.

14. *Ibid.*, p. 29.

15. This anecdote appears in an unpublished Thaler paper titled "Mental Accounting Matters."

16. McKean, 1985, p. 31.

17. Redelmeier and Shafir, 1995, pp. 302–305.

18. Tversky and Koehler, 1994, p. 548.

19. Redelmeier, Koehler, Lieberman, and Tversky, 1995.

20. Ellsberg, 1961.

21. Fox and Tversky, 1995.

22. *Ibid.*, pp. 587–588.

23. Tversky and Kahneman, 1992.

24. Kahneman and Tversky, 1973.

25. Thaler, 1995.

26. Kagel and Roth, 1995, p. 4.

27. Von Neumann and Morgenstern, 1953, p. 5.

CHAPTER 17

1. Personal conversation.

2. Bell, 1983, p. 1160.

3. "The recent rally in long-term bonds is driven by short-term speculation," Roger Lowenstein, INTRINSIC VALUE, *The Wall Street Journal,* June 1, 1995, p. C1.

4. Keynes, 1936, p. 158.

5. Personal correspondence.

6. The following anecdote is from Thaler, 1991, pp. xi–xii.

7. *Ibid.*, p. xii.
8. Statman, 1982, p. 451.
9. Thaler and Shefrin, 1981.
10. Shefrin and Statman, 1984.
11. Miller, 1987, p. 15.
12. Bernstein, 1986, p. 805.
13. Lakonishok, Shleifer, and Vishny, 1993.
14. Kahneman, Knetsch, and Thaler, 1990, pp. 170–177.
15. French and Poterba, 1989.
16. Keynes, 1936, pp. 155–156.
17. Bernstein, 1992, p. 34.
18. *Ibid.*, p. 143.
19. For a detailed examination of this question, and related literature, see Shiller, 1989.
20. Vertin, 1974, p. 10.

CHAPTER 18

1. Quoted in "Unemployment and Mr. Keynes's Revolution in Economic Thought," *Canadian Journal of Economics and Political Science*, Vol. 3 (1977), p. 113.
2. See Garber, 1989.
3. For details on this note, see Smithson and Smith, 1995, pp. 26–28 (which contains an illustration), and Ball, 1991, pp. 74–79 and Appendix E.
4. For the full story on the evolution of the option valuation formula, see Bernstein, 1992, Chapter 11. The narration here draws generously on that chapter. All quotations here are taken from that source.
5. For the full story on the evolution of portfolio insurance, see Bernstein, 1992, Chapter 14. The narration here draws generously on that chapter. All quotations here are taken from that source.
6. Source: Office of the Comptroller of the Currency, published in *The New York Times* of June 15, 1995.
7. "Global Market for Derivatives," *The Wall Street Journal*, December 19, 1995, p. 1.
8. The primary source and all the quotations for this part of the story is Loomis, 1995.
9. Unless otherwise specified, all quotations from here to the end of the chapter are from Loomis, 1995.
10. Quoted in *Grant's Interest Rate Observer*, March 17, 1995.
11. Address to Garn Institute of Finance, University of Utah, November 30, 1994.

CHAPTER 19

1. Kendall, 1972, p. 42.
2. Quoted in Adams, 1995, p. 17.
3. Chesterton, 1909, pp. 149–150.
4. Chorafas, 1994, p. 15.
5. *Ibid.*, p. 16.
6. See especially Hsieh, 1995, and Focardi, 1996.
7. For interesting and lucid descriptions of advances in these areas, see Focardi, 1996, and Leinweber and Arnott, 1995. *The Journal of Investing*, Winter 1995, has five excellent articles on the subject.
8. See "Can the Complexity Gurus Explain It All," *Business Week*, November 6, 1995, pp. 22–24; this article includes reviews of two books on this subject.
9. Kruskal and Stigler, 1994, p. 7.
10. Keynes, 1921, p. 323.

Bibliography

Note: References identified with an asterisk were especially valuable.

Adams, John, 1995. *Risk.* London: UCL Press.

Alderfer, C. P., and H. Bierman, Jr., 1970. "Choices with Risk: Beyond the Mean and Variance." *Journal of Business,* Vol. 43, No. 3, pp. 341–353.

American Academy of Actuaries, 1994. *Fact Book.*

American Demographics, 1995. February.

Ansell, Jack, and Frank Wharton, eds., 1992. *Risk Analysis, Assessment and Management.* Chichester, England: John Wiley & Sons.

Arrow, Kenneth J., 1951. "Alternative Approaches to the Theory of Choice in Risk-taking Situations." In Arrow, 1971, pp. 1–21.

Arrow, Kenneth J., 1971. *Essays in the Theory of Risk-Bearing.* Chicago: Markham Publishing Company.

Arrow, Kenneth J., 1992. "I Know a Hawk from a Handsaw." In M. Szenberg, ed., *Eminent Economists: Their Life and Philosophies.* Cambridge and New York: Cambridge University Press, pp. 42–50.

Arrow, Kenneth, and Frank Hahn, 1971. *General Competitive Analysis.* San Francisco: Holden-Day.

Baker, H. K., and J. A. Haslem, 1974. "The Impact of Investor Socio-Economic Characteristics on Risk and Return Preferences." *Journal of Business Research,* pp. 469–476.

Ball, Douglas B., 1991. *Financial Failure and Confederate Defeat.* Urbana: University of Illinois Press.

Bank Credit Analyst, 1995. Special Supplement, December. Montreal, Canada.

Barnett, A., and A. J. Lofasco, 1983. "After the Crash: The Passenger Response to the DC-10 Disaster." *Management Science,* Vol. 29, No. 11, pp. 1225–1236.

Bassett, Gilbert W., Jr., 1987. "The St. Petersburg Paradox and Bounded Utility." *History of Political Economy,* Vol. 19, No. 4, pp. 517–522.

Bateman, W. Bradley, 1987. "Keynes's Changing Conception of Probability." *Economics and Philosophy,* pp. 97–119.*

Bateman, W. Bradley, 1991. "Das Maynard Keynes Problem." *Cambridge Journal of Economics,* Vol. 15, pp. 101–111.

Baumol, William J., 1966. "Mathematical Analysis of Portfolio Selection." *Financial Analysts Journal*, Vol. 22, No. 5 (September–October), pp. 95–99.

Baumol, William J., 1986. "Productivity Growth, Convergence, and Welfare: What the Long-Run Data Show." *American Economic Review*, Vol. 76, No. 5 (December), pp. 1072–1086.

Baumol, William J., and Hilda Baumol, 1994. "On the Economics of Musical Composition in Mozart's Vienna." *Journal of Cultural Economics*, Vol. 18, No. 3, pp. 171–198.

Baumol, William J., and J. Benhabib, 1989. "Chaos: Significance, Mechanism, and Economic Applications." *Journal of Economic Perspectives*, Vol. 3, No. 1, pp. 77–106.

Baumol, William J., Richard R. Nelson, and Edward N. Wolff, 1994. *Convergence of Productivity: Cross-national Studies and Historical Evidence*. Oxford and New York: Oxford University Press.

Bayes, Thomas, 1763. "An Essay Toward Solving a Problem in the Doctrine of Chances." *Philosophical Transactions*, Essay LII, pp. 370–418. The text also appears in Kendall and Plackett, 1977, with Price's transmission letter, pp. 134–150.

Bell, David E., 1983. "Risk Premiums for Decision Regret." *Management Science*, Vol. 29, No. 10 (October), pp. 1156–1166.

Bell, Eric Temple, 1965. "Gauss, the Prince of Mathematics." In *Men of Mathematics*, New York: Simon & Schuster. Abstracted in Newman, 1988a, pp. 291–332.

Bernoulli, Daniel, 1738. "Specimen Theoriae Novae de Mensura Sortis (Exposition of a New Theory on the Measurement of Risk)." Translated from the Latin by Louise Sommer in *Econometrica*, Vol. 22, 1954, pp. 23–36.

Bernoulli, Jacob, 1713. *Ars Conjectandi*. Abstracted in Newman, 1988, pp. 1425–1432.

Bernstein, Peter L., 1986. "Does the Stock Market Overreact?" *Journal of Finance*, Vol. XL, No. 3, pp. 793–807.

Bernstein, Peter L., 1992. *Capital Ideas: The Improbable Origins of Modern Wall Street*. New York: The Free Press.

Besley, Timothy, 1995. "Nonmarket Institutions for Credit and Risk Sharing in Low-Income Countries." *Journal of Economic Perspectives*, Vol. 9, No. 3 (Summer), pp. 115–127.

Blaug, Mark, 1994. "Recent Biographies of Keynes." *Journal of Economic Literature*, Vol. XXXII, No. 3 (September), pp. 1204–1215.

Blinder, Alan S., 1982. "Issues in the Coordination of Monetary and Fiscal Policies." In *Monetary Policy Issues in the 1980s*. Kansas City, Missouri: Federal Reserve Bank of Kansas City, pp. 3–34.

Bodie, Zvi, Alex Kane, and Alan J. Marcus, 1992. *Essentials of Investments*. Homewood, Illinois: Irwin.

Boge, Steve, 1988. *Exploration into the Lives of Athletes on the Edge.* Berkeley, California: North Atlantic Books.

Bolen, Darrell W., 1976. "Gambling: Historical Highlights and Trends and Their Implications for Contemporary Society." In Eadington, 1976.

Brenner, Reuven, 1987. *Rivalry: In Business, Science, Among Nations.* New York: Cambridge University Press.

Breyer, Stephen, 1993. *Breaking the Vicious Circle: Toward Effective Risk Regulation.* Cambridge, Massachusetts: Cambridge University Press.

Bühler, Walter, 1981. *Gauss: A Biographical Study.* New York: Springer-Verlag.

Cardan, Jerome, 1930. *De Vita Propria Liber: The Book of My Life.* Translated from the Latin by Jean Stoner. New York: E. F. Dutton & Co.*

Chichilnisky, Graciela, and Geoffrey Heal, 1993. "Global Environmental Risks." *Journal of Economic Perspectives,* Vol. 7, No. 4 (Fall), pp. 65–86.

Chesterton, G. K., 1909. *Orthodoxy.* New York: Lane Press (Reprinted by Greenwood Press, Westport, 1974).

Chorafas, Dimitris N., 1994. *Chaos Theory in the Financial Markets.* Chicago: Probus.

Cohen, John, and Mark Hansel, 1956. *Risk and Gambling: The Study of Subjective Probability.* New York: Philosophical Library.

Cone, Carl, 1952. *Torchbearer of Freedom: The Influence of Richard Price on Eighteenth Century Thought.* Lexington, Kentucky: University of Kentucky Press.*

Darvas, Nicholas, 1994. *How I Made $2 Million in the Stock Market.* Reprint. New York: Carol Publishing Group, A Lyle Stuart Book.

David, Florence Nightingale, 1962. *Games, Gods, and Gambling.* New York: Hafner Publishing Company.*

Davidson, Paul, 1991. "Is Probability Theory Relevant for Uncertainty? A Post Keynesian Perspective." *Journal of Economic Perspectives,* Vol. 5, No. 1 (Winter), pp. 129–143.

Davidson, Paul, 1996. "Reality and Economic Theory." *Journal of Post Keynesian Economics,* Summer. Forthcoming.

DeBondt, Werner, and Richard H. Thaler, 1986. "Does the Stock Market Overreact?" *Journal of Finance,* Vol. XL, No. 3, pp. 793–807.

Dewey, Donald, 1987. "The Uncertain Place of Frank Knight in Chicago Economics." A paper prepared for the American Economic Association, Chicago, December 30, 1987.

Dewey, Donald, 1990. "Frank Knight before Cornell: Some Light on the Dark Years." In *Research in the History of Economic Thought and Methodology,* Vol. 8, pp. 1–38. New York: JAI Press.

Dewey, Donald, 1997. "Frank Hyneman Knight." *Dictionary of American National Biography.* Forthcoming. New York: Oxford University Press.

Dixon, Robert, 1986. "Uncertainty, Unobstructedness, and Power." *Journal of Post Keynesian Economics,* Vol. 8, No. 4 (Summer), pp. 585–590.

Durand, David, 1959. "Growth Stocks and the Petersburg Paradox." *Journal of Finance*, Vol. XII, No. 3 (September), pp. 348–363.

Eadington, W. R., 1976. *Gambling and Society: Interdisciplinary Studies on the Subject of Gambling*. London: Charles C Thomas.

Edwards, W., 1953. "Probability Preferences in Gambling." *American Journal of Psychology*, Vol. LXIV, pp. 349–364.

Ellsberg, Daniel, 1961. "Risk, Ambiguity, and the Savage Axioms." *Quarterly Journal of Economics*, Vol. LXXV, pp. 643–669.

Environmental Protection Agency (EPA), Office of Research and Development, Office of Health and Environmental Assessment, 1992. *Respiratory Health Effects of Passive Smoking: Lung Cancer and Other Disorders*.

Environmental Protection Agency (EPA), Office of Research and Development, Office of Health and Environmental Assessment, 1994. *Setting the Record Straight: Secondhand Smoke Is a Preventable Health Risk*.

Eves, Howard, 1983. *Great Moments in Mathematics (Before 1650)*. The Mathematical Association of America.

Finney, P. D., 1978. "Personality Traits Attributed to Risky and Conservative Decision Makers: Cultural Values More Than Risk." *Journal of Psychology*, pp. 187–197.

Fischoff, Baruch, Stephen R. Watson, and Chris Hope, 1990. "Defining Risk." In Glickman and Glough, 1990, pp. 30–42.

Flower, Raymond, and Michael Wynn Jones, 1974. *Lloyd's of London: An Illustrated History*. Newton Abbot, England: David and Charles.

Focardi, Sergio, 1996. "From Equilibrium to Nonlinear Dynamics in Investment Management." Forthcoming. *Journal of Portfolio Management*.

Fox, Craig R., and Amos Tversky, 1995. "Ambiguity Aversion and Comparative Ignorance." *Quarterly Journal of Economics*, Vol. CX, Issue 3, pp. 585–603.

Forrest, D. W., 1974. *Francis Galton: The Life and Work of a Victorian Genius*. New York: Taplinger.*

Frankfort, Henri. *The Birth of Civilization in the Near East*. Garden City, New York: Doubleday, 1956, p. 9.

French, Kenneth, and James Poterba, 1991. "International Diversification and International Equity Markets." *American Economic Review*, Vol. 81, No. 1, pp. 222–226.

Friedman, Milton, and Leonard J. Savage, 1948. "The Utility Analysis of Choices Involving Risk." *Journal of Political Economy*, Vol. LVI, No. 4 (August), pp. 279–304.

Galton, Francis, 1869. *Hereditary Genius: An Inquiry into Its Laws and Consequences*. London: Macmillan. Abstracted in Newman, 1988a, pp. 1141–1162.

Galton, Francis, 1883. *Inquiries into Human Faculty and Its Development*. London: Macmillan.

Garber, Peter M., 1989. "Who Put the Mania in Tulipmania?" *The Journal of Portfolio Management*, Vol. 16, No. 1 (Fall), pp. 53–60.

Garland, Trudi Hammel, 1987. *Fascinating Fibonaccis: Mystery and Magic in Numbers*. Palo Alto, California: Dale Seymour Publications.*

Georgescu-Roegen, Nicholas, 1994. "Utility." In *The McGraw-Hill Encyclopedia of Economics*, 2nd Ed., Douglas Greenwald, ed. New York: McGraw Hill, pp. 998–1010.

Glickman, Theodore S., and Michael Gough, 1990. *Readings in Risk*. Washington, DC: Resources for the Future.

Graunt, John. "Natural and Political Observations made upon the Bills of Mortality." Abstracted in Newman, 1988, pp. 1399–1411.

Greenspan, Alan, 1994. "Remarks before the Boston College Conference on Financial Markets and the Economy." Boston, Massachusetts, September. (Published by Federal Reserve Board, Washington, DC.)

Groebner, David F., and Patrick Shannon, 1993. *Business Statistics: A Decision-Making Approach*, 4th Ed. New York: Macmillan.*

Guilbaud, G. Th., 1968. *Éléments de la théorie mathématique des jeux*. Paris: Dunod.

Hacking, Ian, 1975. *The Emergence of Probability: A Philosophical Study of Early Ideas about Probability, Induction, and Statistical Inference*. London: Cambridge University Press.*

Hald, Anders, 1990. *A History of Probability & Statistics and Their Applications Before 1750*. New York: John Wiley & Sons.

Hancock, J. G., and Teevan, R. C., 1964. "Fear of Failure and Risk-Taking Behavior." *Journal of Personality*, Vol. 32, No. 2, pp. 200–209.

Hayano, David M., 1982. *Poker Face: The Life and Work of Professional Card Players*. Berkeley and Los Angeles: University of California Press.

Heilbroner, Robert L., 1995. *Visions of the Future*. New York: New York Public Library/Oxford University Press.

Herrnstein, Richard J., 1990. "Rational Choice Theory: Necessary But Not Sufficient." *American Psychologist*, Vol. 45, No. 3, pp. 356–367.

Herrnstein, Richard J., and Drazen Prelec, 1991. "Melioration: A Theory of Distributed Choice." *Journal of Economic Perspectives*, Vol. 5, No. 3 (Summer), pp. 137–156.

Hodgson, Godfrey, 1984. *Lloyd's of London: A Reputation at Risk*. London: Allen Lane.

Hoffer, William, 1975. "A Magic Ratio Recurs Through Art And Nature." *Smithsonian*, Vol. 6, No. 9 (December), pp. 111–124.

Hogben, Lancelot, 1968. *Mathematics for the Millions: How to Master the Magic Art of Numbers*. New York: Norton. Originally published 1937.*

Howard, R. A., 1984. "On Fates Comparable to Death." *Management Science*, Vol. 30, No. 3, pp. 407–422.

Howey, Richard S., 1983. "Frank Hyneman Knight and the History of Economic Thought." In *Research in the History of Economic Thought and Methodology,* Vol. 1, pp. 163–186. New York: JAI Press.

Hsieh, David A., 1995. "Nonlinear Dynamics in Financial Markets: Evidence and Implications." *Financial Analysts Journal,* Vol. 51, No. 4 (July–August), pp. 55–62.

Huff, Daniel, 1959. *How To Take A Chance.* New York: Norton.

Ignatin, George, and Robert Smith. "The Economics of Gambling." In Eadington, 1976.

Jackson, Norma, and Pippa Carter. "The Perception of Risk." In Ansell and Wharton, 1992.

Jeffrey, Robert H., 1984. "A New Paradigm for Risk." *Journal of Portfolio Management,* Vol. 11, No. 1 (Fall), pp. 33–40.

Jevons, W. Stanley, 1970. *The Theory of Political Economy.* Harmondsworth: Penguin Books. First published 1871. Second edition 1879.

Johnson, Dirk, 1995. "More Casinos, More Players Who Bet Until They Lose All." *The New York Times,* September 25, p. A1.

Jones, Charles P., and Jack W. Wilson, 1995. "Probability Estimates of Returns from Common Stock Investing." *Journal of Portfolio Management,* Vol. 22, No. 1 (Fall), pp. 21–32.

Kagel, John H., and Alvin E. Roth, eds., 1995. *The Handbook of Experimental Economics.* Princeton, New Jersey: Princeton University Press.

Kahneman, Daniel, and Amos Tversky, 1979. "Prospect Theory: An Analysis of Decision under Risk." *Econometrica,* Vol. 47, No. 2, pp. 263–291.*

Kahneman, Daniel, and Amos Tversky, 1984. "Choices, Values, and Frames." *American Psychologist,* Vol. 39, No. 4 (April), pp. 342–347.

Kahneman, Daniel, Jack L. Knetsch, and Richard H. Thaler, 1990. "Experimental Tests of the Endowment Effect and the Coase Theorem." *Journal of Political Economy,* Vol. 98, No. 6, pp. 1325–1348.

Kaplan, Gilbert Edmund, and Chris Welles, eds. 1969. *The Money Managers.* New York: Random House.

Kelves, Daniel J., 1985. *In the Name of Eugenics.* New York: Knopf.

Kemp, Martin, 1981. *Leonardo da Vinci: The Marvellous Works of Nature and Man.* Cambridge, Massachusetts: Harvard University Press.

Kendall, Maurice G., 1972. "Measurement in the Study of Society." In Kendall and Plackett, 1977, pp. 35–49.

Kendall, Maurice G., and R. L. Plackett, eds., 1977. *Studies in the History of Statistics and Probability,* Vol. II. New York: Macmillan.*

Keynes, John Maynard, 1921. *A Treatise on Probability.* London: Macmillan.*

Keynes, John Maynard, 1924. *A Tract on Monetary Reform.* New York: Harcourt Brace. In Moggridge, 1972, Vol. IV.

Keynes, John Maynard, 1931. *Essays in Persuasion.* London: Macmillan & Co.

Keynes, John Maynard, 1933. *Essays in Biography*. London, Macmillan. This work also appears as Vol. X of Moggridge, 1972.

Keynes, John Maynard, 1936. *The General Theory of Employment, Interest and Money*. New York: Harcourt, Brace.*

Keynes, John Maynard, 1937. "The General Theory." *Quarterly Journal of Economics*, Vol. LI, February, pp. 209–233. Reprinted in Moggridge, 1972, Vol. XIV.

Keynes, John Maynard, 1971. *Two Memoirs*. New York: Augustus M. Kelley.

Knight, Frank H., 1964. *Risk, Uncertainty & Profit*. New York: Century Press. Originally published 1921.*

Kogelman, Stanley, and Barbara R. Heller, 1986. *The Only Math Book You'll Ever Need*. New York: Facts on File.

Kritzman, Mark, 1995. *The Portable Financial Analyst*. Chicago, Illinois: Probus.*

Kruskal, William H., and Stephen M. Stigler. "Normative Terminology: 'Normal' in Statistics and Elsewhere." Unpublished manuscript, September 15, 1994.

Lakonishok, Josef, André Shleifer, and Robert Vishny, 1993. "Contrary Investment, Extrapolation, and Risk." Cambridge, Massachusetts: National Bureau of Economic Research.

Laplace, Pierre Simon, 1814. "Concerning Probability." In Newman, 1988a, pp. 1301–1309.

Lease, Ronald C., Wilbur G. Lewellen, and Gary G. Schlarbaum, 1974. "The Individual Investor, Attributes and Attitudes." *Journal of Finance*, Vol. XXIX, No. 2 (May), pp. 413–433.

Leinweber, David J., and Robert D. Arnott, 1995. "Quantitative and Computational Innovation in Investment Management." *Journal of Portfolio Management*, Vol. 22, No. 1 (Winter), pp. 8–16.

Leonard, Robert J., 1994. "Reading Cournot, Reading Nash: The Creation and Stabilisation of Nash Equilibrium." *Economic Journal*, Vol. 104, No. 424 (May), pp. 492–511.

Leonard, Robert J., 1995. "From Parlor Games to Social Science: Von Neumann, Morgenstern, and the Creation of Game Theory." *Journal of Economic Literature*, Vol. XXXIII, No. 2 (June), pp. 730–761.

Loomis, Carol J., 1995. "Cracking the Derivatives Case." *Fortune*, March 28, pp. 50–68.

Macaulay, Frederick R., 1938. *Some Theoretical Problems Suggested by the Movements of Interest Rates, Bond Yields and Stock Prices in the United States since 1856*. New York: National Bureau of Economic Research.

Macaulay, Thomas Babington, 1848. *The History of England*. Reprint. New York: Penguin Books, 1968.

Macrae, Norman, 1992. *John von Neumann*. New York: Pantheon Books.*

Markowitz, Harry M., 1952. "Portfolio Selection." *Journal of Finance*, Vol. VII, No. 1 (March), pp. 77–91.

Markowitz, Harry M., 1952. "The Utility of Wealth." *Journal of Political Economy*, Vol. LIX, No. 3 (April), pp. 151–157.

McCusker, John J., 1978. *Money and Exchange in Europe and America, 1600–1775.* Chapel Hill, North Carolina: The University of North Carolina Press.

McKean, Kevin, 1985. "Decisions." *Discover*, June, pp. 22–31.

Miller, Edward M., 1995. "Do the Ignorant Accumulate the Money?" Working paper. University of New Orleans, April 5.

Miller, Merton H., 1987. "Behavioral Rationality in Finance." *Midland Corporate Finance Journal* (now *Journal of Applied Corporate Finance*), Vol. 4, No. 4 (Winter), pp. 6–15.

Millman, Gregory J., 1995. *The Vandals' Crown: How Rebel Currency Traders Overthrew the World's Central Banks.* New York: The Free Press.

Mirowski, Philip, 1991. "When Games Grow Deadly Serious: The Military Influence on the Evolution of Game Theory." *History of Political Economy*, Vol. 23, pp. 227–260.

Mirowski, Philip, 1992. "What Were von Neumann and Morgenstern Trying to Accomplish?" *History of Political Economy*, Vol. 24, pp. 113–147.

Moggridge, Donald, ed., 1972. *The Collected Writings of John Maynard Keynes*, Vols. I–XXX. New York: St. Martin's Press.

Moorehead, E. J., 1989. *Our Yesterdays: The History of the Actuarial Profession in North America, 1809–1979.* Schaumburg, Illinois: Society of Actuaries.

Morgan, M. Granger, and Max Henrion, 1990. *Uncertainty: A Guide to Dealing with Uncertainty in Quantitative Risk and Policy Analysis.* Cambridge, Massachusetts: Cambridge University Press.

Morley, Henry, 1854. *Jerome Cardan: The Life Of Girolamo Cardano Of Milan, Physician.* London: Chapman and Hall.

Morningstar Mutual Funds. Chicago, Illinois. Bi-weekly.

Muir, Jane, 1961. *Of Men and Numbers: The Story of the Great Mathematicians.* New York: Dodd, Mead.*

Nasar, Sylvia, 1994. "The Lost Years of a Nobel Laureate." *The New York Times*, November 13, 1994, Section 3, p. 1.

Newman, James R., 1988a. *The World of Mathematics: A Small Library of the Literature of Mathematics from A'h-mosé the Scribe to Albert Einstein.* Redmond, Washington: Tempus Press.*

Newman, James R., 1988b. "Commentary on an Absent-Minded Genius and the Laws of Chance." In Newman, 1988a, pp. 1353–1358.

Newman, James R., 1988c. "Commentary on Lord Keynes." In Newman, 1988a, pp. 1333–1338.

Newman, James R., 1988d. "Commentary on Pierre Simon De Laplace." In Newman, 1988a, pp. 1291–1299.

Newman, James R., 1988e. "Commentary on Sir Francis Galton." In Newman, 1988a, pp. 1141–1145.

Newman, James R., 1988f. "Commentary on the Bernoullis." In Newman, 1988a, pp. 759–761.

Newman, James R., 1988g. "Comment on an Ingenious Army Captain and on a Generous and Many-sided Man." In Newman 1988a, pp. 1393–1397.

Oldman, D., 1974. "Chance and Skill: A Study of Roulette." *Sociology*, pp. 407–426.

Ore, O., 1953. *Cardano, The Gambling Scholar.* Princeton, New Jersey: Princeton University Press.*

Osborne, Martin J., and Ariel Rubinstein, 1994. *A Course in Game Theory.* Cambridge, Massachusetts: MIT Press.

Passell, Peter, 1994. "Game Theory Captures a Nobel." *The New York Times*, October 12, p. D1.

Phillips, Don, 1995. "A Deal with the Devil." *Morningstar Mutual Funds*, May 26, 1995.

Poincaré, Henri, date unspecified. "Chance." In Newman, 1988a, pp. 1359–1372.

Poterba, James M., and Lawrence H. Summers, 1988. "Mean Reversion and Stock Prices." *Journal of Financial Economics*, Vol. 22, No. 1, pp. 27–59.

Pratt, John W., 1964. "Risk Aversion in the Small and in the Large." *Econometrica*, Vol. 32, No. 1–2 (January–April), pp. 122–136.

Rabinovitch, Nachum L., 1969. "Studies in the History of Probability and Statistics: Probability in the Talmud." *Biometrika*, Vol. 56, No. 2. In Kendall and Plackett, 1977, pp. 15–19.

Raiffa, Howard, 1968. *Decision Analysis: Introductory Lectures on Choice Under Uncertainty.* New York: McGraw-Hill.

Redelmeier, Donald A., and Eldar Shafir, 1995. "Medical Decision Making in Situations That Offer Multiple Alternatives." *Journal of the American Medical Association*, Vol. 273, No. 4, pp. 302–305.

Redelmeier, Donald A., and Amos Tversky, 1990. "Discrepancy Between Medical Decisions for Individual Patients and for Groups." *New England Journal of Medicine*, Vol. 322 (April 19), pp. 1162–1164.

Redelmeier, Donald A., D. J. Koehler, V. Z. Lieberman, and Amos Tversky, 1995. "Probability Judgment in Medicine: Discounting Unspecified Alternatives," *Medical Decision-Making*, Vol. 15, No. 3, pp. 227–231.

Reichenstein, William, and Dovalee Dorsett, 1995. *Time Diversification Revisited.* Charlottesville, Virginia: The Research Foundation of the Institute of Chartered Financial Analysts.

Rescher, Nicholas, 1983. *Risk: A Philosophical Introduction to the Theory of Risk Evaluation and Management.* Washington, DC: University Press of America.*

Rubinstein, Mark, 1991. "Continuously Rebalanced Investment Strategies." *Journal of Portfolio Management*, Vol. 18, No. 1, pp. 78–81.

Sambursky, Shmuel, 1956. "On the Possible and Probable in Ancient Greece." *Osiris*, Vol. 12, pp. 35–48. In Kendall and Plackett, 1977, pp. 1–14.*

Bibliography

Sanford C. Bernstein & Co., 1994. *Bernstein Disciplined Strategies Monitor*, December.

Sarton, George, 1957. *Six Wings of Science: Men of Science in the Renaissance.* Bloomington, Indiana: Indiana University Press.

Schaaf, William L., 1964. *Carl Friedrich Gauss: Prince of Mathematicians.* New York: Franklin Watts.*

Seitz, Frederick, 1992. *The Science Matrix: The Journey, Travails, and Triumphs.* New York: Springer-Verlag.

Shapira, Zur, 1995. *Risk Taking: A Managerial Perspective.* New York: Russell Sage Foundation.

Sharpe, William F., 1990. "Investor Wealth Measures and Expected Return." In Sharpe, William F., ed., 1990. *Quantifying the Market Risk Premium Phenomenon for Investment Decision Making.* Charlottesville, Virginia: The Institute of Chartered Financial Analysts, pp. 29–37.

Shefrin, Hersh, and Meir Statman, 1984. "Explaining Investor Preference for Dividends." *Journal of Financial Economics*, Vol. 13, No. 2, pp. 253–282.

Shiller, Robert J., 1981. "Do Stock Prices Move Too Much?" *American Economic Review*, Vol. 71, No. 3 (June), pp. 421–436.

Shiller, Robert J., 1989. *Market Volatility.* Cambridge, Massachusetts: Cambridge University Press.

Siegel, Jeremy J., 1994. *Stocks for the Long Run: A Guide to Selecting Markets for Long-Term Growth.* Burr Ridge, Illinois: Irwin Professional Publishing.

Siskin, Bernard R., 1989. *What Are the Chances?* New York: Crown.

Skidelsky, Robert, 1986. *John Maynard Keynes.* Vol. 1: *Hopes Betrayed.* New York: Viking.

Slovic, Paul, Baruch Fischoff, and Sarah Lichtenstein, 1990. "Rating the Risks." In Glickman and Gough, 1990, pp. 61–75.

Smith, Clifford W., Jr., 1995. "Corporate Risk Management: Theory and Practice." *Journal of Derivatives*, Summer, pp. 21–30.

Smith, M. F. M., 1984. "Present Position and Potential Developments: Some Personal Views of Bayesian Statistics." *Journal of the Royal Statistical Association*, Vol. 147, Part 3, pp. 245–259.

Smithson, Charles W., and Clifford W. Smith, Jr., 1995. *Managing Financial Risk: A Guide to Derivative Products, Financial Engineering, and Value Maximization.* New York: Irwin.*

Sorensen, Eric, 1995. "The Derivative Portfolio Matrix—Combining Market Direction with Market Volatility." Institute for Quantitative Research in Finance, Spring 1995 Seminar.

Statman, Meir, 1982. "Fixed Rate or Index-Linked Mortgages from the Borrower's Point of View: A Note." *Journal of Financial and Quantitative Analysis*, Vol. XVII, No. 3 (September), pp. 451–457.

Stigler, Stephen M., 1977. "Eight Centuries of Sampling Inspection: The Trial of the Pyx." *Journal of the American Statistical Association*, Vol. 72, pp. 493–500.

Stigler, Stephen M., 1986. *The History of Statistics: The Measurement of Uncertainty before 1900.* Cambridge, Massachusetts: The Belknap Press of Harvard University Press.*

Stigler, Stephen M., 1988. "The Dark Ages of Probability in England: The Seventeenth Century Work of Richard Cumberland and Thomas Strode." *International Statistical Review,* Vol. 56, No. 1, pp. 75–88.

Stigler, Stephen M., 1993. "The Bernoullis of Basel." Opening address to the Bayesian Econometric Conference, Basel, April 29, 1993.

Stigler, Stephen M., 1996. "Statistics and the Question of Standards." Forthcoming. *Journal of Research of the National Institute of Standards and Technology.*

Thaler, Richard H., 1987. "The Psychology of Choice and the Assumptions of Economics." In Thaler, 1991, Ch. 7, p. 139.

Thaler, Richard H., 1991. *Quasi-Rational Economics.* New York: Russell Sage Foundation.

Thaler, Richard H., 1992. *The Winner's Curse: Paradoxes and Anomalies of Economic Life.* New York: The Free Press.

Thaler, Richard H., 1993. *Advances in Behavioral Finance.* New York: Russell Sage Foundation.*

Thaler, Richard H., 1995. "Behavioral Economics." *NBER Reporter,* National Bureau of Economic Research, Fall, pp. 9–13.

Thaler, Richard H., and Hersh Shefrin, 1981. "An Economic Theory of Self-Control." *Journal of Political Economy,* Vol. 89, No. 2 (April), pp. 392–406. In Thaler, 1991.

Thaler, Richard H., Amos Tversky, and Jack L. Knetsch, 1990. "Experimental Tests of the Endowment Effect." *Journal of Political Economy,* Vol. 98, No. 6, pp. 1325–1348.

Thaler, Richard H., Amos Tversky, and Jack L. Knetsch, 1991. "Endowment Effect, Loss Aversion, and Status Quo Bias." *Journal of Economic Perspectives,* Vol. 5, No. 1, pp. 193–206.

Todhunter, Isaac, 1931. *A History of the Mathematical Theory of Probability from the Time of Pascal to that of Laplace.* New York: G. E. Stechert & Co. Originally published in Cambridge, England, in 1865.

Townsend, Robert M., 1995. "Consumption Insurance: An Evaluation of Risk-Bearing Systems in Low-Income Economies." *Journal of Economic Perspectives,* Vol. 9, No. 3 (Summer), pp. 83–102.

Tsukahara, Theodore, Jr., and Harold J. Brumm, Jr. "Economic Rationality, Psychology and Decision-making Under Uncertainty." In Eadington, 1976, pp. 92–106.

Turnbull, Herbert Westren, 1951. "The Great Mathematicians." In Newman, 1988a, pp. 73–160.

Tversky, Amos, 1990. "The Psychology of Risk." In Sharpe, 1990, pp. 73–77.

Tversky, Amos, and Daniel Kahneman, 1981. "The Framing of Decisions and the Psychology of Choice." *Science,* Vol. 211, pp. 453–458.

Tversky, Amos, and Daniel Kahneman, 1986. "Rational Choice and the Framing of Decisions." *Journal of Business*, Vol. 59, No. 4, pp. 251–278.

Tversky, Amos, and Daniel Kahneman, 1992. "Advances in Prospect Theory: Cumulative Representation of Uncertainty." *Journal of Risk and Uncertainty*, Vol. 5, No. 4, pp. 297–323.

Tversky, Amos, and Derek J. Koehler, 1994. "Support Theory: A Nonextensional Representation of Subjective Probability." *Psychological Review*, Vol. 101, No. 4, pp. 547–567.

Urquhart, John, 1984. *Risk Watch: The Odds of Life*. New York: Facts on File.

Vertin, James, 1974. "The State of the Art in Our Profession." *Journal of Portfolio Management*, Vol. I, No. 1, pp. 10–12.

Von Neumann, John, 1953. "Can We Survive Technology?" *Fortune*, June 1955.

Von Neumann, John, and Oskar Morgenstern, 1944. *Theory of Games and Economic Behavior*. Princeton, New Jersey: Princeton University Press.*

Wade, H., 1973. *The Greatest Gambling Stories Ever Told*. Ontario: Greywood Publishing Ltd.

Waldrop, M. Mitchell, 1992. *Complexity: The Emerging Science at the Edge of Order and Chaos*. New York: Simon & Schuster.

Wallach, M. A., and C. W. Wing, Jr., 1968. "Is Risk a Value?" *Journal of Personality and Social Psychology*, Vol. 9, No. 1 (May), pp. 101–106.

Warren, George F., and Frank A. Pearson, 1993. *The Price Series*. New Jersey: The Haddon Craftsmen.

Whitman, Marina von Neumann, 1990. "John von Neumann: A Personal View." *Proceedings of Symposia in Pure Mathematics*, Vol. 50, 1990.

Wildavsky, Aaron, 1990. "No Risk Is the Highest Risk of All." In Glickman and Gough, 1990, pp. 120–128.

Willems, E. P., 1969. "Risk is a value." *Psychological Reports,* Vol. 24, pp. 81–82.

Williams, John Burr, 1938. *The Theory of Investment Value*. Cambridge, Massachusetts: Harvard University Press.

Wilson, R., 1981. "Analyzing the Daily Risks of Life." *Technology Review*, pp. 40–46.

Winslow, E. G., 1986. "'Human Logic' and Keynes's Economics." *Eastern Economic Journal*, Vol. XII, No. 4 (October–December), pp. 413–430.

Name Index

Subject Index